WITS
A University in the Apartheid Era

Wits Press RE/PRESENTS

Wits University Press celebrates its centenary in 2022. Since its inception, the Press has been curating and publishing innovative research that informs debate to drive impactful change in society. Drawing on an extensive backlist dating from 1922, **Wits Press Re/Presents** is a new series that makes important research accessible to readers once again. While much of the content demonstrates its historical provenance, it remains of interest to researchers and students, and is re-published in e-book and print-on-demand formats.

WITS
A University in the Apartheid Era

MERVYN SHEAR
Foreword by Firoz Cachalia

WITS UNIVERSITY PRESS

Published in South Africa by:
Wits University Press
1 Jan Smuts Avenue
Johannesburg 2001

www.witspress.co.za

Copyright © Mervyn Shear 1996
Foreword © Firoz Cachalia 2022
Published edition © Wits University Press 2022

First published 1996

http://dx.doi.org.10.18772/12022088042

978-1-77614-804-2 (Paperback)
978-1-77614-805-9 (Hardback)
978-1-77614-806-6 (Web PDF)
978-1-77614-807-3 (EPUB)

All rights reserved. No part of this publication may be reproduced, stored in a retrieval system, or transmitted in any form or by any means, electronic, mechanical, photocopying, recording or otherwise, without the written permission of the publisher, except in accordance with the provisions of the Copyright Act, Act 98 of 1978.

Cover image: Protest by students at University of Witwatersrand, photographer: Gideon Mendel, courtesy of Gideon Mendel/SAHA

For
Caryll and Keith
and for
all those courageous Wits students
as well as those throughout South Africa
who opposed apartheid tyranny
in the face of harassment, intimidation
and incarceration without trial

As far as criticism is concerned, we don't resent that unless it is absolutely biased, as it is in most cases.

> John Vorster, Prime Minister 1966-1978
> Sayings of the Week, *Observer*, 9 November 1969

Universities should resist any attempt by the state to undermine their autonomy and academic freedom. The autonomy of tertiary institutions is enshrined in the interim constitution.

> FW de Klerk, former State President
> Addressing students at the University of Pretoria,
> 15 May 1995

Contents

Foreword by Firoz Cachalia ix
Acknowledgements. xvii
Preface. xix
Introduction. xxix

1 Racial Discrimination at Wits 1
2 The Threat to the 'Open' Universities 20
3 Activists Under Pressure. 37
4 Student Politics in Black and White. 61
5 The 1980s 80
6 Wits and the First State of Emergency 91
7 Resistance Escalates 121
8 Challenge to the Government. 149
9 The Struggle Reaches a Climax. 201
10 Transition to Democracy 257
11 Epilogue. 274

Notes 282
Appendices. 306
Index 348

Foreword

The late Professor Mervyn Shear's book, *Wits: A University in the Apartheid Era*, was first published in 1996. This was also the year in which the legal superstructure of the apartheid system was brought to an end and a new non-racial constitution for a democratic South Africa was adopted with great hopes for a more just future. I am honoured to write this preface to the republication of Professor Shear's book, which was lovingly prepared through careful and rigorous research in the best traditions of truth-telling scholarship. I do so with a deep sense of responsibility to the Wits community, past and present.

The book begins with Shear's tribute to 'all those courageous students as well as those throughout South Africa who opposed apartheid tyranny in the face of harassment, intimidation and incarceration without trial'. It is appropriate that I begin this preface with a tribute to the author himself. Mervyn Shear became a courageous, clear-minded and principled opponent of apartheid tyranny, as well as an advocate of a negotiated transition to a constitutional democracy. As Deputy Vice-Chancellor with the portfolio of student affairs, he gave unstinting support to staff and students protesting against apartheid, and was indefatigable in his commitment to defending their rights and well-being in the face of assaults, banning orders and detention without trial. He is remembered with a great deal of affection and respect by the student leadership of the turbulent 1980s, the period of his service as a senior and distinguished administrator at one of South Africa's leading academic institutions.

Although a reading of the book reveals much about Shear's character and opinions, its historical method is essentially documentary in the sense that it provides a record of facts from the beginnings of the university in

1919, although focusing on the apartheid era. It provides an invaluable resource to the present Wits community, and for the wider South African public, for reflection and deliberation on many of the questions that continue to engage us. Was the relationship between the university and the apartheid state one of resistance or accommodation, or both? Does this have any bearing on how we might understand the university's place and identity in a constitutional democracy committed to the freedoms of the people as well as the of the person and the intellect? Does Shear's account of the history of the university's opposition to encroachment on its autonomy by the apartheid state contribute to our ability to understand, articulate and defend of the values of academic freedom and freedom of expression in institutions of higher learning in South Africa today? Does the history of Wits in the era of colonialism and apartheid documented by Shear throw any light on the challenges of transformation of higher education in the post-colony? In the light on these questions of contemporary interest, I reflect critically on the content of the book.

Shear begins by confronting the university's history of racial discrimination factually and truthfully. His record shows that despite J H Hofmeyr's suggestion in his installation address as its first Principal that the university should 'know no distinctions of class or wealth, race or creed', in practice, 'Wit's admission policies reflected the prejudices of the society to which it belonged. While it never officially adopted a policy of excluding students on the grounds of race or colour, it was very hesitant to accept black students in substantial numbers'. In fact, before the National Party came to power in 1948, determined to implement its policy of apartheid rigorously, the university lobbied the government to introduce legislation to enable it to discriminate on the basis of race after being advised by its lawyers that it needed a legislative basis to do so. Shear notes, 'It seems clear ... that in the 1930s and 1940s the Council of the University was in advance of the state in its desire to implement university segregation'.

The Medical School and the School of Dentistry were particularly notorious. Both actively enforced an odious policy of crude and offensive discrimination at least until the end of the 1960s. Black students who were admitted to the medical school in small numbers were not to be 'allowed access to white patients or even to autopsies conducted on white subjects'. And similarly, black dentistry students were not to be allowed access to white mouths. Shear's factual record shows that the university's governing bodies and administrators 'at that time' regarded the establishment of separate facilities as 'progressive and liberal'. Throughout this period and through the early 1970s, the university also pursued a policy of social segregation, excluding black students from the swimming pool for instance, presumably because the pool water had to be kept pristine for white bodies. Student residences were for whites only. There were 'very few black students on campus' at that time, Shear observes, 'and those who were there were not part of our lives'. So the conclusion is inescapable that at the University of the Witwatersrand, as elsewhere in South Africa 'at that time', the universalist commitments of 'European liberalism' yielded, from a mix of conviction and external 'conservative pressure', to the pervasive 'common sense' racial prejudices of the colonial order on the most basic questions of justice. Shear, to his credit, did not airbrush this shameful history from the historical record.

From the 1950s onwards, Wits University's relationship to the apartheid state is not simply one of complicity, as it was in the pre-1948 era of segregation. It is also one of growing opposition and criticism of the National Party's policies in higher education. This opposition was framed early on as a defence of its autonomy against interference by the state, and its right to exercise control over its admission policy as an 'open university'. But in that period, the university was not unambiguously committed to the principles of non-racialism and non-discrimination. As Shear describes, a significant evolution occurs in the university's understanding and articulation of the basis of its opposition to the plans of the National Party from the early 1950s onwards to introduce 'total educational apartheid'.

On 12 June 1956, a special meeting of Convocation considers a motion opposing the 'continuous threats by the Government's spokesmen to introduce apartheid in open universities and urges Council to re-affirm the long established principle of academic non-segregation', by which it meant segregation in lecture theatres, and nothing more. On April 1959, however, in response to the enactment of the Extension of University Education Act 45 of 1959, at the first General Assembly of the university in the Great Hall, the Council, Senate Staff, Convocation and the student body gathered to express their strong opposition to the Act and adopted a solemn affirmation in the following terms:

We affirm in the name of the University of the Witwatersrand that it is our duty to uphold the principle that a university is a place where men and women, without regard to race and colour, are welcome to join in the acquisition and advancement of knowledge; and to continue faithfully to defend this ideal against all who have sought by legislative enactment to curtail the autonomy of the University.

Here, as it appears from Shear's history, is an articulation for the first time of the principles of non-discrimination and academic freedom as integral to the university's understanding of the purposes of its defence of its autonomy from state inference. Shear does not tell us who drafted the resonant language of the affirmation, which would be of interest because it embodies a new ethical content significantly different from the more truncated version of the idea of 'university autonomy' that had hitherto held sway in the consciousness of the university's decision makers. Nor does Shear reflect on how the growing resistance to apartheid and repression outside the university's precincts throughout the 1950s might have had an impact on internal tensions within the university and its understanding of its role and place in the wider society. But it is clear that opposition to the Extension of Universities Act produced a significant inflection point in the history of Wits University by foregrounding the issue of academic freedom. As Shear remarks, 'the University's affirmation of its commitment to Academic Freedom was to be reiterated in a number of ways in the coming years and would be received with varying degrees of hostility by Government, the Afrikaans press and the police'.

In the 1970s, the university's commitment to a more robust conception of academic freedom evolved as tensions between the university and the government deepened, and the government responded with threats of financial sanctions, which were successfully challenged in court. In 1972, the Senate established an Academic Freedom Committee 'to respond to all matters impinging on it'. And increasingly, under the rubric of academic freedom, the university defended the right of students and staff to protest and oppose government policy in general, not only its educational policy, and to take a stand against state repression. Today, academic freedom is specifically protected as a constitutional right in the country's first democratic constitution.

Ending racial discrimination in admissions was still some way off. In May 1976, shortly before the Soweto uprising in June of that year, and in the face of 'an increasingly severe academic boycott', the Council authorised Professor Bozzoli to 'request the Minister of National Education, Dr P J Koornhof, to open the university once again to students of all races', as the university 'wished to be free to select its students on the grounds of academic merit alone'. The result of introducing this policy, the university submitted, would be that 'the University would probably have no more than 15 per cent black students in the foreseeable future'. At a referendum to test the 'assumption that all constituent parts of the University were in favour of "opening"', the result was overwhelmingly in favour of the proposition. The referendum was, however, opposed by the Wages and Economic Commission, which has been established to investigate the conditions of African workers, as a 'burlesque of university autonomy and academic freedom', which gives some indication of the sentiments of more radical opinion in the university community, impatient with the administration's anxious equivocations on a basic question of justice. It should be acknowledged that towards the end of his term of office, Vice-Chancellor Bozzoli produced a statement on academic freedom which made it clear that this freedom included a commitment to the defence of the principle of non-discrimination: 'academics maintain that in a university, where knowledge is stored, taught, shared and uncovered, those who teach and research, and those who are taught and study should be permitted to join the body of teachers and students on academic grounds only, and should never be selected on the grounds of their race or religion. The freedom to do this is called academic freedom.'

One of the most valuable aspects of this book is the attention given to the tradition of anti-apartheid activism by both students and staff, and to recording police violence and surveillance, arbitrary arrests, detentions without trial and banning orders, as well as assassinations suffered by members of the university community over the decades. Whenever the police confronted protesting students, and particularly when they came onto the campus, Shear was always in the thick of things protecting students and their rights, as page after page of the book attests. The university also provided as much support as it could to students in detention and to staff members who had been detained.

In decade of the 1970s, resistance burst through once more in public domains after the apparent slumber of the 1960s. This period saw the emergence of a generation of impressive student leaders in the SRC and Nusas, who put forward political demands that far exceeded what the university's administrators would or could publicly endorse. In the lecture halls, an open intellectual culture enabled a radical critique of the political economy of apartheid and the history of colonialism to flourish.

The turbulent 1980s was in retrospect the harbinger of great change in the university, and in wider society. Black students from the so called 'Bush Colleges' were admitted in far larger numbers, although they required ministerial consent, and remained a minority. They brought with them their harsh experiences of apartheid and repression, unmediated by the apartheid state's limited accommodation of the autonomy of white universities and 'liberal opposition'. Many lived in 'townships' and 'group areas' like Soweto, Riverlea and Lenasia, where they were politically active, or in a residence for black students. This experience found expression in a radical national liberation paradigm that emphasised resistance and fundamental change.

Black students organised politically in the Black Student Society (BSS) did not participate in SRC elections and boycotted sports facilities on the basis that there could be no normal sport in an abnormal society. They responded actively on campus to the growing resistance in their communities and throughout the country. This often led to confrontation with the police. Although the relationship with the university administration was sometimes fraught in these difficult circumstances, as Shear attests, the university upheld students' right to protest peacefully, and supported them when they were assaulted and detained.

This period produced an impressive group of black student leaders who emphasised black students' self-determining role, but who also embraced non-racialism as a principle and cooperated actively with SRC and Nusas leaders. Many of the relationships of friendship and solidarity that developed at that time endure to this day. The BSS leadership demonstrated considerable strategic acuity in mobilising student radicalism, encouraging peaceful protest and accommodating the perspectives of university administrators. This was most difficult when militant students disrupted speaking events by outsiders on campus, as this raised questions both of freedom of speech and academic freedom in the context of the apartheid state. Liberal opinion was emphatic in its condemnation, ignoring the moral complexities that Justice Cameron pointed out in his minority report to Senate. What the critics blithely ignored in the name of free speech absolutism was the context of the 'empire of force' behind the partial and selective and distorted life of 'free speech' in apartheid South Africa. Nobody seeking fundamental change could be under any illusion that they enjoyed any such freedom. But we have surely learnt from these experiences that the freedoms that are essential to the academic project and to the practice of democracy must be defended today.

The 1990s produced yet another moment in the history of Wits University. It has been a paradoxical one, since the democratisation of our political institutions have only served to emphasise that transformation, both of higher education and our society, is incomplete. New questions of financial exclusion, equitable access, and profound questions about how knowledge is produced and what counts as knowledge have come to the fore. Wits's earliest efforts to deal with these questions are discussed in the closing chapters. I have every confidence that Wits has the resources, goodwill and openness to tackle these questions, though this process will not be free of tensions.

Shear's carefully composed record of Wits University's history, which includes its history of racial discrimination and segregation, and of critique, dissent and resistance to injustice, gives us the means to move beyond denial and blame and to build our university's present and future on shared foundational commitments to equality, non-discrimination, social justice, decolonisation and the pursuit of knowledge, which are also values enshrined in our country's non-racial and democratic constitution.

I end with a tribute to the gentle and courageous David Webster, and to the formidable and indefatigable Bheki Mlangeni, both of whom were slain by 'the empire of force' while on duty in the struggle for freedom at Wits University. Mlangeni's comrade Chris Ngcobo passed away during the Covid-19 lockdown. Together with Lawrence Boya, they formed the backbone triumvirate of the BSS, which played a central role in transforming Wits University forever. It is now no longer a 'white university'. It can finally authentically claim its mantle as an open university, albeit one that is an unfinished project. We have travelled a long way with Professor Shear, and with countless others not mentioned, on the road the Wits community have chosen. But there are still miles to go before we can sleep.

Firoz Cachalia, Adjunct Professor, School of Law, University of the Witwatersrand, Johannesburg and Director of the Mandela Institute
July 2022

Acknowledgements

In July 1991, Robert (Bob) Charlton, Vice-Chancellor and Principal of the University of the Witwatersrand asked me to prepare a document on the University's anti-apartheid activities over the years. I agreed, provided that I was able to produce an objective account that would record the negative as well as the positive aspects. He accepted this proviso without hesitation. When it became clear that the document would have to be a book, Bob Charlton again agreed. He has been consistently encouraging as work progressed and has at no time even hinted that any part of the work should be cut for fear that it might be embarrassing for the University. His support has been much appreciated.

Numbers of people have read parts or all of the manuscript. Their perspectives, suggestions and factual corrections have been invaluable and it is a pleasure to acknowledge the input of Noel Garson, Debra Nails, Howard Philips, Catherine Burns, Keith Breckenridge, Keith Shear and Caryll Shear. The encouragement and advice received from Tim Couzens provided incentive and impetus at a time when I really needed it.

Wits University archivists Joan Biddles and Diana Arnott have been immensely helpful in seeking out documentation in response to innumerable requests. Jo Waltham of the University's Central Graphics Unit, Valerie Diesel of the University's Department of Information and Public Affairs and Rowan Bruwer of *Wits Student* made a considerable and greatly appreciated effort to find photographic material that I wanted for use in the book.

There were some support staff colleagues with whom I worked very closely on student matters during my tenure as Deputy Vice-Chancellor. Their concern for the welfare of the students was inspiring and it is a pleasure to acknowledge them. Geoff Blurton, Jonathan Stead and Pauline Cuzen were successive dedicated Deputy Registrars with the student affairs portfolio. Ken Standenmacher was University Registrar and Bruce Dickson Deputy Registrar, and their protective presence during student confrontations with the police was invaluable. Peta Stevens was Assistant Registrar (Student Affairs) and was a wizard at finding accommodation for desperate students when none seemed to be available. Victor Gordon and Jocelyn Cairns were successive SRC Administration Coordinators and Jocelyn also administered the SRC funds and ensured that every item of expenditure was accounted for. Victor and Jocelyn provided warm support to SRCs and BSSs. Libby Borkon and Marian Seabrook did wonderful work in the Campus Health Service as did Andrew Swart and his staff in the Counselling and Careers Unit. Hazel van Lingen and Joyce Beffon and others in the bursaries and scholarships office did their utmost to see that financial aid went to as many of the needy as funds, never enough, would allow. Kathy Jagoe and Kirsty Fraser developed remarkable facilities for disabled students with limited resources. John Baxter and his staff oversaw the transition to non-racial sport with sensitivity and insight and were an example to sports administrators throughout the country. Phyl Latter and Heather Forder were secretaries who had a welcoming smile and encouraging words for processions of students with all sorts of problems. Their diligent care for my files and documents has made it possible to prepare this record. And after hours, residence wardens and subwardens were also there to advise and encourage.

Preface

In May 1948 the National Party of Dr D F Malan came into power in South Africa on the basis of its apartheid policy. In February 1990, Mr F W de Klerk, the leader of the same party, announced in Parliament that the apartheid era was to end. As I write this, a year has passed since the first democratic election on 27 April 1994. The country is ruled now by a multiparty Government of National Unity under the Presidency of Mr Nelson Mandela, the leader of the majority party, the African National Congress.

During the apartheid era, the National Party Government, in their attempt to entrench political rights and economic privileges in the hands of the whites, inflicted injuries of the most abominable kind on black South Africans. In the process, the country earned international condemnation and was isolated and rejected by the world community.

These events did not leave the universities of South Africa untouched. During the apartheid era, the residential universities could be divided into three categories. There were the English-language so-called 'open universities' – Cape Town (UCT), Natal, Rhodes and Wits – whose doors were, at least in theory, open to all who were academically qualified for admission. From the promulgation of the Extension of University Education Act 45 of 1959 until 1984, the admission of black students was severely restricted. The second group of South African universities included the Afrikaans-medium institutions – Pretoria, Potchefstroom, Rand Afrikaans University, Orange Free State, Stellenbosch and, despite its nominal 'dual language' designation, Port Elizabeth, all of which supported the Government and apartheid education. The third category comprised the universities that were the creation of apartheid tertiary education, established to provide separate institutions for African, Coloured and Indian South Africans. They were rigidly run by administrations appointed by the Government, whose educational policies they implemented with fervour. Those established for Africans were located in areas so remote that they were referred to contemptuously as 'bush' colleges. Today, most of them are under enlightened and progressive administrators who are strongly committed to transforming their universities in such a way as to redress the apartheid legacy, and are referred to with some pride as the historically black universities, or HBUs.

This book is about how one of the 'open' universities, the University of the Witwatersrand, or Wits, as it is commonly known, handled the apartheid era. I was a member of Wits for almost the entire period, having arrived there as a first year student in 1950 and left at the end of 1990. For the last eight years I was a Deputy Vice-Chancellor with the portfolio of student affairs, the first person to occupy this position. They were turbulent years, coinciding as they did with a massive rise in black militancy that was met with a brutal response from the apartheid state, obsessed with its fear of a 'total onslaught' against it. My job kept me close to the students' role in this conflict during the 1980s which is why that decade receives particular attention in this book.

The story of Wits could equally justifiably have been told about the University of Cape Town and also, with perhaps some different emphases, about the Universities of Natal and Rhodes. Throughout the apartheid era there was a particularly close relationship between Wits and UCT in their struggle against this racially discriminatory doctrine, particularly as it applied to academic freedom.

The publication of two booklets, *The Open Universities in South Africa* in 1957 and *The Open Universities in South Africa and Academic Freedom* in 1974, were collaborative projects of these two institutions. The principles enunciated in the two publications reflected the attitudes of large numbers of their staffs and students as well as those of Natal and Rhodes and formed the intellectual thrust of anti-apartheid activities over more than four decades. Similarly, the intensity of student responses over this period was frequently co-ordinated by their respective representative councils and by the white and black national student movements; and my descriptions of student demonstrations on the Wits campus may readily be transposed to reflect similar activity on the others. If there appears to be any suggestion in the course of my narrative that Wits acted alone or even that it was 'first among its peers', this is unintentional.

Although a comparative study of student activism against the apartheid state with similar movements in other countries is outside the scope of this book, it is nevertheless apposite to make a few observations on the subject. The Nationalist Government in South Africa was deeply concerned about the danger to its own stability from student movements and from academics on the left, whereas it encouraged and supported the student movements on the right such as the Afrikaner Studente Bond (ASB) and the National Student Federation (NSF). Black student structures such as the South African Students' Organisation (Saso), the Azanian Students' Organisation (Azaso), the Azanian Students' Movement (Azasm) and the South African National Students' Congress (Sansco) were all part of the mass resistance movements and they flourished from the late 1960s despite being banned and their membership harassed, detained, tortured, murdered or driven into exile.[1] Nusas, originally a non-racial liberal[2] organisation was eventually rejected by black students who withdrew from it in 1968 to form Saso. It then functioned as a white student movement strongly committed to the anti-apartheid struggle. Its leadership was targeted by the state and its supportive media and subjected to vilification, intensive harassment and detention.

The fear of the South African Government and its security establishment of these student movements was well grounded. In India, student activism had played a prominent role in the struggle for independence from British rule; while in South American countries student political activity had forced extensive reforms of the higher education system. This reform movement or *reforma* was responsible for achieving significant student participation in university decision making but was weakened in latter years by the military regimes and political and economic pressures.[3] In 1978 students joined workers in a strike and participated in alliances that led to the formation of the Sandinistas in Nicaragua and the civil war in opposition to the oppressive military regime of General Anastasio Somoza.

In the United States student activism was at its height in the 1960s with the civil rights movement and the campaign against the Vietnam war, when there were disruptions on campuses throughout the country and massive demonstrations in Washington DC. Bewildered academics in that country who had 'learned to expect students in underdeveloped countries to lead unruly demonstrations against the status quo' could just not comprehend that similar activities should be 'sweeping across America, France, Germany, Italy and even Eastern European countries like Czechoslovakia and Poland'. And what was even more difficult to come to grips with was that this should be happening 'not at the most backward universities, but at the most distinguished, liberal and enlightened – Berkeley, the Sorbonne, Tokyo, Columbia, the Free University of Berlin, Rome and now Harvard'.[4] The US President's Commission on Campus Unrest identified three issues on which protest had been focused – the war, racial injustice and the university itself.[5] These were precisely the issues addressed in demonstrations on South African campuses during the 1980s: the wars in Namibia, Angola, Mozambique and in the townships; the racial injustices of the apartheid system; and the need to transform the structure and governance of the universities. The latter process is still a matter of contention on most campuses in the country.

Student activism has also been identified as having played a substantial role in the political transformation in Eastern Europe at the end of 1989 where the students' motivation was partly to see their countries freed of Soviet influence, partly a desire for freedom of expression and representative government and partly a dissatisfaction with the economic situation.[6] In Islamic countries previously secular and leftist-oriented student movements have been transformed into Islamic fundamentalist organisations and are likely to remain so.[7] In China, Deng Xiaoping had warned that without the unquestioned rule of the Communist Party the university students would become 'unbridled and brazen. They will run wild.' In June 1989 10 000 Chinese students demonstrating peacefully for democracy, better jobs and an end to corruption were holding a vigil in Tiananmen Square in Beijing when many were massacred by government troops.[8]

I was to become involved in a period of intense student activism when in January 1983 I joined the University administration. While the two terms I served over the next eight years were exciting and rewarding in many respects, the portfolio was intensely stressful and at times rather hazardous. I believe that there was only one other candidate when my first term expired and when at the end of my second term I declined the offer of a third, it was difficult to persuade any candidates to make themselves available for appointment.

In 1981 when the establishment of such a post was first mooted, the SRC was strongly opposed to it, believing that it would relieve the Vice-Chancellor of the responsibility and they would no longer have access to him. By the following year the SRC had had a rethink and supported the creation of the post.

How did I come to be appointed? Deputy Vice-Chancellorships were established at Wits in the 1960s and all DVCs were drawn from the ranks of the five members elected by Senate to represent it on the Council. The appointments were made by the Council on the recommendation of the Senior Appointments Committee. Representatives of the Senate, staff and students were consulted. Candidates from both inside and outside the University could be nominated or apply.

My membership of Council had come about under rather unusual circumstances. Not long before the DVC post was announced I was invited to lunch by two colleagues, Professor Geoff Blight of the Department of Civil Engineering and Professor Tim Moelwyn-Hughes, Director of the Academic Staff Development Centre. Blight had been a Senate member on Council for only a brief period of his five-year term when he decided that he could not continue and intended to resign. Moelwyn-Hughes was a person with a very strong commitment to the University and liked to take the role of 'king-maker'. We had served on staff association committees together for many years and he had been a good friend and supporter of mine. Blight and Moelwyn-Hughes indicated that they wanted me to stand for election when the former resigned.

While I had for some years wanted to be on the Council because it was through the committees of Council that one could get things done, I had previously been an unsuccessful candidate and was not anxious to fail again. They persuaded me however that I would have considerable support and urged me to let them nominate me. Soon after I was elected, the DVC post was announced and I was approached by Chris Cresswell, Professor of Botany, to be a candidate.

Why me? I would only find that out when, after my retirement, I read the contribution to my Festschrift written by Professor Bob Charlton, a fellow DVC for five years and then my chief as Vice-Chancellor for three. He had written: 'The original nomination by fellow-members of Senate for his appointment as Deputy Vice-Chancellor listed the following grounds: his international repute as a scholar; the respect of his academic colleagues for his sound and fair judgement and his integrity; the high regard of his students for his willingness at all times to listen to their requests and to react in a positive and helpful manner; and his vision of the University's future.'[9]

My academic background was in dentistry and my postgraduate speciality was oral pathology. When I left school at the end of 1948 I went to Rhodes University in Grahamstown where I did the first year of an arts degree, because although I had done reasonably well in my matriculation examination I was not admitted to the dental faculty at Wits in the face of competition from many ex-servicemen who had priority. I made it in 1950, graduated at the end of 1954, and joined the academic staff of the dental school in January 1955. With the exception of periods in Britain where I did postgraduate studies, and various sabbatical leaves, I had spent twenty-nine consecutive years on the academic staff, fourteen of them as professor of oral pathology.

How did all this prepare me for my job and my responsibility for student affairs during a state of emergency and at the height of a student campaign to help bring down the apartheid regime by making the country ungovernable? Very simply, it did not. Shortly after my appointment, Vice-Chancellor Professor D J (Sonny) du Plessis, previously the Professor of Surgery, who occasionally failed to distinguish between his DVCs and his surgical registrars, said to me: 'You know Mervyn, you mustn't think you are important. Half the people here don't know who you are and the other half don't know what you look like.' I'm sure that he was right and equally sure that I deserved the reminder. The extraordinary truth about appointments to top executive positions in universities throughout most of the world, is that they are filled almost always by senior academics who have had no formal managerial training and whose administrative experience is developed on the job. I had been a departmental head for many years, had been deputy dean for six months and had served on innumerable university, national and international professional committees, sometimes as chairperson.

Teaching was something I always enjoyed and relations with my students had been good except for the first few years when I was more or less the same age as they were and not much more experienced.

In an attempt to conceal my insecurity, I adopted an aloof and rigid attitude which was not popular. This was unfortunately the manner used by most of the senior staff of the dental school in those days. Students were under exceptionally strict disciplinary control and were frequently subjected to the sort of verbal abuse they would not tolerate today. Fortunately I was soon able to work my way beyond that attitude and developed a growing empathy for the students and their problems; and particularly for the black students and their special difficulties when eventually they were admitted for study in our school in the late 1960s.

Among the problems they encountered was the fact that their clinical experience was limited because they were not allowed into the segregated surgeries for white patients and were only allowed to work on black patients. It was humiliating for them to be separated in this way. At the same time they suffered the social problems of inaccessibility to university housing, transport and exclusion from student sport and other amenities.

As chairperson of the Academic Staff Association and of the University Teachers' Association of South Africa[10] in the late 1960s and early 1970s I had been involved with the liberal white student movements in their opposition to apartheid education and the detentions and bannings of students, and had spoken at some of their protest meetings. In my younger days I was passionately interested in cricket, and although I was not much good as a player, as a junior member of staff I involved myself in the affairs of the University cricket club which I served as chairman for a number of years and represented the club on the University All Sports Council and at meetings of the Transvaal Cricket Union. This involvement in traditional white activity helped me to adapt to the situation as DVC in which I was responsible for a wide range of student activities from sport to radical political confrontation with police.

Politically I was a fairly typical well-meaning white South African liberal, vehemently opposed to the Nationalist Government policies. As a student I had been a reasonably active member of the United Party Youth. I learned a lot about Afrikaner politics and attitudes from friends in the dental faculty and we had endless discussions and arguments. On one occasion I was persuaded by them during the 1953 general election campaign to attend a huge Nat (Nationalist) rally in the Johannesburg City Hall addressed by J G Strijdom, the Lion of the North, who succeeded Malan as Prime Minister the following year. I have never forgotten the intensity of the passion of the people in the hall and I realised then that it would be many years before people with such views could be induced to support an opposition party. When the Progressive Party was established I joined it and then its successors and voted for it until the last all-white general election in 1989; although by 1987 I had become disillusioned with some of their policies and the public utterances of some of their parliamentary representatives.

While I considered myself relatively well-informed on political issues in South Africa and followed them closely and with interest, when I assumed office as a DVC I had very little insight into black political movements and had naïve perceptions about what I would encounter and be required to handle with regard to political activity on the campus. Although temperamentally I am impatient and easily irritated, with students I can be a good and tolerant listener. This was just as well because I realised very soon that I had an enormous amount to understand and my learning curve was very steep.

I assimilated a vast resource of information about the development of the black student movements; their determination that apartheid had to be abandoned not reformed; their widespread support for the African National Congress, its leaders and Umkonto we Sizwe; the courage of black students in the face of intimidation, harassment, detention and physical abuse from the security police; the politics of boycott; the work of street committees and the rallying of the masses in the townships. I observed at close quarters the politics of the toyi-toyi,[11] the singing of freedom songs, the rallying cries of 'amandla ng'awethu' and 'viva'. For the first time I recognised the importance of 'Nkosi sikelel' iAfrika'.[12] I saw masked students run across the campus with ANC and Communist Party flags, attended the funeral of a black apartheid victim, witnessed real resistance by students to establishment discipline and quickly learned that the University must be very wary about introducing rules that would be impossible to enforce; that consultation and democratic decision-making on various issues were essential if they were to enjoy student acceptance. And I also had to learn how to deal with the police, particularly the riot squad and the security police.

At the same time it was important for me to concern myself with no less interest or energy with the white students and their myriad clubs and societies and activities and needs. They also needed financial aid, housing, health care, career and psychological counselling, spiritual support, sports facilities, and assistance in dealing with compulsory military conscription. Although many white students were apolitical others had decided views ranging from the Students Moderate Alliance on the right to the Students for Social Action on the left. I tried to be fair and even-handed with all political activity on campus, but had many problems with the SMA as this book will reveal. They tried hard to discredit me over the years, and so I was quite surprised (and secretly pleased) that some of their leaders came to a farewell party arranged for me by the SRC; although (and now perhaps I am being unfair) they may very well have been there to celebrate my departure.

Just before retiring from office at the end of 1990 I had another party. This one was arranged by me and it was a dinner in the University for the presidents of the SRC and BSS who had been in office during the previous eight years. In the course of the evening there were many spontaneous speeches, all under the control of Terry Tselane who announced that he was appointing himself the undemocratically non-elected master of ceremonies. One of the speeches was given by James Maseko, a person of fine leadership qualities who is now Director-General of Education in Gauteng Province. He reminded me, and my guests, of my steep learning curve, and I think that he did so with approval.

Hence I think that I may claim that despite my lack of training and qualifications, I managed to handle my job without doing too much harm or damage to the students who were my responsibility over those years. At times I had a bad press, particularly from those who perceived my actions as biased towards the black students; and from time to time my wife and I were subjected to anonymous abusive telephone calls. There were some in the University, including members of Council, who believed that I was harming the institution, but from messages I received in 1990 I think that there was fairly general regret that I did not wish to make myself available for another term of office.

Mervyn Shear
June 1995

xxviii A UNIVERSITY IN THE APARTHEID ERA

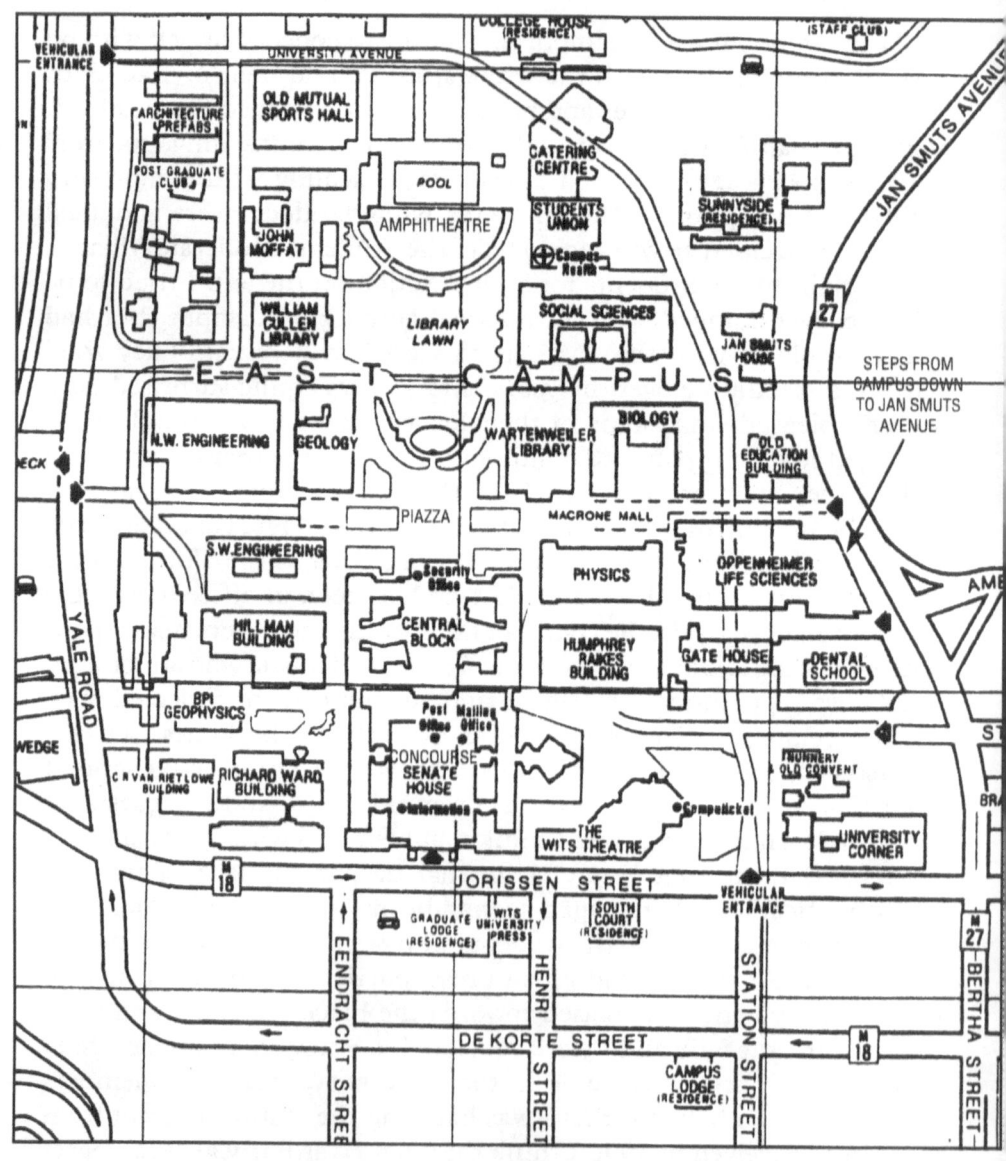

A map of the campus showing many of the sites of meetings, demonstrations and confrontations with the police

Introduction

In August 1993, during what was possibly the most destructive week in its history, the Wits University community was riven by angry and often violent demonstrations by some members of the South African Students' Congress (Sasco)[1] which led to unprecedented and unfortunate polarisation among students and staff. The Sasco group was demonstrating essentially on three issues. The first was against a court interdict which the University had obtained in June 1993 against Sasco (National), Sasco (Wits) and certain individual members of those organisations prohibiting injury to staff and students; disruption of classes or other academic or administrative activities; occupation of, or impeding lawful access to, University premises; damage to property; and incitement of any person to commit any of these acts.[2]

The other issues were a demand for the dissolution of the Council of the University and the establishment of a Transformation Forum 'to deal with the structure of a new democratic Council, financial exclusions and the continuing racial bias in admissions ...' A later demand was for the release of the students detained by the police during demonstrations on the campus on 19 August 1993.[3]

As recently as March 1995 sporadic conflict between a relatively small group of Wits students and workers on the one hand and the university administration on the other, continued to unnerve the campus; and undisciplined vandalism and 'trashing' of the campus which were widely condemned, attracted lurid headlines in the newspapers and extensive coverage on radio and television. The issues were now no longer the struggle against the apartheid regime but questions relating to the high expectations of students in the post-apartheid era, such as financial aid, improved access to higher education and democratic and transparent university governance. All these issues were being taken up by students in many tertiary educational institutions throughout the country, but at Wits there was another contentious matter. University members of the National Education Health and Allied Workers' Union (Nehawu) were demonstrating for the reinstatement of some of their colleagues who had been dismissed after a disciplinary hearing had found them guilty of holding two members of the administrative staff hostage for nine hours until they were released by the police.[4]

Wits had been facing severe criticism from Sasco since May 1993, when the student body had issued a rhetoric-laden statement in which it had the following to say about the University:

> We cannot idly spectate or lamely acquiesce while the racial oligarchy via its university administration tentacles viciously unleashes high intensity academic terrorism and total intellectual onslaught against the endangered black students and African students in particular. History will not forgive us for failing to challenge window dressing exercises and demystify the myth that Wits is an untouchable island, free of contradictions inherent in the repugnant system of apartheid colonial rule.
>
> We have no option but to sharpen these contradictions ... Our view of Wits is that it remains a white university preserving white minority privileges through a myriad of reformist window dressing tactics ... The pretentious toothpaste smiling face of the white Wits Administration has to as a matter of necessity be ripped apart ...

The statement was followed by a number of demands, among them a call for the 'disbandment of the undemocratic University Council', a call which they continue to make at the time of writing, some two years later.

Wits University has, in its seventy-year history, come under attack from every possible political quarter, either for doing too little, or doing too much to develop a democratic and non-racial structure. It received warm praise from Mr Nelson Mandela, at that time

President of the African National Congress, when on 6 September 1991, he was awarded an honorary degree of Doctor of Laws. Mandela acknowledged the University's 'proud record in defence of academic freedom, in opposition to apartheid oppression and repression, while also maintaining high standards of academic excellence'. He also recognised the University's justification for its conflict with the apartheid government by stating that 'no institution committed to the pursuit of truth can flourish in a social order committed to the pursuit of racism and the presentation of racial domination,' and made a commitment to the autonomy of educational institutions which in his view functioned best when independent of political organisations and the State.

> That being said, we do share much and we must build on what we share. What we share is values that are universally respected and this we must advance and defend. Among these values are a belief in democracy, peace, equality, non-racialism and non-sexism. This naturally provides room for cooperation but it also makes us allies in opposition to apartheid and in our dedication to secure peace, which necessitates a democratic foundation.

While Mandela's view of the University's record would be shared by many thousands of its alumni and by past and present members of its staff, a survey conducted in 1986 of the perceptions of the University[5] in the black community,[6] indicated that some of those interviewed about the institution held decidedly negative views. The results revealed that Wits was indeed perceived by many to represent 'mainly groups which are opposed to the interests of the majority of South Africans'. These groups included big business, the Government, and the white community.

> As a result the University does not cater to the needs of members of disadvantaged communities and is isolated from the experience of ordinary people. Wits is also seen by unionists as a place where whites are trained as managers to exploit workers ...

A significant body of opinion saw Wits as racist 'in both overt and subtle ways,' in that there were only small numbers of black academic staff, even in those departments with radical reputations and that there was a lack of representation of black students in decision making.

The alien 'white' image of Wits was not put down simply to the fact that there had been a historical minority of black students there. More importantly, there was a perception that the University had been co-operating with the Government, especially with regard to the apartheid laws.

The liberal character of Wits was also questioned. Some saw it as more liberal than other South African universities, an institution to look up to because of its high standards and a place to which more and more black students would wish to come. Others questioned its claim to being a liberal institution, criticising its style in reacting to social injustices, which was 'behind-the-scenes, covert and non-confrontationist, (and) leads some observers to conclude that Wits avoids taking a clear position on injustice.'

> Wits' present low profile regarding social injustices is widely perceived as a lack of commitment at the very time that (it) should be seen as speaking out. (It) is seen as failing to fulfil its role as a university in society because it is not seen to be in the forefront of calls for change.

Following the divisive and controversial conflict between the former Deputy Vice-Chancellor Professor William Malegapuru Makgoba and a group of senior academics that began in October 1995 and was resolved in April 1996, Professor Es'kia Mphahlele, who was Professor of African Literature at the University during the 1980s, wrote:

> There was a time in Wits's history, not long ago, when its administration hoped to maintain the old-fashioned stance of liberalism by playing the buffer-advocate to protest and plead by turns to Government on behalf of the students. As more and more white students sought

their destiny among the black masses fighting for freedom, it was going to render the liberal stance at Wits indefensible, irrelevant. Besides, black students want to speak for themselves today. Once the sons and daughters of privileged middle-class whites saw their situation as part of the larger blistering pain of blackness and deprivation, the die was cast. For it became for them more than the mere chanting of freedom slogans and dancing along with blacks. They were going to share the physical and emotional pain. Most of them were not willing to go this far. But it was enough to shake up the Wits campus. So in confronting new issues the administration could not for long rely on its traditional reflexes, which suited an Ivy League institution, and its lofty ideas about academic excellence and standards. The university would sooner or later, if ever, discover that these have little to do with the needs and demands of the huge black masses all round.

But the liberal-paternal posture was never going to attain the grace of self-justification. Not ever. And there's the rub. It is the students who will yet change Wits; by extension, other universities, colleges, technikons as well. The high priests and their academic minions tried desperately hard to pretend that the institution could sleep through the real revolution – that of minds, and be content with declarations of intent and protestations of political correctness:

(a) they took it for granted that the admission of a few blacks at a time would be enough to prove their goodwill: blacks would settle for an education 'superior' to what they were coming from, and that would be enough;

(b) while police were constantly invading the 'bush universities', arresting political suspects, Wits and the other 'open' universities cuddled up in a false sense of academic excellence, reputation in the esteem of the British cultural establishment and a measure of political correctness;

c) by the same token these 'open' (white) institutions had never experienced student revolts and other forms of unrest by the time they found themselves plunged in the current conflicts;

(d) with the clamour and increasing pressure from the student body for a higher rate of admissions, more accommodation, tinkering with the inner structures merely to satisfy calls for democracy and transparency is not going to be sufficient.

Expressed in another way, white institutions, 'open' or 'exclusive', have lost their virginity. When active political awareness began to expose their supremacist motives for their hollowness pretty early in the history of the white campuses, it must have become clear, except to the most obtuse, that the great predator called apartheid was not far off.

Finally, one only hopes that tertiary institutions that have always been a white preserve will realise what a microcosm they are of the larger South African malady. In the end it will not matter any more that the 'open' universities ever stood against the apartheid rulers. What will matter is the extent to which they search for and realise the full meaning of such statements of belief as 'academic excellence', 'standards', 'academic freedom', 'transformation', in relation to the multicultural enterprise that is South Africa. For indeed they now appear to us to have become, in their current formulations, children of a doubtful pedigree.

Ironically, while the views that had been advanced through the *Perceptions of Wits* study were being presented to the University community, and the anguish of Zeke Mphahlele on these issues went largely unheard by his colleagues, the institution was being assailed, as it had frequently been in the past, by the Government and the Afrikaans press for encouraging 'radical leftist and revolutionary activity' on the campus, and for pandering to the wishes of black to the disadvantage of white students. In addition, it was now finding itself the target of strident criticism by elements in the English press, particularly in the correspondence columns, and by groups of white students and their parents.

Where does the truth lie? Did Wits do too little to promote racial justice, or did it do too much? Could it have done more, or were its responses just adequate? Did it collude with the authorities in the implementation of campus apartheid? It seems important to try to address these questions even if, in the end, we do not find all the answers; because, to a greater or lesser extent in various respects, the Wits record reflects that of all the English-language 'open' or 'historically white' universities.

What I have done is to look at the documented record of the University of the Witwatersrand in an attempt to assess its position on racial discrimination, its opposition to infringements of fundamental human rights in South Africa and its contribution to the anti-apartheid struggle and to the promotion and maintenance of academic freedom. Let us see to what extent these questions can be answered.

CHAPTER 1

Racial Discrimination at Wits

In 1956 the Nationalist Government announced that it intended to prohibit the 'open universities' from admitting non-white students and to establish separate universities for these students in their 'own areas'. The definition of the term 'open universities' as it applied to the Universities of Cape Town and the Witwatersrand was that 'they admit non-white students as well as white students and aim, in all academic matters, at treating non-white students on a footing of equality with white students, and without segregation'.[1]

In fact, the situation was not quite that clear. Wits University was not entirely 'open', even in respect of its academic admissions policy. The role of the University as a centre for liberal thought and criticism in South Africa during its early years and its policy regarding the admission of black students and the appointment of black staff during that period, have been documented by Professor Bruce Murray in the first volume of the official Wits history.[2] He has pointed out that at its inception Wits's admissions policies reflected the prejudices of the society to which it belonged. While it never officially adopted a policy of excluding students on grounds of race or colour, it was very hesitant to accept black students in any substantial numbers.

When a campaign was launched in 1916 to establish a university in Johannesburg it had been emphasised that the new university would be for 'Europeans'. However, in his installation address as Principal in August 1919, J H Hofmeyr indicated that the new university's policy should be to be open to all who possessed the necessary qualifications: 'It should know no distinctions of class or wealth, race or creed.'[3]

Regrettably, the new University's Senate and Council were not prepared to be led along the liberal path suggested by their young Principal and Murray has indicated that in the 1920s and early 1930s these bodies seriously contemplated officially adopting a restrictive admissions policy when blacks – first Coloureds and then Indians and Africans – began to apply for admission. In 1925 Council decided to take legal advice when the University received a letter from a Mr Du Randt, who was not white, seeking admission for his son.[4] The University Attorney, Mr H J Hofmeyr, reported to Council on 24 November 1925 that after careful perusal of the University Act and Statutes he found no provision that would warrant the exclusion from the University by the Council of a non-European student. The Council resolved to take no action and the young Du Randt was admitted to the Faculty of Medicine in 1926 and graduated MB.BCh at the end of 1933.

In 1926 Council appointed a joint committee of Council and Senate to consider the question of non-European students in the University. This committee recommended that legal advice again be sought as to whether the Council had the power to exclude students on the grounds of colour 'with or without regulations'. Council received the opinions of Advocates Solomon and Nathan on 2 December 1926 that 'having regard to past practice, to the terms of the Statute as it stands, and to the University regulations made thereunder, there is in their opinion no power to exclude candidates from admission on the ground that they are coloured persons'.[5]

But Council was not to be deterred. It decided to appoint a committee to determine what procedures would be necessary to give the University the power to exclude students on the grounds of colour. The committee was advised that legislation, either general or specifically for the University, would have to be introduced by the Government. Although the Minister's attention was drawn to the matter, no action was taken, and from that time until the Extension of University Education Act of 1959, the question of legality was dropped. The proposal was not raised when the University initiated amendments to its Private Act in 1936 and 1952.[6] It seems clear however, that in the 1930s and 1940s the Council of the University was in advance of the State in its desire to implement university segregation.

Prior to the Second World War, black students had been refused admission to the Faculty of Medicine on the grounds that there were inadequate facilities for their clinical training. At the outbreak of war it became University and Faculty of Medicine policy to admit black medical students, although there were continuing difficulties with their training because they were not allowed access to white patients or even to autopsies conducted on white subjects. Moreover, there was opposition from the University branch of the Afrikaanse Nationale Studentebond (ANS), Afrikaner organisations including the churches, the Afrikaans press and the National Party in Parliament to the admission of black students. The University Council responded to this conservative white political pressure by accepting that as a general principle black medical students would receive their instruction in the 'non-European' hospitals.[7] However, when the Government stopped the award of state scholarships for African medical students at Wits in 1949, the then Principal, Humphrey Raikes, insisted that the Faculty of Medicine continue to reserve second year places for Africans who received scholarships from other sources.[8] The students responded to the Government's action by setting up an African Medical Scholarship fund and a general meeting of students agreed to the imposition of a 10 shilling SRC levy for all except those who opted not to pay.[9]

The official policy of the University was to endeavour to establish its own separate medical school for black students and intensive attempts were made, particularly by Raikes, to dissuade the government from opening a medical school for blacks at the University of Natal.[10]

At the same time, the Faculty of Dentistry, although prepared to accept black students for pre-clinical training, consistently refused to admit them in the clinical years on the grounds that there were inadequate facilities for their training. There were also concerns that the admission of black students might lead to political conflict with some of the white students and that in view of the overcrowded facilities in the existing dental hospital, it would be difficult if blacks were to be admitted to the exclusion of whites.[11]

In August 1944 the Board of the Faculty of Dentistry adopted a recommendation by one of its committees that the faculty agree in principle to the provision of facilities for the training of black dental students and that every endeavour be made to provide such facilities.

However, in its representations to the Ministers of Education and Native Affairs on this matter, the University expressed the view 'that the number of non-Europeans likely to qualify for admission to the clinical years of study would not justify the establishment by the University of a separate non-European Dental Hospital'.[12] The University suggested as an alternative, that necessary clinical facilities could be provided by establishing a dental clinic under its control in association with an existing hospital or clinic in a 'native township'.

In August 1946 a Government Committee of Inquiry recommended 'that the training of non-European dentists not be regarded as a matter of urgency since, for some years to come, very few non-Europeans are likely to present themselves for training and consequently it will be necessary, and probably best, that the dental health of the non-European community be catered for through the medium of European dentists.'[13] This was consistent with the representations that had previously been made to the responsible ministers, but it contradicted the evidence presented to the Government Committee by the faculty that there was 'a considerable need for dental services for non-Europeans', that bursaries should be provided for the recruitment of non-European dental students, and that facilities for their training should be provided in a new dental school either at Wits or at another university, or in special clinics in the townships.

At that time, a proposal that facilities be created for the training of black doctors and dentists, albeit that these facilities would be separate within Wits or even in other universities, would have been regarded as progressive and liberal.

The Wits Student Representative Council did urge the University to provide dental training for black students. However, in a letter of response on 17 December 1948, Raikes indicated that the matter had been taken out of the University's hands by Education Minister, J H Hofmeyr, who had said that 'it would be contrary to the policy of the Union Government for us to make provision for the training of non-European dental students. We understand that provision for such training may be considered in connection with the non-European medical school at Durban but we have no definite information on the point.'[14] This was an extraordinary change in attitude by Hofmeyr, in view of his commitment of the University to non-racialism at his installation as Principal.

When the new Oral and Dental Hospital was opened in September 1952, Raikes once again raised the question with the Dean, Professor J C Middleton Shaw, but received a cursory reply that referred to the Minister's decision 'to have non-Europeans trained in Natal'.[15] Shaw continued to be adamant in his position that 'the new Hospital was not designed to train non-Europeans'.[16] Neither Raikes nor Shaw was prepared to take issue with the Government over the matter, and it was only much later, in the mid-1960s, that the first black students were admitted to study dentistry, and then only in very small numbers.

Black students were also not admitted to courses in physiotherapy and occupational therapy and there were no facilities for blacks wishing to study logopedics. The BA in Fine Arts was closed to them as white models were often used in the life drawing studios. There were no impediments to the admission of black students to the Faculty of Engineering, although it was envisaged that students in mining engineering and mining geology would be unable to do practical work during the vacation in terms of the Mines and Works Amendment Act of 1926 which precluded the employment of blacks in certain occupations.[17]

In 1953 the Faculty of Medicine imposed a quota for the admission of black students and discriminatory selection procedures were followed in the same year for admission into second year. This led to a fierce reaction from the Students Medical Council (SMC), the SRC, Nusas and Convocation, and the excluded students and the SMC threatened the University with legal action.[18] In response, the Senate resolved that black students who had passed the first year of study in the Faculty of Science in November 1952 be admitted to second year in the Faculty of Medicine as soon as possible. Council agreed to consider in 1954, or soon thereafter, the position of as many as possible of this group of students.[19]

At the other extreme, some members of Council were becoming concerned about the numbers of black students in the University as a whole. The chairman, Mr P M Anderson, was disturbed at the increase in black enrolments in 1952 from seventy to 101, and wanted to prohibit all Asiatics from outside the Transvaal from admission and to have a quota of fifty for those from within the Province. Raikes was not happy about this and submitted a memorandum to a Council committee recommending that there should be no change in the general policy of the University but that there should be a strict quota for the admission of black medical students. Council responded with a decision to reconsider its admissions policy periodically to allow for changing circumstances such as any appreciable increase in the number of 'non-European' students.[20]

Early in 1954, Professor J C Middleton Shaw, Dean of the Faculty of Dentistry, and Professor Pde V Pienaar, Head of the Department of Phonetics and Logopedics[21] wrote to Sutton that 'the continued admission to the University of non-European students is not in the interests of either the white or the non-European members of the community'.[22] They introduced a motion in the Senate during March 1954, proposing that this body refuse to endorse the University's policy of academic non-segregation. The motion was defeated by twenty-four votes to ten. Senate then approved an alternative motion, proposed by Professor E Harris of the Department of Philosophy and Professor J S Marais of the Department of History, which rejected the principle of 'discrimination in academic matters on racial grounds' and resolved that the Senate 'holds that the policy so far followed by the Council has been in keeping with academic principles, has promoted racial harmony and understanding and has won international prestige for the University'.

Social Segregation on Campus

When I joined the University as a dental student early in 1950 the campus was very different from what it is today. It was also quite unlike the Rhodes campus where I had spent the previous year. Rhodes had about 900 students then, almost all of whom lived in residences, and the campus was a close-knit community where everyone knew everyone else and where, during the terms, the University was central to our lives. Except for occasional forays into the small rural town for shopping, for an evening at the 'scope (Rhodes jargon for the cinema), or to one of the fifty or so churches, the students spent their working and leisure lives on the campus. I had just turned seventeen and this was a comfortable, socially secure and supportive environment for young people far away from their homes, often, like myself for the first time.

By comparison, the Wits environment was much more harsh; an urban institution, not geographically a part of the commercial district of downtown Johannesburg as it is today, but still a longish train, tram or bus trip or even two from the suburban areas where most of us lived. There were a few residences but relatively few students lived there, and they were intended for those whose homes were in other parts of the country. Public transport in Johannesburg then, as now, was inadequate, and the University, located in Milner Park, was poorly serviced. When I travelled to the main campus from my home in Parkwood, only 5km away, I had to take a feeder bus to the Zoo on Jan Smuts Avenue extension in order to get the bus to campus. The feeder buses in particular were irregular and unreliable and I came late for my chemistry practical examination at the end of first year because the bus did not arrive and I had to run all the way for a connection. For dental students who took some of their courses at the medical school on Hospital Hill, there was a long walk 'up the hill', as we described it, between lectures, from the dental school on campus.

To the south and east of the campus were the residential suburbs of Milner Park and Braamfontein with their rows of small single storey houses on small plots, built in the early part of the century. Many of them were boarding houses which accommodated students, providing them with lodging and nutritious meals for about £10 a month. To the south of the Great Hall was the Milner Park School which was bought by the University in the 1970s for the extension known as Senate House.

Very few students had cars, so parking on campus was not the issue it has become today. Anyone with a car could park virtually anywhere. A public road ran east-west through the campus right in front of the Central Block and the Great Hall, where the piazza and a tree-lined walkway are now located, and there was no restriction as far I remember on who could park there. Then as now, students sat between lectures on the steps outside the Great Hall, or the physics and chemistry block to the east and the engineering block to the west, facing north and enjoying the sun. Passing women were vulnerable and, in this male-orientated sexist community, bravely suffered the whistles, catcalls and hoots inflicted by the crass males.

Rules were strict and the authorities laid down a dress code that was observed with little dispute. Men wore long trousers, white shirts (were there any other than white and blue in those days?), jackets and ties. The official Wits blazer, blue with yellow and white vertical stripes was favoured by many students, men and women, although this disturbed some of the academic and administrative staff who thought that they should be worn only on sporting occasions. The women wore dresses below the knees and were not allowed to wear trousers. Contemporary photographs show students attending protest meetings or pre-intervarsity sing-songs in the swimming pool amphitheatre, dressed in this, now strangely formal, way.

Substantial numbers of students were ex-servicemen who had been given priority admission to Wits on an affirmative action programme initiated by Raikes. They were older than the rest of us and were regarded with some awe and considerable respect. Some of them held strong political views and were members of the Springbok Legion and the South African Communist Party (SACP). They exerted considerable influence within the SRC and Nusas, capitalising on the sense of idealism generated by the war against Fascism.[23] Among them was Joe Slovo, who became a prominent member of the ANC and the SACP and Chief of Staff of Umkhonto we Sizwe (the ANC's liberation army). He was the first Minister of Housing in the post-apartheid Government of National Unity.

There were very few black students on campus and those who were there were not part of our lives. It was an exciting time for me to be at Wits but our academic requirements were stringent and there was little time for leisure. The highlights of the University social calendar for me were Rag, the annual intervarsity rugby match against the Tukkies (University of Pretoria), sport over the weekends and endless dances and parties. In order to get seats on the grandstand for the intervarsity one had to attend sing-songs in the amphitheatre during the lunch hours, learn the rugby songs and war-cries, and rehearse them until we were hoarse. Then on the day itself we had to be able to drown out the roars of the opposing supporters, and urge our side to glorious victory. In the early 1970s the SRC insisted that black students be allowed to sit on the stands. Pretoria University would not agree to this so relations were broken off and there were no more intervarsities for about twenty years.

So self-obsessed was I that I was not really aware at that time of the immensely difficult problems young black people had in gaining access to the privileges that I was enjoying; or that once they came to

Wits they were excluded from so many of the activities that I took for granted. I can remember being surprised to see a sign on one of the tennis courts at the far end of the campus that indicated that the court was reserved for the use of 'non-European' students. Although I was not happy about this, or about the exclusion of black students from the swimming pool, and I thought segregated seating in the Great Hall was 'a bad thing', I did nothing active about it. I did attend mass protest meetings in the Great Hall and enjoyed listening to the furious debates of the early 1950s. I remember well the contribution to these polemics of people such as Harold Wolpe, George Bizos, Michael O'Dowd and Godfrey Getz[24] and supported the SRC in the votes to condemn social segregation on campus, although in my first year I was among the politically naïve who believed that the SRC should be there to serve the needs of the students and not participate in politics. I blush to think of it.

There were no black students in the Dental School (and for a long time only one woman) but there were some in the Medical School where we attended courses for three years. There relationships between white and black students were courteous and sometimes cordial, but it was rare to find a close friendship. In our third-year pathology classes we found ourselves joint victims of discrimination because Professor Bunny Becker and his wife Dr Chatkidakis had poor opinions of both dental students and black students and we were ordered to sit at the back of the class.

We thought it a bit of a joke, but of course it added to the humiliation of the black students who already suffered exclusion from autopsies on white bodies. If an autopsy on a black subject followed that on a white, they would have to wait outside until the white body was removed. Why did some of us not go out in protest and solidarity with our black colleagues as numbers of white medical students did in the late 1980s in protest against the exclusion of their black colleagues from the wards for white patients at the main academic hospital in Johannesburg? The answer is that this sort of discrimination was part of life then and far too few white South Africans took personal stands on incidents of this kind. It is part of the guilt that we must bear.

There was no formal discussion at student meetings about the exclusion of black students from the Dental School, let alone attempts to pressure the University on this issue. We were so terrified of Middleton Shaw and some of his senior staff that the possibility of crossing them on important points of principle was never considered. We were guided by our obsession with survival. In 1964 two Indian students were admitted. One of them, Dr Ismael Dockrat, and I became good friends and did some research together on a condition known as submucous fibrosis which affects Indians almost exclusively and in South Africa mostly women. An epidemiological study we did in Johannesburg and Durban showed for the first time that the condition was caused by chewing the areca or betel nut.

Dockrat has talked to me about those early days and how lonely it was to be the only black student in the dental school. He often spent days alone when off duty because all but two of his white classmates, he believes, were afraid to be seen in public with him. In subsequent years some coloured students were admitted and eventually some Africans. Professor Trevor Arendorf who was one of the first coloured dental students at Wits and graduated in 1973, told me that he had a number of white friends and they used to play sport together on the campus. But after the games, he noticed that these friends were reticent about being off campus with him.

There was a pervasive fear among white liberals during the Vorster era when the Bureau of State Security (Boss) were ruthless in their response to all forms of dissidence. During the campus turbulence of 1972 while I was chairperson of the Academic Staff Association I addressed a student protest meeting in the Great Hall and referred to the fear of the oppressive regime and of people's reluctance to come out publicly in opposition in case they were marked.

When I and other members of staff in the 1960s raised the prohibition on black students even looking at white patients, let alone performing any clinical procedures on them, and suggested that clinical facilities should be open to all students, we were told by Evans Dodds, the dean at the time, that if we raised the matter with the Government, the Dental School would be closed down. As a result our black students were not able to see the breadth of material that was available to their white colleagues and suffered some humiliating experiences when reprimanded for passing through a surgery for whites or having a quick look at a rare and interesting case involving a white patient.[25]

Dockrat experienced other difficulties with Dodds. One Friday Dodds called him into his office because he had discovered that Dockrat had been to mosque. He was told that if he persisted in this activity Dodds would have to reconsider admitting others 'of his type'. Dockrat told him that in that case he would not go again. On another occasion Dodds ostentatiously refused to dry his hands on a towel that Dockrat had just used. There were other similar humiliations and Ismael Dockrat, a gentle and quietly spoken man tells me euphemistically that this was not the happiest period of his life. Trevor Arendorf had similar experiences.

This was more than social segregation, it was academic segregation, something we proclaimed was not the University's policy.

Until the late 1970s there was virtually no social integration on the Wits campus. Black students were not admitted to the main residences, were not free to use the sports facilities and were excluded from formal student social functions. The official policy, as propounded by Raikes, was one of 'academic non-segregation, coupled with social segregation'. On 13 June 1932 Raikes responded to a letter from the Secretary of the Student Representative Council, that permission must be sought from the Principal to admit 'natives and coloured persons to meetings of University Societies', and that 'proper provision (must be made) for the accommodation of natives or coloured persons, in order that the susceptibilities of all the guests may be duly safeguarded'.[26]

On 8 October 1952, Raikes issued a statement headed 'Position of the University in relation to politics and the duties of students and student societies in relation thereto and to the University'. His explanation of the policy of 'academic non-segregation but social segregation' was that 'the Non-European student has access to every educational facility which the University provides, but he is not admitted to the sports facilities provided for Europeans nor to European dances or other social functions'. He added: 'Some persons hold that this policy is impossible of implementation. If they are right, then the only thing to do in the best interests of both parties is to stop the admission of Non-European students.'[27] He went on to castigate students who had recently taken part in a march, writing that 'any demonstration against the operation of the duly established laws of the country is wrong, but demonstrating in University blazers and in close association with Non-Europeans makes things worse – it brings the University into contempt.' One reads this sort of statement today with dismay, but Raikes was clearly expressing the viewpoint prevailing in white South African society at that time.

The march in question had been organised by the Students' Liberal Association (SLA) and led by Harold Wolpe to join a demonstration at the Magistrate's Court protesting against the arrest of two medical students, Deliza Mji and Nthatho Harrison Motlana, President and Secretary of the African National Congress Youth League, for their involvement in the Defiance Campaign. Wolpe had been President of the SRC the previous year and was a leading figure on the SLA which had been established on the campus in August 1948, soon after the Nationalists came to power, in order to 'resist attempts from any quarter to introduce racial or political discrimination in the academic sphere'. It effectively replaced the Forum of Progressive Students (Fops) which had previously represented similar views on campus.[28]

After the accession of the National Party to power in 1948 there was pressure on the universities to observe strict apartheid. The response of Raikes and the Council was that the University should ward off attempts at Government intervention by tightening up on social segregation and limiting the intake of black students. This policy, described by Murray as 'essentially one of appeasement',[29] met with strong opposition from the student left.

As was to be the case in subsequent decades at Wits and in many of the other South African universities, the student leadership and relatively small numbers of academics were in the vanguard of progressive political thought in the country. They faced formidable resistance to change from the established authority of conservatively-minded members of Council and administrators. In 1948 Raikes and the Council were defied by the SRC when they attempted to prohibit black students from participating in the Rag procession. During the SRC presidency of Godfrey Getz in 1952 the SRC undertook a comprehensive review of discrimination on campus. The restrictions that the University imposed on its black students were set out in a letter from the Registrar, Mr I Glyn Thomas to the SRC on 6 May 1952. Black students were excluded from University sports and dances, segregated seating in the Great Hall was to be imposed for all University functions for which members of the public could purchase tickets and black students could not participate in productions in the Great Hall unless the entire cast was black.[30] The All Sports Council was the one student body to demonstrate discriminatory policies. While it was prepared to accept blacks as members of sports clubs, they might not participate in league events and they could use the grounds only when they were not being used by whites. Moreover, these concessions were to be subject to the law and conventions of the land, municipal regulations, the parent bodies of the clubs and the decision of the Council.[31]

On 13 May 1952 the SRC adopted a motion proposed by Harold Wolpe that no student club or society that imposed discrimination against any student on the basis of race, colour or creed would be recognised by the SRC or allowed to function on the campus and that the SRC could no longer agree to or passively accept the restrictions placed by the university authorities on the full participation of non-European students in the activities of student clubs and societies.[32] In October 1952 the SRC called on the Principal to withdraw the provisions for segregated seating in the Great Hall. If this restriction were not withdrawn, the SRC threatened to propose to a general meeting of the student body that they decline to make any further use of the Great Hall for any function at which the authorities imposed a colour bar.[33]

These events happened concurrently with Raikes's angry outburst against the students who had demonstrated at the Magistrates Courts and others who had taken part in the Defiance Campaign during the vacation, and this evoked an equally angry response from Getz against the policies of Raikes and the Council. Getz argued that the nature of South African society made it impossible for the University to remain politically neutral and that the Government's policies of apartheid education and its infringements of the fundamental liberties of freedom of speech and organisation made it imperative for a true university to take a stand on these issues. He also defended the rights of individual students to act on their own consciences provided they did not purport to represent the University in their actions.

Getz accused Raikes and the University authorities of failing to protect the independence of the University and of capitulating to Government pressure.[34]

Getz's courageous and principled stand on these issues was far in advance of the thinking of most South African whites at the time and his speech split the campus. His presidential address at a student meeting in the Great Hall on 9 March 1953 was drowned out by howls, heckling, bells and whistles and the meeting had to be postponed (an infringement of freedom of speech which was to be echoed at many meetings in the 1980s).[35] After two adjournments a motion of no confidence in the SRC was lost by a narrow margin of 693 to 725. In a subsequent referendum, the motion was carried by 1 314 to 1 035 in an 80 per cent poll. The SRC resigned, but most of the former members were returned in the subsequent election in April, and Getz was re-elected President.[36]

Getz was succeeded by Mr D J Goldstein who was equivocal about the social segregation issue. In a memorandum prepared in September 1953, he was strongly supportive of academic non-segregation but wrote '... There is no absolute dividing line between social and academic non-segregation, but one may draw the line wherever one wishes. Naturally, one must not be completely neglectful of the mores of the time, and one must take into consideration the feelings of all sections of the student body. Experience at Wits has shown that the system at present in use here works admirably ... The present situation is regarded by almost everyone as a tolerable compromise under the circumstances.'[37]

Raikes retired from the University on grounds of ill-health in 1953 and was succeeded by Professor W G Sutton, Head of the Department of Civil Engineering. Murray paints a sympathetic picture of Raikes, believing that he was genuinely committed to black educational advancement but was determined not to challenge the social customs of the country.[38] His middle of the road approach was rejected by consecutive SRCs and dismissed contemptuously by the Malan government. He dreaded political activism, strongly opposed student involvement in political protest and believed that his soft approach would persuade the Government to refrain from imposing university apartheid. His policy clearly failed and, in effect, the University was colluding with white conservatism in imposing social segregation. When apartheid university education was imposed by legislation, social segregation was an inevitable consequence. In its long struggle with the Government on academic freedom should it

Students Clash with Council

A motion passed by the student body in March 1954 instructed all student societies and clubs not to make use of the Great Hall for segregated functions. The Choral Society defied this motion and the SRC threatened to withdraw its recognition and financial support. This led to a clash with the University Council and Sutton who regarded the action as a challenge to their authority. Council resolved to permit the SRC to proceed under its existing constitution but subject to the veto of the Principal, on its behalf, in the case of any SRC decision or action which he considered to be undesirable.[39] The statutory recognition given to the SRC in terms of the University's Private Act was then used to impose a constitution on the SRC which it regarded as undemocratic and unacceptable. The next step was that Council dissolved 'the body hitherto known as the SRC', a move seen by many as another attempt by the University to pacify the Government.[40] Later in the year one concession was made. The principal was empowered to rule whether lectures held under the auspices of the Visiting Lecturers' Trust Fund and the Hoernlé Memorial Lectures under the auspices of the South African Institute of Race Relations might be regarded as academic occasions (despite the presence of the public) on which racial separation would not be required.[41]

By 1962 the Council was still intransigent in respect of social segregation on campus. Letters from Mr Neil Callie, President of the SRC to Sutton on 28 December 1961 and 8 February 1962 referred to the fact that its motions condemning social segregation had not been implemented on campus. Callie indicated that the SRC intended to organise an inter-faculty sports and cultural tournament and wished the Graduation Ball to be open to all graduate students.[42] Council decided to reaffirm the policy of the University regarding social segregation, and turned down both requests.[43] It merely noted a subsequent resolution of the SRC on the question and agreed to inform the student body that the Council was 'unable to deviate from its present policy'.[44]

Some years later there was a row on the campus and outrage was expressed by sections of the Afrikaans press when, on 19 May 1969, a pamphlet was distributed by two Conservative members of the SRC, Mr Barry Keyter and Mr Henry Vorster. In the pamphlet headed 'Important Message to the Students of Wits' they accused the SRC executive of secretly introducing social integration on the campus without informing the full SRC and contrary to the policy of the University Council.[45] In response to a question from the Acting Minister of National Education, Senator J de Klerk, Vice-Chancellor Professor G R Bozzoli sent a telegram on 22 May confirming that

> Council policy remains academic but not social integration. Decisions about academic character of functions at discretion of Principal. Daily campus life has always been regarded as academic activity. Naturally there are occasional marginal problems as one has the desire as far as circumstances allow to let all bona fide registered students use facilities which have been provided from fees, donations and state funds. Facilities range from libraries to refectories to recreational amenities. Until this year swimming pool excluded but recently and with misgivings I acquiesced in students giving some tightly controlled access to swimming facilities to non-white students as experiment. I know of no incidents having occurred but in view of pending meeting of students on the issue I have deferred decision whether experiment to proceed or not.[46]

By the very next day Bozzoli had taken the decision. He sent another telegram to De Klerk in which he confirmed that Council accepted the principle of social segregation and that he had therefore cancelled the concession permitting non-white students to use the swimming bath. In a recent conversation he assured me that Council had not forced him to take the decision, but that the enormous pressure from the Government had left him with no other choice. In this second telegram, Bozzoli also asked De Klerk for an early opportunity to discuss with him this issue and the position of over 120 Chinese students. The Government regarded Chinese South Africans as non-whites and they were subjected to the same humiliating discriminatory measures as other groups in this category.

On 26 May 1969 Bozzoli wrote the following to Mr Mark Orkin, President of the SRC:

> Earlier this year you asked me to give permission for non-white students to use the swimming bath. After due consideration and by virtue of the discretion vested in me by the Council, I decided that recreational swimming by individuals during the academic day was part of the academic life of students and gave my permission, provided the privilege was extended to bona fide registered students only.
>
> Very recently, as the result of extensive press publicity, the Hon. the Minister of National Education has advised me that in his opinion swimming is a social and not an academic activity, thereby implying that my decision constituted a breach of understanding between the Council and the Government.
>
> Following upon an exchange of correspondence between the Minister and myself, I now have to advise you, with regret, that I have no option but to withdraw this permission.
>
> In my latest telegram to the Minister I have asked him to grant me a personal interview in order that the matter might be discussed further.[47]

A motion of no-confidence in the SRC introduced by Vorster and Keyter at a mass meeting of students on 27 May was defeated.[48] Speaking against the motion, Miss Lindsey Collen, a member of the SRC executive said that the decision to open the pool to all students could only be successful if it was introduced in an unsensational way. Orkin told the meeting that integration was the wish of the majority of students. 'We chose what we judged at the time to be right and acted upon it. We stand by what we have done and are proud of it.'

On the following day, Keyter and Vorster were suspended from the SRC for six weeks for breaking the confidence of an earlier SRC meeting held in committee.[49]

De Klerk informed Bozzoli that he could expect a letter from him. When this eventually came, from Mr S P Muller, then Acting Minister of National Education, it was a directive, instructing him to close the pool to non-whites.[50] It was an unfortunate setback for Bozzoli who rejected the very concept of social segregation. I doubt whether he had any alternative given the angry mood in the Afrikaans press and the rage from the Government at this threat to the fabric of white survival. If Bozzoli had stood firm against the Government, the Council would have pressured him to back down.

For Trevor Arendorf the exclusion from the swimming pool was a bitter experience and he no longer felt that Wits was his university. He loved to swim, and when he came to Wits, assumed that he would be able to use all the facilities. He says that when during the controversy the University argued that the pool was private and therefore not subject to the restrictions on public facilities, the authorities had sent two young undercover policemen who swam in the pool without being challenged, thus rendering the privacy argument invalid.

Another humiliating experience abides in Trevor's memory. He went to buy two tickets for a Choral Society performance of *The Gondoliers* in the Great Hall and was refused the tickets by a fellow student on the grounds that the hall had a permit only for a white audience. It was a blatant untruth but Trevor was not familiar with the Council ruling on this matter and in any case was far too embarrassed to argue about it.

Residential segregation, too, was a source of considerable hardship for black students. In 1945 the University had opened Douglas Smit House as a segregated residence for the accommodation of twenty-five students.[51] At the end of 1963 it had to be closed; restrictions on the admission of black students to the university meant that there was insufficient demand for accommodation and the residence was running at a loss.[52] The closure of Douglas Smit meant considerable hardship for those students who had no alternative accommodation. The other residences were closed to them and the provisions of the Group Areas Act prevented them from living in private lodgings close to the University.

Single black men and women were not allowed to own houses but might be given permission to live in single-sex state hostels with their appallingly bad facilities that were particularly unsuitable for studying.

Wits students protested at the closure and passed a resolution rejecting 'any form of racialism at this university, as exemplified by separate residences'.[53]

A partial solution would later be provided by the opening in 1976 of Glyn Thomas House in Soweto, adjacent to Baragwanath Hospital, but this was also segregated and was a long distance from the campus. Suitable accommodation for black students continued to be a major problem until the early 1980s when desegregation of the residences was effected. In the latter part of the 1970s and during the 1980s the policy of social segregation gradually and steadily fell into disuse without having been formally withdrawn. There is no record in the University Archives that Council has documented a change in its policy.

CHAPTER 2

The Threat to the 'Open' Universities

The Government's intrusion into the autonomy of the universities during the 1950s was part of its plans for total educational apartheid. The Bantu Education Act of 1953 enabled the Department of Native Affairs to take control of all African schools. The religious missions were coerced by a threat of suspension of all state financial aid into handing their schools over to the control of the Department of Native Affairs. A syllabus specifically for Bantu schools was designed in terms of the notorious statement by the then Minister of Native Affairs, Dr Hendrick Verwoerd (later to become Prime Minister) when he opened the debate on the Act in parliament:

> Racial relations cannot improve if the wrong type of education is given to Natives. They cannot improve if the result of Native Education is the creation of frustrated people who as a result of the education they receive have expectations in life which circumstances in South Africa do not allow to be fulfilled immediately, when it creates people who are trained for professions not open to them, when there are people who have received a form of cultural training which strengthens their desire for white-collar occupations to such an extent that there are more such people than openings available. Therefore, good relations are spoiled when the correct education is not given...
>
> What is the use of teaching the Bantu child mathematics when it cannot use it in practice? What is the use

of subjecting a Native child to a curriculum which in the first instance is traditionally European? I just want to remind Honourable Members that if the Native inside South Africa today in any kind of school in existence is being taught to expect that he will live his life under a policy of equal rights, he is making a big mistake.[1]

I have read these words many times and still shudder at their cold callousness. But Verwoerd meant every word he uttered that day, and he and his minions set about implementing them with zealous fervour. When Verwoerd left the Department of Native Affairs to become Prime Minister, and after his assassination, his successors continued in the same brutal direction, possibly with declining conviction, but until almost the end, in the mid-1980s, with unflagging hope. The harm wrought by the policy is immeasurable, both in terms of the appalling human deprivation that resulted and the catastrophic economic consequences for the country and the continent.

Protest and Affirmation

Despite the conflicting voices within Council, the *de facto* exclusion of black students from a number of courses and the expressed desire of some members of Council and Senate to limit the intake of black students, the protest evoked among all constituencies of the University against the proposed threat to the open admissions policy, was more intense than any in its previous history.[2] This event, more than any other, moulded an institutional attitude to the iniquity of apartheid and evoked determination that this philosophy should have no place within its precincts. It must not be forgotten however, that there had been considerable tension in the preceding years between the conservative governing bodies and administrative officials of the University and important sections of the staff and student body who, as a progressive opposition, had long been pressing for a more enlightened policy on black student matters.

In April 1954, the University submitted a memorandum to the Government-appointed Holloway Commission of Inquiry into Separate Training Facilities for Non-Europeans[3] whose terms of reference were 'to investigate and report on the practicability and financial implications of providing separate training facilities for non-Europeans at universities'. Wits strongly opposed both separate facilities within the University and segregated institutions. The University's view was that the range and standard of facilities available to 'Non-Europeans' at Wits were such that it would be impracticable to parallel them. It was submitted that the policy of academic non-segregation and restricted social contact had fulfilled its academic purposes with great success and the minimum of social difficulties, and there was no reason to depart from it. The University cautioned that academic segregation might result in racial prejudice and hatred being cultivated among the intellectual elite of the less-privileged races.

While the views expressed might have been regarded as enlightened in the context of contemporary white South African values, the insistence on the maintenance of a 'predominantly European character' which meant 'white' rather than 'European', and the restriction of 'social contact outside the academic sphere' have distinct racist connotations today. It seems naïve moreover to have suggested that while academic segregation held certain dangers, social segregation did not.

On 12 June 1956 a special meeting of Convocation took place to consider the motion:[4]

> That Convocation is perturbed by the continuous threats of the Government's spokesmen to introduce apartheid in the open universities and urges the Council of the University publicly to re-affirm the long-established principle of academic non-segregation at the University, and to resist with all the means at its disposal any attempt made by the Government to interfere with the independence of the University.

The student body also responded angrily to the Government's threats and established an 'Academic Non-Segregation Committee'. A general meeting in the amphitheatre on 13 September 1956 attended by about 1 400 students reaffirmed the student body's belief in university autonomy and the principle of university admission based on no criteria other than those of academic qualifications.[5] It was also decided to mount an hour-long lecture stayaway.

Although permission for this was refused by the acting Principal, Professor I D MacCrone, who threatened disciplinary action against the organisers, it was decided to go ahead with the stayaway as 'a principled stand taken in accordance with our belief in academic non-segregation'.

Approximately 1 000 students withdrew from classes, and a protest meeting on 19 September was addressed by the Rt Rev Ambrose Reeves, Anglican Bishop of Johannesburg, Dr Ellen Hellman, former President of the S A Institute of Race Relations, and Dr S S Israelstam, President of the Convocation of the University. More than 250 professors and lecturers signed a statement calling for the University to remain open and for entry to be based only on academic merit.[6]

The Open Universities Liaison Committee (Witwatersrand) was established in October 1956 under the chairmanship of Professor J S Marais of the Department of History, and resolved to hold a protest meeting.[7] This took place on Friday 7 December 1956 in the Great Hall. The Chancellor of the University, the Hon Richard Feetham, was in the chair, and addresses were delivered by Dr A W Hoernlé, Professor MacCrone, Dr W F Nkomo, and Mr W Pollak QC.[8]

Among the points made by speakers were that the legislation would convert the institution into an 'ethnic' university, that the University would be coerced into adopting a policy which it found repugnant and degrading, and that the proposed separate universities would be inferior both academically and in respect of their equipment. Dr Nkomo informed the meeting of the poor facilities at the South African Native College, Fort Hare, at which he had been a student. The meeting concluded by passing a resolution formally protesting against the proposed legislation[9] and declaring its belief 'that the University of the Witwatersrand should continue to be free, as it has been ever since it was established, to decide for itself whom it will admit to be taught within its walls and how they shall be taught'.

On 14 December 1956, Sutton reported to the Council that a deputation had seen the Minister of Education and had been told that the Government intended to introduce legislation at the forthcoming session of Parliament to provide for the establishment of new universities for non-whites and that those universities admitting 'non-white' students would no longer be permitted to do so. The Council passed a resolution opposing the legislative enforcement of academic segregation on racial grounds and issued a public statement enunciating the principles embodied in it.[10]

In Council's view, the statement read, 'the policy of academic non-segregation accords with the highest university ideals and contributes to interracial understanding and harmony in South Africa ... It desires that the University be permitted and enabled to carry on its functions under the same conditions as hitherto, and that nothing be done to change or impede the University's policy of academic non-segregation.'

Though it cannot be doubted that the abhorrence of the proposed legislation expressed by many staff, students and members of Convocation was sincere, there must have been considerable compromise and a range of motivations in the process of drafting these two resolutions. After all, it was this same body which had been prepared to risk the country's interests by excluding black students from some courses and faculties and by applying a rigid policy of social segregation.

Throughout this period, the reactions and responses of the various constituencies within the University of Cape Town were very similar to those at Wits, and representatives of the two universities held a joint conference.[11] The monograph *The Open Universities in South Africa*, emanated from the papers presented at the conference. This, with the revised edition published in 1974,[12] became one of the most frequently cited works on the subject during the long years of university apartheid and government harassment of the English language universities. The publication also brought the reaction of the open universities to the attention of the international academic community. An article in *Nature* pledged the universal support of the international community of universities for the stand taken by the open universities 'against a measure which they believe will prevent them from fulfilling their true function and rendering their most effective service to the community in which they are placed'.[13] This support waned as international opposition to the policy of apartheid led to ever-widening sanctions against South Africa, including an academic boycott which affected opponents as well as proponents of apartheid.

The University Council determined to be vigilant on these matters and appointed a standing committee consisting of the Chancellor, the Vice-Chancellor and the Council's representatives at the Cape Town conference to watch developments and advise it of any action that might be deemed necessary in the future.[14]

By March 1957 the 'Separate University Education Bill' had been introduced, and Sutton addressed a meeting of the academic staff on 22 March on the proposed legislation. The object of the Bill, he said was to close the open universities to 'non-white persons' and to transfer to the Government the University College of Fort Hare and the 'Medical School for Non-Europeans of the University of Natal'. The staff passed a resolution expressing its strong opposition to the Bill.[15]

In a detailed statement, Council reaffirmed the tenor of its evidence to the 1953 Holloway Commission on university apartheid. It deplored the proposed interference with the autonomy of independent university institutions; contended that the proposed university colleges for 'non-whites' could not provide the equivalent of the university education available at the 'open universities' and maintained that the proposed provisions of the Bill were repugnant to university tradition. Particular exception was taken to the provision that the Council, Principal, Senate and staff of the proposed university colleges should be appointed by a Minister and controlled by ministerial regulations.[16]

The Council also recorded its belief that the Bill was 'grievously injurious' to university education in South Africa and its alarm at the implications of the Bill, particularly the danger of future Government interference with the academic freedom of independent universities. It was agreed that a petition would be sent to the Speaker and House of Assembly with a plea that it be heard at the Bar of the House.[17]

On 1 April 1957, a deputation of Council members met the Minister of Education, Arts and Science, Mr J H Viljoen. The deputation consisted of the Chancellor, the Hon Richard Feetham, the Vice-Chancellor and Principal, Professor W G Sutton, the Vice-Principal, Mr I Glyn Thomas, and Professor I D MacCrone, a member of Council.

The Minister was urged to appoint a Select Committee to hear representations from the University and the University of Cape Town. The Minister asserted that not more than 300 'non-white' students would be affected, but if the University were to be allowed to continue its present policy, twenty or twenty-five years later there might be 1 500 to 2 000 'non-whites' seeking admission. How could the University retain its European character if it admitted so many 'non-whites'? The deputation emphasised the principles at stake and that their importance could not be measured by the fact that initially only small numbers were directly affected.[18]

A full record of the meeting as well as correspondence on the matter between the Registrar of the University and the Secretary for Education, Arts and Science, was published by the Council of the University in May 1957.[19] One of the reasons for publishing this record was a speech made to Parliament by the Minister on 8 April (Hansard, 4240) in which he quoted the Chancellor as having said that 'We will never take more (non-white students) than we have today.' The University delegation objected to this speech in strong terms. The Registrar wrote to the Secretary on 17 April denying that the Chancellor had made the statement attributed to him, and asked that the Minister take steps to remove the misconception as soon as possible. The Minister conceded in a letter dated 26 April that he had intended to give a general impression gained during the interview and that the Chancellor had said that the 'University Council could safely be entrusted with the responsibility of regulating the admission of Non-European students.'

In his reply of 30 April, the Registrar denied that the word 'regulating' was used by any member of the deputation in the sense implied in the letter. All members adhered to the University's policy that the admission of students, 'European and Non-European', should depend on the application of academic criteria. The Chancellor had, however, 'undoubtedly indicated that the Council could safely be entrusted with the responsibility of continuing to exercise its present powers in regard to the admission of students'.

An amended Bill was read a first time on 8 April 1957 and was published on 10 April. At the beginning of May, the University organised, jointly with the University of Cape Town, a petition to Parliament, which all members of the academic staff were invited to sign.[20] The Bill passed its Second Reading in May 1957. It was then referred to a Parliamentary Select Committee which was transformed into a Commission of Inquiry during the Parliamentary

THE THREAT TO THE 'OPEN' UNIVERSITIES

The front page of Wits Student *on the day of the historic march against the Separate University Education Bill aimed at bringing apartheid to the 'open' universities*

recess.[21] Evidence was submitted by Council, the Lecturers' Association, the Executive Committee of the Convocation, and the Student Representative Council.[22]

The Commission of Inquiry reported in August 1958 and recommended that a new Bill be drawn up, to be called the Extension of University Education Bill. This was introduced on 26 February 1958 and became law as the Extension of University Education Act 45 of 1959. Its provisions were summarised in *The Open Universities in South Africa*:

> The Extension of University Education Act is mainly devoted to providing for the establishment, management and control of separate university colleges 'for Bantu persons' and for 'non-white persons other than Bantu persons'. Only four of its 42 provisions are directly concerned with the question of university segregation. Section 17 prohibits the attendance of a White person as a student at any of the colleges created by the Act. Sections 31 and 32 provide that no black student who was not registered at an established university when the Act came into operation might attend such a university without the consent of the responsible Minister ... Contravention of one of these sections is punishable by a fine of R200 or by imprisonment for six months.[23]

The Government had originally intended to take control of the medical school of the University of Natal which in practice admitted only black students. In an impressive stand of principled opposition to this intention, the teaching staff announced that they would resign if their school was brought under Government control, and the plan was abandoned.[24]

The University Registrar notified the Deans of Faculties and Faculty Secretaries on 12 November 1959 that Proclamations No 221 and 223 of 1 October 1959 declared that Section 31 of the Act would operate from 1 January 1960.[25]

In 1959, the Wits student body consisted of 297 black students and 4 813 whites.

During the period before the Bill became law, the anger of substantial numbers of the University staff, students and Convocation about the legislation and their frustration at the intransigent attitude of the Government to all objections were so intense that it was decided to hold the country's first academic procession of protest. The date was set as 22 May 1957.

Picture courtesy The Star

A procession of 2 000 professors, lecturers, students and members of Convocation marches to the City Hall on 22 May 1957

Such a procession, wrote the Open Universities Liaison Committee to all members of the academic staff and Convocation, could 'only be justified by the gravest objections to a measure like the proposed legislation. We are convinced that the objections to the Bill are of the most grave, and the decision to protest against it in this way was not taken lightly. It is because the Bill constitutes an attack on the fundamental nature and purpose of a university that we ask members of Convocation to demonstrate their opposition.'

Participants in the procession included members of Council, Senate, academic staff, Convocation and the student body. Vice-Chancellor W G Sutton addressed the assembly from the steps of the main block before the procession left and I D MacCrone gave an address at the City Hall at which it ended.[26] Academic dress was worn and the procession moved in columns of thirty-five files, six persons deep, with an interval of five yards between columns. It was an impressive and moving ceremony which has become part of the folklore of the University, and is frequently referred to by members of the institution who participated.[27]

One group of students, campaigning for election to the SRC and referring to themselves as a 'Liberal Ticket', criticised the policy of 'academic non-segregation'. They regarded the idea of an 'open university' as practised at Wits as hypocritical, were opposed to all forms of apartheid on the campus, and urged the Council 'to ignore the Universities Apartheid Bill when it becomes law'.[28]

On 16 April 1959 the first General Assembly of the University met in the Great Hall. Members of the Council, Senate, staff, Convocation and the student body gathered to express their strongest objections to the Act, and to make a solemn affirmation which has been recalled and reaffirmed every year since.[29] The affirmation reads:

> We affirm in the name of the University of the Witwatersrand that it is our duty to uphold the principle that a university is a place where men and women, without regard to race and colour, are welcome to join in the acquisition and advancement of knowledge; and to continue faithfully to defend this ideal against all who have sought by legislative enactment to curtail the autonomy of the University. Now therefore we dedicate ourselves

to the maintenance of this ideal and to the restoration of the autonomy of our University.

On the second anniversary of this dedication ceremony, an Academic Freedom Week was held. A plaque on which the affirmation was

A banner, strung across the pillars of the Central Block, bears the statement of affirmation later to be inscribed on a plaque outside the entrance to the Great Hall

inscribed, was unveiled by the Chancellor of the University, Richard Feetham in a ceremony held on Monday 17 April 1961 in the foyer outside the Great Hall before a Congregation of Council, staff, Convocation and students.[30] This plaque is affixed to the wall in the lobby outside the entrance to the Great Hall. The SRC organised a petition to the Minister of Education, Arts and Science, to reopen the University.

The University's affirmation of its commitment to Academic Freedom was to be reiterated in a number of ways in the coming years and would be received with varying degrees of hostility by Government, the Afrikaans press and the police.

During 1961, the University instituted 'The Chancellor's Lecture'. This was to be a triennial public event at which it would reaffirm the ideals enshrined in the dedication. In 1963 the Student Representative Council established the annual Richard Feetham Memorial Lecture to supplement the Chancellor's Lecture.[31] The Senate established an Academic Freedom Committee in 1972 which was to remain vigilant on all matters affecting academic freedom and to respond to all matters impinging on it.

The tenth anniversary of the Day of Affirmation on 16 April 1969 was observed by a partial closure of the University, and by a Second General Assembly on the piazza in front of the Central Block. More than 3 000 students and staff were addressed by Professor G R Bozzoli, previously a Professor of Electrical Engineering at the University, who had been appointed Vice-Chancellor and Principal in 1968.[32]

On the previous night students holding a placard demonstration in the thoroughfare outside the University had been attacked by a group of about 100 men, many of whom claimed to be from the Air Force School of Technical Training. In another incident, nineteen students, including Mark Orkin, President of the SRC, had been arrested by railway police while distributing academic freedom pamphlets and invitations to attend a public meeting. Six of the students paid admission of guilt fines, but the others refused to back down and were all subsequently acquitted on a charge of contravening a railway regulation by unlawfully distributing literature on railway property.[33]

A petition signed by many thousands of students, lecturers and members of the public was presented to the Minister of National

Education, Senator J de Klerk, calling on him to reopen Wits to students of all races. Nusas campaigned strongly nation-wide for the opening of the universities, and received messages of support from civil rights groups, churches and student organisations throughout the world. However, students of the Rand Afrikaans University presented a resolution to Vorster condemning the protests at Wits and other universities.[34]

The SRC had arranged a week of education and protest and published a commemorative booklet.[35] Seminars held throughout the rededication day culminated in a public meeting, attended by 2 000 people, who were addressed by Professor Philip Tobias, Dr Zac de Beer and Mark Orkin.[36]

In the course of his address, Tobias paid tribute to the courage of the students who had held vigils at the edge of the campus on a number of successive nights, in the face of police action and other forms of intimidation. The story of student activism at Wits and at other South African universities against apartheid and human rights infringements is an honourable one; and it will be seen to be a recurring theme as this tale unfolds.

Vociferous though the opposition was, the English-language universities had lost the battle. The Government pursued its objective of developing university apartheid and only limited numbers of African, Coloured and Indian students were allowed to study at Wits, Cape Town, Natal and Rhodes, and then only provided they received Ministerial permission; and this was only given when the courses and subjects followed were not available at the apartheid institutions.

In the face of national and international criticism, the Government claimed success for its policy by increasing the numbers of students from about 22 000 in nine residential universities in 1957 to over 73 000 in fifteen residential universities by mid-1973.[37] There were three universities for African students, Fort Hare, Zululand and the University of the North; the University of Durban-Westville for Indians; and the University of the Western Cape for Coloured students. The remaining ten residential universities were reserved for white students. The 'white' universities fell under the aegis of the Minister of National Education whereas the others were under the control of the Ministers of Bantu Education, Coloured Relations and Indian Affairs.[38]

Criticism of the system continued to be heard regularly from within the English-language universities and opposition from academic institutions abroad led to an increasingly severe academic boycott. Ironically, many of those attacked by the boycott were among apartheid's most vigorous opponents. The Government was unmoved. The academic boycott did not affect the National Party's performance at the all-white elections and, if anything, the strong-arm tactics against protesting students and academics probably enhanced its image among conservative whites who ardently approved of measures that promoted what they saw as 'law and order'.

Every academic success, like every accomplishment in the field of sport, was hailed by the Government-supporting media, particularly the South African Broadcasting Corporation, as a triumph for a South Africa in isolation, under siege. The inferior facilities and absence of academic freedom at the apartheid universities were disregarded until increasing militancy on the part of the black students at these institutions rendered them virtually ungovernable and led to their forced closure for prolonged periods.

A Referendum

Some years later, Bozzoli tried a different approach. On 21 May 1976, the University Council authorised him to request the Minister of National Education Dr P J Koornhof, to open the University once again to students of all races.[39] A committee of senior professors, including a number of faculty deans, prepared a cautiously worded draft working paper for the meeting on 20 October 1976.[40]

The University stated that it wished to be free to select its students on grounds of academic merit alone. While it was acknowledged that it was not possible at that time for integrated residences to be established 'it will be desirable for more opportunities to be provided for blacks and whites to study together. Our previous experience of mixed student bodies here has shown that relationships between black and white students have always been amicable'. While a quota should not be introduced, it was thought that on grounds of academic merit alone it would be most unlikely that the current number of black students would more than double during the following five years, and the University would probably have no more than 15 per cent black students in the foreseeable future.

In a controversial move, a referendum was suggested to determine the extent of support for this stand.[41] Bozzoli reported to Senate on 31 August 1976 that the Academic Freedom Committee had asked for the assumption that all constituent parts of the University were in favour of 'opening' it to be tested.[42] While a memorandum from the Senate Academic Freedom Committee supported the move and urged members of the University to vote on the issue,[43] an organisation affiliated to the SRC and known as the Wages and Economics Commission, questioned the University's sincerity, referred to the referendum as a 'burlesque of university autonomy and academic freedom', and called on students not to support it.[44] It was not a burlesque, although most of us realised that an approach to the Government was likely to be a futile exercise.

Bozzoli addressed the University and pointed out that numbers of black matriculants were rising and the time would undoubtedly come when the admission of all students on academic merit would lead to white students being rejected in favour of better black ones.[45]

The referendum, which was held at the end of September 1976, took the form of a secret postal ballot. Respondents were asked whether they supported the decision of the Council of the University that the Vice-Chancellor should approach the Minister of National Education to seek the removal of legislation which prevented blacks from registering at the University without ministerial permission. The result was an overwhelming vote in favour of the reopening of the University. In a 52,5 per cent poll, students voted by 5 143 votes to 415 in favour (92,5 per cent). The academic staff poll was 73 per cent with 1 658 voting in favour and 128 against the proposal (92,8 per cent).[46]

Bozzoli and Vice-Chancellor-elect Professor D J du Plessis, former Head of the University's Department of Surgery, together with the Vice-Chancellor of the University of Cape Town, met Koornhof on 29 October and were told that his Department would study the proposals and their implications in relation to existing legislation, and would raise the issue with the Minister of Bantu Education.[47] Nothing came of the representations. Bozzoli described Koornhof as cordial and 'promising' (he was known to the media as 'Piet promises') but said he had explained that no change in Government policy could occur in under three years – a year each to convince the Prime Minister, the party and the officials. Koornhof referred to the whole setup as 'the tortoise'.[48]

He submitted that under extremely difficult circumstances, and contrary to some uninformed public opinion, a good deal of success had been achieved in the handling of unrest in the past. While conceding that on some occasions minor disruption had been tolerated to avoid greater disorder, he pointed out that overseas experience had proved that such a policy was wise, effective and should be followed judiciously.

Council would continue to take strong action against those who attempted to disrupt the University's activities. However, indications were that *agents provocateurs* linked to outside agencies had been active on campus, and under such circumstances the currents of unrest could not always be excluded whatever measures might be taken.

Stutterheim suggested that the conditions might become counterproductive and lead to more problems than they were intended to avoid, and that they would be administratively unmanageable.

With his letter, he submitted a copy of the legal opinion and recommended that the Minister accept the Council's assurances that it intended to continue to implement its existing policy in a 'vigorous and appropriate manner', and take the matter no further.

Finally he mentioned that the Council, the Senate and the University as a whole stood united and resolute in retaining the institution's autonomy and preserving its academic freedom.

Clase's response to Stutterheim's letter was dated 13 October 1987. To it he appended amended conditions which would come into effect on 19 October 1987 and would remain in force until further notice. He indicated that the representations made by the universities had been considered carefully by the relevant departments and new conditions had now been laid down which differed markedly in certain respects from those contained in the previous letter. He gave only one example, stressing that 'the obligation to report on incidents and occurrences as set forth in paragraph 2 of the conditions does not mean that your Council has to report to me on, for instance, typical student pranks, horseplay or similar trivialities'. He again urged that the conditions be kept confidential and expressed the hope that it would never be necessary for him to use them as a basis for reducing the subsidy of the University. 'Your Council' he wrote 'is the authority under whom all aspects of your University's

the Minister's proposals should be only one aspect of a broader programme of action which should include vigorous internal debate, discrediting the Minister's conditions, and, in the end, challenging the conditions in court. The entire University community needed to have an opportunity to make its views known and a University Assembly was an appropriate and solemn way of allowing this to happen.

The students were, of course, correct. The Government was not going to be dissuaded from its course by a reasoned response from the Council. Only through massive public campaign and an application to the courts, might it be possible to convince the Government that it could not manipulate the Council to do its bidding. The Council, perfectly properly, sent a reasoned response to the Minister's letter, but as will be shown later in this chapter, the Minister acceded only to minor amendments to some of the most legally offensive requirements. In the end, it was the immense public reaction, including general assemblies at all the English-language universities and applications to the Supreme Court, that caused the Government to climb down.

In Stutterheim's reply to the Minister (see Appendix 11),[45] he emphasised the importance of autonomy to universities and reminded him that the University's Private Act vested exclusive authority in the Council for 'the general control of the University and all its affairs, purposes and functions'. While the Council welcomed the Government's public commitment to academic freedom, the requirements contained in his letter would in fact curb academic freedom on campus and constituted an invasion of the autonomy of the University. He reiterated the University's commitment to strive for nationally and internationally recognised excellence and the maintenance of the highest standards and the greatest possible contemporary and local relevance.

He reiterated that violence, intimidation, harassment, incitement, discrimination, or wilful disruption of University activities (particularly teaching and research, classes and meetings) were not acceptable, and that abrogation of freedom of speech whether by students, staff or outsiders was rejected by the academic community. The principle of freedom of speech, wrote Stutterheim, was instilled in students throughout their stay at the University.

universities had led to an orientation towards the needs of underprivileged communities and an emphasis on equal opportunity for all communities to gain access to and benefit from the resource of knowledge that they provided. The search for objectivity had often exposed truths which were politically embarrassing to the Government. Apartheid laws directly affected many of the students, and repressive acts had curtailed more than the academic freedom of several students and academics.

Wits's collegial autonomy had led to a critical climate of intellectual endeavour. An internationally controversial political system such as apartheid would inevitably be under the intellectual spotlight and subjected to academic dismemberment. Wits's search for truth and social relevance had led to greater contact with black communities, trade unions and alternative views on the education crisis. The Minister's demands sought to supervise the way in which the University managed its internal political climate and thus constituted a fundamental assault on its chosen direction.

The demands had been publicly projected as an attempt to restore 'freedom of speech' and to counter the ongoing disruption of the academic programme which was leading to an abuse of taxpayer's money, wrote the students. They were convinced that the Minister was well aware of the fact that the image portrayed in the press of a campus in turmoil with regular disruptions of lectures was untrue and that Wits with its high quality record of research and degrees was not wasting taxpayers' money. They believed the target was the critical and open climate of political debate and the resultant anti-apartheid sentiment that prevailed at the University.

The conditions they contended, were directed pointedly at student organisations and specifically at Nusas[44] which they pointed out, was the only 'affected' organisation in South Africa. The history of the open universities and their quest for academic freedom was inextricably tied up with the history of Nusas and its leaders and no evidence had ever come to light to suggest that the organisation was anything other than open and legal despite a protracted commission of inquiry. If the Government's conditions were implemented, they would render Nusas and all its aims illegal.

It was important, the students stated, to mobilise maximum support for the chosen direction of the universities. A private response to

ensuring the free expression of views and the peaceful continuation of teaching and research, it must protect life, limb and property.' The Senate would support those who were responsible for controlling events on campus but regarded outside interference in this function as wrong in principle and unworkable in practice.

The Senate would not acquiesce, let alone participate, in measures that sought to limit its academic freedom and right of free speech and would not surrender to coercion from within or from without. The conditions set out in the Minister's letter were inimical to the maintenance of academic standards, the realisation of the research potential and the retention of the international reputation of the University of the Witwatersrand. They were in direct conflict with the most cherished ideals of the University. If enforced they would destroy a national asset.[41] Council met on 21 August to consider Senate's response. It also gave attention to a statement by the Executive Committee of the Academic Staff Association, a memorandum from the three student observers on Council, a letter from the Chairman of the Postgraduate Association and a document entitled 'The truth about Wits' prepared by the Deans.

The statement of the Executive Committee of the ASA[42] also made a commitment to high standards of academic excellence which they believed could flourish only in a climate of academic autonomy. The ASA rejected as mischievous distortions of the truth the impression that had been cultivated in certain quarters that the University was in a constant state of turmoil and/or that it was being manipulated by a radical clique which sought to bend it to its own ends. In the ASA's view the gravest threat of disruption to the normal operation of the University was posed by attempts by the state to interfere in its autonomy and to impose on the Council a policing role in the enforcement of Government policies. These would have damaging effects not only on the university but on the country as a whole. The conditions which the state now sought to impose on the allocation of university subsidies violated its autonomy, and the ASA totally rejected them.

The memorandum from the three student representatives on Council was the result of discussion among student leaders and was signed by Etienne Marais, Scott Hazelhurst and Rosemary Hunter.[43] The memorandum pointed out that the autonomy of the open

should therefore not be defensive, apologetic or appear too anxious to look for common ground.

A Special Meeting of Senate on 19 August debated the Minister's letter and approved a response.[40] There was considerable concern about the conflict between the principles the Minister had released to the media and the confidential conditions conveyed in his letter. Although the Government's published statement expressed a commitment to freedom of speech and implied a desire to preserve the autonomy of the universities, much of what it required of the universities entailed a denial of free speech on campus, constituted an invasion of autonomy and usurped the University's legitimate field of authority.

The statement drew attention to the high standards of excellence the University had achieved in educating students and in scholarship and research. The research done at Wits was a national asset of great and increasing value at a time when links with the outside world were becoming ever more difficult to maintain. Over the years, as admission requirements had become increasingly competitive, the proportion of undergraduates and postgraduates who had completed their degrees had increased. No one could have any doubt that the University was making a significant contribution to the country's high-level manpower needs and it could not be said that taxpayers' money was being wasted.

The statement went on to say that the University, while sensitive to national needs and accountable to all its constituent communities for its use of public funds, must at the same time be autonomous. It could not be accountable to any one sector of the public, and outside interference and pressure, from whatever source, were unacceptable. Equally unacceptable was any form of violence, intimidation, harassment, or discrimination; any wilful disruption of University activities (particularly teaching and research, classes and gatherings); and any abrogation of freedom of speech, whether by students, staff or outsiders.

The core of academic freedom was freedom of expression and freedom of enquiry. 'The University must therefore continue to do all that it can to ensure that these freedoms prevail within its walls, exposed neither to restriction nor to intimidation, neither to disruption nor to censorship. At the same time while (it) is dedicated to

ignorance of those who had drafted it about the nature of a true university, how it was run, and the principles underlying the search for truth and academic integrity with which knowledge should be conveyed to students.

From a purely legal point of view, the letter was a monstrous, confused and complicated document, flawed throughout, and it reflected very badly on De Klerk's legal advisers.

The University's Response

During the discussion that followed the presentation of the opinion to the Executive Committee of Council the SRC observers objected to the fact that the conditions set out in the letter were being kept under wraps. In their opinion the issue was serious enough to warrant holding a General Assembly so that the University's reaction could be made public. While the possibility of a General Assembly was not ruled out, the committee felt that the situation would be exacerbated if it were to be held before the University had responded to the Minister. Some thought that this would be staging a confrontation and that the University would be weakening its position simply in order to make a public protest. This was an extraordinary view in the light of the fact that the universities were in a powerful position legally.

Stutterheim informed the committee that the request for confidentiality had come from the Minster. Although some points had been made public, details of the conditions had not been released. However, the chairman of the Academic Staff Association was given permission to refer the matter to his executive committee, and Tober was able to use his discretion as to what he told the executives of other University constituencies.

By calling for confidentiality the Government won a considerable strategic advantage. While it could continue to feed the press with statements about the importance of taking action against the universities on issues such as 'the need for freedom of speech' and 'the wastage of taxpayers' money', the universities were constrained from responding publicly. In the circumstances, the University's response to the Minister would have to be worded carefully. It would become a public document and form part of the history of the University and

do in order to comply with the conditions. The Minister could not lawfully require a council to take any steps which were not within its powers under the relevant Acts of Parliament or any statutes framed by the Council under them. If, therefore, any such steps were contemplated they should be spelt out so that Council could consider whether they were within its powers, and regulate its conduct accordingly.

The advisors also believed that the conditions were null and void and would probably be set aside by a court.

They also pointed out certain other provisions they regarded as questionable, for example, the requirement that the Council would be precluded from authorising any departure from the 'predetermined academic calendar'. Clearly if such a decision was considered necessary in the interests of the University, to prevent Council from taking it would constitute an unwarranted interference with its responsibility for the general control of the affairs of the University.

The legal advisors also commented on the requirement that any incidents of unrest or disruption which merited disciplinary action should be reported to the Minister accompanied by an explanation of the circumstances that had given rise to them and by a report from the Council setting out the steps that had been taken or were intended to be taken to prevent similar incidents in the future. After receiving this report the Minister would notify the University whether it had complied with the relevant conditions.

The underlying assumption appeared to be that the fact that an incident happened showed *prima facie* that there had not been compliance. This assumption was unjustified, said the advisors, citing the fact that, although the state of emergency had been in force for many months, all the powers of the state had not been able to prevent incidents of unrest. There was no reason to believe that a university, with its limited powers and different approach, would be any more successful even if all 'reasonable steps' were taken.

It was, they believed, undesirable that the university should be pressured into taking the Ministers possible response into account when considering the proper punishment for a disciplinary offence.

This legal opinion demolished the Government's case and it was clear that if the universities were to take the matter to court they would win. It also exposed the absurdity of the document, and the

to the development of the 'Freedom of Speech on Campus' document discussed in Chapter 6[38] (see Appendix 7).

The Executive Committee of Council met on 14 August to consider the legal opinion of Nicholas, Kentridge and Zeffert[39] (see Appendix 10). They had concluded that the conditions as a whole were *ultra vires* of the Minister, were 'void for vagueness'; and were 'liable to be set aside by the Court'.

The Minister, they said, did not have the power to make conditions such as those set out in the letter. It was a fundamental principle of South African administrative law that when a public body or a public official was given a power for a particular purpose, it could not be used to obtain any other object, however laudable. If a person exercising a power used it for some other purpose, he acted contrary to law.

Under section 25(1), the relevant section of the Act, the Minister was not entitled to impose any conditions which he might choose to make. Conditions must be germane to the payment of subsidies. They might not have as their object the promotion of extraneous matters, such as the maintenance of law and order. The Minister might determine the purposes for which a subsidy was granted, the basis on which it was granted and the conditions subject to which it was granted.

The section in question did not authorise the Minister to impose conditions which were not related to finance. More especially, it did not authorise him to dictate to the University Council on matters which the legislature had entrusted to the University and particularly the Council. The conditions contemplated in the letter cut into the autonomy of the University and would encroach on and interfere with powers which Parliament had vested in the Council alone. They would interfere with the exclusive authority of the Council; with the Council's 'general control of the university and all its affairs, purposes and functions'. There was no doubt that the Minister did not have the power under section 25(1) to determine the proposed conditions.

They went on to point out that the paragraph in the letter which enjoined Council to take 'all reasonable steps' was vague. It was not possible to ascertain objectively what 'reasonable steps' were. Council would be left in ignorance of what it would be required to

Students use chairs on the Library lawn to send a graphic message to police helicopters

The extent to which the BSS leadership was able to direct the responses of the membership from the top is debatable. While many of its leaders had impressive personalities and considerable credibility in the organisation, the BSS was to a great extent driven by the 'grass roots' members. If there was pressure from the members for a demonstration on a political issue, the leadership would organise one. Though there is little doubt that once a demonstration was in progress, the leaders could modify its course, they were aware of their limitations and of the importance of the appropriately selected phraseology and rallying cry.

The BSS supported a suggestion made by Tober that there should be a procedure whereby a collegial decision could be taken by all the constituencies of the University on controversial figures who were invited to speak on campus. This proposal was later pursued and led

- The uninterrupted and undisturbed tuition of and study by students;
- The functional, constructive and educationally responsible utilisation of taxpayers' money;
- The application of effective measures to maintain good order and discipline;
- The maintenance of traditional academic values and standards.

Tober referred to the detailed set of conditions and procedures the University would be required to meet and said failure to do so would entitle the Minister to withhold all or part of the University's subsidy.

On 12 August, Tober presided over a meeting which was called at short notice at the request of the SRC and the BSS and which included members of the executives of the Academic Staff Association (ASA), the SRC and BSS. I was present, as were the Vice-Principal, Professor Robert Charlton and Tober's personal assistant, Mr Derek Swemmer.[37] Mr James Maseko, president of the BSS, said the organisation appreciated that the University administration was facing a difficult period and was prepared to support it. He felt it was more crucial than ever to strategise together. Mr Etienne Marais, President of the SRC, said it was necessary to have maximum student mobilisation on the issue and, as the SRC intended protesting as soon as possible, asked that a further meeting be held during the coming week. Tober agreed to hold a further meeting as soon as Senate had discussed the issue.

It was an important meeting in another respect. During its course, the BSS acknowledged that some of its recent actions might have contributed to the adverse public opinion which had been mobilised against the University. The BSS delegation said that although they did not apologise, the organisation had decided to be sensitive in the future to the consequences for the University of its members' actions. Protests would be contained within certain parameters, they would be peaceful, and they would be defensible. Although the BSS had been observed as being in the forefront of violence, in their view there had been neither academic disruption nor intimidation. There was a need to explain the BSS's position to the University and to white opinion outside it and they suggested that this might be done by advertisements in the papers or by means of letters to parents.

On Wednesday 5 August 1987, the Chairmen of all University Councils and the Vice-Chancellors and Rectors were summoned to a meeting with De Klerk.[34] Also present at the meeting were the 'Own Affairs' Ministers of Education and Culture, the Minister of Education and Development Aid, the Minister of Law and Order and several other senior officials of the Government departments concerned.[35] De Klerk stated that the purpose of the meeting was to discuss the events that had occurred on various campuses in recent months. Parliament, the Government and the general public had expressed their concern about the disturbances that had taken place. The Government viewed these events in a very serious light and should the universities fail to meet certain conditions, a reduction in the subsidy might result.

De Klerk told them that the universities would be expected to fulfil the conditions and follow the procedures that had been set out in letters that they would receive, and that the Councils would be responsible for ensuring that they did so. The universities would be expected to prevent unrest incidents and disturbances on their campuses, and if these arose, they would have to be reported to the Minister by their Councils. While reasonableness would be the guiding factor, financial constraints would be applied if appropriate steps were not taken. De Klerk agreed to give the universities until 31 August to respond to the letters. These responses would be considered and a set of guidelines and rules would be published thereafter.

On 5 August 1987, the Chairman of Council received the letter signed by Mr P J Clase.[36] The same letter was received by other universities under the control of the 'Own Affairs' Ministries of Education and Culture of the House of Assembly, the House of Representatives, the House of Delegates and from the Minister with responsibility for the Department of Education and Development Aid (see Appendix 9).

Council noted the contents with concern and decided to ask its members who were lawyers to study the letter and advise it on their interpretation of the clauses. Mr Justice H C Nicholas, Mr S Kentridge and Professor D T Zeffert agreed to do so.

On 11 August, Tober informed all staff and students of the situation by means of a circular letter and listed the issues that had been released to the media by the Minister. These were

Cruise O'Brien, as justification for his own lamentable, totalitarian actions.

In fact, he acted on his own. If he does not like the consequences of what he did, he must blame himself alone.

That there was a vigorous debate, in which this newspaper participated, about conditions on the English campuses is perfectly true. English South Africa does not have a Broederbond in which secretly to thrash out its internal differences; it does so in the open. That is the Anglo-Saxon way ...

He must have known that he was picking a fight when he set out to blackmail the universities into complying with his wishes ... The point is that his intervention is unnecessary. The English universities have already, in response to trenchant public criticism, taken a fresh look at themselves and have embarked on a sensible, and sensitive, course of action to overcome their problems and to remedy their mistakes. There was not the slightest need for some ham-handed cultural alien to blunder into the campuses, making threats and issuing orders.

In fact, the English-language universities were on no different course of action in November than they were in March. The situation on the campuses was just as delicate as it had been earlier when the universities were as acutely sensitive to the political dynamics affecting the campuses as they were to those in the rest of the country. Owen was clearly bruised by the fact that the Government had claimed his editorial approval of firm action against the English universities, and it was arrogant of him to claim that the universities had contritely modified their policies in response to his criticism. Nor should it be thought that the Wits of the 1980s ever considered that it was attempting to thrash out its 'differences' with the media in 'the Anglo-Saxon way'.

When yet another election which excluded the majority of South Africans was announced for 1989, the University developed different procedures for dealing with electioneering on campus.

I mentioned my belief that the campaign of letter-writing and statements to the press was orchestrated by malice towards the University.

Wessels praised the role of the Vice-Chancellor and said that he felt there was more evidence of discipline than there had been previously.

In summing up, De Klerk said the meeting had greatly assisted him and his colleagues in reporting back to Cabinet. He held no brief for any organisation on the Wits campus and wished the University well in coping with the situation. His personal evaluation was that unrest would continue in South Africa. The Government realised that the real remedy lay in its hands and it was working at constitutional development. However, though it was prepared to share power, the Government would not satisfy radicals who supported a socialist system and wanted to take over. De Klerk felt that discipline was necessary to deal with 'committed revolutionaries'. He said he would do what he could to correct perceptions in the light of what he had learnt from us.

Nothing further was heard until August 1987. In the meantime unrest on campus continued as the state of emergency progressed and almost every avenue for extra parliamentary expressions of anti-Government opinion was closed. The venomous anti-Wits campaign in the media continued and was aggravated by the unfortunate decision to prevent Helen Suzman from speaking.

The usual spate of letters to the press by people inimical to the University was now supplemented by contributions from normally well-disposed liberals who regarded the decision as a violation of freedom of speech.

The greatest harm to the University came, however, from a series of vitriolic leading articles by the editor of *Business Day*, Mr Ken Owen. These, among others, were used by the Government as propaganda, a fact which was noted by Owen!

> National Education Minister F W de Klerk, trying to defend his indefensible assault on the autonomy of English universities, is now seeking to put the blame on English newspapers. He cites editorial criticism of the universities, in particular the treatment of liberal Conor

of freedom of speech and that some promoted the concept of revolution as a vehicle of change, Tober replied that there were always ideologically committed people in universities but that if complaints of indoctrination were received from students, they were investigated and the matter was discussed with the lecturers concerned.

I said the University had considered its strategy very carefully. It was aware of experiences on campuses in the United States during the late 1960s and of the situation on certain campuses in South Africa which had had to close down for periods of time. It seemed very clear to the administration that an attitude of '*kragdadigheid*' towards our students would lead to conflict between them and the administration and that this could immobilise the University. This attitude should not be seen as weakness on the part of the University administration.

Within an hour of the Unita meeting I had seen leaders of the BSS and had strongly reprimanded them for their action in breaking up the meeting. Similarly, very soon after the O'Brien meeting, the Vice-Chancellor and I had spoken to the executive of the BSS and had persuaded them that their actions had not been correct. The fact was that 18 000 students had completed their courses with minor interruptions and all 18 000 were writing the end-of-year examinations.

The University had been very active in trying to defuse conflict situations on the campus and prevent conflict occurring between students and the police. I said that I had arranged to see General van Eyck, the newly-appointed Divisional Commissioner for the Witwatersrand the following week, together with Major Oberholzer who had led the recent police raids onto the campus; and that I hoped to discuss ways of avoiding conflict.

For instance, both the BSS and the SMA had been requested not to set up rival meetings. The BSS had agreed but the SMA had refused on the grounds that it was their fundamental right to hold meetings whenever they wished.

When I was asked about the alleged assault on Mr Phillip Powell of the National Student Federation on 28 August 1986, I replied that the University never condoned violence but said that Mr Powell had been advised by University security and members of the administration to remove himself from the area of conflict as there was some fear that he might be in danger.

exaggerated, but there seemed to him to be little doubt that certain things were happening.

The Government, he said, supported the traditional view of the missions of the universities, freedom of speech and the principle of fair funding, but it was nevertheless the duty of the state to take steps if it was convinced that these were necessary. The Government regarded Wits as a centre of excellence in tertiary education and it would be a tragedy if the University were to find itself in a position where it was blackmailed into abandoning this position. The use of force, or at least discipline was sometimes needed to support freedom of speech.

De Klerk said that he did not ask the University to subscribe to the policies of the Government but felt that radical ideologies and revolutionaries, if given enough rope, might destroy those things on which Government and university agreed. He asked whether Professor Ampie Coetzee's views that, given the political situation at the time, freedom of speech was dispensable, were those of the University.[33] He extended an invitation to the University to cooperate as he did not wish to impinge on its autonomy.

Tober's response was that the Universiy's opposition to violence was unchanged and it used the powers it had to curb violence. He pointed out that the Senate had condemned the actions of students in the O'Brien affair. Statements like that attributed to Professor Coetzee, he said, could be freely made by individuals on the staff in their personal capacities but they could not speak on behalf of the University.

Though punishment was one form of action, it was also important to convince wrongdoers that certain actions are wrong and unjust. Despite isolated unjustifiable incidents the University continued to run without interruption and it was untrue to say that it was in turmoil. It sought solutions not confrontations. He spoke of the Commission of Inquiry and handed copies of its report to the Ministers present. If the Government were to insist on a judicial commission of inquiry, he said, it would be seen to be harassing the open universities.

Tober explained in detail the disciplinary procedures and how they operated.

In response to a question from Minister Coetzee about the perception that some members of the teaching staff exceeded the privileges

Viljoen should have appreciated that there would be no docile acquiescence and cooperation from the universities, and that his scheme to entice them to practise educational apartheid as surrogates of the Government would surely fail.

De Klerk's Threat

On Thursday 20 November 1986 a delegation from the University was summoned to the office of the Minister of National Education, now Mr F W de Klerk. The other English-language universities had received similar calls and their delegations also met with the Minister at about that period. The University delegation comprised Stutterheim, Tober, members of Council – Dr Albert Wessels, Dr Keeve Steyn and Mr Steven Anderson, Professor Peter Tyson (also Chairman of the Senate Academic Freedom Committee), and myself. Supporting the Minister of National Education were the Minister of Justice, Mr Kobie Coetzee; Mr Piet Clase; the Deputy Minister Designate for Law and Order, Mr Roelf Meyer; Brigadier Johan van der Merwe of the Security Police; the Director-General for National Education, Dr Rue Venter; the Chief Executive Director of the Department of Education and Culture, Mr J D V Terblanche; and a member of the Minister's Secretariat.[31]

The meeting, said De Klerk, had been called after a discussion at Cabinet level. The situation at some of the universities was causing concern to the State President for a number of reasons. There were perceptions that some universities had lost control of the situation; that they pampered radical students; that they did not protect moderate students; and that they wasted the taxpayers' money. Events such as the Conor Cruise O'Brien affair, the burning of effigies, a reported remark of Professor Tober in the USA that compared with the Student Moderate Alliance the Ku Klux Klan looked like a heavenly choir;[32] and the statements of certain professors and senior lecturers had led to the perception that things were out of hand. This in turn had led to pressure on the Government from parents, students and voters. Demands were being made that the facilities of the universities not be offered to radical students. Pressure was being placed on the Government to use its financial muscle to get the situation under control. De Klerk felt that these perceptions were probably

as Vice-Chancellor replied on 14 January strongly refuting this suggestion as it applied to Wits and insisting that 'we have always admitted, and shall continue to admit, students solely on the basis of academic merit and potential, while continuing to raise our admission standards ... We consider it vital that academic work at our University continues in a peaceful atmosphere. The reintroduction of restrictive measures is quite unnecessary, and would seriously endanger peace on our campus and also aggravate the unrest among black communities in our country.'[28] Tober also referred to the growing isolation of South African universities from the international academic community through the academic boycott and the danger that renewed threats of the imposition of admission quotas would seriously aggravate this situation.

On 13 December 1985 the Chief Executive Director of the Department of Education and Culture wrote to the University removing the restrictions requiring ministerial consent for the admission of black students in medicine, dentistry, nursing, pharmacy and surveying.[29] The letter also stated that 'these students must still be included in the quota of non Whites as was previously arranged by your University with the Minister'. Tober replied on 7 January 1986 that no such agreement existed. Fortunately nothing came of the threats although the Act remained on the statute books until 1991.[30]

Why did the Minister and the Government capitulate on this issue when their predecessors had been adamantly inflexible? There can be little doubt that the Minister was under an unprecedented amount of pressure from the English-medium universities. Dr Gerrit Viljoen was an intelligent intellectual who had been a professor of classics and a university rector. He, more than most, would have realised what a negative image was being projected, both nationally and internationally, of the Government's education policy at a time when the regime was moving slightly and slowly away from rigid apartheid under the pressure of sanctions and escalating insurrection.

In the period after 2 February 1990, F W de Klerk, then State President, frequently stated during interviews that the decision to move away from apartheid was taken when the previous Government, under P W Botha, realised that this policy had failed. Perhaps this realisation also influenced the Government's shift on university apartheid.

the health and welfare of the people of South Africa, matters which were of primary concern to medical educators.

Du Plessis wrote a conciliatory letter to Viljoen on 6 September 1983 saying that the University was 'very pleased indeed' that he did not propose to impose a quota and that this had greatly reduced the tension on campus, which would undoubtedly have been seriously aggravated by such an imposition.

This was effectively the end of restrictions on the University's right to admit suitably qualified applicants, irrespective of race. In 1983 there were 1 737 blacks registered, representing 11 per cent of the total student enrolment. By 1990 black student numbers had increased to 4 642 (24 per cent).[23] Between 1986 and 1990 white enrolment declined by 380 students, whereas in the same period African enrolment doubled.[24] At the start of the 1995 academic year and before registrations had been completed, there were 6 573 black students at Wits (40 per cent) of whom 4 063, or roughly one-quarter of the student population, were Africans.[25]

In the Faculty of Medicine the numbers of black students increased from 369 (18 per cent of the Faculty) in 1984 to 871 (33 per cent) in 1990 and in Dentistry from 64 (15 per cent) in 1984 to 103 (31 per cent) in 1990.[26] It is not clear whether any applications for admission to these faculties were refused by the Minister. Although Mrs P R Hyde, Secretary of the Faculty of Medicine has told the University archivist that the provisions of the Act were not applied in the faculty, it was pointed out by a member of Council at the meeting on 10 February 1984 that in past years about 90 per cent of black applicants to the medical school had received ministerial consent, whereas in 1984 the figure had dropped to 50 per cent. This indicated to him that a more restrictive policy was being applied.

It came as a considerable surprise when Mr P J Clase, Minister of Education and Culture in the House of Assembly (responsible for 'white' education) wrote a menacing letter on 20 November 1985, referring to the powers of the Minister to impose a quota for the registration of 'students of other population groups' and accusing the universities under the control of his department of being guilty of 'a conspicuous transgression of the accepted criterium (sic)' for admission.[27] Professor Karl Tober, who had, by then, succeeded Du Plessis requested that the practice of racially classifying registered students and staff be terminated and that representation be made to the Department of National Education to abandon the category of 'race' or 'population group' in the returns it required.

It deprecated the decision to continue restricting entry to the Faculties of Medicine and Dentistry and the branch of Surveying, and called on the Minister to remove these restrictions. Senate also called for the repeal of the sections of the Act which provided that the Minister or his successors retained the power summarily to revoke the University's authority of free admission.

The SRC passed a resolution asking Council not to implement racial classification as a criterion for acceptance and requested it to consider the removal of any reference to racial grouping from the University application and registration forms.[18] The Academic Staff Association also called on the University to resist implementing the racial provisions of the Act and to reject any imposition of a racial quota system.[19]

Meeting a few days later, Council agreed that although the matter appeared partially resolved, certain sections of the Act remained unacceptable and the University would continue to campaign for its withdrawal.[20] Council also pointed out that it had already approved the removal of any reference to racial classification on the application forms but that, in terms of the law, the University was required to obtain statistics on race for the purpose of applying for the Government subsidy.[21]

Council was satisfied that the Senate statement was in line with Council policy. It would continue to urge the Minister to respond to matters of concern to the University, but 'timing was crucial and ... care should be taken to select an appropriate time to approach the Government'.

The Executive Committee of the Board of the Faculty of Medicine deplored the fact that black applicants for admission to the Faculty would continue to require ministerial permits.[22] They pointed out that the need for highly trained black doctors and paramedical personnel was so great in South Africa that no racial, geographic or political deterrents should be permitted to stand in the way of black students receiving training at the medical school of their choice. They rejected the Minister's policy, stating that it was not in the interests of

The University believes that the admission of students to the University should be the responsibility of the University Council, that the decisions should not be based on race and that existing legislation which restricts admission of certain race groups should be repealed.[15]

The Senate reiterated the objections contained in its statement in March.

It rejected the Government notion that Wits was a 'white university' or 'a university mainly for whites' or a university 'established to serve a specific population group'. On the contrary, it emphasised that the University welcomed students of all races who met its admission requirements and strove for the abolition of all discriminatory procedures.[16] It held that it should be free to determine for itself who shall be admitted to study and the criteria and methods of selection of students. This was no less important a part of its autonomy than its freedom to determine who shall teach, what shall be taught and how it shall be taught. This policy and these fundamental principles would be violated by the enforcement of the proposed quota system.[17]

Senate expressed its confidence that the University would not act in any way which was not in conformity with those principles 'and therefore urgently and earnestly calls on the University to decline in any way to implement, or aid in the implementation of, any form of racial quota system governing admissions to the University.'

> To give effect to this charge, Senate adjures the University:
> (a) not to come up with a 'desired' racial quota in response to any request for such;
> (b) not to furnish racially-categorized estimates of the expected intake of students for any year;
> (c) henceforth not to require details of population group from applicants for admission to study at the University.

Senate also regretted that members of the University were classified racially for purposes of official returns to the ministry. Accordingly, it

Universities of Cape Town and Natal and had urged them to raise their standards of admission in order to reduce the number of undergraduate students in favour of increasing the number of postgraduates. He would be discussing the University's proposals with the Cabinet and senior officials of other education departments, and would send a written reply to the University. In due course he would make a public statement in which he would announce the conditions for admission to universities. He did state however, that he would reserve the right to impose certain restrictions on the intake in particular faculties which also existed in universities reserved for other race groups.

By the end of August the University had received a letter from Viljoen stating that 'in the light of the assurances you have given me in your letter of 1 August 1983, regarding your University's policy on the admission and selection of students and on restricting your annual growth rate, I have decided not to determine at this stage any condition in terms of the amended section 25(2) of the Universities Act 1955 in the form of a so-called "quota" for the registration at your University of students other than White. It would appear from the information you made available that your policies are unlikely to result in an immediate substantial change in the composition of your student body.'[14] The Minister retained the power to impose a quota system on the University should he wish to. While the University was encouraged to admit students for degrees in disciplines which would benefit the development of the country, ministerial consent was still required for admission of black undergraduates to medical, dental, agricultural, paramedical, surveying and veterinary science courses at the four English-medium universities.

Du Plessis issued a press statement which read:

> The University of the Witwatersrand is pleased that it will not be required to implement a quota based on race which is contrary to our basic philosophy of equal educational opportunities. However, there are still racial restrictions on the admission of black students to certain faculties which we believe to be educationally, socially, morally and financially undesirable. In addition, the possibility still remains that a quota might be imposed.

The SRC called on the University to defy the Act, regardless of the consequences. Council however, decided to send a delegation to the Minister of National Education.[10] The idea of defying a law, however objectionable, was anathema to most members of Council and would not have been countenanced. The delegation consisted of the Chancellor, Mr M Rosholt; the Chairman of Council, Dr N Stutterheim; Mr SAG Anderson, Dr C Skeen and Dr A K Steyn (who was not present at the first meeting). The members, other than the Chancellor, were selected by Stutterheim who, surprisingly, did not include the Vice-Chancellor, any of his deputies or any member of Senate. Presumably he intended the delegation to present a conservative image.

The delegation saw Viljoen on two occasions and submitted a proposal that Council should be responsible for the University's admission policy and that the Minister should not impose any racial criteria for admission.[11] During the first meeting, Viljoen stated that he was prepared to withhold the application of a quota under certain conditions. He was assured that the University would continue to raise its standards and that no affirmative action would be taken in favour of any particular race group either on admission or during any course. It was pointed out to him that the growth in numbers at the University was not attributable to an increase in the number of black students only. Statistics indicated that the main area of growth was in white student numbers.[12]

Within a short time however, although it would not be formal policy, the University would be applying affirmative action in regard to admissions. Recognising that black students were severely disadvantaged by their poor schooling, a means had to be devised whereby those with potential to complete a degree course could be identified despite relatively poor matriculation marks.

At the meeting with the Minister on 14 July, Viljoen was assured that although the University believed strongly that Councils should be free to determine their own admission policies, the University in no way wished to seek confrontation with him over the issue. In fact, the mood of many members of the Senate, academic staff and student body was strongly confrontational, but the conciliatory tone may have given the Minister the space to back down.

At the second meeting, Viljoen confirmed his acceptance of the delegation's proposals.[13] He had seen the Vice-Chancellors of the

Provision had been made in the Bill for the Minister of National Education to determine the conditions of entry into universities for all races, and the courses that could be taken. On 11 April, representatives of the four English-language universities met in Cape Town and, the following day, issued a statement signed by the four Vice-Chancellors.[6]

Following an unsuccessful meeting between the Chairmen of the Councils of the Universities of Cape Town and of Wits with the Minister of National Education, all four English-language universities expressed their abhorrence of the concept of racially determined admission criteria, by holding General Assemblies on 3 May 1983. At Wits, an outdoor gathering on the library lawns was attended by about 6 000 staff, students and members of Convocation who heard strong statements by the Chancellor, Vice-Chancellor, Chairman of Council, Professor Phillip Tobias representing the Senate, the President of Convocation and the President of the SRC, condemning the quota provision of the Bill and rejecting its implications.[7]

The Council was informed at its meeting on 24 June 1983 that the Bill had passed its second and third readings and had become law.[8] Its official designation was the Universities Amendment Act, No 83 of 1983. The purpose of the relevant section of the Act was stated in the title to be 'to further regulate the determination of conditions regarding subsidies to universities'. Section 9 stipulated that the Minister might lay down, as a condition for the determination and granting of the state subsidy, 'a basis for the calculation of a number of persons of a population group or population groups mentioned therein who may at any time be registered at a relevant university as students ...'[9]

In the course of the discussion of the Bill in the Council, it was pointed out that the implication that the University would have to apply a racial quota was totally contrary to its philosophy and could have a devastating effect on its image among the black population and internationally. Senate had expressed its absolute opposition to the measure and had appointed a committee to draft suggestions on the steps that could be taken now that the Bill had become law. Although the Senate and the SRC appeared restrained, it was made clear that neither body would continue to withhold action if Council was not seen to take an active part in opposing the Act.

proposals) which would prescribe an upper limit to the intake of students from a particular group; and the system of affirmative action which had been used in the United States of America, which set a minimum for the intake of disadvantaged students in an attempt to overcome centuries of discrimination.

In this context, the Wits Senate referred to the much-cited Bakke case in the United States. Here, although the system of positive racial quotas was rejected by the US Supreme Court, four members of the Court had dissented from the majority view that the California Supreme Court's judgement should be reversed. They dissented because they believed that the judgement prevented the defendant (the Regents of the University of California) from according any consideration to race in its admissions process and they did not wish to prevent 'voluntary preferential treatment of racial minorities as a means of remedying past societal discrimination ...', subject to certain limits and conditions. In the accompanying documents, the University argued that whether or not one agreed with the judgement in the Bakke case, two elements in the argument could not be used to justify the proposed racial quota for universities in South Africa. These were the element of voluntary or autonomous preferential treatment by an educational institution; and the use of preferential treatment to remedy past societal discrimination. The proposed quota in South Africa would limit rather than increase the number of places available to disadvantaged students.

The University strongly opposed the proposed amendment by which the Minister would retain the power to control the admission of students. 'The power of the Minister is essentially arbitrary and the University deplores the fact that the proposal will not restore to the University its unfettered right to determine the admission of students ... The University considers this right to be a crucial component of university autonomy and academic freedom, which for higher educational institutions are of the most vital importance ... That the University legislation urgently needs to be changed is undoubted; but a change from ministerial control with permits to ministerial control with quotas is not the kind of change the universities need or want. It merely replaces one morally and socially offensive system with another.'

Council was informed on 8 April 1983 that the Universities Amendment Bill had been through its first reading in Parliament.[5]

believed they could lead to more flexibility when universities made their decisions regarding admissions.

Du Plessis had spoken against the proposal at the CUP, stating that the University would not wish to implement a racially discriminatory system on behalf of the Government and that the system contained no advantages for black students.[1] The concept of racial quotas for the admission of students was anathema to the University at that time, and an extended and bitter battle followed to persuade the Minister to withdraw this section of the Bill. Attitudes were now very different from those in 1953 when the University had itself imposed a racial quota for the admission of black students into the Faculty of Medicine.

Council responded at its meeting in December 1982 to the request by the Department of National Education for comments on the proposed amendments. It indicated that while the proposed quota system had practical advantages in that Ministerial permission would no longer have to be sought for the admission of the given quota of black students, it nevertheless adhered to the policy of open universities and to its strong desire for complete freedom in formulating its own admissions policy.[2]

A special meeting of the Senate on 8 March 1983 considered a statement prepared by the Senate Academic Freedom Committee.[3] Senate opposed the retention by the Minister of the power to make regulations controlling the admission of students to Wits and to South African universities in general, the imposition of racial quotas on the university and 'the compelling of the University Council to become an instrument of, and active participant in, the Government's policy of discrimination against students on grounds of race'.

Numerous arguments in accompanying documents supported the University's rejection of a racial quota.[4] Among them was a quotation from Professor R Dworkin of Oxford who argued that 'We are rightly suspicious of racial classifications. They have been used to deny, rather than respect, the right of equality, and we are all conscious of the consequent injustice.' This statement is particularly relevant to the South African Government's educational policy. The slogan 'separate but equal' had long been known to be a myth. A clear distinction must be drawn, one argument went, between the negative or exclusive quota system (such as that envisaged by the Government's

CHAPTER 8

Challenge to the Government

In the course of the turbulent 1980s five South African universities – Cape Town, Natal, Rhodes, Western Cape and Wits – were involved, to a greater or lesser extent, in two major confrontations with the Government on important issues of both principle and practice. In both instances, after debilitating effort on the part of these universities, the authorities backed down. There were pitifully few occasions during its forty-six years of power on which the Nationalist Government responded to public pressure on liberal issues and these two episodes are political landmarks in the regime's retreat from apartheid. The first concerned the 'Quota Bill' and the second was the threat of financial sanctions posed by F W de Klerk as Minister of National Education in his attempts to coerce the universities into clamping down on political activity on their campuses.

The 'Quota Bill'

In July 1982, Dr Gerrit Viljoen, then Minister of National Education, informed the Committee of University Principals (CUP) that the Government was considering amendments to the Universities Act (Act 61 of 1955 as amended). Section 4 related to a proposed quota system to be instituted in 1984, which would regulate the admission of black students to the so-called white universities. This could be done by inserting an enabling clause to that effect in the Act and by requesting Parliament to approve such an amendment. The Minister's justification of these measures was that he

demonstrations, and about their fears of possible danger to themselves during these events.[35] Meetings were held with these people in an attempt to give the best possible advice about what to do under conditions that were often unpredictable.

when most other white organisations feared harassment ... Contrary to Mr Bruce's assertion that the NSF was a liberal organisation, many observers have recognised that it was part of a state strategy to counter the influence of anti-apartheid organisations on the campuses.'[33]

Student demonstrations and confrontations with the police continued. There was mounting outrage at the state of emergency and the repression prevalent in schools and on campuses throughout the country; and considerable hostility to the presence in the schools and on some campuses of the South African Defence Force which was being used to bolster the police in maintaining the state of emergency.

On 8 October 1986 a meeting organised as part of the Campaign for National United Action was banned by the Acting Chief Magistrate of the Johannesburg. A notice issued by the BSS after the banning stated that the Campaign was 'a genuine attempt by our organisations to engage people in action that will lift this country out of the mess into which the government has plunged it. It is a genuine attempt to urge our people to peacefully oppose and bring to an end the widespread violence perpetrated by apartheid and its agents. If these peaceful endeavours to establish democracy are met with this kind of action, the question becomes what is to be done? Should the people of this country fold their arms and watch our country disintegrate under continued dictatorship of irrational men?'[34]

On 23 October a meeting was held in the Great Hall to mourn the death of President Samora Machel of Mozambique, who was killed when his aircraft crashed in South African territory and security force involvement was suspected. The meeting was followed by a march to the edge of the campus and once again the police intervened and fired teargas. On this occasion, the gas drifted into one of the buildings and affected some students attending a mathematics class. One of these was a paraplegic who suffered considerable breathing difficulties.

Complaints and expressions of anxiety were received from members of staff about the disruption of classes, about the intrusion of students fleeing from the police into laboratories and libraries, about the damage to their motor cars parked in the vicinity of the anti-Wits and anti-SRC-BSS positions appeared to dissipate. This may have been the result of the humiliating criticism by the Commission, or perhaps its sources of funding dried up. The University did not conduct an inquiry into those sources, but some years later it was revealed that it had received financial support from secret State funds and from numbers of businessmen.

On 26 July 1991 the *Weekly Mail* disclosed, after receiving a secret document, that there had been security police involvement with the NSF. On 2 August 1991 the police confirmed that they had given partial financial assistance to the NSF to 'promote freedom of speech' and to further cooperation between different groups on South African campuses. They said in a statement that the NSF was supported in an effort to promote stability and law and order on campuses in the mid-eighties when there was 'campus unrest, disruption and boycotts of classes, damage to university property and intimidation of students'. They claimed that strict financial control had been exercised and that all expenditures had been properly audited and accounted for. In view of the changed circumstances in the country it had been decided to terminate SAP involvement.

The previous day the NSF had announced that it had disbanded following an admission that it had received Government funding. [31]

Business organisations which the NSF was reported to have claimed supported it included the Anglo American Chairman's Fund, the Free Market Foundation, Pick 'n Pay, Anglo Alpha, and Everite. The *Financial Mail* also provided funding for the NSF to attend an overseas conference.

The editor of the *Financial Mail*, Mr Nigel Bruce, was reported to have said: 'If we are getting to the stage where the security police are funding a liberal organisation, then we are definitely making progress'. He was not disturbed by the fact that the NSF had allegedly been started to counter Nusas because 'Nusas needs combating'. The NSF supported free enterprise and 'the sort of liberal philosophies that we subscribe to here. The funding was in furtherance of those ideals. The managing director of Times Media Limited knew about the financial assistance.'[32]

Stevan Silver, National President of Nusas had to remind Bruce of the organisation's 67-year-old track record of opposing 'inequalities, repression and government interference in our universities at times

detained and even tortured by the security police. At the same time they had an extraordinary sense of solidarity. The slogan 'an injury to one is an injury to all' was heard frequently. Critics alleged that the solidarity was brought about by intimidation and coercion. I doubt that very much. But, be that as it may, it was a powerful weapon at the time.

This is not to say that the University abdicated its responsibility to maintain discipline. When there were breaches of the rules of student conduct and offenders could be identified, disciplinary procedures followed. Although this did not deter the critics from demanding summary expulsions, the University was not prepared to dispense with due process.

The SMA ceased to play the same significant role in student activities on the Wits campus. Although it did not formally disband, and on a few occasions invited controversial speakers, its aggressively

Picture: Paul Weinberg

I and other peacekeepers try to restrain angry BSS members from another confrontation with the members of the SMA

Though Van Eyck was grateful for the opportunity to discuss the problems, he stressed that whenever law and order were threatened, and especially when an order banning a meeting was ignored, he had no alternative but to act, and with strength. Although he was not a student basher, he would give orders for all students attending or organising such banned meetings to be arrested. He said he had received complaints from members of the University community as well as the public regarding the actions of some Wits students and it was his duty to investigate the complaints and ensure that the rights of the complainants was not interfered with. In response to our anger and horror at the sjamboking incidents in Jorissen Street the previous May, Oberholzer expressed his deep regret and said that he had been away in Pretoria. He would be open to the University's mediation to prevent confrontation.

We left with some hope that the police might in future handle campus confrontations with greater sensitivity. Unfortunately, this was not to be the case. Oberholzer, who had been praised at the meeting for the restrained manner in which the past few crises on campus had been handled, was transferred. It would seem that our praise might have been the 'kiss of death' for him and that he was considered too soft to deal with student activists. Further meetings with senior police officers were held from time to time over the following few years, without any evidence that our exhortations were taken seriously.

It proved impossible to give effect to the Commission's recommendations on unorganised marches and stone throwing. Neither the administration nor the leaders of the BSS and SRC who officially condemned this method of protest were able to influence what was only a very small group of students and we were not prepared to coerce them. We were also not prepared to ban unorganised marches because we acknowledged the right of students to demonstrate peacefully and we knew we could not enforce such a ban.

Although the media, the SMA, the parents of some of the students, and some members of the public were 'screaming' for aggressive disciplinary action against demonstrating students, we knew that iron-fisted responses at some of the country's universities had led to their having to close down. The angry, militant students felt that they had nothing to lose. Some had already been expelled from other institutions for their political activities; many had been harassed,

structure of student government should be reviewed. Although a full public disclosure of the findings in regard to the SMA would have been invaluable in countering the public perceptions of the University which had been conveyed by the SMA's propaganda campaign, Council decided that only a brief summary of the Commission's report should be released to the media, but that it would include the summary of the findings and recommendations. Regrettably, Council decided that the annexure by Cameron, which provided an insightful view of the attitudes and motivations of black students in the University which were so poorly understood by members of the white community inside and outside the University, would not be included in the release.

The University administration took the recommendations of the Commission very seriously, though attempts to implement them were not uniformly successful. Although it actively seeks to appoint blacks to responsible positions in the administration, this community is still under-represented, a fact which remains a source of dissatisfaction and controversy.

A Meeting at Police Headquarters

On 27 November 1986 I and Mr Jonathan Stead, Deputy Registrar for Student Affairs, had a meeting at police headquarters, John Vorster Square, with General Mulder van Eyck, Commissioner of Police for the Witwatersrand, and Major Oberholzer, who had been the senior officer in charge of recent riot squad incursions on the campus.[30] The purpose of the meeting was to attempt to persuade Van Eyck to keep his forces off the campus and allow the University to control student demonstrations in its own way. It was pointed out once more that the black students in the University were highly politicised, that the country itself was in turmoil, and that the mere presence of the South African Police on campus was sufficient to escalate tensions. Many sympathetic students who were not activists became involved when police moved onto campus. We emphasised the University's view that it was the democratic right of students to voice their opposition to apartheid and to demonstrate publicly this standpoint. We said that stone throwing was strongly condemned but it was often difficult to identify those responsible.

'radical', more particularly black students; and on the other, the University Administration which is alleged to be turning a blind eye to wrong-doing. In the course of the hearing and in our discussions afterwards we asked ourselves what steps the University's critics could possibly want it to take. Should the University abandon its present measures and call in the police or army; double its own security force; effect a mass expulsion of part of the University community; introduce electronic monitoring equipment? Would this not create a state of siege at Wits in which all debate and all differences are stifled and in which the life of the University is quelled? These methods have been tried at other universities in South Africa and at the secondary school level. The results of the adoption of such methods have not only failed to solve any problems; they have plunged the country's educational system into an unparalleled crisis.

The Commission praised many of the students, black and white, who had testified before it and who had displayed 'talent, leadership ability, eloquence and promise'. It was important, the members thought, that the incidents of disruption and confrontation which had occurred should be seen in their appropriate context: firstly, in that of a country being brought almost to standstill by opposing social forces in the determination of the majority to secure a new social order; and secondly, in the context of an academic institution, the normal activities of which were disrupted only on a very small number of days in the course of the whole year.

A Disappointing Response

The response of the University Council to the Commission's report was disappointing.[29] Some members expressed concern 'that the philosophies of the members of the Commission may have permeated the report,' and criticised the close scrutiny that had been given the SMA. Although the Commission had confirmed the authority of the SRC, the mandate of the student body was questioned because of the low poll in the SRC elections, and it was suggested that the

assault on the University's public credibility and, far from wishing 'to promote and re-establish the integrity of Wits in the eyes of all thinking South Africans,' it appeared to be committed to undermining the University's public credibility in a scurrilous manner.

The Commission also found evidence that the SMA and its parent body, the NSF, were provided with lavish funding from anonymous sources. Yuill had refused to give any information about the source of this funding except to say that the SMA's funds came from 'donations' from the NSF.

> The NSF has, we gather, at all times, absolutely refused to disclose the source of any of its funding, which may come from private individuals, business corporations or overseas institutions.
>
> The presence of covert government funding in campus organizations is a relatively recent memory. The possibility of its recurrence cannot be excluded. The NSF's refusal to disclose any information about its sources of funding gives credence to speculation along these lines.

The Commission reported at length on the extent of the attack on the University and on the integrity and judgement of its principal officers in certain sections of the media. It accepted the view of many who had testified before it 'that the University's image should not be located only in the opinions of the white community, still less in those of a small section of the white community which is represented over-vocally in the letter columns of the daily press and in the emanations of the official broadcast services'.

While recognising that the views of the public corporations who in part funded the University, and the state, which provided it with a subsidy, had to be taken into account to a perhaps disproportionate degree in assessing the University's public image, nevertheless for a balanced impression of its own public image the University should look to the broader South African community.

> The attacks upon this University to which we have referred seem to take as their focus on the one hand, the

not share its 'moderate views'. On the basis of 'patriotism', government actions are supported and critics of the government are derided. An instance is a pamphlet which casts the police actions at Sharpeville in 1960 in a favourable light. While the 'Sharpeville tragedy' is said to be 'a regrettable event in South Africa's history', this pamphlet takes as its main theme the suggestion that Sharpeville has been 'manipulated to produce anti-SA propaganda: The radical left will predictably rave on about the fact that trigger-happy policemen gun down as many unarmed blacks as possible, who were peacefully protesting about the pass laws. This distorted picture of events cannot be seen in isolation.'

The Commission considered that it was the overt displays by the SMA, particularly on or near certain specific dates in the calendar, which triggered disruption and tension.

Nevertheless, it did not consider that what had been called the 'mob veto' should be applied to the right of expression on the Wits campus. The Commission was particularly critical of the tone of publications distributed or sponsored by the SMA on the Wits Campus.

> ... In SMA publications, the University Administration ... is represented as being, at best, supine in the face of or, at worst, deliberately collusive with, flagrantly illegal beha-vi-our. There is ... no room for factual nuance or moral debate as far as the SMA is concerned, and the University has in its view lamentably failed in its obvious duty in declining to act with severity against the sole causes of the conflicts on campus, namely the 'radical elements.'

The Commission regarded this view as 'distorted, partial and misleading'. The strident attacks on the University and its principal officers in much of the SMA literature seemed, the members thought, to echo harsh criticism of the University expressed in SABC programmes, in the letters columns of the daily newspapers and in rightwing political tracts. The SMA seemed to be deeply implicated in an

activity 'constitutes, in many people's eyes, a desperate act of opposition amongst a population deprived of amenities, profoundly mistrustful of the police, excluded from all legitimate democratic means of expression and deprived by large-scale detentions of responsible leaders'. However it considered stone throwing on the campus to be evidence less of deprived social conditions and justified anger at the police than of indiscipline and self-indulgence, and recommended that disciplinary steps be taken against perpetrators.

Detailed consideration was given to the SMA and its relations with the SRC, the BSS and the University.[28] The Commission was unable to determine precisely who ran the organisation, how it was financed, the extent of its support on campus and what activities it undertook. Questions relating to these matters put to the chairman, Mr Martin Yuill, were 'either not answered or were evaded on the basis that they were "irrelevant" or that some sort of "legal enquiry" which the SMA itself was conducting would be prejudiced if the questions were answered.' The Commission concluded that neither of these grounds had any substance and that they constituted 'a subterfuge to enable the SMA's chairman to avoid disclosure of relevant information which might have contradicted the SMA's professed objectives'. Yuill's attitude towards the Commission was described as 'not only uncooperative but truculent and obstructive'.

The Commission found that the SMA had contravened the rules of the SRC by not providing it with a constitution or with copies of minutes of its committee meetings; nor had it provided the SRC with a list of its office bearers or a list of persons said to have paid subscriptions. This information 'must have a bearing on its entitlement to SRC facilities, such as rooms ... the use of Wits venues for meetings; displaying of posters ... (and) using the name of this University in SMA literature and on its letterheads ... '

With regard to the relations between the SMA and the BSS, the Commission reported that Yuill adopted an attitude of belligerence towards any suggestion that special recognition of any kind should be given to black students on campus.

> The SMA constitutes a highly vocal presence on campus, distributing at evidently high cost elaborate tracts and pamphlets attacking as 'radicals' all those who do

of the NSF, who was 'observing' the proceedings, was allegedly assaulted. He had been advised by campus security and members of the administration to remove himself from the area of conflict as they feared he might be in danger.[26] The incident was raised by De Klerk at his meeting with representatives of the University on 20 November 1986 (see Chapter 8).

Bizos Commission

In addition to its specific findings on freedom of speech issues, the Bizos Commission made some general observations.[27] It referred to the conditions created in the country and pointed out that academic freedom and freedom of thought and expression must be considered 'in the light of the passions of the search for a new social order'.

The Commission considered it likely that clashes between the police and the university community would continue because of the general situation in the country. It was important therefore that 'the University should seek at the highest levels to assert ... (that) while the South African Police can be expected to adopt the view that they cannot "stand idly by" while illegal gatherings and other events occur on campus, (it) ought in the end to be left to regulate affairs on its own campus ... The detention or restriction of student leaders, moreover, not only serves as a source of anger but deprives the student body of responsible leadership, often during critical times.'

The Commission praised and indeed encouraged what it referred to as 'organised marches', while it was critical of 'spontaneous, unorganised marches'. With regard to organised marches, it stated that 'there is much warrant ... in the traditions of dissent, liberalism and humanism upon which this University as an institution draws for the toleration of the sort of deliberate expression of conscience which occurred ... on 30th May 1986'. Spontaneous unorganised marches, however, while also arising from the deeply felt grievances and beliefs of the participants, held 'considerably more danger than the first both for the safety and well-being of the participants and for the attainment of the ideals to which the University aspires' and should be discouraged.

While strongly condemning stone throwing as a form of expression or activity on the campus, the Commission recognised that such

walls. So I could see right into the third cell and there at a table sat the huge man, with a grin on his face. Clearly our cell was wired for sound and he was able to listen to our conversation.

Chris came in first and I got up to give him a bear hug, facing the glass panel. The huge man gave a derisory sneer. I discussed the students' work with them and asked about their plans for the examinations. I had been told not to discuss anything other than work, but I did manage, by whispering, to get some other information from them about their conditions of detention. Chris told me that the huge man was a security policeman and that his comment in the corridor was 'Watch out Chris, I'm going to get you'. This exchange was obviously heard by the warder who had been taking notes because at the end of the visit he approached me and Chris and said that he had heard the comment about the threat and asked me whether I wished to lay a complaint against the other person. I answered that I would like to, but as I would be leaving Diepkloof and Chris would be left behind to face possible retribution from the policeman concerned I would only do so if Chris agreed. Chris said 'Leave it, it's better that way.' I left, feeling again very strongly the loss to student leadership that resulted from the detention of people like Chris.

Subsequent visits were refused despite numerous requests.

Repeated applications were made to the Minister of Law and Order for the release of the students and staff, to no avail. There was a standard response, that the Minister had given the application his consideration but that the request could not be granted. It was almost certainly the security police who were taking these decisions, and the Minister was signing the *pro forma* letters. In one instance a letter of refusal signed by the Minister arrived two weeks after the student for whom the request had been made had been released.

Some student leaders in the SRC and Nusas were detained for questioning. Others were made aware that they were under surveillance, and their cars and, in one instance, a motorcycle, were damaged by tyre slashing, by acid poured on the paintwork or by arson. While they were obviously very distressed by these incidents, in not a single instance was any of them intimidated into abandoning his or her commitment to a democratic South Africa.

On 28 August 1986 there was yet another clash between students and the police. Among other incidents on that day, Mr Phillip Powell

the detained students were allowed to receive study material. Lecturers prepared study material and projects, as indicated by the AGD guidelines, which were taken to the prisons and were later collected and marked. Arrangements were made for the students to write examinations which were invigilated by warders. To their considerable credit, numbers of these students were successful and a few even completed their degree requirements and graduated *in absentia*.

By October 1987 when the second edition of the guidelines was produced, about forty departments in six faculties and scores of individuals had provided academic support to both students and staff. It was a remarkably successful operation, and did a great deal for the morale of the detainees, as well as easing somewhat the spartan conditions under which they were held.

Not unexpectedly, one of the effects of detention was psychological depression and after their release the detainees were advised to seek counselling, which was available at the University. Some, particularly those who had been subjected to prolonged periods of detention, had, during their period in prison been referred to hospitals for psychiatric treatment. It was easier to call on the detainees in hospital as their guards tended to be flexible in allowing contact visits.

I was given permission for only one contact visit in Diepkloof Prison but was kept under constant surveillance during the visit. A warder was posted outside the visitors' cell and notes were ostentatiously taken of the conversation. The opportunity arose before an examination period. Chris Ngcobo, Bheki Mlangeni and Lawrence Boya had been detained during the raid on Glyn Thomas House and I had not been able to get permission for a visit earlier. On this occasion I sought permission to make arrangements for their examinations if they were still in detention.

After a long wait, I was taken to the visitors' cell and found Chris, Bheki and Lawrence waiting in the corridor outside, accompanied by a warder. Just as we were greeting, a policeman in plain clothes walked by. He was one of the largest men I have ever seen, gigantic in both height and girth. As he passed he muttered something to Chris then moved on and entered a door two cells away from the one we were to use. When I was shown into 'our' cell, the students stayed with the warder and were allowed in one by one. To the left of the table at which I was sitting was a large glass panel and the cell on my left had glass panels in both lateral

Ms Kathleen Satchwell, who represented all the students and staff who were detained, and she was informed immediately news of a detention was received. She visited all the detainees, drew up affidavits for them, and sought whatever recourse to law was available, although as the state of emergency proceeded one legal remedy after another was removed by Presidential proclamation.

Whatever they were able to achieve, her visits, as well as those of Judge Richard Goldstone, gave the detainees just that little bit more confidence in a desperately isolated situation. Judge Goldstone performed most conscientiously his duties of visiting detainees in prison and observing the conditions under which they were kept. He played an important role in ensuring that our students and staff as well as others in detention in many parts of the country were treated satisfactorily.

The powers of the state, conferred by proclamation, were formid-able, and were the subject of a workshop arranged by the University's Centre for Applied Legal Studies in April 1987.[25] The State authorities had 'powers of preventive and interrogative detention without trial; powers to ban books, persons and organisations on the basis of secret and untested information; powers to ban meetings and gatherings without representations from the affected parties'. For nearly ten years all outdoor gatherings at which more than two persons were present had been prohibited in terms of Section 46 of the Internal Security Act, 74 of 1982. The Public Safety Act granted the State President powers 'to legislate by the proclamation of regulations and, further, to confer substantial law-making and policing powers to subordinate officials. These law-making powers enabled policemen effectively to rule over regions, more particularly the black townships in these regions …' The regulations granted the widest possible power to arrest and detain by granting this power to 'raw recruits' of the South African Defence Force, South African Police and other agencies of the 'security forces'. They attempted to exclude legal process and legal supervision from the exercise of emergency powers; and they sought to prohibit or inhibit public accountability over police conduct by a ban on information on 'unrest events' and police conduct.

Every week, members of the AGD would visit the prisons in which the University's students were detained, taking items such as warm clothing and pocket money. After repeated representations,

the detainees had been held for nearly two months only three had been charged, and the charges related to being in possession of banned literature. In terms of the emergency regulations, I was prevented from telling the students how the detentions had taken place, or about the conditions under which the students had been detained.

The University administration, together with members of the academic staff and student bodies, developed a programme under the auspices of the Academic Staff Association, to assist those in detention. The staff members constituted the Advisory Group on Detentions (AGD) which worked tirelessly throughout the state of emergency to provide assistance to students in detention. The group was constituted and administered by Debra Nails, a lecturer in philosophy and education, and Isabel Hofmeyr, a lecturer in African literature. The other members of the AGD were Harold Annegarn (Nuclear Physics), Godfrey Ashby (Religious Studies), Lorraine Chaskalson (English), Michael du Plessis (English), Tim Hinton (Education), Nol Loubser (Psychology), Mary Metcalfe (Education), Gill Noero (English), Jane Starfield (History), Gillian Straker (Psychology), Glenda Webster (Academic Support Programme), and Anne Wright (Sociology).

Arising out of a meeting of the Academic Freedom Committee and the Academic Staff Association on 11 September 1986, a booklet was prepared by Gillian Straker and Debra Nails for the use of departmental heads. This set out the procedure to be followed by the head or by the departmental nominee whenever a detention was reported.[23] Straker brought the matter to Senate which committed itself to the principle that departments had an obligation to assist students and staff in detention and after their release and that heads of departments must appoint nominees who would liaise with the AGD.[24] (See Appendix 8.)

A detailed register was kept in my office of all Wits detainees and amended as soon as new information became available.

The security police were contacted immediately to confirm detentions and to determine where people were being held – a procedure that was by no means simple. Parents were contacted as soon as possible and reassured that the University would provide whatever support it could. Detainees were provided with clothing, toiletries and pocket money. The University was fortunate enough to be assisted by

detained children. If necessary, we arrange for clothing and toiletries to be taken to the detainees.

The relevant faculty is informed and, where necessary, deferred examinations arranged. The department is then contacted to determine what examinations are involved and to obtain recommended study material. The departments concerned, and in particular the library staff, have been most responsive to requests and have jointly gathered many books, journals, past examination papers and other reading material. We arrange for this material to be delivered to the students' places of detention. We have not yet been successful in all cases in having study material delivered to detainees, but will not cease in our efforts in this regard. An application has been made for access to the detained students in order to make arrangements for the deferred examinations to be written in prison.

All student detainees have been visited by a judge of the Supreme Court. The administration has spoken to senior police officers and have been assured that all the Wits student and staff detainees are in good health, are visited regularly by judges and magistrates, have regular access to a district surgeon and receive medication if necessary.

During all of the above actions, the administration has worked closely with the executives of the Student Representative Council and the Academic Staff Association. I repeat our opposition to the State of Emergency and the detention of members of this University and urge the authorities either to charge or to release them. We shall continue to maintain contact with the detainees and shall not cease our efforts to secure their release.

We shall keep students and staff informed of future developments.

On 6 August 1986 I addressed a student meeting and informed them that eight of the students who had been detained had been released. Many of the student leaders had been detained. Although some of

Chancellor Charlton and the Chairman of Council saw the Minister of Education and Culture, and the Vice-Chancellor and Chairman of Council met the Minister of Law and Order during the first week of August.[22]

On 21 July 1986 I addressed a circular to all members of staff and students in order to keep them informed about the detentions and what the University was doing about them.

ACTIONS TAKEN BY THE UNIVERSITY WITH REGARD TO THE DETENTION OF STAFF AND STUDENTS

Many of you will be aware that a number of students and staff of this university have been detained. In view of the emergency regulations we are unable to publish their names, but 20 students and 2 members of the academic staff are currently in detention. Naturally this is a matter of grave concern to the University and I therefore wish to inform you of the steps that have been taken to ensure their well-being and to obtain their release.

On 20th June, the acting Vice-Chancellor issued a statement that was reported in the press, deploring the State of Emergency and the detention without trial of some of our students and staff, and assuring students of sympathetic consideration of applications for deferred examinations. Following a meeting of the University Council on 27th June, the Chairman of Council and the acting Vice-Chancellor were granted an interview by the Minister of Education and Culture. At this meeting grave concern was expressed regarding the welfare of our detained students and staff and the Minister was urged to ensure that they were either charged or released.

The Student Affairs office has proceeded in the following manner. We maintain a detailed register of all Wits detainees and upon learning of a detention, send a telex for confirmation to the Commissioner of Police. We then contact the parents and families wherever possible. A number of parents have been able to visit their

was threatened with arrest for failing to produce a record of the students who had put this 'subversive' material in the box room. As they were leaving the Warden asked the brigadier in charge of the operation for the names of the detained students but he refused to give them or even to say how many there were. The operation lasted for about four-and-a-half hours.

Thirty students had been arrested and all but thirteen were released later that morning. These thirteen were detained in terms of the emergency regulations.

At 3am the following Friday the police raided Mofolo residence and stayed until 5.30am searching rooms and questioning students. Mofolo residence, also in Soweto, was owned by the YMCA who by arrangement with the University, allocated a certain number of rooms each year to Wits students. Three doors were broken and pamphlets and student newspapers were torn up. More than 100 heavily armed men, their faces painted black, conducted the raid. When the students opened the doors of their rooms, firearms were pointed at them.

At midnight on 26 June, there were further raids – on Jubilee and Barnato Halls, two on-campus residences – and more students were detained. The police entered Barnato Hall without informing either the Warden or the Deputy Warden of their presence.[21]

Students at all the affected residences were badly shaken, and the Deans of faculties and heads of departments were as sympathetic and helpful as possible in agreeing to defer mid-year examinations when this was requested.

That week Claire Wright, President of the SRC, and Dali Mpofu, President of the BSS were detained and held for a month before being released without being charged. The only reason for this move can have been to intimidate the student body and discourage them from further political activity.

These events were reported to the University Council who were urged to send a high level delegation to the Minister of Law and Order to express grave concern at the harassment of our students and the scandalous treatment of one of the Wardens who had committed no offence and who had suffered great indignity. The matter was discussed by the Council on two occasions and by the Executive Committee of Council once. A delegation consisting of Acting Vice-

indiscriminate acts of terror against the civilian population'. No individuals ever identified themselves as 'concerned academics' and nothing more was heard of them, but the pamphlet was another component of the orchestrated campaign of vilification to discredit the University, its administration and its SRC.

Student and Staff Detentions

Within days of the declaration of the second state of emergency, two incidents occurred which had a major effect on campus life and which profoundly touched the personal lives of a number of students.[19] At about 3am on Sunday 15 June, more than 200 police and military personnel raided Glyn Thomas House, a university residence housing only black students, situated adjacent to Baragwanath Hospital in Soweto.[20]

Casspirs were used in the raid and the surrounding fence was cut to enable them to gain access. A security guard who refused to allow them into the house was assaulted. The police took up positions in the corridors and a security guard was ordered to take some of them to the Warden's flat. The Warden was woken by a plain-clothed balaclava-wearing man who pointed a firearm at his head. Behind him were two uniformed men with rifles. The first man grabbed the Warden's arm and led him through the flat, looking into every room. He was told to get the master keys and was forced to make five copies of student lists containing the names and room numbers of residents.

He was frog-marched at gun point to the students' rooms and made to open each one. Two men wearing balaclavas would storm into the room and in many instances hold a gun to the student's head. Plainclothes men and women would then follow to search the room while two uniformed men would stand with their rifles crossed barring the door. When doors could not be opened, they were kicked in and some were kicked in before the Warden was asked to open them. The rooms were searched, books and pamphlets were confiscated and some were torn up. In the process, numbers of students were detained.

Finally, the men searched the rooms in the administrative block, including the students' box room and the house committee room, removing boxes full of books, magazines and leaflets. The Warden

opinion are present in the University student community, and leads to an escalating degree of confrontation'.[14]

A leading article in *The Star* stated: 'There must be a fancy word for a state in which the biggest danger to public order can come from the police. Whatever that word is, it is beginning to apply to more and more situations in South Africa. The latest occasion during which the major danger to public order was the very people supposed to ensure it, was at Wits University yesterday.'[15]

The leader of the Progressive Federal Party in the Transvaal, Mr Douglas Gibson, said he was appalled at the over-reaction by the authorities to the legitimate expression of opinion by students. 'Whether people like it or not, university students have the right to participate in political life.'[16] The police did not agree.

A few years after these events, Charlton and I were asked to attend a meeting in the offices of the District Commissioner of Police for the Witwatersrand to discuss campus unrest. There we were told by the District Commissioner in the presence of General Basie Smit, head of the security police, and Colonel du Toit, head of the security police on the Witwatersrand, that the police had the right to shoot to kill if they saw a student about to throw a stone. *Kragdadigheid*[17] was the culture of the times and student protest was seen as part of the total onslaught and was to be fiercely suppressed.

On 3 June Tober made a statement in which he again deplored in the strongest terms the action of the police and in an address to students on the same day, called on the police to end their harassment and arrest of students and staff on campus. In a television interview that night he said that police should only come onto campus when he requested it.

Tober requested a meeting with the Minister of Law and Order, Mr L le Grange. The meeting, also attended by the Chairman of Council, took place during the first week of August.[18]

At the same time as the Academic Staff Association was expressing its support for the students, an anonymous letter on a university letterhead and purporting to come from 'Concerned Academics at Wits' was sent to parents of students. The sender gained access to the confidential address list of students by fraudulent means. The circular attempted to smear the SRC and Nusas by linking them with organisations which 'claim responsibility for cowardly and

Ironically, the student whose arrest and denial of bail the previous day had sparked the day's events, was released during the afternoon, but forty-nine students and staff were now being held in custody. We made strenuous but unsuccessful efforts during the evening to secure their release and then decided to make an urgent application to the Supreme Court. This was prepared during the night and heard by a judge in his chambers on the following morning, a Saturday, when the courts do not routinely sit.[12] The application was not opposed, and they were all released on their own recognisances by midday. Forty-eight of them appeared in the Magistrate's Court on the following Monday morning on charges under the Internal Security Act relating to attending an unlawful meeting.

The Commander in charge of the Hillbrow Police Station where the students were being held, was a Colonel Blignaut who had steadfastly refused to grant bail on the Friday afternoon and night. However, when I encountered him in the corridor of the Supreme Court on the following morning his reaction was 'What's the problem professor? There's no problem. Of course we'll give them bail!' He was also very co-operative in front of the judge.

On 30 July five members of staff and thirty-six students pleaded guilty and were each fined R50 or 10 days imprisonment, suspended for one year.[13] Charges against the others had been withdrawn. A statement signed by all of them stated that 'we believe that we are entitled and obliged to protest our support of a fellow-student. We believe that we should be entitled to express our views in a direct and public manner'. The magistrate commented that it appeared that the accused had been a nuisance more than anything else. It had taken dozens of heavily-armed police acting with appalling aggression to suppress this 'nuisance', and countless hours were involved in the legal process required to bring it to a conclusion.

A well-attended meeting of the Academic Staff Association on 2 June passed, by 217 votes to one, a resolution expressing its anger and concern *inter alia* about the disruption of protest meetings on campus by the police and the harassment and arrest of colleagues and students. On 30 May the Executive Committee of the Academic Staff Association had condemned the presence of police on campus which 'inflames tempers, exacerbates whatever disagreements of

Street, a block away from the University. When they disregarded an order to disperse and instead sat down in the road, the police attacked them brutally and indiscriminately, beating women and men. A few more were arrested and forty others were treated in the Campus Health Clinic for lacerations, bruises and dog bites. The incident was filmed and screened world-wide that night, but not on SABC TV. Those who witnessed the attack were appalled but when I showed a copy of the BBC's footage after a meeting of the Executive Committee of Council a few days later, I was stunned to hear one member, Mr Michael O'Dowd, retort that 'it served them right'.[10]

More student marches were planned and Tober contacted the Divisional Commissioner of Police for the Witwatersrand and urged him to withdraw his men. He also requested him to ensure that the police exercised extreme restraint in off-campus confrontations. After a number of further incidents during the afternoon, including police charges, stone throwing by students and the use of teargas to disperse them, the police finally withdrew and the student gatherings broke up.[11]

Mayhem in Jorissen Street. Police take out their fury on a group of seated protestors.

I was asked to be one of thirty-nine staff and students who marched towards the Hillbrow Police Station to protest against police incursions on campus in May 1986. I am flanked by Claire Wright and Dali Mpofu.

Within a few days however, trouble flared up again. As part of a week-long campaign, the End Conscription Campaign (ECC) arranged a meeting in the arcade of the Students' Union on 29 May.[9] The SMA decided to commemorate Republic Day on the same day. This led to a confrontation between the BSS and the SMA similar to that which had taken place on 20 May. During the encounter the police arrived and the students dispersed. After discussions, the police agreed to leave the campus but while they were withdrawing they arrested one student whom they alleged had thrown an object at them. Attempts to secure the release of the student on bail failed, and the University retained a human rights lawyer, Kathleen Satchwell, to represent him.

The following morning a mass meeting of students gathered in the arcade to protest at the presence of the police on the campus the previous day and to demand that the police did not enter the campus again and that the student who had been arrested be released. After numerous proposals and counter-proposals, the meeting agreed that a representative group of some thirty-nine students and staff should march to the periphery of the campus, confront the police with their demands, and be arrested if necessary. I was asked to accompany them.

The police were not present at the edge of the campus and so the marchers decided to proceed up Jorissen Street, one of the main thoroughfares through Braamfontein, towards the Hillbrow Police Station, where they intended to present their demands. When the march moved off campus, I continued to accompany them. They reached the Hillbrow Police Station, but not the way they had intended to. About half-way there, on the east side of the Civic Centre, the march was intercepted by a squad of riot police who ordered them to disperse. The marchers sat down on the pavement and refused to budge. I tried to persuade the officer in charge that the march had been entirely peaceful thus far and that he should allow it to proceed. I shouldn't imagine that the major had the authority to exercise any flexibility, and my request was summarily refused. After a further warning the marchers, a few journalists and an unfortunate group of bystanders, were arrested.

Instead of intimidating the student body, this sparked further marches. The second group was intercepted by the police in Jorissen

faction was prepared to move away although this would have defused the conflict. After about thirty minutes a small squad of police appeared and the students scattered.

The University was gravely concerned about the antagonism which continued between the SMA and the BSS despite the attempts to implement the recommendations made in this regard by the Browde Commission the previous year. We had had numerous discussions with both parties, separately and together, in an attempt to encourage dialogue and promote tolerance. We recognised that in the prevailing political situation there were bound to be differences in ideology, but believed, probably naively, that it should be possible for differing points of view to be propagated freely on campus.

A disturbing aspect of the student demonstrations was that in an attempt to recruit support, some members of the BSS would enter lecture theatres and libraries and coerce fellow students into leaving their studies and joining the protest. This angered the lecturers involved and was resented by the students affected. Although they would offer to submit affidavits in support of their complaints, they never did. The BSS leadership claimed, when challenged on the matter, that it was not BSS policy to coerce any students into joining demonstrations, but they were ineffective in stopping the practice. In the absence of formal complaints that included names of alleged offenders, it was never possible to bring anyone before a disciplinary inquiry for this objectionable activity.

Much of the planning of protest meetings and marches took place in the residences at night and by early on the morning of the event, plans had already been formulated and it was extremely difficult to persuade the organisers that an alternative strategy might be wiser or more successful. Not only the students involved but the security police were inevitably fully apprised of the plans by early morning.

In a graduation address on 24 May 1986, Tober referred to the recent demonstrations and to the turmoil in the country into which the University had been drawn. He stressed the University's abhorrence of violence and intolerance, and called for the repeal of the entire body of legislation requiring separate facilities in education, health and welfare on the ground of race. He urged the police to refrain from intervening on the campus, stating that such actions exacerbated tensions.[8]

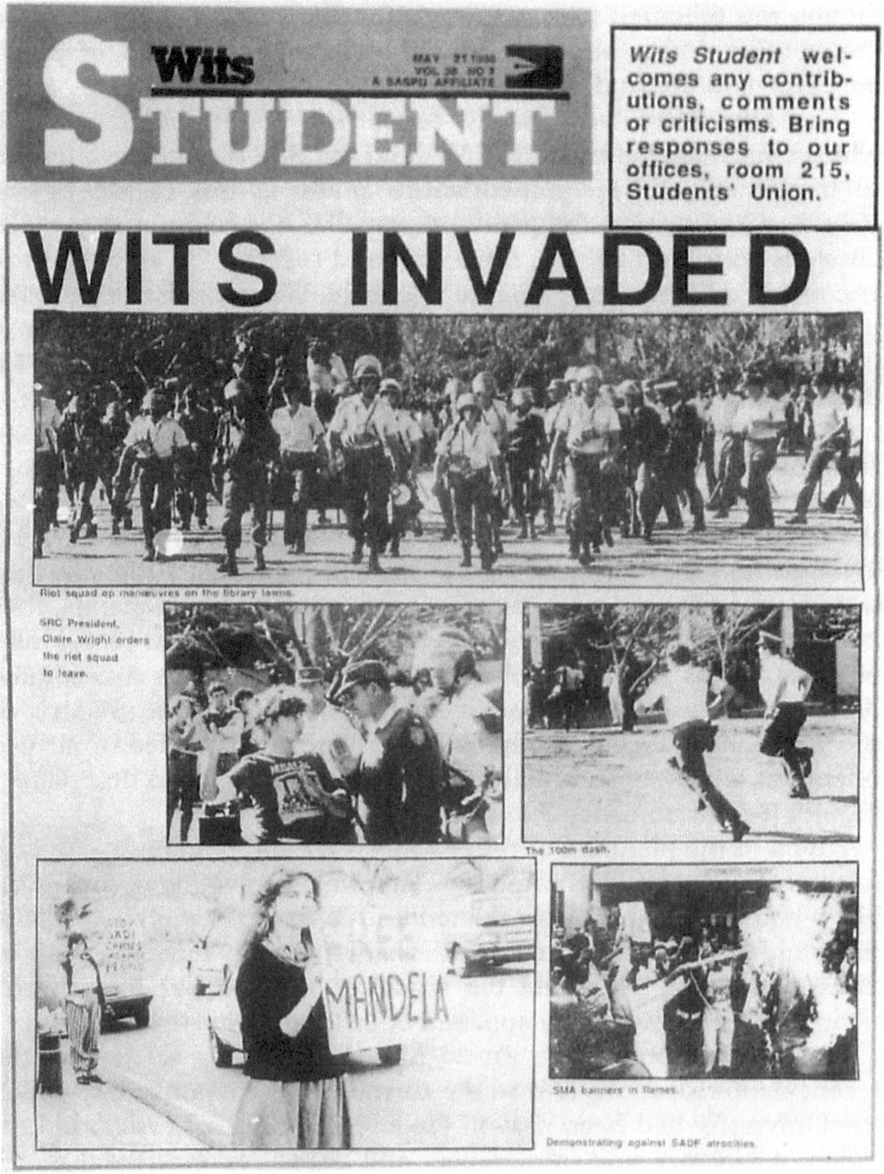

Wits STUDENT

Wits Student welcomes any contributions, comments or criticisms. Bring responses to our offices, room 215, Students' Union.

WITS INVADED

Riot squad op manœuvres on the library lawns.

SRC President, Claire Wright orders the riot squad to leave.

The 100m dash.

SMA banners in flames.

Demonstrating against SADF atrocities.

Courtesy University Archives

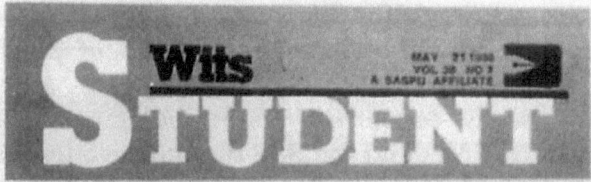

The front page of Wits Student *of 21 May 1986 graphically illustrates the invasion of police onto the campus*

action against those responsible. Although he was able to give the Minister the registration number of one of three Casspirs involved, no action was taken. On 26 May 1988, fifty students and two security guards brought an action against Malan in which they claimed a total of R245 000 in damages. The SADF members denied that they had used teargas, claiming that they had wished only to search the bus for unlawful literature.[3] The claimants were awarded a total of R50 000 plus costs, with individuals being awarded amounts ranging from R350 to R3 000.[4]

On 19 May 1986 South African commandos launched pre-dawn raids on what were claimed to be ANC bases in Harare and Gaborone, and the airforce bombed a 'base' in Lusaka. The Harare 'base' was a house that had been evacuated and the planes hit the wrong target in Lusaka, bombing instead a United Nations camp full of Angolan and Namibian refugees. Political commentators believed that President P W Botha was 'thumbing his nose' at the Commonwealth Eminent Persons Group (EPG) which had been appointed to determine whether the South African Government was serious about moving away from apartheid to a negotiated democratic constitution. A positive report from the EPG might have enabled those Commonwealth countries opposed to the imposition of sanctions to avoid a split on the issue.[5]

The campus was tense the day after the attacks as angry students determined to hold a demonstration despite a warning from the police early that morning that if such a meeting were held outdoors it would be illegal and the police would intervene.[6] As always, the security police were well informed about activities planned on campus.

Before arrangements could be made to transfer the meeting indoors, a group of students had gathered on the library lawns. A squad of police was on campus in a very short time and thirteen students were arrested. After negotiations, the police agreed to withdraw from campus and release the arrested students if the meeting was transferred indoors. Subsequently a meeting attended by about 3 500 students proceeded peacefully in the Sports Hall.

An alternative outdoor display by the SMA commemorating a bomb blast in Pretoria on 20 May 1983[7] led to a confrontation with a group of BSS members and to a menacing situation which required the intervention of members of the administration, university security and SRC leaders as buffers between the opposing groups. Neither

CHAPTER 7

Resistance Escalates

Student unrest on campus continued in the period leading up to the declaration of the second state of emergency on 12 June 1986. The BSS informed the University that it was unlikely that black students would attend lectures on 1 May (Labour Day), or on 16, 17 and 18 June, in recognition of Soweto Day.[1] Although there was no official University policy on 'making up lost time', some lecturers rescheduled lectures which they were to have given on sensitive days. Others gave their lectures as scheduled, but repeated them at a later date. Yet others insisted on sticking to the timetable.

On 1 May, a number of students attended a May Day rally in Soweto. After the rally a bus containing about ninety students and some security guards was stopped outside Diepkloof, a suburb of Soweto by troops of the South African Defence Force who ordered the occupants off the bus and almost simultaneously smashed the front doors. Attempting to obey the instruction, the occupants were alighting as quickly as possible, but before many had had a chance to do so a teargas canister was fired into the bus. Terrified students broke the emergency exit window while more teargas was fired at them. Several were injured by broken glass, and many were overcome by teargas. No medical treatment was offered by the SADF, no attempt was made to question the students, and no explanation was given for the action. They were ordered to leave the area about forty-five minutes later.[2]

The acting Vice-Chancellor, Professor R W Charlton, sent a telex to the Minister of Defence, General Magnus Malan, urging him to order an investigation of the incident with a view to taking disciplinary

the incident was 'symptomatic of the absurdity of holding a general election for the minority,' but adding, 'even under the most repressive circumstances opportunity for debate and discussion should be used'.[43]

In planning their action, the BSIC had infringed the procedures set out in the 'Freedom of Speech' document and some of the offenders who had been identified were summonsed to appear before University disciplinary committees. The BSIC refused to recognise the validity of the document, averring that they had not been party to its acceptance.[44] There were hints of a major confrontation with the administration on the issue.[45] The SRC took a conciliatory line with the BSIC and in an angry reaction to that, five SRC members resigned on 1 August.

As was frequently the case with incidents of this kind it was not possible to identify all the offenders. At a Vice-Chancellor's Summary Enquiry, one of a variety of student disciplinary hearings available to the University, seven students pleaded guilty to contravening Rule R7(g) of the General Rules for Student Conduct in that they took part in the disruption of the meeting. They were severely reprimanded, warned that if they were found guilty of a similar offence in future they would face severe consequences, including possible expulsion, and were fined R200 each. The BSS expressed its regret that the meeting was disrupted and undertook to work with the University administration to prevent such disruptions in the future.[46]

Despite this incident, I believe that these debates and discussions led to a greater tolerance on campus of opposing political viewpoints. Black students seemed to appreciate the fact that their concerns about certain speakers were being heard and addressed and that the procedures followed were transparent and democratic. Particularly after February 1990 when the political process was opened up, the BSS tended to stay away from meetings organised by the SMA.

The level of political tolerance on the campus has been good. During the course of 1993 a meeting addressed by both the African National Congress and the Inkatha Freedom Party was attended by a large audience. There was considerable heckling, but the meeting proceeded without disruption and concluded peacefully.[47]

During the period leading up to the first democratic election in April 1994, there was no evidence of political intolerance on the Wits campus. As I write this in May 1995, the political issues on the campus are different and concern 'transformation and democratisation'.

arranged by the Wits Debating Union to discuss the role of parliamentary politics.[42] Although the invited speakers, Dr Frederik van Zyl Slabbert, Dr Zach de Beer and Mr Steven Friedman, were widely respected opponents of the Government, they were not given a hearing. The reason given was that there were objections to De Beer, co-leader of the Democratic Party, being allowed to speak on campus in the run-up to an apartheid election.

Using a carefully planned strategy, a group of about 120 students started chanting and singing from the time the chairperson tried to introduce Slabbert. When Slabbert went to the rostrum and tried to speak he could not be heard over the chanting, and returned to his seat. The President of the SRC, Bettina von Lieres, who attempted to persuade the crowd to allow the speakers a hearing, was ignored. Some of the crowd were now standing and swaying while they chanted and sang and senior members of the staff who tried to remonstrate with them were jostled and ignored.

Although the meeting was then closed by the chairperson and about half of the students left the hall, the Acting President of the BSIC, Mr Nepo Kekana, stood up on a chair and addressed the group of protesters. In a display of political intolerance that shocked many who heard it, he said that 'no National Party or Democratic Party leaders will make speeches here for as long as we are on this campus. What you are seeing here today is just the beginning'. He said it was time for white students to stop hiding in their luxury areas and become committed to the cause of ending oppression. The University, he said, should belong to the people; their parents had built it with their own sweat and blood. The senior administration would be replaced.

Outside the hall, Kekana addressed the crowd again, referring to a campaign of the Mass Democratic Movement which was due to start on 2 August and would take several forms including the defiance of restriction orders placed on ex-detainees, the mass invasion of hospitals which practised apartheid, and a general challenge to existing apartheid regulations.

Charlton apologised to the would-be speakers, saying that the disruption was a gross violation of one of the University's most cherished values, freedom of speech. The guests, who must have been extremely embarrassed, responded graciously, Slabbert saying that

many occasions on which the panel was called together and it was never necessary to prohibit a meeting. On one occasion the panel grappled with objections brought by the SRC, BSS and South African Union of Jewish Students (SAUJS) to an invitation from the SMA to Marc Henri Glendinning, a member of a far-right British conservative group which was alleged to have published anti-Semitic views. His proposed topic was 'The case against apartheid'. The SMA described him as a libertarian. The panel allowed the meeting to proceed on the assurance from the SMA that if racist views were expressed, the chairperson would immediately close the meeting. Access to the meeting was restricted to staff and students, and security precautions were taken. There was a considerable amount of heckling but the speaker was able to conclude his speech.

In October 1989, the Freedom of Speech panel was convened to consider an objection raised by the chairperson of the Namibia Solidarity Committee (NSC), to a meeting arranged by the SMA, which was to be addressed by Mr Edward Ndopu, a journalist on *The Times of Namibia*. His subject was 'The contravention of human rights in Swapo detention camps'. In objecting, the NSC voiced the opinion that the SMA's motives were 'to create an incident or a reaction, which in turn will be used to discredit the Mass Democratic Movement (MDM) and its campus components, Nusas and BSS/Sansco, as well as the youth of Namibia who are studying in our universities ... It seems to us ironical that the South African government and its supporters are suddenly the defenders of human life and dignity in Namibia, or anywhere else. This sudden wave of sympathy with victims of a guerilla war instigated by SA, the total hypocrisy, is enough to anger any young student who has been through the hands of the SAP or conscripted into the SADF ...'[40]

The Freedom of Speech panel included members of the SRC, SMA and BSS. It concluded that there were no grounds for prohibiting the meeting, and Charlton conveyed this decision to the Namibia Solidarity Committee.[41] The meeting went ahead as planned and was ignored by the BSS.

Unfortunately, the Black Students' Interim Committee (BSIC), established by the BSS as an alternative organisation when it was restricted in 1989, was guilty of a severe infringement of the procedures when, on 31 July 1989, some of its leaders prevented a meeting

which believed that there should be no restrictions whatsoever on the freedom of speech on campus. However, once it had been approved formally, the SMA abided by its requirements but the BSS was very inconsistent in its response.

The essential features of the document were that freedom of speech could not be absolute. The University would not countenance the advocacy of racism, sexism or violence. The document set out the procedures to be followed when meetings, functions and displays were planned on the campus.

If the person responsible for assessing the application submitted believed that the proposed activity conflicted with the University's enunciated principles, the application would be referred to a panel made up of representatives of various constituencies on campus. Similarly, any person or organisation on campus concerned that a proposed activity might conflict with the same principles, might also object and the objection would be considered by the same panel.

If the panel, after careful consideration, supported the objections the activity could not proceed, but if the panel rejected them it would be an offence for any person or group to interfere with the meeting other than to be present and to register displeasure by means of mild heckling.

The document was idealistic. It reflected the wishes and met the anxieties of the group that had laboured through eighteen drafts. I do not know whether all of them were confident that student groups would abide by it. I was hopeful that the procedures would satisfy both the University's commitment to academic freedom and those who would not countenance the presence on campus of people known to have racist views.

In March 1988 an early draft of the document was leaked to the press after it had been sent for comment, marked 'confidential', to various University constituencies. Some newspapers erroneously interpreted this as 'tightening up on student discipline despite protestations that they would ignore government threats to cut subsidies unless conflict on campus was eliminated.'[39]

In general, the procedure worked reasonably well. Different student groups made their applications with varying degrees of accuracy, and on occasions there were gaps in the information provided. These were considered with some flexibility. There were, in fact, not

was arranged in the Great Hall the following week in order to encourage discussion of the document. The film deals with the controversy in the American town of Skokie over the planned march through the centre by a neo-Nazi group and how the matter was resolved. The showings were poorly attended and only two students attended the planned discussion, so the meeting was cancelled.

Interestingly, at the same time as the freedom of speech debate was proceeding in South Africa, a similar controversy was evoking intense reactions in the United Kingdom where section 43 of the Education (No 2) Act 1986 which had come into force on 1 September 1987, was causing concern.[37]

The section provided that heads of institutions should try as far as possible to ensure that 'freedom of speech within the law was secured for members, students and employees of the establishment and for visiting speakers'.

The use of any premises within these institutions should not be denied to any individual or body because of their beliefs, views, policy or objectives.

The motivation for this section was that for some years government ministers, Conservative Party MPs and other politicians had been badly received by student audiences and were sometimes prevented from speaking. Of concern was the fact that 'speakers expressing views on immigration and race, for example, however anathema to students' unions and left-wing political societies, will not necessarily infringe the law on inciting racial hatred and they will therefore enjoy the statute's protection'.

Zellick enunciates very similar views to those that were being canvassed on the Wits campus.[38] He identified the danger that section 43 would lend itself to exploitation by extreme political student groups who might invite known extremist speakers as a provocative gesture. This would result in much the same dilemma that we had had – whether to prevent the meeting on grounds of potential conflict, and risk alienating the public and the media or allow it to proceed and risk disorder, injury and adverse publicity.

The freedom of speech document (see Appendix 7) was finally approved by all the constituencies of the University with the exception of the BSS which had been consulted at every stage but had not responded or made any commitment to it; and the SMA were: the qualifications of the speaker; who invited the speaker; the makeup of the audience and the point and purpose of the invitation.

'If in all cases the answer to these four questions is an academic answer,' Prof Suzman wrote, 'then I believe that such people should enjoy the full protection of the University. To the extent that they are not, claims for academic freedom on their behalf are muted or even perhaps absent, and the requirements on the University to exercise its powers and prerogatives in defending such rights are to that extent lessened.'

If it was believed that a meeting might constitute a 'clear and present danger', and specifically might pose a danger to life, limb and property, 'the University authorities may prevent such a meeting from taking place'.

After extensive discussion, Senate was not able to take a decision, another indication of the complexity of the issue. Nevertheless, following on proposals made at a meeting with the executive committees of the Academic Staff Association, SRC and BSS on 12 August 1987 (see Chapter 8), the senior administration decided to draw up a document for consideration by all constituencies of the University.

The document was drawn up by a large committee which included representatives of the administration, teaching and support staff, and students. Existing procedures for booking venues and holding meetings were consolidated and new ones added, providing for the refusal of permission for a speaker, a meeting or a display. This would not be done without careful consideration by a panel specially constituted for this purpose. A corollary was that if permission was granted after careful consideration by the panel, then the speaker, meeting or display must be allowed to proceed without interference.

It was an extremely difficult document to prepare, and eighteen drafts were necessary before it was approved by the committee. It was then considered in detail with student representatives and approved by various university committees for implementation from 1 September 1988.[35] Originally headed 'Arrangements and code of practice for the holding of meetings or functions' the title was later changed to the more simple 'Freedom of Speech on Campus'.[36] In order to publicise it, the University arranged showings of the film *Skokie* during lunch hours over a period of four days, and a meeting

effective it was in bringing about the collapse of the Nationalist Government is difficult to gauge. While economic, financial and sports sanctions hurt immeasurably, it is doubtful whether the Government was ever greatly concerned about the academic and cultural boycotts. Relatively few individuals were affected, and these did not constitute a significant political pressure group. Nor would the Government have been greatly concerned about the cumulative effects on cultural values, teaching and research resulting from a prolonged period of academic isolation, because this would not have disempowered them.

The Commission also reported at length on the extent of the attack in certain sections of the media on the University and on the integrity and judgement of its principal officers. The campaign of vilification was grist to the mill of the Government which was intent on clamping down on political protest on the campuses of the English-language universities. It led to yet another attempt by the state to coerce these universities into political submission through the threat of subsidy cuts. The agent for this assault on the autonomy of the universities was to be F W de Klerk, Minister of National Education. An account of this affair is given in Chapter 8.

A Code of Practice

In view of the controversy and the conflicting views both on and off campus after the Unita incident, the Senate Academic Freedom Committee was asked to consider what action should be taken on occasions when it might be wise to refuse permission for a speaker or speakers to address a meeting on the campus. The committee reported to the Senate on 10 June 1986 and the subject was debated at considerable length.[34] The Academic Freedom Committee used as the basis for its consideration of the matter, a memorandum entitled *Academic Freedom and Freedom of Speech*, prepared by Professor Jonathan Suzman of the Philosophy Department (see Appendix 6).

It concluded that although the University had an obligation to defend the rights of freedom of speech of its full members, that obligation did not extend to all meetings held on the campus, nor to all visitors invited to speak in the University.

The extent to which it had an obligation could be determined by reference to the criteria set out in the Suzman memorandum. These

debate about the appropriate means by which our goal of greater freedom may be achieved. We believe that the coercive approach taken by students on Dr O'Brien's visit last week was inappropriate.'

The majority of the Commission saw the O'Brien meeting as evidence of the dangers inherent in departing from the principle of freedom of speech.

A minority view was submitted as an annexure to the report by Adv E Cameron[33] who regarded it as necessary 'to give greater recognition to the fact that the students involved were themselves giving expression to profoundly held moral views when they took the action which prevented the Unita speakers from being heard. How best could the students who disrupted the meeting give vent to their views? ... In the end, they decided to express their viewpoints most forcibly – though entirely non-violently – by singing and chanting until the meeting could no longer be held ...'

Cameron's carefully-reasoned argument (Appendix 5) is a useful contribution to the debate on freedom of speech which has international relevance on campuses and elsewhere. It is regretful that the Council, in an ill-judged act of censorship, decided not to include it in the release to the media, because it provided an insight into the attitudes and motivations of the black students in the University and also probably of a wide spectrum of black opinion in the country as a whole.

Cameron concluded his thoughtful contribution by stating his view that the coercive approach adopted by the students in O'Brien's case was inappropriate.

Few members of the academic staff would have disagreed with him. Many of them had been victims of the academic boycott and had been excluded from attending international meetings for a number of years. Some of those excluded had been committed and vocal opponents of apartheid over a long period and had thereby exposed themselves to possible victimisation at the hands of the authorities of the apartheid state. That such people should have been distressed and offended by an indiscriminate boycott is beyond dispute. The debate on the academic boycott has been intense and the arguments for and against have been canvassed *in extenso*. However one feels about it, the motives of those who propagated it should be respected given the intensity of the anger evoked by the apartheid policy. How

campus to the extent of making it impossible for the speaker to make his views heard is always out of place at an academic institution such as Wits...

'Students should realize that there are alternative ways of expressing their opposition to the views sought to be aired at meetings to which they object. These include the use of question time, the passing of resolutions, the holding of an alternative meeting or the staging of a walk-out to express their dissent.'

The majority of the Commission concluded that the interruption of the Unita meeting was unacceptable and the behaviour should be rejected. They took the view that

> toleration in principle of disruptions of this kind embodies grave dangers to important values which ought to prevail on a university campus. Relaxation of the principle that maximum toleration of the freedom of expression of views ought to prevail may be construed as licence to groupings representing either the majority or a minority to silence opposing viewpoints. Whatever the merits or demerits of the invitation to the UNITA speakers, particularly in Sharpeville week by a society whose bona fides as a student organization is questioned, the majority nevertheless feels that arrangements having been made to hold the meeting, it should not have been disrupted.

No direct evidence was placed before the Commission about the disruption of the Conor Cruise O'Brien meetings.[32] While they were hesitant to express unequivocal views about the incidents, the Commissioners tended to agree with the sentiments expressed by the executive of the Academic Staff Association on the issue. The latter body had issued a statement in which it reaffirmed its commitment to the goal of academic freedom in a free South Africa. It noted that many who habitually attacked the University had been quick to demand draconian action against the students who opposed Dr O'Brien's visit although they had been conspicuously silent on the restrictions placed by the state on the University community.

The statement went on: 'In the present context the academic freedom which we enjoy is limited and partial. There is a critical need for

Picture courtesy University Archives

Sharpeville Day commemoration, 22 March 1972

the University environment where rationality and restraint are important values.

(The student's) resort to the rhetoric of 'the right of free speech' is in our view not only spurious but misleading, for it creates an atmosphere of opprobrium for the University and some of its students around an incident for which Mr H was in our view chiefly to blame.

The Commission was of the view that violent disruption of meetings' on campus, as distinct from boisterous interjections, was always wrong and constituted a clear disciplinary offence. No evidence had been presented to indicate that any meetings had been disrupted by violence. The Unita speakers' meeting had been disrupted by means of chanting, singing and rowdy interventions. The Commission was divided on its attitude to such an event. The majority took the view that 'any disruption of a meeting properly scheduled to be held on

G Bizos SC. The other members were Advocate W H R Schreiner SC and Advocate E Cameron.

The Commission's sessions were open to all students and staff of the University and a number of members of Council, the Senate, the Administration, staff organisations and student bodies attended the sittings. Written and verbal evidence was submitted by twenty-three students and members of staff and the administration submitted a portfolio of documents.

The Commission gave careful consideration to the question of freedom of speech and the disruption of meetings. It also studied much of the derogatory published material.

It focused specifically on the public comment by the student who had supported the actions of the police at Sharpeville. The student claimed that he had been exercising his right to free speech when he said that 'I believed that the police were doing a good job and that they had only defended themselves at Sharpeville. I also said that they should kill more (referring to terrorists and anarchists).' The Commission rejected his claim, stating that these were 'fighting words' within the famous formula applied by the United States Supreme Court: those words 'which by their very utterance inflict injury or tend to incite an immediate breach of the peace':

> Such utterances are no essential part of any exposition of ideas, and are of such slight social value as a step to truth that any benefit that may be derived from them is clearly out-weighed by the social interest in order ...[31]
>
> If this limitation on 'free speech' can be justified in the United States, we have no doubt that it should apply to statements on the Wits campus. (The student) therefore does not seem to us to have been exercising any right of 'free speech' in uttering the words to which he confesses. We regard his statement as offensive, deliberately provocative and dangerous. To tell a group of black South Africans commemorating the Sharpeville tragedy that the police 'should kill more' constitutes in our view grossly and foreseeably inflammatory conduct. This does not, of course, condone the attack on (him), which is to be deplored, particularly in

Most of the letters in the correspondence columns of the press during this period were critical of Wits. Many of them took the SMA line and were clearly part of an orchestrated campaign to discredit the University. Sometimes the same letter appeared in different papers within a few days.[29]

I was invited to respond to this criticism in a guest column in the *Saturday Star* on 1 November 1986.[30] The column began, 'The anguish of the townships extends to our campus. The poverty, the misery of daily life, bad schooling, the back-breaking labour which ages people prematurely, unemployment, the young people out of school, uniformed men in Casspirs, the fires, the detentions, friends and family lying low in fear of detention; these are things not lightly cast aside when a young person becomes a university student.

'It is clear to us on this campus that we are not immune from the restlessness that racks our land.'

I then referred to the episodes of unrest on campus during the year and the infringements of freedom of speech. Addressing the accusations that the University was not preventing the disruption of meetings and was not taking disciplinary action, I wrote that we were not prepared to use physical force against our students. Universities in South Africa which had attempted to use force to discipline their students had become ungovernable whereas, despite the ten incidents of campus unrest in the past year, the University had continued to function normally.

I described the disciplinary procedures followed by the University and stated my belief that we should use educative processes in handling student misdemeanours because this could be just as salutary as punishment and was much more effective in maintaining a student body which identified strongly with the institution.

Police intervention in campus protest meetings exacerbated the situation because it attracted the attention of thousands of students and led to polarisation and conflict.

Our role when students faced the police was to attempt to defuse the situation. We deprecated the incidents of stone throwing while condemning unnecessary police action on campus.

The Commission of Inquiry appointed by Council to investigate the events at the University between August 1985 and October 1986 met on 3, 6 and 7 October under the chairmanship of Advocate

In a notice issued on 20 March, Tober wrote that normal academic debate and discussion on election issues were not affected by the ruling but attendance at these events was to be restricted to staff and students of the University.

The bar on Mrs Suzman's speech enraged many people. Suzman was a graduate of and former lecturer at the University which had awarded her an honorary doctorate, and she had a superb record as an anti-apartheid campaigner both within parliament and outside it. She had frequently addressed meetings on campus at the behest of student groups. She was greatly admired in the University and it was extremely difficult to have to tell the organisers of the decision.

In retrospect it is clear that the strategy was not wise, but at the time it seemed to be an appropriate decision.

The controversy was not confined to the campus. Mrs Suzman was understandably furious, and contemplated returning her honorary degree. The matter was also taken up with vigour by the press and even, laughably, by the Government, who unblushingly accused the University of not upholding freedom of speech.

Particular prominence was given to a mischievous campaign of letter-writing to the press and to an endless flood of telex messages to various members of the university administration and the Government (with copies sent to newsrooms), by one J R Lambson. Lambson, who claimed to be chairman of the 'University Freedom of Speech Association', was a one-man-and-a-telex-machine operation, and no other person ever claimed to be a member of his organisation. Although an advertisement in *The Star* of 3 April 1986 called for 'students and members of the public who are interested in a stable future for the RSA' to write to him so that a meeting could be convened to form the Association, there is no record that any such meeting was ever held.

Lambson had no connection with the University.[27] A man of pronounced right wing views, he seemed to work closely with the National Student Federation and the Student Moderate Alliance and was probably funded by the same sources.[28] With the development of telefax technology in the 1980s, Lambson's funders enabled him to graduate from his telex to a fax machine, after which the flow of his communications proliferated. It was unfortunate that the press granted him some credibility by publishing his communiqués, without ever investigating whether his 'Association' had any substance.

An independent inquiry at the University of Cape Town found that O'Brien's actions had been provocative. At Wits, the students who had prevented the postgraduate seminar from taking place appeared before a summary inquiry called and chaired by the Vice-Chancellor and were charged with disobeying a lawful instruction by a senior officer of the University. The charges were not denied and the students were severely reprimanded.

In response to the anger within the University and the criticism in the media, a special meeting of the Senate on 17 October debated the issue of disruption of academic meetings and drew up a policy statement. The statement was discussed by Council and a joint statement emanated from the two meetings.[26]

In the statement, they deplored what had happened and affirmed that it was a universally accepted principle of academic freedom that a scholar who had been invited to speak at an academic gathering should be heard courteously by his audience. They condemned, in the strongest possible terms, the disruption of these academic meetings and reaffirmed their commitment to ensuring compliance by all members of the University with universal standards of academic behaviour.

At the same time, they condemned the infringement of academic freedom that had occurred the previous day when a meeting arranged by a number of student organisations on the campus in order to protest against apartheid had been banned.

During the year, the flood of criticism of the University and its senior officers had continued in the press and in various programmes of the South African Broadcasting Corporation and these criticisms became sharper after the O'Brien incident.

They reached their peak in the course of 1987 when it was decided not to allow veteran opposition MP, Mrs Helen Suzman, who was campaigning for re-election to the House of Assembly in the forthcoming General Election, to address a meeting in the School of Law. There was so much tension and anti-Government feeling on campus at the time that the University was extremely anxious about the potential danger to life, limb and property if candidates of the National and Conservative parties were to be invited to address meetings during the campaign. The solution, it was decided by the Vice-Chancellor's Board, a committee consisting of the senior members of the administration and the Deans of faculties, would be to ban all electioneering activities on campus.

to demonstrate solidarity,' he wrote, 'But I shall be glad to have my visit taken as a demonstration of solidarity with the staff and students of the University of Cape Town. Also as a gesture of defiance against an intellectually-disreputable attempt to isolate what I know to be an honest, open and creative intellectual community.'[22]

The publicity which preceded O'Brien's visit was regarded as a challenge by the University Boycott Committee of the University of Cape Town who alleged that he had described the academic boycott as 'Mickey Mouse stuff'.[23] There were at the same time eleven other visiting lecturers from overseas at UCT, none of whom experienced any problems.[24] O'Brien's attempt to lecture was prevented by a large group of students who had organised themselves to ensure that the proceedings would be disrupted. The threats of violence on the campus were such that O'Brien cancelled the remainder of his stay.

During his time in South Africa, Wits's Department of Political Studies, then unaware of the controversy surrounding his visit, had invited him to give a lunch-hour lecture to undergraduates and a seminar to postgraduates and staff. When it was learned that there were plans to disrupt the talk, Dr Tom Lodge, a senior lecturer in the department, met the audience, before O'Brien appeared, to discuss the matter with them. A group of BSS leaders insisted that the scheduled lecture would be disrupted but said they would be prepared to engage in 'open debate' with O'Brien on the issue of the academic boycott. O'Brien refused to accept this alternative, and the lecture was cancelled. Similarly, the scheduled seminar was 'sat in' by a smaller group of BSS leaders who refused to leave when called upon to do so by the Dean of the Faculty of Arts.

O'Brien was understandably distressed by the experience which he described as an 'academic necklacing'. Debra Nails, a lecturer in philosophy, has said that those who like herself had attended both sessions scheduled for O'Brien, were more disturbed by what happened at the second. There had been a long and informative debate between academics and Tiego Moseneke, the only spokesperson for the BSS, but when all the arguments were against him, he fell back on his mandate to do what had been decided, as he put it 'democratically', before the meeting.[25] The fact is that in the circumstances prevailing at that time, once given a mandate, the BSS representatives had little room for manoeuvre.

which infringed the claims of all opinions to be heard on campus and which might encourage a spirit of intolerance or even violence, which it unequivocally rejected in all its forms.

Not all the statements emanating from the University during that week were as tolerant. One, purporting to have been issued by 'the newly formed Student's (sic) Committee for Action' stated 'What we have to say to these hooligans is that we will no longer tolerate their barbarism! We have come so far and will go no further! It would appear that these thugs only understand one thing... VIOLENCE, VIOLENCE AND MORE VIOLENCE!!!!! We as students are now forced to meet this violence on equal terms. Admin. cannot garuantee (sic) our safety. TAKE NOTE YOU THUGS... YOUR DAYS OF STREET VIOLENCE ON OUR CAMPUS ARE OVER!!!!!'

The people responsible for this type of notice (and there were others from time to time) never identified themselves, but the statements contributed to the tension on the campus. It was widely thought that they might not even have been produced by students but by right wing provocateurs bent on provoking confrontation; or might have been part of the security police's 'dirty tricks' campaign.

The O'Brien and Suzman Episodes

The next 'freedom of speech' issue has come to be known as the 'O'Brien episode'. On 9 October 1986, two lectures which were to have been delivered by academic and journalist, Dr Conor Cruise O'Brien, were disrupted by students. This unfortunate occurrence caused considerable harm to the academic integrity of the University and led to outraged reactions both within and outside the institution.

O'Brien had a considerable reputation as an academic and had been a prominent critic in Britain of the academic boycott of South Africa, and particularly of the exclusion of South African academics from the World Archaeological Congress in Southampton.[21] He was Pro-Chancellor of the University of Dublin and had been Vice-Chancellor of the University of Ghana from 1962 to 1965 and Editor in Chief of *The Observer* from 1979 to 1981.

He had accepted an invitation from the University of Cape Town to teach there for five weeks. 'I did not accept the university's invitation

Executive Committee of Council. The Vice-Chancellor's Office did not interfere with this legal process.

The Unita incident raised problems. Against whom should action be taken? About two hundred people had been involved and it would clearly be impractical to hold hearings involving all of them. It was decided that the best way to handle the situation would be to call in the leaders of the BSS and to urge them to accept that despite the absence of freedom of speech in South African society generally, the concept should be sacrosanct on the Wits campus. Though the leadership responded positively, they had immense difficulty in persuading their grass roots membership to accept this view.

The Disciplinary Adviser had similar problems with the assault charges. Clearly the students who laid these charges were aggrieved, and understandably so. There can be no excuse for the physical assaults, they were appalling, and those responsible deserved to be punished. The actions of the students who assaulted the suspected informer earlier in the day were equally reprehensible. In the event, the Disciplinary Adviser could not bring any charges because he had insufficient *prima facie* evidence with which to do so.

The events of the week were considered by the Senate at a special meeting on 2 April. After an extensive and sensitive debate, Senate passed a resolution (Appendix 4) with which the Council subsequently associated itself.[20] While the Senate resolution steered away from reference to retributory action, the Council reaffirmed 'that in instances where members of the University contravene the disciplinary code governing behaviour on the campus, the appropriate disciplinary procedures will be invoked'.

The resolution reaffirmed the Senate's commitment to the principle and practice of freedom of speech and fair debate on the campus but noted the widespread intolerance, insecurity, fear and alienation in South African society and believed that it would be inconceivable that higher education were not affected by this. However, even though deviations from the practice of free speech in the University might be seen as a spill over or spin-off from society, they were to be deplored and discouraged.

Senate appealed to the members and leaders of University communities to exercise restraint and tolerance in the face of the many provocations of life in South Africa and to refrain from behaviour

said that they should kill more (referring to terrorists and anarchists).'

The student claimed he was then stoned, attacked with sticks and kicked by the crowd. Dali Mpofu came to his aid and suffered an injured hand in the process.

In his statement, the second student said that he, objecting to a speaker's claim that 'incidents of unrest were the product of a desire for individual freedom', called out 'Bullshit' and was then 'pushed, kicked and punched by people whom I hesitate to call students – they bore no identity cards but many of them wore yellow T-shirts indicating membership of a certain society of students'.

His statement ended with the angry declaration that 'I see no reason why I should be intimidated by mob violence on my own University Campus. I suggest that today's incident of the assault I suffered is proof enough that these "freedom meetings" are nothing but a sham and an opportunity for all idle students to waste time.

'To avoid intimidation and if I feel that the University Administration is impotent in such matters to protect a student and ensure his basic rights, I will feel the necessity of carrying a firearm to ensure the enforcement of such rights ...'

During the afternoon there was a confrontation with police in Yale Road, which separates the east from the west campus. Stones were thrown and there was considerable concern when the police drew their weapons. Rubber bullets and tear gas canisters were fired, but fortunately the students heeded our appeals to stop the stone throwing, and dispersed.

The public, the media and members of the University reacted angrily to the infringements of freedom of speech and the violence on campus and there were calls for the administration to take disciplinary action against the students responsible. In a statement Tober explained that the University administration did not itself initiate disciplinary hearings. The procedures laid down by Council were that campus security prepared a report on all instances of misdemeanour and a dossier was then sent to the University Disciplinary Adviser. If there was *prima facie* evidence that an offence had been committed, the matter was referred to a disciplinary committee which was usually chaired by a senior member of the School of Law. Reports of the disciplinary committees and their sentences were all reviewed by the

is undoubtedly necessary for the sake of good order in the institution and democracy. But this will in no way change the views of the BSS supporters. Political mission work is necessary for this. The worrying question that hangs over us is to what extent and for how many black people has the government and the Afrikaners themselves become unacceptable, even hated.'[17]

Sharpeville Day brought more problems to the campus when a meeting arranged by the BSS to commemorate the killings at Sharpeville and the more recent ones at Langa went very badly.[18] During the morning a woman alleged by some students to be a police spy and who was found to have a forged student card, was forced to the platform on the library lawns from which the meeting was being conducted. She was interrogated by a number of students, and at one stage was in some physical danger. She was rescued by members of the administration, security staff and SRC and BSS leaders who formed a shield around her and removed her to a room in the Students' Union where she was guarded by security.

I remained outside the door with Ken Standenmacher and Bruce Dickson, fending off angry students who were demanding that we hand her over so they could complete their interrogation! With student leaders helping to defuse the situation, tempers later cooled, and the woman was removed through the back of the building and escorted off the campus. She gave a statement to the University security staff in which she admitted that she was not a student at the University and had fraudulently obtained a student card.

She said she had been on campus the morning of the meeting to go to the library and had met some friends who had taken her to the BSS offices where she had been assaulted and told she was believed to be an informer. She had then been forced in front of the crowd.

Later in the day, two white students were injured in scuffles on campus and laid formal complaints with the University.[19]

Both of them made statements and these give some perspective on the attitudes of some white students at Wits during this period.

One of them said that when he saw a crowd on the West Campus with placards 'denigrating the police and Defence Force and lauding Swapo, the ANC and MPLA', he had decided to exercise his right to free speech and said he 'believed that the police were doing a good job and that they had only defended themselves at Sharpeville. I also

A woman reporter from one of the latter approached me as soon as I entered the room, told me who she was, and started to abuse me verbally, blaming me and the University for this occurrence. She was joined by some of the SMA office bearers who also berated me.

Registrar Standenmacher and Deputy Registrar Student Affairs Jonathan Stead had reached the meeting before me and had been trying in vain to persuade the students to stop the shouting. I tried to attract the attention of the demonstrators by raising my hands in a 'please quieten down' gesture and called for silence, but got no response. This resulted in further abuse from the journalist and the SMA members. I spotted Dali Mpofu, President of the BSS standing on one of the benches and, climbing over the benches to reach him, I told him that I was appalled by the behaviour, which would receive very bad publicity and was making my position untenable. He said he would try to stop the noise, shouted 'Amandla!' and called on his members to sing the anthem, 'Nkosi Sikelel' iAfrika'. They did so and then trooped out.

Although there would still have been time for the Unita party to be heard, they had by then been ushered out by the SMA and university security personnel, and had convened a press conference in the nearby NSF offices. The University was again faced with the embarrassment caused by the abuse of its policy of freedom of speech. In addition, the SMA had scored a propaganda victory which they used with considerable effect for some time.

What became clear at that meeting was that senior members of the University administration were ineffective in controlling crowds and approaches had to be made through the student leadership. At a meeting with three members of the BSS executive immediately afterwards, when horror was expressed at what had transpired, the explanation was that Unita were bandits; that blacks in South Africa did not enjoy freedom of speech or many other fundamental freedoms; that life on campus could not be separated from events in the rest of the country; and that they could give no undertaking that it would not happen again.[16] The University refused permission for a repeat Unita meeting on 21 March, Sharpeville Day, as it was thought that to hold it on that particular date would be unashamedly provocative.

In a perceptive and soul-searching comment, a writer in *Die Vaderland* stated that 'disciplinary action by the University authorities

short of admitting joint culpability for the consequences of apartheid. It did however concede that universities (and by implication Wits) had tended to take an official position only on matters that bore directly on their nature and function. It was conceded that the situation demanded that Wits now speak out on broader issues and that it was morally obliged to protest at gross injustice. Failure to do so could be taken to imply tacit acquiescence in an outrageous state of affairs.

Both documents represent important statements of principle in that they unequivocally condemn aspects of government policy outside the academic domain, and recognise that as academic freedom and general freedom are indivisible, it is incumbent on the University to speak out without hesitation against infringements of freedom of any kind. (See Appendix 3.)

Issues of Freedom of Speech

Between 17 and 21 March 1986, a series of student demonstrations took place which were very distressing to many members of the University because they involved the issues of freedom of speech and intimidation on campus and led to extremely negative comment in the media.[13] These and other incidents of student unrest and police intervention on campus during the course of the year would lead to a second Commission of Inquiry in October, and an attempt by the Government to coerce the universities into clamping down on campus activism under the threat of withdrawal of state subsidy.[14]

On Wednesday 19 March, the NSF, through its SMA affiliate, arranged a lunch-time meeting which was to be addressed by three members of the National Union for the Total Independence of Angola (Unita), including two brigadiers. Unita was supported by the South African Government during its civil war against the Popular Movement for the Liberation of Angola (MPLA).[15]

I received an urgent summons during the lunch hour to come to the lecture theatre in which the meeting was being held as it was being broken up by black students. When I got there, large numbers of BSS members were standing on the seats and benches. They were chanting, singing and heckling, making it impossible for the speakers to be heard. There were also numbers of journalists and photographers present, some representing right-wing European newspapers.

it. The majority of South Africans and a substantial proportion of the Wits community saw the state of emergency not as preserving the security of the state, but rather that of the apartheid regime.

It was an unfortunate experience for Tober, who was committed to a non-racial and democratic South Africa, to an unfettered admissions policy based on merit, and to providing for the financial, residential and academic needs of black students. He had also consistently supported the students' right to demonstrate peacefully on campus. The episode did however, lead to the University making a more powerful statement of commitment to the anti-apartheid struggle beyond the academic terrain.

Taking a stand

The concern of many members of the academic staff about the critical situation in South Africa, about the way in which the state of emergency was interfering with the lives of staff and students and their ability to pursue their academic interests, and about what was perceived to be the University's inadequate response to these issues, led to a joint special meeting of the Boards of the Faculties of Arts, Education and Science on 9 October 1985.[7]

The meeting was initiated by Professor C F Cresswell, Dean of the Faculty of Science, who chaired it.[8] Those who attended it approved by a vote of ninety-eight for, one against and five abstentions, a document containing a preamble and a statement of principle, which had been drafted and approved by each of the three boards.[9]

The Academic Board Executive (ABEX) welcomed the initiative and agreed to give the seven other faculties an opportunity to add their reactions which would be forwarded to Senate. A drafting committee was established to prepare a succinct policy statement on the University's attitude to the current situation.[10] The preamble and statement of principle were approved with certain amendments by Senate and with certain other amendments by Council, as was the policy statement.[11]

The first document[12] was in essence an admission of joint responsibility for a less than total commitment to the anti-apartheid struggle. The second, which required the approval of a wider constituency, fell

uphold the rights of students to demonstrate peacefully. The petitioners expressed their support for these rights and for their restoration to the University. They declared their belief that it was the duty of the University, of its staff and of its students, as privileged groups in South African society, to address all issues which affected freedom of expression and of educational institutions and called for the reaffirmation of these principles as espoused by the resolution of the General Assembly of the University on 8 June 1972 (see Chapter 3).[6]

Where Tober displayed faulty judgement was in his unreserved acceptance that the existing restrictions could only be lifted if members of academic institutions refrained from acts of violence and the use of force. The minimal force displayed by students in throwing stones, reprehensible as it might be, was a reaction to the violence of the police in carrying out regulations which prohibited the free expression of opinion; and could not be regarded as justification for

Picture courtesy *The Star*

A typical General Assembly on the library lawns. This one was held to protest against the 'Quota Bill' in 1983.

all further restrictions on the admission of black students to the University and for the introduction of equal educational opportunities. Tober quoted from a speech he had made on 29 February 1984:

> If a University allows itself to be used as a political weapon, even for the noble cause of eradicating injustice, we may endanger the very functions of the University which alone enable it to make real contributions to change. No single university in this world has enough power to end all social evils, least of all by posturing and clamouring for publicity. The abuse of academic freedom can only lead to its ultimate destruction ...
>
> This does not mean that universities should be divorced from social reality or absolved from social responsibility. But universities must serve the people as institutions of learning. It is not for us to solve the problems of the day by publishing political manifestos. But we can and should respond to grave national problems as scholars in our specific disciplines, be it as human and social scientists, in community medicine and dentistry, in the exploration of our material resources, in the defence of human rights and liberties, or in the design of new skills and technologies.
>
> Nor does it mean that the University will remain silent, when actions by the authorities hinder staff and students in the pursuit of their academic objectives, or worse, curtail their freedom.

In his anxiety to maintain academic objectivity on a highly sensitive and emotional political issue, Tober succeeded only in releasing a flood of anger against himself from a substantial body of staff and students. A petition organised by the SRC and issued by an anonymous 'Ad-hoc Students and Staff Committee', signed by about 150 staff members 'including many senior members of the academic community' and about 500 students, was sent to him on 30 August.

The petition rejected his suggestion that it was possible to separate academic freedom from other forms of freedom, and regretted his failure to condemn the recent actions of the police on campus and to

disperse. On a number of occasions the senior officer in charge would tell me that he had orders from Pretoria to break up the demonstration.

Students gathered again the following morning, but announced that they would disperse after lunch. I was telephoned during the morning by a senior police officer who asked the University authorities to assist in controlling student protests and offered to release the detained students if the demonstrations stopped. He was told that meetings would end after lunch that day. During the lunch period the students were addressed by Bishop Desmond Tutu, after which they dispersed. With excruciatingly bad timing, a strong force of police arrived at the entrance to the campus just then. The news spread, and the students started to gather again on the steps of the Great Hall. The senior police officer was persuaded on this occasion that the students would disperse if the police left, and this is indeed what happened.

Tactical Error

On Friday 16 August Tober addressed the sixth General Assembly of the University.[5] Unfortunately the event was to have unhappy consequences for him. In some respects, his speech was a good one. He started by reaffirming the principles which formed the foundation of the University, and challenging those who wished to bring down the institution to 'remember that it is indestructible ... firmly resting on the three cornerstones which are the basis of all the great universities of the world: freedom, scholarship and service'. He recapitulated the University's repeated affirmations about academic freedom.

He was, however, extremely cautious in his condemnation of the state of emergency, arguing that although 'within the confines of a university campus, this proclamation of 21 July 1985 constitutes a serious curtailment of our freedom of expression', he accepted 'unreservedly, that the present restrictions could only be lifted if members of academic institutions refrain from acts of violence and from the use of force. Personal responsibility cannot find shelter behind institutional privilege. Our University must remain a place where differences are settled by argument, not by fists, by words, not by stones. We must seek solutions not confrontations ...' He then called for the lifting of

head with a thick rubber baton. Although he was prepared to proceed with an action against the police, a Senior Counsel advised that the action would not succeed as, in terms of the emergency regulations, it would be necessary for him to show that the police were aware that he had not been part of the demonstration. The matter therefore unfortunately fell away.[4] Recently, Maphai, describing the incident to me, spoke of the look of enjoyment on the policeman's face while he was hitting him. He still experiences a sense of injustice at what was done to him and frustration at the inaccessibility of legal remedy at the time.

Attempts to confirm the names of the students arrested and to secure their release that day, were unsuccessful. That night, at an urgent meeting of representatives of all groups on campus called by Tober, there was a pervasive sense of outrage at the police action as well as a deep feeling of helplessness in the face of emergency regulations which precluded access to the normal legal processes. It was decided to call another General Assembly of the University later in the week.

Student anger at the events of the previous day led to a further meeting on the library lawn on Tuesday 13 August. In the course of the morning, a deputation of students called on Tober to address the gathering. In doing so he strongly criticised police action and expressed sympathy with black students whose lives were so tragically affected by the situation. He released a statement to the same effect to staff and students. Strongly worded statements condemning the police action were also released by the Academic Staff Association, the SRC and the Law Students' Council.

Efforts continued during the day to secure the release of the students who had been arrested.

During the lunch period there was another march. The police were again present, but on this occasion took no action, and the students dispersed.

It was observed on numerous occasions that if the police took no aggressive action, the student demonstration would end peacefully. I put this argument to senior police officers several times in urging them to assume a low profile when reacting to protest marches but they were rarely responsive. If the emergency regulations forbade open air assemblies, the only response was to force the crowd to

Firoz Cachalia was one of several students arrested on the campus on 12 August 1985

Despite encouragement, not one injured student was prepared to sign an affidavit about the events of the day. There were probably two reasons for this, one that the students were afraid of a vindictive response from the police, the other that many of them did not want their parents to know about their involvement. There was however, an affidavit from a lecturer in philosophy, Mr Vincent Maphai, who had inadvertently become involved in one of the skirmishes as he was leaving a religious service at the Holy Trinity Catholic Church, which is just off campus. A policeman had hit him about eight times on his

present. I informed the SRC President and the BSS Chairperson, as was the usual procedure, that an open air meeting was illegal in terms of the emergency regulations, but that the University did not forbid it.

The University stood by its 1972 resolution that 'it is the right of university students as of other bodies of citizens to express peacefully by public assembly and procession their opinions on matters of public policy'. The administration did not feel constrained to enforce the provisions of the state of emergency, with which we strongly disagreed. Students were nevertheless cautioned about the possible consequences and were warned that violent behaviour such as stone throwing was not acceptable. It was University policy not to make rules that were unenforceable, and students would certainly not have acceded to a ban on protest meetings.

Throughout the morning the gathering, which was orderly and peaceful, was addressed by student leaders. At about 1.30pm some 300 students started a march and moved, toyi-toying and singing freedom songs, to the periphery of the campus where they were joined by an equal number of onlookers. The demonstrators were met by a squad of about thirty riot police armed with sjamboks,[3] batons, teargas equipment and side arms. The students sat down on the road, still within the campus, chanting 'Peace!' There was no response to an order from the senior police officer that the group must disperse within four minutes. He then called out 'Your time is up,' at which the squad, flailing indiscriminately at the crowd with their sjamboks and batons, charged the students, who turned and fled back onto the campus. At this stage numbers of rocks were thrown at the police. The police broke up into small groups, chasing students who were running and seeking shelter in different parts of the University. Some students were pursued into the Wartenweiler Library.

In the course of this exercise, eight students were arrested and forty were treated in the Campus Health Clinic for various injuries, most of them to the back, arms and legs. The medical officers made detailed notes, clinical photographs were taken of the injuries, and the injured students were asked to prepare statements, all with a view to instituting legal proceedings. It was an appalling attack on a peaceful demonstration.

study or to enrol for any studies. Tober urged that the interpretation be reconsidered or the ruling changed as the academic progress of students was being hindered and their success in examinations jeopardised.

He also asked that lecturers be given access to reading material for bona fide study purposes. The University would supply the material, which could be scrutinised by whomsoever Government saw fit to delegate, and passed to detainees by the prison officials.

Tober also urged that the University be allowed to supplement the prison diet with fresh fruit, or that the detainees be able to buy fresh fruit from the prison shop.

On the previous day, a telegram had been sent by the Deans of all the Faculties to the Minister of Law and Order, L le Grange, and the Minister of National Education, F W de Klerk. It read:

> We, the Deans of the Faculties at the University of the Witwatersrand, wish to express our grave concern over the denial of reasonable study and reading privileges to students and staff detained in terms of the emergency regulations. It seems to us unconscionable that those who are detained, without trial, presumably for preventative purposes, should be denied privileges accorded – and properly accorded – to those actually convicted in the courts. We believe the authorities should reconsider this indefensible policy forthwith, and allow detained students and staff access to written material relevant to their areas of study and reasonable facilities to make use of them.[1]

It is difficult to say whether these communications influenced the authorities. The fact is that after a period of intransigence the policy was changed. Detained students were allowed to study, and the police appointed a student liaison officer at Diepkloof Prison, near Johannesburg, where most of the detainees were held.

As a peaceful protest against the state of emergency, the BSS called for a lecture boycott on 12 and 13 August.[2] Early on the morning of 12 August, a group of students gathered on the library lawns. The numbers grew throughout the morning until about 1 000 were

CHAPTER 6

Wits and the First State of Emergency

The United Democratic Front (UDF) was set up at a mass rally in Cape Town in August 1983 in response to the constitutional proposals for a tricameral system. The organisation grew rapidly to a membership of over two million. The UDF rejected the new constitution and campaigned vigorously among Coloureds and Indians to boycott the first election held in terms of the new dispensation. Opposition to the system from the African population was fierce, and there were widespread strikes and boycotts of schools.

The Government's response to the unrest was to declare a state of emergency which took effect on 21 July 1985 and which led to a period of more intense oppression, together with abrogation of the Rule of Law, than had ever been experienced in the land. The police and military had wide powers and, protected by indemnity, were able to detain and interrogate people at will. Within a few months thousands of individuals had been detained. Hundreds of Wits students were affected in different ways.

Shortly after the declaration, four students and two members of the University staff were detained. Urgent representations for their release failed, and subsequently further detentions took place.

On 8 August 1985 Tober wrote a letter to the Director-General of the Department of Justice about the conditions under which the students and members of the academic staff were being detained in terms of the Public Safety Act of 1953. He referred to three specific and practical concerns relating to their physical and mental well-being. In terms of the regulations, detainees were not entitled to any reading matter except the Bible or other holy books and were not permitted to

showed concern for all the students of the University and did whatever was possible to defuse the situation as soon as it was reasonably possible. All the student witnesses who were asked the question agreed that the doors of those responsible for the administration of the University were always open to them, including those of the Vice-Chancellor. Needless to say, it is highly desirable that this state of affairs, which is a credit to Wits, continues in the future.'[14]

In general Council accepted the recommendations, except the one which proposed the exclusion of 'a graduate and a member of Convocation' (Russell Crystal) from the University. Nevertheless, they indicated that the recommendation should be brought to his attention. Dogs would only be used for crowd control as a last resort, and the administration should continue to warn students of the possible consequences of a march off campus. Stone throwing should not be countenanced.[15]

It was decided not to release the full report, a decision which is difficult to explain, but I suspect that some members of Council might have been anxious about the criticisms of the SMA being made public. The Commission's perspicacity could have helped to create a better understanding among the public, the media and the students.

The report is an interesting and important document because of the insight the Commissioners showed into the dynamics of campus politics and the motivation which influenced the actions of the antagonistic student organisations. The criticisms of some aspects of the University's handling of student protest were constructive and helpful and I certainly found the report immensely useful in dealing with subsequent episodes of campus unrest.

Unfortunately it was difficult to get the opposing student factions to accept all the recommendations of the Commission. Numerous meetings were arranged so representatives of the groups could meet over a table for constructive discussions, but these did not progress very far. The SMA would not accept the report at all. It argued that it did not recognise the legitimacy of the Commission and continued to arrange provocative meetings. Stone throwing episodes continued during confrontations with the police, but it was well-nigh impossible to identify offenders. The BSS insisted that it was not their policy to indulge in stone throwing, but it could not be responsible for individuals who did. The University ceased to use dogs to control student disorder.[16]

they insist on doing so; the BSS and SMA should, if possible by mutual agreement but if necessary by the authoritative intervention of the University, be prevented from holding meetings in response to each other, particularly on politically-sensitive days; liaison between the University authorities and the BSS; the BSS and University security; and University authorities and security should be improved.

The Commission also commented that Russel Crystal's presence on campus provoked the members of the BSS and recommended that he should be informed that he would not be allowed onto the campus on particularly sensitive days. Students should be aware of the importance of carrying their student cards with them at all times. Finally, the Commission recommended that no prosecutions or disciplinary proceedings should follow from the events of 14 May 1985. (See Appendix 2.)

The Commissioners observed that they had been enormously impressed with the calibre of a number of the witnesses who testified before them. They believed, however, that the students responsible for drafting the SMA report deserved censure. 'Many of the statements of fact we find to be palpably false and we regret to say that the report appears to have been drafted in an attempt to mislead us into making wrong findings of fact against their fellow-students (members of BSS). That the SMA chose not to participate in the viva voce proceedings, in our view, renders their motives in submitting the report suspect.'

The Commission did, however, recommend that the University make it clear that stone throwing would not be tolerated. Student leaders in the SRC, BSS and SMA and those involved in University publications should be called upon publicly to condemn violent or even unruly behaviour and should take steps to ensure that intemperate students did not resort to such behaviour.

The Commission concluded that the black students involved in the events of the day should be criticised for their unruly and even dangerous reaction to provocation, but added that the deliberately taunting and inciting conduct of the members of SMA should not be allowed to coincide with meetings of the BSS on commemorative days. Security police should treat black students with greater sensitivity and do so without dogs.

In the Commission's view the administrators of the University could not have done anything to prevent the events of 14 May. 'They

University has for most of its existence been engaged on many levels in a struggle against many of the laws which oppress and degrade black people in this country. The University cannot contemplate a situation in which (it) should become a battleground between its authorities and its students as the townships have become a battleground between their inhabitants and the South African Police.'[12]

Other important observations made by the Commission concerned the relations between the black students and the University in the context of the general situation existing in South African society.

The University could not exist separately from the system of which it was a part, said the Commission, but that did not mean that it should be equated with that system and injustices which might occur on campus should not be responded to the same way as those in society.

Though the University could not expect to be unaffected by the growing social conflict which surrounded it and the articulation of black anger and aspirations would undoubtedly become a feature in the future, the Commission believed that 'the University's concern should probably be that this anger is not directed at itself'.

The fact that the attempt to restrain students from confronting the police off campus, which the University saw as being in the interests of both the students and of the institution should be seen by black students as 'condescending', the Commission observed, 'is a signal indication to us of the gulf which has emerged between the University authorities and the black students'.[13]

This last comment is accurate. The University administration, myself included, was slow to comprehend that black student politics was substantially different from that which had obtained when the institution comprised predominantly white students. Black students fiercely resisted the imposition of rules and regulations drawn up by the authorities without any prior consultation. Brought up in a society in which they were entirely disempowered by a white hegemony which had imposed unjust laws on them, they would not accept this in their university where complete equality was the policy.

The senior officers of the University learned fast, and the report of the Commission assisted the learning process.

In brief, the Commission recommended that dogs should not be used for crowd control on campus; that students should be persuaded not to demonstrate against the police off campus but not be coerced if

Addressing angry students in the Senate House concourse ... 'I learnt an important lesson about the democratic process'

cross-examination. Reference was made in evidence to the difficult socio-economic circumstances which afflict many of the University's black students and to the intensity of their grievances against the system which governed South African society. It was extremely enlightening to be able to hear their perspectives in the calm judicial atmosphere.

The Commission had 'no doubt that socio-economic deprivation as well as the manner in which most black people experience the exercise of authority must lead to most black students having a different appreciation of the role of authority from that held by their white counterparts'. But, its report continued: 'The University authorities are neither the government or the police. Indeed, this

said that he would expect a full report on the day's events from members of staff who were involved and would welcome statements from anyone else. By the time that Standenmacher returned to the concourse, however, I had already agreed to the inquiry.

Tober was extremely angry when I told him of my decision, but by the next day he had been convinced that the inquiry would be a useful exercise and helpful in resolving student tensions.

The violence in the concourse could probably have been avoided if I had agreed to address the crowd earlier, and I erred in not doing so. Nevertheless, I had learnt an important lesson about the democratic process. It is not easy to negotiate in a situation where one is in a minority of one to 150, but the students were able to leave with their demands met and their anger ameliorated. I was also able to witness the control which an elected and respected leader such as Ngcobo was able to exercise on his followers.

The details of the inquiry were settled on 28 May through negotiation between the administration and student representatives. The Commission, which considered both written and oral evidence, sat on 13 and 14 June 1985. It was chaired by Jules Browde SC, and the other two members were George Bizos SC and Edwin Cameron, an advocate and a member of the staff of the Cals. Its sessions were open to all students and staff of the University and between twenty and sixty people were present throughout the hearing. Observers were invited to put points or questions to the witnesses. No members of the SMA were prepared to testify personally, but the organisation submitted a written report.

By the time the Commission met, there had been another angry face-to-face confrontation, on 30 May, between the SMA, who had arranged a table display on campus to commemorate Republic Day, and the BSS, who were incensed at the display of the South African flag and at what Republic Day stood for. Members of the administration, security and student leaders had a hard time defusing the situation and we had to position ourselves between the two factions to prevent physical harm being caused. In the process we were severely jostled. These experiences were undoubtedly in the minds of those who gave evidence to the Commission of Inquiry.

The proceedings were among the most democratic the University had ever experienced and no witness was immune from intensive

forum for them to express their views. The function of the security staff was to see to the safety of students and to safeguard University property and I regretted greatly that the sequence of events during the morning had led to a breakdown in trust between the students and security staff who had in the past been very sympathetic.

Chris Ngcobo then invited students to address their questions one at a time and ensured that I had the opportunity to respond. I was given a generally quiet hearing interspersed with heckling when they disagreed with an answer. The questioning was sharp, and the students were supported by Mr Raymond Suttner, a lecturer in the School of Law, who was particularly critical of University security staff and their use of dogs. The process of question and answer, demand and response continued for about an hour.

At first the students made two demands: that the University should undertake not to institute any disciplinary procedures against any of the students involved in the day's activities; and that it must undertake an investigation of the role of the security staff that day. I was not prepared to give an undertaking on either of these demands, insisting that there were established procedures and that it would be improper for me to do so.

After some time, Grant Rex made a compromise proposal that the University agree to hold an independent inquiry into all the events of the day. This seemed to me to be a reasonable solution, but I was reluctant to agree without consulting the Vice-Chancellor who was still tied up in the Academic Board meeting.

I tried to get a message to him through Deputy Registrar Bruce Dickson and Registrar Mr Ken Standenmacher who were standing by, but it was clearly an unsatisfactory way to consult under pressure. The students would not agree to wait until the following day for an answer, and I felt that it was important to defuse the tension immediately to avoid the possibility of further damage and the real danger that demonstrations might go on indefinitely.

After further negotiation, the students agreed to disperse and I agreed that the University would accede to the proposal for an independent inquiry, the details to be agreed upon by negotiation between the administration, the SRC and the BSS. In the meantime, it transpired later, Tober had left the meeting to speak to Standenmacher and Vice-Principal Charlton. He had not agreed to an inquiry but had

dogs were a symbol of the repression to which they were subjected in the townships by the South African Police. According to the Commission, 'their mere presence is an affront to the black students and their use in crowd control exacerbates the situation rather than assisting in defusing it'.

An angry crowd of students moved to the concourse of Senate House. There Chris Ngcobo, Chairperson of the BSS told me the students were demanding that the Vice-Chancellor, Professor Tober, address them, and failing him, that I do so.[10] The Vice-Chancellor was unavailable as he was about to chair a meeting of the Academic Board and I was reluctant to address the large crowd in the concourse, but suggested that I would meet a delegation of students in my office.[11] The Vice-Chairperson of the BSS, Jennifer Mohamed, said that this was not the way 'our democracy' worked and that I should address the whole group. She said that the students were very unhappy with the way that security had handled events during the course of the day. I insisted that I would only speak to a delegation and left the concourse to attend the meeting of Academic Board.

A short time later, I was called out of the meeting by Grant Rex and asked to come to the concourse immediately as the situation there was very tense and he believed it would help to defuse things if I were to agree to address the whole group. Students had attempted to storm the stairwell to make their way to the Vice-Chancellor's office on the eleventh floor of Senate House and had been restrained by campus security, again with dogs.

When I arrived at the concourse I saw chairs being thrown at the dogs and their handlers. Students had forced their way into the Central Admissions Office and the Coffee Shop, both of which lead off the concourse, and had damaged some of the furniture. After advising the head of security to withdraw the dogs, I agreed to address the group.

It was a difficult situation for me. I was facing about 150 to 180 highly emotional students who were mourning two comrades and had been involved in the conflict with campus security and their dogs. They gathered around me angrily but were called to order by Chris Ngcobo, who chaired the session. I expressed my sympathy over the tragic deaths in detention and said that I appreciated their distress and that the administration wanted to assist in providing a

was particularly inflammatory in the light of the belief, widely held on the campus, that members of the SMA might have links with the security police, or that they might make material in their possession available to the security police. The SMA claimed that they were merely taking photographs for their newsletter. The response of some of the demonstrators was to throw clods of earth at the two.

The crowd split at this stage, but both groups converged on Jorissen Street where numbers of police vehicles were present.[9] A sequence of events following an attempt by University security staff to prevent the one group from entering Jorissen Street, led to a serious confrontation between security and students. In the course of this, a few students and security staff were injured and two students were detained by security for a brief period. The situation was aggravated by the fact that Wits's security staff were accompanied by dogs. Evidence before the Commission was that to black students, the

Picture courtesy Mayibuye Centre

Russell Crystal (pointing), Philip Powell (with camera) and other SMA/NSF members confront the BSS

the DPSC were arrested and charged under the Internal Security Act with participating in an illegal gathering.

Thirty-five people were arrested including sixteen students, among them Grant Rex, President of the Wits SRC, and a previous President, Lloyd Vogelman.[4] When they appeared in court the following day, charges were dropped pending further investigation.[5] It was an extraordinarily strong-arm reaction to a peaceful demonstration that in no way endangered the security of the state. Large numbers of plainclothes police were involved in confiscating placards, taking names and addresses and making arrests. This overreaction, indicative of the state's sensitivity to any challenge to its authority, heralded the states of emergency that were to follow, when citizens were to be deprived of all right of dissent outside of Parliament.

The Browde Commission

The events which took place on campus on 14 May 1985, and the friction which was to lead to the establishment of a Commission of Inquiry,[6] are illustrative, although not typical of, a number of similar occurrences during the following months and years of the decade. The origin of the conflict was concurrent meetings of rival student groups held in adjoining venues during the lunch period that day.[7]

In one place the SRC and BSS were holding a joint meeting to commemorate the deaths in detention of Mr Andreas Raditsela and Mr Sipho Mutsi. In another an SMA meeting on 'Terrorism', organised some weeks in advance, was addressed by Mr Peter Stiff, an ex-Rhodesian. Outside the second venue, and located in such a way that it was bound to be seen by those attending the SRC/BSS meeting, the SMA had placed a table on which was displayed an eight-page pamphlet entitled 'Special Report – Target Terrorism'.

The conflict began when members of the SRC/BSS group snatched pamphlets, tore them up and threw them in the air. The group then toyi-toyied towards Jan Smuts Avenue.[8] Before they reached their destination, a member of the SMA leadership, accompanied by the chairman of the SMA, raced ahead of the group and positioned himself to photograph it. This was not the first time that this practice, which was to be described by the Commission as 'flagrantly provocative and objectionable behaviour', had taken place. It

While overt student activism during 1984, the first year of open admissions, was relatively subdued, there was an increase in tension on campus, particularly between the BSS and the SMA. The BSS was vigorous in establishing structures to represent black student interests. Working with the SRC they set about trying to 'conscientise' black and white students as well as the staff, about the disabilities suffered by black South Africans and the need for the University to take an uncompromising anti-apartheid stand.

The BSS worked not only for black students at Wits, but also for those in other institutions in South Africa. To this end, they applied pressure on the Wits administration to admit black students who, because of political activities, had been expelled from the 'bush colleges'.

The University was sympathetic because of the allegedly unfair manner in which the affected students had been treated. A procedure was set up to investigate the academic records of those who had applied for admission to Wits, and a substantial number was accepted. Many of these students were marked by the security police and were detained without trial during subsequent states of emergency.

Anger among young blacks at the poor quality of black education led in May 1984 to a nation-wide boycott of schools, colleges and universities. The Azanian Students' Organisation (Azaso) and Cosas deliberately chose 30 May, the day before Republic Day, for a day of national protest in solidarity with the boycotting students. At Wits, students observed a three-hour boycott of lectures, while the SMA manned a kiosk on the campus, distributing South African flags and anti-Nusas pamphlets, and occasionally taunting the boycotters. The black consciousness-aligned Azanian Students' Movement (Azasm) strongly condemned the day of protest calling it 'liberal, sympathetic and pitiful'.[3]

On 29 November 1984 a National Day of Protest against State repression was called by the Black Sash, the Johannesburg Democratic Action Committee (Jodac) and the Detainees' Parents Support Committee (DPSC). In the course of a peaceful picket demonstration, Professor John Dugard, a distinguished academic who was Director of the Centre for Applied Legal Studies (Cals) in the University's Faculty of Law, and Dr Max Coleman, chairman of

CHAPTER 5

The 1980s

My tenure as DVC coincided with the years during which student activism at the English-language universities was at its most intense.

With all the furore over the Quota Bill (see Chapter 8), there was surprisingly little student activism in relation to the referendum of white voters called at the end of March 1983 and scheduled for 2 November of that year, to approve the new constitution which would establish a tricameral parliament.[1] White voters were asked to accept the Constitution Act and two-thirds of them did. Coloured and Indian opinion was tested, not by referenda but by two separate general elections in which there were massive abstentions. Black African opinion was not tested at all.

Although anger about the new constitution spilled over onto the campus and the issue was extensively debated, the debates were generally peaceful. There was some support for the constitution from members of the University who regarded the proposals as 'a step in the right direction'. The Chairman of Council, Nico Stutterheim, and a senior member, Charles Skeen, caused a stir when they signed a newspaper advertisement in which a group of prominent business people advocated a 'yes' vote. Fortunately, this was not picked up by the students. At a mass meeting in the Great Hall on 2 June, Dr Allan Boesak, President of the World Alliance of Reformed Churches, said the proposals endorsed apartheid. The new constitution would fail to 'represent a historical moment to begin anew ... and correct the mistakes of the past ... We who struggle for human rights have no option but to reject these constitutional proposals, not only for the sake of honesty but for our own sakes as human beings.'[2]

a theoretical physicist and a Fellow of the Royal Society, brought together an effective group who devoted three years to their task. The plan was published in 1980.[52] It recognised that the University had historically served predominantly the white middle-class community of the Witwatersrand and that efforts should be made to open it effectively to all who were qualified and wished to receive an education in the English language.

It acknowledged that the University was not serving society to the best of its ability in the setting of contemporary South Africa. Students were not being educated to be fully aware of the social and economic problems which surrounded them and the University was not doing enough to equip able students from the disadvantaged sectors of the South African educational system to overcome their early educational disadvantages so that they might benefit fully from their studies at Wits. Moreover, not enough research in the University concentrated on the problems of its immediate environment. The conclusion of the academic planners was that the University should 'maintain and develop (its) pure scholarship and rigorous advanced teaching, while using the intellectual strength that this provides to plan, to educate skilled staff for, and to assess the success of activities which will develop in all the surrounding communities.'

The University would have to grow to about 22 000 students to accommodate the large numbers of black students who would be admitted, the committee concluded. At that time the total enrolment was 13 126 of whom 8 per cent were black. By 1990 there were 19 341 students, of whom 24 per cent were black.[53] More staff would be needed 'to do research in matters of local concern such as the utilisation of solar energy at low cost, the study of the use of English as second language, adult education, (and) the problems of urbanisation'. Most importantly, the committee recognised that the University must be prepared to offer special curricula including bridging courses for students of high potential who had suffered educational disadvantages.

The Academic Plan was a substantial document, the product of much thought, consultation and discussion, and went into considerable detail on its recommendations. It was accepted by the Senate and the faculties and many of its recommendations were implemented during the subsequent decade.

numerous other administration boards, was responsible for all urban black African administration, came to the residences on a few occasions or wrote letters about individual residents, but this pressure stopped towards the end of 1984. The requests to the press were honoured on every occasion.

In the first weeks of his Vice-Chancellorship, though, Du Plessis was to experience an example of the prejudice prevalent among some white English-speaking people in the northern suburbs of Johannesburg to this day. A small suburban newspaper which subsists on revenue from advertisers, published an editorial after an interview with Du Plessis, which referred to Wits's 'almost obsessive preoccupation with the affairs of the Blacks'.[51] The article also stated that 'Wits is an essentially White educational institution and will remain so for the foreseeable future. Not only is it financed by money from the pockets of increasingly hard-pressed taxpayers but the overwhelming majority of its students are there at the direct or indirect expense of White parents, for whom it often means substantial sacrifices. The university's obligation to these White taxpayers and White parents should be its first consideration.'

This sort of thinking demonstrates how the University's administration and staff had to contend, not only with an apartheid government but also with a substantial constituency of the public, in its attempts to open the University. Opposition from this quarter was expressed in letters to the press, phone calls (many of them anonymous) to the University and refusals to contribute funds. Some families who might have been expected to send their children to Wits made their statement by sending them to the Rand Afrikaans University or to universities outside Johannesburg, and frequently announced proudly that they had done so. In later years when more blacks were admitted, some white families whose children were not accepted into faculties with limited intakes, accused the University of lowering its standards.

Early in 1978, Du Plessis, mindful of the rapid political and demographic changes that would inform future policy for the University, delegated to Professor Frank Nabarro, a Deputy Vice-Chancellor, the task of assembling a group of people in the University who would look closely at Southern Africa and the immediate constituency of the Witwatersrand and draw up a long-term academic plan. Nabarro,

and the responsible ministers were more readily giving approval for such registrations. Du Plessis strongly encouraged this process, but as the Act provided for penalties against the students concerned rather than against the registering university, it was still policy that no black student could be registered without ministerial approval.

In an interview soon after taking up his post, Du Plessis identified as the biggest issue facing the University the need to assist black education, and he committed himself at various times throughout his tenure of office to promoting this objective.[50] In the course of this first interview he also said that 'black students have exactly the same facilities as the white students'. This was not entirely correct. While, by 1978, the University's policy of social segregation had in most respects fallen into disuse (although Council had never formally rescinded its policy on this issue), the University's residences were still not fully 'open'. The Group Areas Act was still in force and this was a legal impediment to integration of university housing on the main campus which was located in a white group area.

Du Plessis was fully aware of the urgent need of black students for suitable university accommodation because of the long distances they had to travel from home to the University, and because the abysmal poverty in which many of them lived at home made for poor working conditions. He strove to raise funds to build new residences and was always alert to the possibility of purchasing blocks of flats which could be used to house black students in particular. He also decided that he would gradually increase the proportion of black students in the on-campus residences notwithstanding the Group Areas Act.

This move evoked no overt reaction from white students in the residences, although the matter was clearly widely discussed. From time to time there were questions from reporters about the presence of black students in the previously all-white hostels. These questions were probably often a reaction to hostile reports about this illegal integration. By the time I joined Du Plessis's administration in 1983, it was agreed that the response to the press should be completely frank, but with a request that the facts should not be made public, as the Government might then be forced to take action. We believed that the authorities were aware of what was happening but had decided not to react unless public pressure forced them to do so. Officials from the West Rand Administration Board, which, like the

Aggett's tragic death highlighted the very considerable danger in which detainees found themselves and there was immense concern for them.

After their release from detention, banning orders were served on Haysom, Coleman and Van Heerden. Haysom was prevented from pursuing his studies or contributing to research and teaching in the Centre for Applied Legal Studies. Coleman and Van Heerden, Honours students in Industrial Sociology, were allowed to continue their studies, but the provisions of their banning orders made it impossible for them to undertake their field work, to publish their results, or to take part in discussions about the implications of their work outside the bounds of their course of study.[46]

On 24 August 1983, three students of the University were detained by security police and held under section 29 of the Internal Security Act. They were Daryl Glaser, a Master's student in the Department of Sociology, Karl Niehaus, a third-year BA student and Robert Whitecross, a second-year BCom student.[47] Glaser and Whitecross were released a few days later but Niehaus was tried and convicted on a charge of attempted sabotage. Whitecross, who shared a house with him, gave evidence against Niehaus at the trial. He was revealed then as being a security police spy. During the subsequent states of emergency, Whitecross had 'special responsibilities' for Wits and was evident on numerous occasions.

The Academic Plan

As black student numbers increased in the University, it became clear that there would have to be a considerable amount of creative thinking and planning to provide for their special needs: in particular for academic support, financial aid and residential accommodation. Furthermore it became clear that there was going to be conflict on the campus between students of substantially opposing political views.

When Du Plessis assumed office as Vice-Chancellor in January 1978, there were 650 black students registered at the University.[48] By the time he retired in January 1983, the number had increased to 1 737.[49] In the previous few years, the impression had been gained that the Government was becoming more flexible in its attitude towards the admission of blacks to the historically white universities

the country on an exit permit. Like many other young South Africans who were victims of apartheid, he was unable to return until the plethora of restrictive laws were repealed in 1990.

Detentions of staff and students continued during 1981 and by the end of November nine students and one member of staff were being held without trial under security legislation.[44] On 11 February 1982 the Academic Staff Association, the Administrative and Library Staff Association, the Black University Workers' Association and the SRC held a protest meeting to express their concern for members of the staff and students, as well as for the large numbers of other individuals who were being held in detention by the Security Police. This meeting was planned to coincide with a nation-wide 30-minute period of mourning for Dr Neil Aggett who had died in detention on 5 February.[45]

Picture courtesy *Wits Student*

David Webster speaks at a meeting to protest the death in detention of Neil Aggett. Webster was later to be assassinated outside his home by unknown assailants widely believed to be members of the security forces. The scorch marks on the picture are the result of an incident when members of a men's residence, angered by an article in Wits Student, *trashed the newspaper's offices destroying most of the archives.*

while Conservative white students were persuaded by the Government's 'total onslaught' strategy to regard these movements as the terrorist enemy. The result was that discussions between the opposing factions indicated only that their differences were irreconcilable.[39]

Another issue addressed at the 2 June meeting was the detention of Andrew Boraine which was strongly condemned by Du Plessis and by Adelman. In his address, Adelman also said that it had been agreed that heckling of speakers at meetings would be reduced, no flags or banners would be allowed at meetings, and no cabinet ministers would be allowed to speak on the campus. 'Students who acted in the way they did, acted out of a deep-seated and passionate belief in freedom, justice and democracy. There is not always consensus, but the majority of students on this campus are directly opposed to apartheid and racism in any form', he said.[40]

On 18 June, Adelman was served with a five year banning order and three black student leaders – Azhar and Firoz Cachalia and David Johnson – were detained.[41] At an angry protest meeting at which the students were joined by thirty senior members of the administration and academic staff, the arbitrary actions and the threats to the University were condemned as 'a flagrant violation of human freedom and a threat to the independence of the University and the unity of the student movement'. A motion was passed calling on the University Council to insist on a meeting with the Ministers of Justice and of Police to demand the immediate release of all detained students and the lifting of Adelman's banning order. The Vice-President of the SRC, Jeremy Clark, called on the assembly 'to commit ourselves in the face of repression to a democratic future for our country'.[42] That night, a group of about 100 students held a silent torchlight vigil.

Strong condemnation of the bannings came surprisingly from two newspapers that were invariably supportive of Government policy, the *Citizen* and *Vaderland*, and also from the Chairman of the University of Pretoria's branch of Political Students' Union (Polstu).[43] This was welcome and useful because it gave a signal to Government that even in its traditional support base there was some discomfiture about its disregard for fundamental freedoms. Sadly these warnings were ignored by the P W Botha regime.

The arbitrary banning order served on Adelman was a vicious punishment. Without the freedom to pursue his legal studies he left

Picture courtesy University Archives
Demonstrators hold up the remnants of a South African flag burnt in protest

correspondence columns of the newspapers. Others regarded the burning of the flag as 'unspeakable.'[37]

Du Plessis attempted to cool the situation in a dispassionate address to students on 2 June in which he emphasised that a university was a place where all should feel free to express their ideas and beliefs and exhorted students to approach their differences in a scholarly manner.[38] It was an appropriate speech, but with the advantage of hindsight it is clear that he would not have had a receptive audience. The political climate was not conducive to such rational conduct.

Disenfranchised black students felt themselves to be the victims of apartheid and idolised the banned and exiled liberation movements

hold a function or pursue an activity here and should the possibility exist (in the prevailing climate of opinion) that this might lead to student disturbances, Government should be warned beforehand of the potential hazard'. The fact is that it would have been foolhardy to have arranged any such event on the Wits campus during that entire decade. Student outrage would have led to protest demonstrations which would have been almost impossible to contain.

This threatening meeting was followed by a letter from the Director-General of National Education who asked for written confirmation that amenities of the University would be available for official national events such as the Republic Festival and the South African Games and that disciplinary action be urgently instituted against those students who were guilty of burning the South African and the Republic Festival flags.[36] He added the following paragraph: 'The Minister appeals to you to act in these matters urgently in order to avoid that further build up of public pressure necessitates steps in terms of sections 25 and 27 of the Universities Act, No 61 of 1955, which he would of course prefer to avoid.' (These sections provided for penalties which might be imposed in the event of financial mismanagement.) Council regarded this remark as highly inappropriate and improper. It was indeed. A few years later, attempts by F W de Klerk, as Minister of National Education, to impose financial sanctions on universities if they did not clamp down on political activity on their campuses, were strenuously opposed and defeated in the courts.

Throughout the period of tumult over the burning of the flag, little attention was paid to the feelings of the majority of the population about the national symbols which had been thrust upon them. Most black South Africans felt nothing for the national flag which symbolised only the Dutch and British origins of the whites and the old Boer Republics, or for the national anthem 'Die Stem'. Many were frankly antagonistic and regarded the flag and the anthem as representing the oppressor. Few whites were sensitive to these issues at the time. Hogarth, a *Sunday Times* columnist, wrote about Nationalist antagonism towards the Union Jack when it was the official flag of the Union of South Africa, and how a person who had burnt a Union Jack at the University of Pretoria in 1919 had been regarded with honour. A few letters which drew attention to factors mitigating against general national support for the flag appeared in the

by outdoor demonstrations the same day and on the following two days in support of the Republic.[32] Differences between opposing groups were exacerbated by incidents of provocative and racist behaviour. Members of the University administration had difficulty in restraining the rival parties from violence, and on 27 May, squads of riot police moved uninvited onto campus and, although the crowds had begun to disperse, ordered them to do so in terms of the Riotous Assemblies Act.[33]

During one of the confrontations a South African flag which was being brandished by a member of the SMA was set alight. The incident was filmed by South African Television and the screening, together with extensive newspaper coverage, led to an outraged reaction from the white public. Council was assured by Du Plessis that every effort was being made to trace those responsible for the flag burning, and that if they were students they would be disciplined. Leaders of the SRC, BSS and SMA had agreed that any student guilty of insulting language, provocative behaviour, racism or racial incitement, violence or disruption of classes, should be punished.[34] Attempts to identify the culprits failed and it was concluded that the person depicted in press photographs of the incident was an outsider who had joined the protest demonstrations, a phenomenon that was not uncommon during this decade.

Stutterheim and Du Plessis were summoned to Pretoria to be told by the Ministers of Finance and of National Education that the Cabinet was seriously concerned about the anti-Republic sentiments expressed at Wits and other universities and the Government was considering taking action.[35] The presence of the Minister of Finance was ominous and, bearing in mind Vorster's threats in 1972 and one of the recommendations of the Van Wyk de Vries Commission, was intended to convey a warning that the University might be in danger of forfeiting state subsidy. The Ministers asked whether, since Wits was heavily subsidised by the State, the University's premises and facilities would be available for any national needs or for any function which Government might wish to organise there. Council inexplicably recorded that it would have no objection to hosting Government-sponsored functions or activities but felt that these would be more successful if the University could be seen to associate itself with them. Wisely, it added the rider 'that should Government propose to

Staff Association released a statement supporting the student action.[27] Adelman argued: 'We are accused of being undemocratic for not allowing Dr Koornhof to speak on our campus. However, I do not see how a Minister who is denying the most basic rights to millions of South Africans can, in turn, demand the right of freedom of speech in order to campaign for a thoroughly racist regime on a campus where he is not wanted. When Mandela, Sisulu and Toivo are allowed to exercise their democratic rights to speak on Wits campus, we will allow Koornhof to speak as well.'

While this incident was undoubtedly an infringement of freedom of speech, the action of the SMA and the Political Forum in inviting the Cabinet Minister responsible for enforcing some of the most shameful apartheid measures to speak on such an emotional day, was particularly insensitive.[28] It was a pattern which the SMA was to repeat on numerous occasions in the following years, to the extent that the only conclusion that could be drawn was that it was using this device to discredit the SRC and the BSS by demonstrating that these bodies had no respect for freedom of speech and similar values, and that their activities were bringing the University into disrepute. It was difficult to persuade the black students that they were being provoked and that they were responding just as the SMA hoped they would.[29]

Also in 1981, it was announced that the twentieth anniversary of the establishment of a republic in South Africa would be celebrated with a Republic Festival. In the week preceding Republic Day on 31 May 1981 anti-Republic demonstrations were held on the campuses of the Universities of Cape Town, Durban-Westville, Natal, Rhodes and Wits. Nusas came out in favour of a boycott of the celebrations and its President, Andrew Boraine, was detained under the General Laws Amendment Act which provided for detention for fourteen days without trial. Boraine had also been held in solitary confinement for eight weeks during the previous year and released without trial.[30] During his second detention Boraine was interrogated by the security police for two days because he had given a 'black power' salute when as Nusas President he had addressed a student meeting at the University of Durban-Westville.[31]

Not everyone on the Wits campus was against the celebrations. An anti-Republic Day meeting in the Great Hall on 25 May was followed

police held a workshop in March (1990) to assess and make plans for the year; (and) the Durban Student Alliance (DSA) was instructed to improve links with Inkatha and to launch a programme of relief to victims of violence in order to gain positive publicity.' In 1986 Crystal established the International Freedom Foundation (IFF) which has now been exposed as a South African Military Intelligence front intended to garner international support for the apartheid government to campaign against the African National Congress.[21]

It was in this context that the SMA and the Political Forum invited Dr P Koornhof, Minister of Co-operation and Development to speak at the University on 20 March 1981, the day before Sharpeville Day, which commemorates the death of sixty-nine people shot by the police in 1960 while protesting peacefully against the Pass Laws. A few months earlier, in October 1980, Koornhof had published draft legislation in the form of the Orderly Movement and Settlement of Black Persons Bill, which proposed a severe form of influx control.[22] Organised as it was on the eve of one of the most emotional days in the lives of black South Africans, the invitation was regarded by the SRC as extremely insensitive, and further polarised relations between that body and the SMA.

Koornhof had been invited to deliver one of a series of speeches by representatives of the political parties contesting the General Election. The meeting went ahead but Koornhof was subjected to such severe heckling by about 300 of the 1 200 students in the Great Hall that he was unable to be heard. While students in the front of the hall were calling out 'Amandla', 'Free Mandela' and 'Remember Sharpeville', others at the back were chanting 'Stem Nasionaal (Vote National)'.[23] The incident caused considerable consternation in the University and the behaviour of the hecklers was regarded by many students and staff as an abuse of the institution's commitment to freedom of speech. Public reaction was generally unfavourable but the Council's reaction was fairly muted.[24] The Chairman of Council, Dr N Stutterheim, telephoned Koornhof to convey Council's apology, and Du Plessis wrote to the same effect.[25] Both the Chairman and the Vice-Chancellor, Du Plessis, addressed angrily worded circular letters to the student body.[26]

However, Sammy Adelman, President of the SRC, rejected criticisms of the students who disrupted the speech and the Academic

SMA claimed to have members from all political groups ranging 'from good conservatives to moderates'.[16] Crystal himself professed to be the National Party on campus.[17] Fierce antagonism between members of the SMA and those of the BSS and supporters of the SRC continued until the end of 1986 when a university-appointed Commission of Inquiry strongly criticised the SMA and its mode of operation.[18] Thereafter the SMA functioned only sporadically until 1992 when its parent body, the National Student Federation (NSF) disbanded after it was exposed as having been funded by the Government and the security police as a covert operation. This did not surprise many of the NSF's opponents. The revelation had resulted in the resignation of six of its ten affiliates and the withdrawal of financial support by several of the NSF's sponsors.

It had been an open secret for many years that the SMA and its affiliates were funded by some politically naïve businessmen, but it had never been revealed which organisations were contributors. It had also been strongly suspected, but never proved until the exposé, that some members of the NSF and its affiliates were colluding with the security police.

In announcing the disbanding of the NSF, its President, Danie Kriel, stated that 'the cause for which the NSF worked is a noble one and to me was more important than the financing thereof. It is a dark day for our students that the only classical liberal organisation has disbanded.'[19]

Mr Anton Harber, co-editor of the *Weekly Mail* which revealed the source of the funding, was reported to have said at a mass meeting at Wits that there was documentary evidence 'that the NSF is a front for covert state operations on university campuses'.[20] Harber said the document describing 'Operation Aristotle' had been verified by the police as an official document. 'In it security police reported on a project run from December 1989 to the end of 1990, in which local NSF officials and police met regularly to discuss strategy and tactics.'

Among other things the document showed that 'local NSF officials have police code names, for example "Source N834 (formerly NG1306)", probably a student at Natal university; police and NSF strategised the shift which occurred in 1989, when NSF affiliates stopped "Nusas-bashing" to concentrate on what the report calls the "more human face" of free market ideals; NSF members and security

campus. By 1981 there were about 1 300 potential members who, because of their increasing numbers, felt more confident of taking stands on political issues.

In the next few years this self-assurance was to grow, particularly as the relatively sheltered environment of a university campus compared with the townships provided political space which was otherwise completely lacking for black South Africans.

The recognition of the BSS was followed by the establishment in 1980 of a right-wing student organisation known as the Student Moderate Alliance (SMA). In statements to the press, the chairman Brian Civin said that the Alliance had been formed because the University was being taken over by radicals bent on disrupting racial harmony at Wits. 'There would have been no need for our birth had not extreme radicals marched through corridors to disrupt lectures. This triggered the wrath of extreme right-wing radicals which has brought about a serious polarisation among students at Wits.' The incident referred to was one in which some students had encouraged a class boycott in solidarity with Coloured school pupils.[13]

The SMA's manifesto called for the retention of 'our cultural heritage and tradition' but the leadership denied that they supported apartheid. They proposed to work towards gaining a majority of black and white student support in order to win the SRC elections. They maintained that only left-orientated students voted in the SRC elections and their candidates would encourage the many moderate students on campus to vote. Although the vote was 10 per cent higher than in the previous elections, the SMA ticket was soundly beaten and only one of its members was elected. It was the last occasion on which the organisation put up candidates.[14]

The SMA chairman in 1981 was Russell Crystal, who claimed that his 'political soul came about because of the Left on campus'. His view was that people who publicly associated themselves with demonstrations were unpatriotic and did irreparable harm to the image of the University. In an interview published in May 1981, Crystal is reported to have said that for him and his supporters, the sounds of 'citizens of Azania', 'comrades', 'death to white rule', 'death to white dictatorship' were insupportable and stirred conservative students into a froth. 'That's when reaction starts and in reply our people get mad enough to shout "death to the coons".'[15] The

reassured after such events that some action had been taken to identify and discipline the 'culprits'. On this occasion members of Council expressed their complete satisfaction with the Vice-Chancellor's report and with his skilful and prompt action in the matter. Bozzoli's attitude had been one of caution, and his apprehension that the violence might spread to the campus was particularly evident in the anxious wording used in his notice to students.

BSS vs SMA

In 1977 the Black Student Society (BSS), originally called the Afro-Asian Society, was formed and aligned itself with Saso.[10] Its formation evoked some controversy in the University as membership of the organisation was restricted to black students. The case in favour was that black students, being victims of apartheid, had distinctive needs and required the special support which could best be provided by peers who suffered the same disadvantages. The argument against was that the constitution of the SRC and the ethos of the University did not allow for racially exclusive bodies, and to allow the BSS to constitute as such was as racist as giving permission for the formation of an exclusively white organisation.

In the event, both the SRC and the University authorities approved the application of the black students but the debate about whether or not the BSS was racist continued until the organisation dissolved at its annual general meeting in 1990 following a referendum. A united student body was created in 1992.[11]

Although it formed a loose alliance with the SRC and Nusas because of shared political ideals, the BSS would not take part in student elections and discouraged all black students from doing so. The motivation for this action was ill-understood by many students and staff who were unfamiliar with the boycott strategy of black democratic movements but it also led to the demise of the organisation when about 75 per cent of its members called for an end to the policy of non-participation in SRC affairs. Successive SRC and Nusas executives, however, were sensitive to the issues and trust grew between them and the BSS.[12]

During the early period of its existence, the BSS had a low profile because it was constrained by the small numbers of black students on

An open air meeting was planned for the lunch hour, but as all open air meetings had by then been banned in terms of the Riotous Assemblies Act, the students were persuaded by Bozzoli and the President of the SRC to hold it indoors. With this, the students' public protest effectively came to an end.

Although Bozzoli attempted, with the assistance of the SRC, to identify a ringleader or leaders of the illegal marches on the previous day, he became convinced that the march was an example of a mass movement of young people who had become emotionally heated.

Bozzoli would not have been so naïve as to believe that students would assist the university authorities in identifying any so-called ringleaders, nor would he probably have wanted to find a scapegoat. He would have realised that such action would merely serve to prolong the campus unrest. However, some members of Council had always to be

A light moment as two students add their signatures to a 'Charge General Van den Bergh' petition on the campus. One of them, Olivia Forsythe, was years later revealed to have been an informer.

Blood streams from a cut above the eye of a woman student, after an attack on students protesting the events in Soweto in June 1976

in another form, with school boycotts and demonstrations against the new constitution.

The upheavals did not, however, diminish white support for the Government, and the National Party won the 1977 general election with a record number of seats.

Wits's Response

It was not long before the news of events in Soweto reached the University and some students immediately mounted a poster picket in Jan Smuts Avenue. The numbers and anger of the students increased when they heard of the violent turn the march had taken. The SRC tried to direct student reaction into discussion groups being held in various places on campus. Bozzoli was asked by a group of students to close the University as a sign of protest, but refused to do so.[9]

On the following morning he advised all members of staff of his attitude and stressed the need to remain calm and obey the law. During the morning further meetings were held on campus and students called for a boycott of lectures. Despite attempts by the SRC to dissuade them, a group of 200 to 300 students went on a protest march to the City Hall and back, without any incidents. However, a second march in the afternoon was intercepted by the police and on their return the marchers were attacked by a gang armed with sticks and chains. No students were arrested.

In an attempt to prevent further marches, Bozzoli issued a notice on Friday 18 June calling on students to remain calm and not to indulge in actions which could inflame emotions. He regarded the illegal march of the previous day as unwise and highly irresponsible and appealed in particular for students to avoid encouraging assemblies of people in the city which could lead to riots. He concluded by warning that the University would take an extremely serious view of any students who organised and led actions of this kind or took part in them.

When Bozzoli received a telephone call that morning from a Brigadier of the South African Police who urged him to dissuade the students from marches into the city, he was able to assure him that such a step had already been taken.

meant the imposition of third language instruction in a system already gravely handicapped by inadequate, run-down schools, over-crowded classrooms, insufficient books and no equipment. It was enough to push the pupils to the limit of their endurance. To the Bantu Education authorities this was just another departmental directive that they expected to be implemented without question. The views of opposition members of parliament, organisations such as the South African Institute of Race Relations or of the teachers and students who were affected by the ruling, were rejected or ignored as were the many warnings to the Minister and his deputy about the rising anger over the ruling.[5]

On 16 June hundreds of Soweto pupils gathered early in the morning in numerous localities, many bearing posters decrying the use of the Afrikaans language. They marched peacefully, chanting and singing, towards Orlando, one of the suburbs. At the Orlando West Junior Secondary School soon after 9am, a contingent of police vehicles arrived and about fifty police formed up to face what was now a crowd of several thousand pupils who had been urged by their leaders to remain peaceful.[6]

A single tear-gas cylinder was fired into the crowd, then a shot. The pupils panicked, started to throw stones, and the police responded with live bullets. A 13-year-old schoolboy, Hector Petersen, who was shot and killed has become the symbol of the tragedy, but there were others killed and many were wounded. Despite police reinforcements the now furious crowd attacked the hated West Rand Administration Board offices and two of its employees were killed. Other property of the Board was set alight and extensive damage resulted.

The schools were closed the next day, but violence continued and there were many deaths and injuries. Extensive damage was done to property including Administration Board buildings, bottle stores, shops, libraries, post offices, banks, buses and private homes. The Government took a tough stand but in the following months a succession of strikes, stayaways and boycotts occurred.[7]

Estimates put the number of deaths at 700 by October 1977, including over 100 children. Large numbers of people were arrested and many detained, among them, Steve Biko.[8]

The Soweto uprising kindled a reaction that spread throughout the country, continued intermittently until 1980 and resurfaced in 1984

CHAPTER 4

Student Politics in Black and White

In December 1968, the South African Students' Organisation (Saso) was established by African and Indian students, heralding the start of the Black Consciousness Movement (BCM) and providing an alternative to black membership of the non-racial Nusas.[1]

Saso's aim was 'to liberate blacks from their own attitudes of inferiority and subservience before political rights could be achieved'.[2]

In July 1972, the Black People's Convention (BPC) was established to co-ordinate the various group which adhered to the Black Consciousness philosophy. In March 1973, Stephen Bantu Biko, President of Saso and other leaders of the BCM were banned in the wake of a series of unofficial strikes by black workers in Durban. Biko was prohibited from addressing public meetings and was restricted to King Williams Town in the Eastern Cape. In 1974, nine members of the Saso leadership were convicted on charges under the Terrorism Act for fomenting student disorder on black campuses and were imprisoned on Robben Island.[3]

In September 1977, Biko died after twenty-six days in detention, in the course of which he was subjected to appallingly inhumane treatment.[4]

The Soweto Uprising

Early in 1976, the Bantu Education Department under its Minister, M C Botha, and Deputy Minister, Andries Treurnicht, directed that Afrikaans would be used together with English as a medium of instruction in secondary schools under its jurisdiction. This ruling

In South Africa, Academic Freedom has a further most important aspect to it. It is argued that the basic requirements are met by providing separate institutions of higher learning for each of the race groups in our country. What does it matter, it is said, if a black student cannot enter a university reserved for whites, provided he has a university of his own to attend?

It matters a great deal, because if the racial groups are segregated in their education, in addition to being segregated in their living, they will have no opportunity of gaining that most important knowledge of all, the knowledge of their fellow countrymen. Without such knowledge, what hope is there of mutual understanding and respect, and it is these latter two aspects of life that have the most vital influence on our living together in harmony ...

Bozzoli retired from the Vice-Chancellorship and from the University at the end of 1977. After his retirement, he continued to play a role in education, and in his frequent public addresses, maintained the consistent line which had won him the respect of his students and staff.

Spy vs Spy. Some members of the 1973-4 Student Representative Council, chaired by Glenn Moss (front row third from left). Moss and Cedric de Beer (front row right) were later detained for periods under the Terrorism Act and stood trial and were acquitted on charges under the Suppression of Communism Act. Among the members of the SRC were no fewer than three informers working for various branches of the security services. They are Arthur McGiven (front row left); Lieutenant Derek Brune (front row second from left) and Major Craig Williamson (front row second from right). The other members are Michael Mendelowitz (front row third from right), and (back row, from left) Jonathan Schwarz, Paul Sarbutt (who is also suspected of having been an 'intelligence agent), Ian Gordon, Andrew Love, Andrew Laxton and Geoff Russell.

Towards the end of his term of office, Bozzoli produced a short statement on academic freedom which was published by the Student Academic Freedom Committee.[62] It read:

> ... The academics maintain that in a university, where knowledge is stored, taught, shared and uncovered, those who teach and research, and those who are taught and study should be permitted to join the body of teachers and students on academic grounds only, and should never be selected on the grounds of their race or religion. The freedom to do this is called Academic Freedom.

by-laws and regulations. The analogy drawn by the Commission did not, in the Council's view, 'do a service to it, the youth or the country'.

The Council went on to say that there were 'many university students who out of genuine concern seek for what they believe will be a better society; and in the pursuit of this end protest in a peaceful and lawful way. It is the belief of this university that they should be allowed to continue to express their convictions – and that any measure that prohibits or constrains them from so doing will cause prejudice to the country.'

While the majority of councillors were clearly supportive of Bozzoli's minority report and sensitive to the political aspirations of the student body, some dissociated themselves from this important and powerfully-worded statement,[58] an indication of a conservatism which had been evident among some members for many years. The more conservative members were often Government appointees and were frequently constrained to take positions supportive of the Government, or of individual ministers, or of authorities such as the police, however cogent might have been the arguments in the course of Council debates against the decisions or actions of such people.

Other strong statements against aspects of the Second Interim Report came from the Senate,[59] the Academic Freedom Committee, the Academic Staff Association and Convocation.[60] The University community was outraged that the extensive evidence given to the Commission on academic freedom, particularly the right to accept students and appoint staff on merit without considerations of race, should have been summarily dismissed by the majority of the Commissioners. There was also considerable anger at the potential threat of punitive cuts in the state subsidy, and at the dismissal by the Commission of the allegations by principals of three universities that police spies were active on their campuses. A photograph of the 1973 Wits SRC features three people who were later exposed as security police spies: Craig Williamson, Derek Brune and Arthur McGiven.[61]

In the event the Government did not proceed at that time with measures to coerce the universities into political conformity by threats of cuts in state subsidies. Whether this was the result of the fierce response of the English-language universities and press is a matter for debate, but wiser counsel prevailed until the theme was resuscitated in 1983 and again in 1987.

Bozzoli also strongly opposed the majority report on the political involvement of the universities. He insisted that members of a university who held opinions contrary to those of the governing party at the time should have the right to express these views in public or in the press and that it would be wrong for any university to interfere with the free expression of such opinion as long as those who expressed it did so within the limits of the law.

Similarly if Government policy conflicted with strongly held ideals of a university, such an institution should have every right to express its disagreement with such a policy, even though it had no alternative in terms of the law but to adhere to it. The university should also have every right, Bozzoli wrote, to express its disapproval of actions taken by officials of the Government in carrying out duties arising from such a policy.

The majority report was extremely critical of Nusas, accusing it of having 'forged a steel ring' around student activities on the campuses of the English-language universities and regarding it as responsible for the 'undesirable state of affairs at certain universities in that students are taking an active militant part in politics'.

There was strong support for Bozzoli's report among various constituencies of the University, and strong condemnation of the majority report. There can be little doubt that in a repressive society the university, as a corporate body, has an onus to speak out strongly against injustice and infringements of human rights beyond those which have an adverse effect on education. As had been affirmed at the General Assembly on 8 June 1972, it was the right of university students to do so.

The University Council associated itself with the Council of the University of Cape Town which had urged the Government not to implement the Commission's recommendations aimed at preventing university staff and students from taking part in lawful political activities. Council stated that there was an absence in the Commission's findings of 'an appreciation of the deep concern shared by many university students for the welfare of their country now and in the years that lie ahead'. Although the Commission had drawn a close parallel between student demonstrations in South Africa and those in other lands that had taken a violent turn, protests by students at Wits had not gone beyond the law, save for a few insignificant breaches of

university existence in South Africa is that it is founded upon a social order based on the principle of multinational separate development.' This implied that all universities in South Africa accepted enforced apartheid in their institutions.

The most objectionable part of the report however, was the implication that it would not be improper for the state to withdraw financial support for universities considered by a minister or a magistrate to be involving themselves in political activities. The relevant paragraph of the report reads:[55]

> An essential condition for state subvention to the university is that the latter should carry out its function properly and that it should not exceed its capacity. If the university fails to comply with this condition the state's function of financing it falls away. This principle is very pertinent where the university as such participates actively in politics…; any active participation in political activities that turns the university into a political instrument is beyond the university's true function, and exceeds its capacity as a statutory corporation. The forfeiture of state subvention in such circumstances should not be regarded as a punishment or sanction – it is no more than a consequence of an irregular action.

Van Wyk de Vries regarded academic freedom as a freedom in respect of academic matters only. In his view, a university whose members participated actively in extra-parliamentary politics would be acting beyond its capacity, and this would be unlawful.[56]

In an interview explaining his minority report, Bozzoli said the English-language universities in South Africa generally regarded their freedoms as having been limited in three respects: the selection of students on academic grounds; the appointment of staff, where colour also came into the decision; and the unavailability because of censorship and banning of a considerable and academically important section of written works. He pointed out that the majority report did not recognise these freedoms and while it did not recommend any further restrictions, it had made no attempt to support the universities in their efforts to regain them.[57]

Among these matters were 'the steps required to ensure efficient education' and 'student relations in general, and in particular the role students and student bodies could play, in co-operation with academic authorities, in maintaining a healthy spirit and code of conduct on the campus of modern universities.'

Of considerable importance was the charge to the Commission to report on a suitable formula for the subsidisation of universities, 'the posts structure and lecturer-student ratio; the salary structure as a determining factor in attracting and retaining lecturing staff and bursaries and loans for students.'

In view of the urgency of the matter, the Commission was to give priority to the financing scheme and, if necessary, to submit an interim report on that aspect.

There was consternation that what had begun as a normal quinquennial revision of the subsidy formula should have escalated into these unprecedentedly wide terms of reference.

It seemed clear that the reason for this was the unrest on university campuses both in South Africa and abroad. As I put it in my report for 1968/69 as Chairperson of the Academic Staff Association (ASA), these events had raised fundamental questions regarding both the nature and function of the university in modern society in general and in South Africa in particular, and there were fears about the universities' capacity to disrupt the norms of the society in which they were set.

The ASA joined the Lecturers' Association to form a number of joint committees that addressed themselves to the vast task of preparing memoranda on the various aspects of the Commission's inquiry.

When the report and two interim reports of the Commission were tabled in Parliament on 30 October 1974, six years after its appointment, there was general satisfaction at the fact that it had recommended that the state accept the major responsibility for the subvention of universities on a more generous scale than before. Other aspects of the report were not acceptable and on these Bozzoli submitted a minority report.[54]

Bozzoli claimed that certain chapters in the report amounted to 'a proposal to bring all the universities into conformity with Government policy as interpreted by the Government presently in power'. He objected strongly to the statement that 'A unique characteristic of

State's respect for the individual's civil liberties, basic human rights and the rule of law as recognised by all civilised nations of the world. There can be no order while the individual in South Africa remains crushed ruthlessly under a burden of suppressive legislation.'[51]

After the meeting, about 1 000 students took part in a placard demonstration on Jan Smuts Avenue and then moved to different suburbs of Johannesburg.[52]

These detentions presaged a much greater onslaught on student leaders by the authorities during the 1980s, particularly during the states of emergency.

The Van Wyk de Vries Commission[53]

When, in June 1972, Prime Minister Vorster threatened that the Government would stop its subsidies to students it identified as 'loafers' it was clear that he was already considering some form of financial sanctions.

In the course of the 1980s the Government initiated two major measures designed to coerce the English-language universities into political conformity. In 1983 the 'Quota Bill' provided for subsidy cuts if these institutions did not fall in line with the state's educational policies. In 1986 and 1987 there was another threat of reduced subsidies if the university authorities did not control the political activities of staff and students on their campuses.

The Government used as grounds for these threats some of the findings and recommendations of the Second Interim Report of the Van Wyk de Vries Commission of Inquiry into Universities in 1974.

The Commission was appointed on 10 September 1968 under the chairmanship of Judge J van Wyk de Vries. Its eight members included three university principals, among them Prof Bozzoli, Professor O P F Horwood of Natal and Prof H B Thom of the University of Stellenbosch.

The Commission's terms of reference were: 'to inquire into and report, in so far as the universities for Whites in the Republic of South Africa and the University of South Africa are concerned, on the educational, academic, financing and developmental aspects of universities, and on any other matters which the Commission may deem to be of importance.'

Gullible members of the public and even of the university community were often deceived by such innuendo into the 'there is no smoke without fire' syndrome. Very seldom were any students brought to trial, and by the time the majority were released, sometimes many months after their detention, the 'just you wait and see' threats had been forgotten. In this manner, decent and concerned people were lulled into silence about infringements of the liberty of their fellow citizens.

In August 1975, the President of Nusas, Mr Karel Tip, and two members of the Executive, Mr Glenn Moss and Mr Gerry Maré were detained in terms of Section 6 of the Terrorism Act.[48] Bozzoli called the fourth General Assembly of the University on Tuesday 26 August 'in order that the University's attitude towards the policy of detention of students without charge or trial may be stated publicly'.

The Assembly was addressed by the Chancellor of the University, Mr B L Bernstein, the Vice-Chancellor, Professor Bozzoli, and Mr Michael Stent, Acting President of Nusas. Bozzoli opened his address by warning, once again, of the presence of informers in the audience. 'We have absolutely nothing to hide, but who can tell what distorted version of an incident might be reported merely to prove they are earning their pay.' The application of the detention laws had become a serious threat to the proper functioning of the University, Bozzoli said, to say nothing of its devastating affect upon the victims.

He stressed that the very essence of a university was to encourage intelligent study and to indulge in unfettered comment. Yet in a climate of fear it was only natural that certain academics should feel inhibited from expressing their real opinions ... 'Our universities have suffered from these harsh methods and from other measures, such as censorship, which have deprived them of academic material ... It is essential that our universities remain free to seek out the truth.'[49]

Another speaker, Professor P V Tobias, said that the detention of the three students had 'attacked and sought to erode our heritage of freedom of speech, freedom to protest, freedom to strive by all legal means for better conditions of life for the underprivileged and the disadvantaged.'[50]

The meeting endorsed a Student Representative Council statement, part of which read 'There can be no law unless it is based on the

his killers have not yet been identified and brought to justice it is widely believed that agents of the security police were involved and that it was his role as a political catalyst for young whites that led to his assassination.[43] The Nusas leadership was accused of 'incitement and agitation' aimed at overthrowing the existing order and replacing it with an anti-capitalistic system.[44]

The bannings were strongly condemned by all constituencies of the University. In a statement released on 27 August 1974 by the University's Academic Freedom Committee on the occasion of the publication of the fourth interim report of the Commission, it was asserted that 'these procedures did not allow for open hearings nor for the weighing and sifting of evidence through cross-examination. Witnesses were allowed only limited legal representation and were not afforded the opportunity to refute previous evidence. Furthermore, the Commission was constituted solely of party politicians who are not qualified to undertake judicial or quasi-judicial functions... As the Commission appeared to adopt procedures contrary to natural justice we have serious doubts about the validity of many of its findings. These doubts are reinforced, in particular, by the partial and selective nature of the evidence published in the Report.'[45]

The Vice-Chancellors of the English-language universities sought an interview with the Prime Minister to protest against the punitive measures, as usual, to no avail. In 1974 Nusas was declared an 'affected organisation' in terms of the Affected Organisations Act and was thus prevented from receiving foreign funds.[46]

Detentions

The contempt of the Government for basic human rights was demonstrated by the leader of the National Party in the Transvaal, Dr Connie Mulder. When he opened the Transvaal Congress of his party on 25 August, Mulder said that 'the National Party would place the security of the state above the freedom of the individual if law and order was threatened'. Critics of detention without trial should 'think twice. When facts came out they might not be so critical'.[47] This type of insinuation was frequently employed by the Government and members of the police to justify the detention without trial of its political opponents.

people connected with it. The eight were immediately issued with banning orders under the Suppression of Communism Act which prevented them from continuing their work with Nusas and from pursuing their studies at any university other than the University of South Africa (a distance learning institution).[42] The eight included the President of Nusas (Paul Pretorius), a past-President (Neville Curtis), two Vice-Presidents (Paula Ensor and Phillipe le Roux) and a lecturer in political science at the University of Natal (Dr Richard Turner) who was banned from teaching. He was assassinated in 1978 shortly before his banning order was due to expire. Although

Picture Times Media Limited, courtesy MuseumAfrica

Members of the Schlebusch Commission, Louis Le Grange (left), who was later to become Minister of Law and Order, George de V Morrison and Lionel Murray are confronted by protesting students after the banning of eight Nusas leaders

Africa... We are convinced that the provision of separate opportunities for the different national groups is completely reconcilable with education of a good quality... We support the provision of separate education for the different national groups as a necessary requisite for full development of each nation. We emphasise that educational integration inevitably implies that integration will take place at all other levels in the society. The cry for educational integration is therefore nothing less than an onslaught on the whole social and political set-up of South Africa. Our conclusion is that the demonstrations are aimed at a radical revolution of the social and political order in our country. We and our universities will oppose this with all our might.

Such public demonstrations of support for academic apartheid played no small part in persuading the international community of scholars to impose the academic boycott.

Despite contentions that the protests were incited by a small group of students, 10 000 members of the public signed a petition distributed by the SRC deploring police violence and calling for equal education for all races.[39]

Nusas, in which many of Wits's student leaders were active, was for many years the victim of Government vilification because of its opposition to apartheid and its criticisms of infringements by the state of human rights. In 1972 the Government appointed a Parliamentary Select Committee to investigate the affairs of the organisation as well as those of the South African Institute of Race Relations, the University Christian Movement and the Christian Institute. The Committee was later converted into a Commission of Inquiry consisting of ten Members of Parliament – six from the National Party and four from the United Party – under the chairmanship of Mr A L Schlebusch MP.[40] The participation of the United Party was widely criticised, particularly when their representatives signed the report containing the recommendations.[41]

On 23 February 1973 the Schlebusch Commission tabled an interim report in which it recommended unanimously that no action be taken against Nusas but that urgent action be taken against eight

The views of students at the Afrikaans-language universities were diametrically opposed to those of their English-language counterparts. The students of the University of Pretoria had considered holding a counter-demonstration in that city to show the world that South African students were not unanimous in their views. They decided however, according to the Chairman of their Students' Council, 'to pay strict attention to the Minister's call for us to confine ourselves to our studies'.[35] This attitude was described in a leading article in *The Star* as 'cringing compliance' and 'the sickly fruit of the kind of academic bondage against which English-speaking students have so appositely been demonstrating'.[36]

Severe criticism also came from the Rectors of six Afrikaans universities who might have been expected to have had a greater sensitivity to, and understanding of the situation. Despite a tradition that the country's universities refrained from public criticism of each other, a statement signed by them was sent to the South African Press Association on 20 June 1972, which condemned the student demonstrations and the lecturers who had supported them. The actions of the authorities in dealing with the demonstrations were praised, and there was an obsequious defense of Government policy on separate education.[37]

Four of the rectors – Bingle, Hamman, Marais and Viljoen – are listed as members of the Afrikaner Broederbond.[38] As such they may well have made a contribution to the development of the policy of racial segregation in education and Viljoen was later to become Minister of National Education.

The policy of separate education no longer exists, although its legacy will continue to plague the country for many years. It is ironic now when it is so difficult to find anyone who admits to having supported apartheid, to recall the words of the leaders of Afrikaans university education twenty years ago. Part of their statement read:

> On behalf of the demonstrators, students as well as university leaders have come out strongly in favour of integration of white and non-white in education at school level as well as at university. We are convinced that such a development would have fatal consequences for the development of the nations concerned as well as for the peace and order and good human relations in South

General H J van den Bergh, head of the Bureau for State Security was invariably in attendance.[29]

On 12 June 1972 a meeting of 1 400 students in the University Great Hall decided on a change of tactics in the struggle for equal education for all South Africans. Instead of confronting the police they would undertake an extensive campaign to inform the public about the inequalities of the education system. This would be done by canvassing and distributing pamphlets.[30] The frustrations of the students at the negative perception of their efforts by large numbers of the white public are easy to understand.

The next tactic employed by the Government was to threaten the universities with legislation which would force them to 'maintain law and order' on their campuses or face a cut in their government subsidies. Speaking to a gathering of the Rapportryers[31] of Stellenbosch on 13 June 1972, Prime Minister Vorster said the Government would stop its subsidies to 'loafers' in South African universities and 'if parents are prepared to let their children have holidays in the universities, they must be prepared to pay for this themselves'.[32]

Although nothing came of the threat to the subsidies at that time, it was an ominous portent. It was to be one of the recommendations of the Van Wyk de Vries Commission's report in 1974, and in 1987, Mr F W de Klerk attempted to implement it during his term as Minister of National Education.

In a further attempt to place the actions of the students in perspective, Bozzoli addressed a meeting of parents, students and members of Convocation on 15 June, and sent an open letter to parents in which he praised the students for their unselfish dedication to the cause of education and of national unity in South Africa, and urged that non-segregated education should be introduced at the earliest possible opportunity.[33]

Although there were supportive articles in the English language press, the Afrikaans press and the SABC were consistently antagonistic towards the anti-apartheid activities of Wits students. One Afrikaans newspaper claimed that student action was not only directed at what they regarded as Government injustices, but also at the existing system of law and order itself. It also reported that 'parents over the entire country were disturbed at the methods used by students to convey their leftist ideas to schoolchildren'.[34]

Prof GR Bozzoli talks to Brigadier H J Schroder after a police baton charge on the campus in June 1972. Among those looking on are Adam Klein, Mark Orkin and Benjamin Pogrund.

contemptuously, referring to it as naive, and promising a fuller statement later. No formal reply was ever received.

Bozzoli had a number of meetings with Vorster, one at the Prime Minister's request, the others at Bozzoli's or the joint request of the Vice-Chancellors of the universities of Cape Town, Natal, Rhodes and Wits. On each occasion, the Prime Minister berated Bozzoli about his students. Vorster was always an intimidating presence and

impersonating the police. Charges against thirty of the students were subsequently withdrawn; the other thirty-eight were acquitted on charges under the Riotous Assemblies Act and discharged.

The fact that they had been acquitted did not deter one Cabinet Minister who, on the day following the judgement is reported to have described the student demonstrators as 'internal terrorists'.[26]

Despite its dangers, student activism, together with that of some of the churches, was to play a significant extra-parliamentary role during years of increasing oppression and suppression of democratic political expression.

Writing about student protest at the time, Benjamin Pogrund referred to the complex and formidable pressures on white students.[27] Their fear, and even more so their parents' fear, was that they would lose social standing and security and be exposed to some form of state action if they overtly opposed the status quo. Black students had even more to fear, Pogrund pointed out. In addition to the formidable body of apartheid legislation with which they had to cope, they became marked people in the eyes of the Security Police and were subject to surveillance and harassment for years after they left university.

Bozzoli's response to the student protests and the Government reactions was thoughtful and insightful. On 7 June 1972 he wrote an open letter to Vorster, in which he drew attention to the serious situation developing in the country in relation to students. He pointed to the experience of other countries that student protest could be contained if the authorities recognised early that the students might have a legitimate grievance, investigated it and attempted to redress it. The real trouble began when the police and the military were called in, a move which generated great support for the students who were attacked, and led to serious clashes.

Grievances of students at the universities for blacks that their education was not equal to that at the universities for whites, were not being addressed, Bozzoli wrote, and the resulting high feelings would never be suppressed by strong-arm action by the police. He concluded by appealing to the Prime Minister to take note that there were grievances and to have them investigated by strictly impartial persons who would report back publicly.[28] Far from responding positively to this well-informed communication, Vorster treated it

intellectual understanding between different groups of people in the same country.' Protest meetings 'of this magnitude (have) the immense value of demonstrating the depth and breadth of our feeling on the issue which brought us together. It permits each and every one of us to show our solidarity on the vital matter of education and records our extreme anxiety and distress at the happenings in our universities.'[23]

This important speech not only made the public aware of the intensity of the opposition to academic apartheid within the English-language universities, it also gave a strong message to the students that it was their democratic right to speak out strongly and to demonstrate publicly and peacefully against apartheid policies and the oppressive measures that were being taken to enforce them.

Far from being intimidated, Wits students held another peaceful demonstration on the periphery of the campus on 9 June. After a warning by the Commissioner of Police for the Witwatersrand that they were contravening the Riotous Assemblies Act, a squad of plainclothes policemen who had been waiting on the other side of the road rushed at the students with considerable force, in two separate attacks, arresting sixty-eight of them as well as two journalists who were reporting the demonstration. Jenny Cunningham, a former SRC President, was grabbed by the hair and manhandled, and had to receive treatment later for suspected concussion. Another student received severe facial injuries which required medical treatment.

Among those arrested was Craig Williamson who was later to achieve notoriety when he was exposed as a Security Police spy.[24] The Executive Committee of the Academic Staff Association held an urgent meeting that night and issued a press statement in which they bore witness to 'horrifying scenes of brutality and violence perpetrated on our campus against defenceless students. This afternoon the situation deteriorated sharply. The baton charge and the brutal beatings were now carried out by men not in uniform. It proved impossible to find out whether these men are plainclothes policemen or thugs. Yet they beat and assault our students in the presence of uniformed police.'[25]

The arrested students were refused bail despite an urgent application to the Supreme Court. The journalists were released on bail after twenty-one hours in custody and charged with assaulting and

Picture Times Media Limited, courtesy MuseumAfrica

In one of the biggest protest meetings ever held at Wits, about 7 000 people cram the University's Sport Centre to affirm the right of students to peaceful public assembly

In his speech, Bozzoli condemned strongly the Extension of Universities Act, saying that 'a university which is compelled to admit only students of one race cannot conceivably provide the same education as one in which the students mix freely with all their fellow countrymen. Segregation can only lead to a complete absence of

of the North after they had protested against the expulsion of Mr Abraham Tiro who, at a graduation ceremony, had condemned the system of Bantu education and white control of black universities.[21]

At Wits, on 8 June 1972, in response to these events, the Chancellor called another General Assembly 'to consider matters of grave importance to the universities of the country'. The meeting had to be held indoors because of the ban on outdoor gatherings and about 7 000 people filled the upper and lower halls of the University's Sports Centre to hear addresses by Professor Bozzoli, Dr F Hill, Chairman of Council, Professor E Kahn, Deputy Vice-Chancellor, and Mr Adam Klein, Vice-President of the SRC, and to pass a resolution affirming the right of students to peaceful public assembly.[22] The resolution read as follows:

> We here present at this Assembly of the University do solemnly resolve to:
>
> Affirm that it is the right of university students as of other bodies of citizens to express peacefully by public assembly and procession their opinions on matters of public policy and their right thereby to seek public support for the opinions thus expressed;
>
> Record our conviction that it is particularly appropriate for university students as a privileged educational group to concern themselves with the inequities, deprivations and other shortcomings resulting from policies which affect the education of less privileged sections of the peoples of South Africa;
>
> Express our extreme distress and indignation at the violent measures taken by the Government to suppress the peaceful public assemblies and processions of university students, and at the exercise by the Government of extreme powers to restrict the free expression of opinion on matters of public policy in circumstances which do not constitute an emergency endangering the security of the State.

The resolution was subsequently supported by the Executive Committee of Convocation.

trial, was held by Wits students on 7 October 1970 and was widely praised by political leaders and academics.[15]

A number of laws provided for the detention of individuals for extended periods without trial.[16] On 24 and 25 October 1971 numbers of students were removed from their homes late at night and detained one week before their examinations. Because of the timing there was no formal reaction from the student body until the start of the new term.

Finally, a student protest meeting was held on 29 February. Addressing it, Bozzoli said that some students had been held for thirty days, some for sixty days, and some were still in detention. No reason had been given for their arrest, none had been tried and there was no evidence that they had committed any crime. 'I cannot sufficiently deplore acts of this kind, designed to intimidate and strike terror into the hearts of young students, and not without its effects on their preparedness to speak and take office, and I wonder, in fact, who are the terrorists,' said Bozzoli.[17]

Bozzoli's frequent public statements in support of fundamental human rights and against apartheid, particularly as it affected education, were frequently criticised by the Afrikaans-language press and by Cabinet Ministers. On 27 April 1972 he and the Chairman of Council, M W Whitmore Richards, were summoned to Cape Town by the Minister of National Education, J P van der Spuy, to be told that the Cabinet viewed his various speeches with displeasure. These speeches, he was told, encouraged a small irresponsible extreme leftist group and took no account of the 'big silent majority' who were thereby not encouraged to express their views.[18]

Generally, 1972 was a turbulent year for the English-language universities. Picket demonstrations had replaced marches as the preferred method of student protest, but these too were frequently prohibited in terms of the Riotous Assemblies Act.[19]

A series of peaceful picket demonstrations by students of the University of Cape Town during June, in support of free and compulsory school education for all races, was broken up by the police. The reaction of the Minister of Justice was to ban, for one month, any outdoor public gathering of a political nature in all cities and towns in which there was a university.[20] The protest had been provoked by the rustication of the entire student body of the University

The march was cancelled, but a teach-in, addressed by Social Anthropology Professor John Blacking, was held in front of the Great Hall. The students then moved to Jan Smuts Avenue where a placard demonstration took place. A group of people, some of whom were thought to be students of the Rand Afrikaans University, pelted the demonstrators with fruit, eggs and paint. The police stood by and did nothing.[9] SRC President John Kane-Berman was defiant in the face of Vorster's threats and told a reporter: 'We are completely undeterred and stand as firm as ever.'[10] MacCrone issued a statement deploring any effort by the Government to try to pressure or influence the decisions of any university council, especially with regard to the appointment of its staff.[11]

Protest marches have long been regarded by students at the open universities as a legitimate means of expressing their opposition to injustices, particularly in matters pertaining to the universities and to education in general. Originally local authorities granted permission for such marches, but in 1970 the General Law Further Amendment Act required the approval of the Chief Magistrate of the district concerned for any procession authorised by the local authority.[12]

In Johannesburg it became unusual for the Chief Magistrate to approve student marches, although exceptions were made on rare occasions when the entire University, including members of the Council, Senate and staff, processed at the conclusion of a General Assembly. Occasionally, when student anger was particularly roused, illegal marches were held, to the admiration of some and the outraged indignation of others.

On 18 May 1970, although permission had been refused, about four hundred Wits students took part in a well-organised and orderly march into the city in protest against 'the erosion of the rule of law and in particular against indefinite arbitrary detention under Section 6 of the Terrorism Act'. When they reached police headquarters at John Vorster Square, they were ushered into the charge office where some were handcuffed.[13] After days of media speculation thirty people were charged under the Riotous Assemblies Act. Among them were ministers of religion, students and lecturers.[14]

Yet another orderly march, this time in protest against banning orders served on nineteen detainees acquitted in a recent political

Picture courtesy The Star

Nusas President, Neville Curtis, attempts to present a protest document to Prime Minister B J Vorster who refuses to accept it

a Government threat to introduce legislation to prohibit such appointments, the UCT Council withdrew its offer to Mafeje. This led to angry student protest at UCT which was taken up by students at Wits. A protest march through the city of Johannesburg was planned, but was prohibited by Vorster, by then Prime Minister, who telephoned the Mayor of Johannesburg and threatened to take swift action if the City Council allowed the march.[8]

May 1966: 3 000 Wits students march to the City Hall in protest against the banning of Nusas President Ian Robertson

route they were subjected to abuse from various groups of people, and were pelted with eggs, water and toilet paper.[6] The march was followed by an all-night vigil on the periphery of the campus. Vorster received a Nusas delegation and was presented with a petition signed by thousands of students and academics but gave no reason for his action, nor did he relent.[7] Robertson had been personally responsible for inviting Senator Robert Kennedy to visit South Africa as the guest of Nusas, and the banning was intended as a sign of Government disapproval.

Although the law did not prohibit the appointment of black staff to the open universities, in 1968, the Government intervened to prevent the appointment of Mr Archie Mafeje to the post of senior lecturer in social anthropology at the University of Cape Town. After

object of some considerable derision, the informers were taken very seriously. The attempts to intimidate students and to pay some to provide information, accurate or inaccurate, which may have led to the arrest and detention of some students, were strongly condemned by the administrations and staffs of the universities affected. Vice-Chancellor Bozzoli was particularly outspoken in his criticism of this kind of action.[3]

On 15 December 1964 the University was informed that the appointment of Professor E R Roux, a long-serving member of the Department of Botany, would be terminated by the Minister of Justice on 1 February of the following year on the grounds that he was a listed Communist and was to be subjected to punitive restrictions. Roux was an excellent scientist and teacher, a kind and gentle man, and was popular with his students and colleagues. He had never attempted to promote communism within the University.[4] His arbitrary dismissal outraged his colleagues and students, but their protests were of no avail. There was a similar outcry in 1967 when Dr Raymond Hoffenberg, a distinguished physician on the staff of the medical school of the University of Cape Town, was banned and thereby prevented from pursuing his teaching and professional work. Despite protests and interviews with the Minister the restriction orders were not lifted and Hoffenberg left the country early in 1968. His departure was a great loss to South Africa. He settled in the United Kingdom where he served the medical profession with distinction and was for some time President of the Royal College of Physicians of London.

In May 1966, Mr Ian Robertson, President of Nusas was banned in terms of the Suppression of Communism Act, by the Minister of Justice, Mr John Vorster. This provoked an outcry throughout the country. Political leaders, the English-language press, and university students and staff strongly condemned the arbitrary action, calling on the Minister either to try Robertson or to revoke the banning order. At Wits, students at a mass meeting on 12 May condemned 'this vicious measure which violates the elementary principles of justice and human decency'.[5]

The following day about 3 000 Wits students carrying scores of banners marched from the campus to the centre of Johannesburg in a dignified demonstration of anger against the ban. At places along the

CHAPTER 3

Activists Under Pressure

The struggle against apartheid education widened into a battle against the implementation of apartheid in general and the draconian methods used by the authorities to suppress almost all forms of extra-parliamentary opposition. At first during the early 1970s, the great majority of student demonstrators at the English-language universities were white. As black student numbers increased during the 1980s, members of the black student movements predominated and frequently took the initiative in setting up the protests.

Harassment of student activists and demonstrators by Government supporters and the police was to become a feature of student protest. One of the first victims of this oppressive legislation was Mr Dennis Brutus, founder of the anti-apartheid South African Sports Association in 1958. In 1961 he had helped organise a national convention of coloured activists at Malmesbury in the Western Cape and this had led to his being banned.[1] In 1962 he was elected to the SRC, but because of the banning, was unable to attend and participate in its meetings. The SRC appealed to Council to make representations to the Minister in this regard, but the Council was unsympathetic, arguing that Brutus was restricted in terms of a legal enactment.[2]

The Government also resorted to a variety of sinister and covert methods to suppress student opposition to apartheid. One of these was the infiltration onto English-language campuses in the 1960s of student informers paid by the police to spy on their fellows. It was also discovered that plain clothes police and police photographers were attending student meetings. Although the police were the

activities fall. Consequently only you are able, by introducing effective measures, to achieve the objects embodied in the conditions.'

The new conditions were substantially the same as those in his earlier letter (see Appendix 12). Details of the revisions are referred to in Professor Zeffert's legal opinion (Appendix 13). The identical letter and list of conditions was sent to the Chairman of the Council of the University of Cape Town on the same date, and presumably to other universities as well.

Zeffert advised that in his opinion the Minister did not have the power to make such conditions.

The most significant concurrence between the new and the old conditions was that which required Council to report to the Minister about incidents of unrest and made provision for the Minister to alter the subsidy if he was not satisfied with Council's response.

Although there was a difference in the scope of the conditions, Zeffert nevertheless believed that they still interfered with the exclusive disciplinary authority of the Council and with its 'general control of the university and all its affairs, purposes and functions'. They prescribed to the Council what disciplinary provisions it must adopt, intruded into the Council's power of control and went beyond the powers granted to the Minister by Section 25(1).

Despite the fact that the words 'take all reasonable steps' had been replaced by 'take steps directed towards', the conditions were still vague and Council had still not been informed with sufficient certainty what steps to take. While some of the worst instances of unreasonable demands and of vague and imprecise drafting had been removed other defects remained. Zeffert referred to one point which seemed to him to be 'an almost text-book illustration of ultimate unreason. The University is precluded from registering any student who has been expelled from another university on the basis of certain acts of misconduct. This presupposes that the student was expelled on good grounds. What if there had been fraud in expelling him from the other university? What if no reasonable man, applying his mind to the facts, could possibly have expelled him?'

Zeffert's conclusion was that the new conditions were as problematic as the old.

At a Council meeting on 16 October 1987 considerable tension arose between those members of Council who wished to take aggressive steps to oppose the measures and others who preferred to take a conciliatory stance.

One major point of difference was whether legal steps should be taken against the Minister. The academic representatives, the Vice-Chancellor, the Deputy Vice-Chancellors, the student observers, and some of the non-academic members believed that the conditions would have very serious and detrimental effects on the University. If the Minister's action was considered to be *ultra vires* then the University should oppose it in the courts. In response to the view that it could take eighteen months to two years before the matter was finalised, by which time the Government could easily amend the Act to validate the new conditions, this group felt that the University should be seen to be taking active steps to oppose the Minister even if the outcome merely provided a tactical victory in the short term.

An alternative suggestion was that an urgent interdict be sought restraining the Minister from imposing the conditions. The opposing view was that such an application would probably be unsuccessful since the University had not yet suffered any harm, and that it would only serve to irritate the Minister and invite more pressure from his constituency. Some members of Council expressed themselves strongly against any court action, either by the University on its own or in collaboration with other universities. They believed that much more would be achieved by continuous discussion and consultation than by confrontation, legal action or threats of legal action. It was also suggested that the Chairmen of the Councils and the Vice-Chancellors of all like-minded universities should meet jointly with the Minister as such action had been effective in the case of the 'Quota Bill'.

For a while it appeared that Council might not be persuaded that it was absolutely essential to take a strong stand against the threat to the autonomy of the University imposed by the conditions. The balance was swayed by the argument that students had behaved responsibly in their effort to support the steps being taken by the University, but that should the University be seen to be refraining from further action, they might take matters into their own hands.

As a compromise and a first step, Council agreed to issue a press statement, together with a copy of the Chairman's reply to the Minister's first letter. The statement, released on the same day, read:

The Council of the University of the Witwatersrand has considered the communication received from the Minister of Education and Culture relating to the conditions imposed by the Minister in regard to the payment of subsidies to the University. It takes this first opportunity to give public expression to its dismay at this, the most serious encroachment on its autonomy in the University's history. In a letter to the Minister dated 25 August 1987, the Chairman of Council expressed the views of Council in regard to the conditions proposed by the Minister. The representations there made have been virtually ignored by the Minister. A copy of the letter is now released for publication so that the seriousness of the crisis now facing the University may be made known.

The Council regards the Minister's conditions as likely to achieve the opposite of what the Minister claims to be his intention. It rejects the implication that it is unfit to control the affairs of the University and regards the conditions as unacceptable.

Acting Vice-Chancellor R W Charlton also released a statement to the media that day, together with a copy of correspondence with De Klerk and other documents pertaining to the issue. Charlton's statement condemned the Minister's action as a completely unacceptable invasion of the University's legitimate field of authority that destroyed its autonomy. The University would now be controlled by the Minister and not by the Council. For centuries, he said, university autonomy had been safeguarded to prevent interference from kings, dictators and governments because universities could not function effectively if there was such interference.

The true purpose of the action was to enlist the University Council and its administration in the stifling of legitimate dissent not, as the Government asserted, to ensure the functional, constructive and educationally responsible use of taxpayers' money.

The conditions created the opportunity for spies, informers and *agents provocateurs* to disrupt the running of the University and to manufacture 'incidents' which would require the University to report to the Minister and which could create a totally misleading impression of the situation on campus.

The conditions were abhorrent and such systematic violation of university autonomy in South Africa would impoverish the country and all its peoples. History would not deal kindly with those responsible for such folly, he said.

A meeting of the University was held on Monday 19 October and was addressed by Charlton, Ms Rosemary Hunter, and Mr Firoz Cachalia of the BSS. In his address Charlton described the restrictions as 'of equal or even greater significance' than the Extension of University Education Act. The interference amounted to nothing less than the usurpation by the Minister of Education and Culture of the authority of the University Council over a considerable part of the day-to-day running of the University. If there was any comfort to be gleaned from this disastrous situation it was that by unremitting effort the University had succeeded in regaining the right to admit students without consideration of race, colour, gender or creed. Although it was true that the shadow of the Quota Act still hung menacingly over the University and it had taken many years before relative freedom had been restored, 'we must nevertheless take heart from that victory and tackle the daunting task of regaining control over our affairs'.

The Minister had made one concession in omitting the so-called 'Affected Organisations' from the conditions. On the other hand there had been a sinister addition, namely the requirement that the University must take disciplinary action on 'proof' furnished by the Minister of Education and Culture. 'From whom will he receive such proof?' Charlton asked, 'from spies, informers, political rivals, the Security Police? The prospect is truly appalling.'

The linking of academic standards and taxpayers' money to measures which were really designed to enlist the University Council and the administration in the ranks of those engaged in stifling legitimate dissent, was a blatant example of the propaganda with which the University had been attacked for the past year or more, obviously to prepare the ground for this imposition of Ministerial control. This propaganda had been only too successful in mobilising white English-speaking opinion against the University and had made it possible for the Government to act. Attempts to counter the vicious propaganda campaign had had little success and those responsible for creating the climate of adverse public opinion, including some who should have known better, had much to answer for.

When Senate met at an extraordinary sitting on 21 October it took a much stronger stand on the issue than had the Council.[46] Professor John Dugard, in his capacity as Chairman of the Senate Academic Freedom Committee, presented a draft statement prepared by the Committee, and drew attention to a number of points raised by it. The Committee believed that the conditions stipulated by the Minister constituted the most serious threat ever to the autonomy of the University. Compliance with the Minister's conditions, the AFC believed, would lead to a drop in academic standards and a loss of freedom of debate. Senate should decline to comply with the Minister's conditions on the grounds of principle, practicability and their dubious legality.

The University should, in concert with other supporting universities, take action as soon as possible to test the legality of the conditions in a court of law and should seek an interdict restraining the Minister from implementing the terms of his proposals pending the outcome of the case. The Committee indicated that the Senate should issue a statement so that the Government and the community would know where the University stood on the matter. The University must not find itself in a position in which it had to enforce the conditions.

A lengthy discussion ensued during which a range of strategies was discussed and Senate agreed to issue a strong statement, unequivocally repudiating the conditions and refusing to comply with them. The wording of the draft statement of the Academic Freedom Committee was modified slightly and approved by a vote of 55 to 1. It read:[47]

> The Senate notes with dismay, consternation and anger the Government's decision to impose conditions upon the granting of university subsidies. These conditions are not designed to promote respect for traditional educational values. Instead they aim to compel the university authorities to suppress freedom of debate on the campuses and to compel the universities to enforce National Party ideology. In effect the universities are

being called upon to act as policemen for the enforcement of Government policy.

Senate finds these conditions to be totally unacceptable and declines to comply with them. Moreover, it believes that they are of suspect legality. If South African universities attempt in any way to enforce these regulations, they will cease to be universities in the true sense of the word and will become tools of the National Party Government. In this process, their degrees will be debased and will cease to enjoy recognition from foreign universities.

Senate expresses its surprise and disappointment at the apparent willingness of some universities to support the Minister's conditions. Senate calls upon these universities to reconsider their positions in the light of the serious threats that these conditions pose to the reputation of all South African universities.

Senate affirms its full confidence in the existing disciplinary code and the implementation of this code and expresses the belief that the existing procedures will continue to ensure the good government of the university.

Senate's decision not to comply was an important one. It was the first occasion on which the academically highly principled body had voted overwhelmingly for an act of civil disobedience. While its members were undoubtedly influenced by the informed view that the conditions were of suspect legality, they had nevertheless been pushed to the limits of their tolerance of state interference in the affairs of the University.

That afternoon, a meeting chaired by Charlton with representatives of all the constituencies of the University except Council and Convocation[48] was told of the Senate resolution and that there would be a meeting of Vice-Chancellors in Cape Town the following day. All present agreed that the conditions should be rejected, that the University should act in concert with the Universities of Cape Town, Natal, Rhodes and the Western Cape and that the University should investigate the issue of taking legal action. It was also decided that a General Assembly should be called on a date in the following week agreed upon by the five universities and that this might be followed by a solemn march, in academic dress, led by the Chancellor and Vice-Chancellor.

The ASA met on 21 October and resolved to support Senate's resolution. It also decided to reject categorically the infringement of the autonomy of the University and to exhort all members of the University not to co-operate in the enforcement of the new regulations. It pledged itself to support the University in exploring the possibility of taking legal action to overturn the regulations and it supported the notion of calling for a General Assembly. It also called for all the constituencies of the University to inform the international academic community of the situation, and to seek its support.

Throughout the campaign waged by the English-language universities, the Afrikaans universities were remarkably and distressingly complacent, and even supportive, of the Government's actions.[49] Although they are reported to have raised minor objections to the original draft regulations they expressed satisfaction with the conditions.

There was some protest at the University of Stellenbosch when about 200 Nusas supporters and black students raised objections with the Rector, Professor M de Vries. By the middle of November De Vries was under pressure at Stellenbosch to change his stance.[50] At the insistence of the university's Senate, the Stellenbosch Council expressed grave doubts about the underlying principles and practicability of the De Klerk conditions, and De Vries announced plans to meet the Government to discuss the issue and to propose guidelines for the maintenance of order on the Stellenbosch campus.[51] Reports suggested that Stellenbosch academics feared that their university could suffer academic boycotts and lose research possibilities while their English colleagues received international recognition for their stance. This seems to have induced *Die Burger*, the official National Party mouthpiece in the Cape, to urge the Government to heed the views of the Stellenbosch academics.

Professor D Joubert, Rector of the University of Pretoria, claimed smugly that there were no problems on his campus and that speakers from the left and the right were always allowed to address meetings. It is to be hoped that he appreciated the lack of wisdom and foresight in that position when, only a few years later, student supporters of the right wing Conservative Party caused a major rumpus on the Pretoria campus when Mr Nelson Mandela was invited to speak there, and when, in September 1993, Mr Walter Sisulu, Deputy President of the ANC, received death threats and warnings from the Afrikaner Volksfront (AVF) when he was due to address a meeting at the University of Pretoria, and the meeting had to be cancelled.[52]

The Rector of Potchefstroom University pronounced himself completely satisfied with the requirements.

A somewhat more perceptive attitude was displayed by Professor G J Hauptfleisch, Vice-Rector (Academic) of RAU. He wrote that the threat of a subsidy cut in an attempt to force a university to adopt a particular course of action was a serious threat to university autonomy even if the requirements were not unreasonable. The precedent that it set for future actions and by different future Governments was exceptionally disturbing.[53]

The Government-supporting Afrikaans newspapers took their usual obsequious line as did the student leadership at five Afrikaans-language universities – Pretoria, Stellenbosch, Free State, RAU and Potchefstroom – who welcomed the imposition of the regulations.[54]

The attitude of the Afrikaans universities did not escape the notice of influential academic circles abroad. A commentator in the scientific journal *Nature* wrote that: 'The new edict has already forced South African universities into two camps. Although the past few years have seen even the Afrikaans universities veer towards opposition of apartheid, the Government could well have calculated in advance that they would reluctantly knuckle down to the new edicts. By doing so, they have isolated the more outspoken universities and made them more vulnerable to further threats to their independence.'[55]

De Klerk used the opportunity provided by the Cape Congress of his party on 10 October to defend his actions, denying that the conditions were intended to infringe on the autonomy of the universities. 'Nothing is further from the truth,' he is reported to have said.[56] 'There were incidents on campus which did not necessarily break the law, but did clash with the ethics of universities such as boycotts of classes, burning the image of the State President and hindering clubs from inviting guests to address them ... The underlying purpose of the Government conditions is to ensure the maintenance of traditional university standards and values.' It was in this speech that, in support of his case, he alluded to the attacks on the English-language universities by newspapers such as *Business Day*. It was this speech which so raised the ire of its editor Ken Owen, that he wrote the venomous 'Cultural Alien' article quoted earlier, p 162.[57]

Representatives of the Universities of Cape Town, Natal, Rhodes, Western Cape and the Witwatersrand met in Cape Town on 22 October together with the national leadership of Sansco and Nusas.[58] After a wide-ranging debate, they agreed that the administrations of the five universities and their student bodies should coordinate their responses until such time as the conditions were withdrawn. The group expressed the hope that those universities that had supported or accepted the imposition of the conditions would reconsider their positions in the light of the serious threats that they posed to all South African universities.

The date set for the General Assemblies of the universities was Wednesday 28 October 1987.

General Assembly

The Wits General Assembly was planned by a committee representing the Council, administration, Senate, Academic Staff Association, the Technical Staff Association, the Administrative and Library Staff Association, the Wits workers' unions National Education, Health and Allied Workers' Union (Nehawu) and Black University Workers' Association (Buwa), the SRC and the BSS.[59] Most of the procedures were readily agreed to by all on the committee. The various constituencies would read statements which would be published in a booklet. The Assembly would be followed by a march or academic procession which would end on the piazza in front of the Great Hall where a statement would be read and be inscribed on a new plaque. An advertisement would appear in the daily press calling on past students to attend. The University would be closed during the Assembly to enable all the staff to attend.

There was a difference of opinion on the venue for the Assembly and on the route that the march would take. In view of the restrictions on outdoor gatherings, the administration suggested the sports hall. The SRC preferred the library lawns because of the need for the demonstration to be visible. The latter venue was agreed to and permission had to be sought from the Chief Magistrate of Johannesburg. The negotiations on the route for the march were protracted. The students wanted to march outside the campus before ending on the piazza but the administration was reluctant, knowing that there was less likelihood that the Chief Magistrate (advised as always by the security police) would agree. We were also extremely apprehensive of police intervention if a march beyond the perimeter of the University got the slightest bit out of hand.

After extensive discussion and undertakings given by the students, it was agreed that part of the march would be off campus and that marshals would direct the procession.

A notice from Tober called the General Assembly for 12pm to comment on 'Government Restrictions on University Subsidies'. On 26 October the Registrar made a formal application to the Chief Magistrate for permission.

In response to a request from the Chief Magistrate for information about the march, Professor Charlton, Vice-Chancellor designate and acting Vice-Chancellor in the absence of Tober who was ill, informed him that the Assembly was being convened by the Vice-Chancellor at the request of Senate and that it would be addressed *inter alia* by the Chairman of Council, the Chancellor, the Vice-Chancellor, the Vice-Chancellor designate and by other members of the University who had a direct and substantial interest in the matter to be discussed.

The Chief Magistrate was also informed that the Assembly, a dignified occasion in academic dress, would be attended by 4 000 to 5 000 people and would end with a formal academic procession to the place where a plaque was to be laid and the wording of the plaque would be read out. The meeting and procession would end by 2pm and classes scheduled for the afternoon would continue as usual. The Assembly and the procession would remain within the boundary of the University campus. Previous Assemblies had been held in the open air on the campus and had proceeded without incident and there was no reason to believe that this one would be any different.

In a letter to the Registrar, the Chief Magistrate gave his approval on the morning of the Assembly. Had it been refused, it is almost certain that the students at least, and possibly also other constituencies of the University, would have decided to proceed anyway. The police would then have intervened immediately and mayhem would have erupted earlier than it eventually did.

> With reference to your application dated 26 October, 1987, permission is hereby granted in terms of section 46(3) of the Internal Security Act, 1982 (Act 74 of 1982) for a meeting of the General Assembly of the University, called for by Professor R W Charlton, Acting Vice-Chancellor of the University, to be held on Wednesday, 28 October, 1987, between 12 noon and 14h30 on the Library Lawn in the centre of the East Campus of the University for the purpose of allowing the various constituencies of the University to comment on the newly imposed conditions for the granting of subsidies to universities and for a formal academic procession to take place.
>
> The assembly and the procession shall remain within the boundary of the Witwatersrand University campus.

I was in the chair at the Assembly which was attended by about 6 000 people. After I had opened the proceedings, there were addresses by the Chairman of Council, the Chancellor, Professor Phillip Tobias representing the Senate, Charlton, Mr Eyvind Finsen, President of Convocation, Ms Rosemary Hunter, President of the SRC, and representatives of the staff associations and unions. (See Appendix 14 for the addresses by Stutterheim, Rosholt, Tobias, Charlton and myself. The addresses of the others are not available.) In powerful statements the speakers drew attention to the gravity of the Government's action, expressed great anger at the assault on the autonomy of the universities, and made clear the determination to oppose vigorously any attempt to enforce them.

Tobias told the Assembly that the Senate found the Minister's conditions totally unacceptable and declared that its members would decline to comply with them. He also expressed the bitter disappointment of the Senate that several universities seemed unperturbed by the conditions; that Stellenbosch had been reported as saying that they 'can go along with them' and Potchefstroom that it gives 'full support' to them.[60]

At the conclusion of the addresses, the Chancellor, Chairman of Council, Vice-Chancellor and Vice-Chancellor Designate led a march through part of the University grounds towards Jorissen Street, the southern boundary of the campus.[61] Many gowned marshals – staff and student volunteers – assisted in organising the procession. Several groups carried banners.

Initially the procession was orderly and extremely dignified, but after more than half had already turned back into the University grounds, a group suddenly moved off the pavement and into Jorissen Street. The riot squad had been nearby but had kept a low profile until this incident. They immediately rushed towards the students, striking out at them with batons. I dashed over to urge the senior police officer, Major du Toit, not to use force but to allow me time to persuade the students to move back to the campus. He threatened me with arrest for interfering with the police in the course of their duties. Robert Whitecross, a plain clothes member of the security police, then ran up and also threatened me with arrest, saying that it was already clear that I could not control the students, and there was no point in discussing the matter.[62] I used a loud hailer to continue urging the students back into the procession and eventually they all got back off the street.

In the meantime, the main body of the procession had reached the piazza where Tober read the inscription on a second plaque that had been installed on the wall outside the Great Hall.

> On the 19th of October 1987 the Government of the Republic of South Africa renewed its systematic violation of the autonomy of the University of the Witwatersrand, Johannesburg. At a General Assembly of the University held on the 28th of October members of the University affirmed that
>
> The University of the Witwatersrand is dedicated to the acquisition, advancement and imparting of knowledge through the pursuit of truth in free and open debate, in the undertaking of research, in scholarly discourse and in balanced, dispassionate teaching. We reject any external interference designed to diminish our freedom to attain these ends. We record our solemn

protest against the intention of the Government, through the threat of financial sanctions, to force the University to become the agent of Government policy in disciplining its members. We protest against the invasion of the legitimate authority of the University. We protest against the stifling of legitimate dissent. In the interests of all in this land, and in the knowledge of the justice of our cause, we dedicate ourselves to unremitting opposition to these intended restraints and to the restoration of our autonomy.

Picture courtesy *The Star*

Another confrontation. On this occasion, after a formal University protest on 27 September 1990, my intercession was successful and the police agreed to withdraw.

> The 19th day of October 1987 will forever remain a day of shame in the history of South African universities. Until full autonomy is restored to the University of the Witwatersrand, the space adjacent to this plaque shall remain empty to bear witness to the continuing diminution of the freedom and status of the University by those who rule this land. On the full restoration of our autonomy an inscription will be added to record the return of Wits to the ranks of the world community of universities enjoying freedom from external control.

The students were now worked up and agitated, both by the occasion and by the police intervention, and a toyi-toying column started to weave its way back towards the periphery of the campus. Our peace-keeping group, comprising senior, caring staff members, tried to persuade them to stay on campus. Our motivation was that a procedure had been agreed upon by all constituencies on campus for a peaceful mass demonstration and that this relatively small group was turning the solemn occasion into a disruptive conflict which would alienate rather than garner support for our campaign against the ministerial conditions.

They did turn back in response to our goading, but, after proceeding a short distance, swung away again towards the streets in response to directions given by a few diehards who had placed themselves in the front of the procession. We were not even sure whether these were students or whether they were politicised youth who had come in from the townships to take part in the protests and were aching to challenge the authority of the police. They might even have been *agents provocateurs*, sent in by the security police to incite a confrontation and thereby discredit the University's avowed peaceful protest.

As the march moved towards Jorissen Street, some of the student leaders took charge and Tiego Moseneke of the BSS called on me and the peace-keeping group to withdraw so that 'we can lead ourselves'. We did this, standing a little to the side and observing the proceedings. They decided to sit down in the street and observe five minutes' silence. The road in which they were sitting was Station Street, not itself a major thoroughfare, but an access route to the University from Jorissen Street, which was a busy road.

No sooner had the students sat down than the riot squad, armed and wearing gas masks, formed up in Jorissen Street, ready for action. Major Du Toit was once again there, sitting in his car nearby. I went over to speak to him, accompanied by Professor June Sinclair and Mr Edwin Cameron who were part of the staff peace-keeping group.[63] I wanted to tell him that the students had decided to observe five minutes of silence and that they would then sing 'Nkosi Sikelel' iAfrika' and disperse. All Du Toit would say was 'You've got one-and-a-half minutes to go'. He then rolled up his car window. This was the end of our attempt to negotiate a peaceful conclusion to the day's activities.

Just as they were ending the anthem, teargas canisters were fired at them from both the front and the rear by a squad of police who had come up behind them from the campus. This meant that as the students turned back towards the campus they ran into another cloud of tear gas. A rather bedraggled group of students and peace-keepers eventually made their way back to the piazza, where freedom songs continued to be sung for the rest of the afternoon, interspersed with speeches by student leaders. Although the police did not come onto campus by foot, a police helicopter repeatedly circled in the region of the piazza and the library lawns for some time, often at low altitude, someone inside it taking photographs. The noise drowned the sound but this did not deter either the singers or the speakers.

A group of creative students used chairs left on the lawns after the assembly to send a message to those in the helicopter: 'FUCK OFF', it read.

Many of those involved in organising the General Assembly felt betrayed by the actions of the small group that had broken out of the procession and led to the police involvement. A considerable unity had been achieved during the consultations before the meeting and some of those involved felt let down. In a rather tense meeting the morning after the Assembly, leaders of the SRC and BSS were challenged by representatives of some of the other groups. The students were in a difficult position. They were not themselves responsible for the breach of agreement and did not defend what had happened. At the same time they found it difficult to condemn the offenders. The peace-keeping group felt particularly peeved because, having been asked to stand aside and let the students 'lead themselves', they had

had to suffer a heavy dose of teargas with them. The student leaders who had given the undertakings bore the brunt of the strong condemnation.[64]

The peace-keeping group, first formed in 1985, consisted of a group of academic and administrative staff who had volunteered to act in that role during periods of student unrest and were alerted by the Student Affairs Office whenever a politically-orientated meeting was scheduled. They were well-disposed towards students and by and large sympathised with their objectives. They believed that their presence at demonstrations could be helpful and protective, particularly when there was likely to be conflict, either between different student groupings, or with the police; and indeed they were. Most of them were people who were well known on campus and were readily recognised at least by the student leadership if not by the student body as a whole.

The academic members of the peace-keeping group who were regularly present were Harold Annegarn, John Dugard, David Freer, David Glasser, Noel Garson, Scott Hazelhurst, David Horsfall, Berend Kolk, Michael Larkin, Carol Lewis, Philip Machanik, Conrad Mueller, Etienne Mureinik, Debra Nails, Noam Pines, Michael Sears, John Shochot, June Sinclair, Mervyn Skuy and Alf Stadler. The administrative staff members were Jocelyn Cairns, Pauline Cuzen, Bruce Dickson, Ken Standenmacher, Jonathan Stead, Peta Stevens, Victor Gordon, various members of the University's security staff under the direction of Cliff Hurst, and myself.

At a meeting after the 28 October march they queried their future role in the light of the snub. They decided that they would continue to play a peace-keeping role but would stand towards the back of demonstrations rather than in front, as had been the practice. They did so on the following one or two occasions, after which the student leaders asked for a meeting and indicated that they would appreciate it if the peace-keepers would revert to their earlier procedures.

In a newspaper interview on 29 October, Charlton said he would resign if the conditions imposed on the universities were not withdrawn,[65] as he would find the situation intolerable. 'In effect, what the Minister wants is for the Council through its administration to implement some of the aspects of the state of emergency ... If the Minister decided to withhold the subsidy it would have such a devastating effect on the University that the Council may indeed be forced to do what he wants.'

Charlton reported to Senate on 1 December 1987 that the Chancellors, Vice-Chancellors and Chairmen of Council, or their representatives, of the Universities of Cape Town, Natal, Rhodes, Wits and Western Cape, had met with Minister De Klerk on 25 November.[66] De Klerk had pointed out that three of the universities represented at the meeting – the Universities of Cape Town and Western Cape and the University of Natal – had challenged him in court, and until the cases, which had been set down for February 1988, had been heard he could not receive representations. Nevertheless, the occasion was used to present him with a written statement from the five universities on how they saw the consequences of his actions.

The debate on this matter at the meeting of Council on 11 December was again difficult and divided.[67] It began with some members disputing the accuracy of the minute of the discussion that had taken place at the previous meeting. Zeffert's updated legal opinion was before the meeting, as were an extract from the Senate debate and the statement released by Senate.

A major difference in opinion surfaced when the question was raised of taking legal action against the Minister in view of the fact that actions had been launched in the Cape and in Natal.

Mr Sydney Kentridge had been consulted and had advised that it seemed that no purpose would be served by a third hearing in the Transvaal as the matter would eventually go to the Appellate Division.[68] He added, however, that he was strongly of the view that the conditions were invalid and should simply be ignored. Only in the unlikely event that the Minister should actually withhold a subsidy, should the University consider taking the matter to court.

Some members of Council, however, believed that the University must be seen to be taking action, and suggested, as an alternative to proceeding in the Transvaal Provincial Division, that Wits might join the University of Natal. The University, it was argued, could not afford to isolate itself particularly in view of the academic boycott. There was a danger that the University's qualifications would be rejected overseas and academic staff would be prevented from visiting institutions abroad and participating in international conferences.

The academic boycott had already severely affected the ability of academic staff to publish in international journals and there was deep concern that the University's international associations would be severed. Moreover, they argued, the University's teaching and research programmes would be jeopardised if it became impossible to attract high-quality academics from abroad, and if its own staff of international standing decided that they would have to leave the country.

The counter-arguments were feeble. Some members felt that since most of the University's income came from the Government, Council needed to be cautious. Others believed that Council had expressed its view in the statement released after the previous meeting and a further statement was unnecessary. It was also felt that in view of the possibility that different opinions might be forthcoming from the two hearings, it would be wise not to take any further action until the outcome was known.

Some members stated frankly that they had difficulty in supporting legal action against the Minister. It was said that the Minister still appeared willing to discuss the matter and that every avenue should be explored before legal action was contemplated. Certain universities had acted over hastily and the matter could be resolved through negotiation.

Another contentious issue was Senate's statement of 21 October. Several members did not agree with its contents, particularly with the comment that it was the Minister's intention to enforce National Party policy. They could also not accept the suggestion that Council investigate the possibility of setting up a special trust, with support from foreign Governments and institutions, with a view to counteracting any possible reduction of subsidy.[69] They believed that Council could not threaten the Government in this way. Some members stated that they could not be party to the Senate proposals and dissociated themselves from the statement.

Members who believed it was unacceptable to allow statements to be released without Council's approval were reminded that Senate was entitled to express its views independently of Council and that it would be most unfortunate if Council were to make a statement that contradicted the Senate's. It was stressed that over the years great efforts had been made to seek common ground on various issues so as to accommodate the views of the various constituencies in the University.

In the end Council rejected a proposal that a further statement be issued. Doubt was expressed about the propriety of supporting one of the litigants. It was suggested, somewhat absurdly, that 'this could be seen as an attempt to influence the outcome of the hearing and that it would be unwise to issue a statement in support of one or all of the parties concerned'. Council decided merely to reaffirm its earlier statement and to maintain close contact with other universities in an attempt to change the Minister's position.

Council also agreed that no reference should be made in the statement to any proposed legal action. Effectively, Council had decided not to take legal steps, a most unfortunate decision which was not in the best interests of the University. It evoked considerable criticism from students and staff both at Wits and at sister universities. Some members of Senate expressed their disappointment and felt that the University should have been seen to protest rather than to have avoided confrontation. They also regretted that nothing had been done beyond holding a General Assembly.

The 'hawks' on Council were not yet satisfied. They proposed that steps be taken to re-examine the University's disciplinary procedures. When it was pointed out that the Council would then be seen as responding directly to the Minister's directives, it was said that executive authority was vested in the Council and that in view of the Minister's statement that taxpayers' money was not being properly used, Council should be seen to be taking greater action.

De Klerk, clearly extremely sensitive to the scathing opposition to his measures, made a further attempt to justify them in the cosily uncritical environment of yet another adulatory party gathering, this time at the Transvaal National Party Congress on 13 November. He also used the occasion to attack Ken Owen for his attempt 'to aggressively create mistrust between English and Afrikaans South Africans, in this case to bolster a weak defence of indefensible tendencies at some of our universities.'[70]

Support from universities abroad was inestimably valuable in boosting the morale of the English-language universities in their opposition to the measures. The presidents of fifteen universities in the USA sent a letter to De Klerk expressing concern.[71] 'These conditions can only further compromise the freedom of speech and enquiry on the campuses of South Africa. You are asking the councils and presidents to police the actions of both students and staff on and off campus in ways that are inconsistent with universal standards of academic freedom and autonomy. To accept such conditions would be to forfeit the respect and the moral authority needed to secure their compliance. Any university of standing must enjoy the independence and freedom required to carry out its essential mission. Accordingly, we urge you, the South African Government, not to impose these conditions.'

Neither the pleas, the protests nor the representations succeeded in persuading the Government to withdraw the conditions. The only remedy lay with the courts.

Victory In the Courts

The case of the University of Cape Town and the University of the Western Cape against the Ministers of Education and Culture of the Houses of Assembly and House of Representatives, the Minister of National Education and the Minister of Home Affairs was heard from 9 to 12 February 1988.[72] The applicants sought an order declaring that certain conditions imposed under the Universities Act 61 of 1955 were invalid.

The orders were granted with costs on 12 February 1988 and reasons for the judgement were handed down on 3 March by Judges Howie and Nel, with Judge Conradie concurring. The court held that the imposition of the conditions in issue had been prompted substantially by the ulterior motive of achieving objects not empowered by section 25, and that the operation of such ulterior motive had rendered the conditions *ultra vires* and invalid. It was also held that the conditions were void for uncertainty and that the provisions on disciplinary steps that Councils were required to take, 'constituted oppressive or gratuitous interference with the unhindered imposition of punishment according to the merits of each case, free from extraneous influence'. They were accordingly invalid and since 'they formed so integral a part of the conditions as a whole ... even if the conditions as a whole had been *intra vires* in the strict sense and enforceably clear in meaning, they would nonetheless be void for unreasonableness.' (see Appendix 15)[73]

The court supported in all respects the opinions of the University's legal advisers. The judgement was a humiliating defeat for De Klerk and a triumph for the universities that had opposed the conditions. Nevertheless, with an extraordinarily naïve view of the way in which the English-language universities functioned, a leading article in *Business Day* (12 April 1988) stated: 'The English universities might ... have been much better off if they had thrown their support wholeheartedly behind the party that best represents their interests (the Progressive Federal Party); instead they encouraged their students to wander off into some non-parliamentary wilderness in search of a socialist Utopia, and now they whimper under de Klerk's lash.' Some wilderness; some whimper! Was this the 'Anglo-Saxon way' referred to so piously by Ken Owen?

In the Natal Provincial Division Judge NS Page sitting in the application brought by the University of Natal reached the same conclusions. The conditions were invalid and of no force and effect; and the respondents were ordered to pay costs[74] (see Appendix 15).

There was little likelihood that a third court would have come to a different conclusion. The question now was, would De Klerk introduce amending legislation to legitimise the imposition of the conditions?

A deputation from the Committee of University Principals met De Klerk on 11 March 1988 and presented him with a memorandum prepared by their Executive Committee.[75] Certain proposals made in the memorandum were unacceptable to Wits and Charlton informed De Klerk that the University would not support them.[76]

One proposal was that, in exchange for an undertaking to manage the universities in the spirit of the academic objectives that had been laid down, the conditions for the granting of subsidies would be withdrawn. If such an undertaking were not fulfilled, the Minister would summon the Vice-Chancellor/Rector and the chairman of Council of the university concerned for discussions. If the problem was not resolved, the Minister would appoint a one-man commission in consultation with the particular chairman of Council, to investigate the affair and would decide on further action on the basis of the findings of such an investigation. De Klerk promised to consider the proposal.

It is highly unlikely that any of the universities which had been strongly opposed to the conditions would have accepted this attempt at compromise. The use of a one-person commission appointed by the Minister to resolve an impasse would have been no less an intrusion on the autonomy of the universities than the original Government intervention, and one must conclude that the Executive Committee of the CUP had gone beyond the brief it received from the full committee. In response to an angry reaction to the proposals from Dr Stuart Saunders, Vice-Chancellor of the University of Cape Town, the Chief Director of the CUP made an unconvincing attempt to justify them. 'At no stage was this viewed by Exco or presented to the Minister as anything more than a possible agenda for further discussions. It was couched in the given terms to illustrate that there are alternative ways to handle this sensitive issue than the route followed up to now, ways which will allow for much reflection, consultation and, if necessary, mediation/arbitration before potential action becomes an issue.'[77]

In his reply to Charlton, De Klerk indicated that the Government was considering its position in the light of the recent court cases. It remained committed to the realisation of the original goals intended by the conditions and was considering ways and means by which they could be achieved.[78]

A public statement by De Klerk in reaction to the Supreme Court rulings suggested that the Government might be considering adopting a less aggressive stance. 'We must continue to maintain the universities' relationship with the State in such a way that we do not become prescriptive, that university autonomy is maintained. But at the same time we must remain faithful to traditional university values. The universities' essential task, that of education and research, should not be hindered, and our taxpayers' money should be used for that purpose and not to further aims that threaten national security.'[79]

However, when replying to the committee stage debate on his budget vote in the House of Assembly on 19 April, De Klerk insisted that, in spite of the Supreme Court decisions, the Government was still intent on achieving the goals it had set out with its subsidy preconditions.[80] He said that the unrest situation at certain universities which had given rise to the original action had still not abated sufficiently for the issue to be dropped. The Government would decide on a course of action within the following few weeks and would make announcements. He insisted that the courts had ruled against the Government's methods and not its goals. The Government had four options: to appeal against the courts' decisions, amend legislation, seek consensus with the universities, or leave the matter alone. He stated that the situation at universities was such that the last was not, in fact, an option.

Responding to De Klerk, Charlton insisted that Wits supported the goals enunciated by the Minister and that there was absolutely no reason why he should contemplate further action to achieve them.[81]

By 3 May, the Government had decided to try negotiating with the universities. In a speech on his budget vote in the House of Delegates De Klerk said the letters to the universities outlining the subsidy conditions would be withdrawn.[82] Each Own Affairs minister would consult the universities under his control to reach agreement on measures on which there was already a large degree of consensus. It was essential that a workable solution be found as the Government could not allow stayaways, class boycotts and intimidation of lecturers on campus to continue. There would still be room for constructive protest, criticism and debate, but this would have to be done in a responsible manner and in a way that would not serve the 'revolutionary onslaught against the country'. It was important, he admitted, that the tension between the Government and the universities be eliminated without losing sight of the four goals to which the Government remained committed. In his view, academic freedom could not exist at a university that aligned itself fully with 'leftist radical views'. Ironically, he appealed to academics at universities to take a stand against philosophies that made a mockery of the concept of academic freedom.

Charlton welcomed the Minister's statement, saying that 'there has been no boycott of classes or examinations and no intimidation of lecturers at Wits and we have always adhered to the goals the minister has repeatedly enunciated'.[83] On the question of the maintenance of discipline, Charlton drew attention to Judge Howie's judgement in which he said: 'The paramount consideration must be that justice must be seen to be done. The disciplinary procedures concerned are required to be conducted according to the rules of natural justice. There must be a fair trial.' Charlton pointed out that Wits had always exercised student and staff discipline according to these principles and would continue to do so. 'Those who have called for arbitrary administrative action against alleged offenders, such as summary expulsions should recognise that that would not only be morally unacceptable but also liable to be overturned by the courts.'

On 4 July 1988 Minister Clase wrote to the Chairman of Council.[84] The letter stated that in the light of the recent court decisions, the conditions for subsidisation had been withdrawn. He asked for an undertaking by the Council that the Government's four aims would be achieved by the University without any further steps being taken. In order to achieve the aims the Government might consider two options: to amend the existing legislation, or to enter into discussions with universities regarding ways in which the aims could be achieved before any further steps were considered. 'Since a mutually acceptable course of action is naturally desirable, the second option is the obvious choice at this stage. If your Council is prepared to give the undertaking desired, it will be appreciated if you would notify me accordingly within six weeks of receipt of this letter. I should also like to be informed whether you accept the proposed procedure or receive your comments on it.' If the Council could not give the undertaking, he requested a discussion as soon as possible.

Stutterheim gave the assurance, in a letter on 9 August, that the Council would continue to govern the University as it had always done, in a manner consistent with the four aims.

This assurance was reiterated by Stutterheim's successor as Chairman of Council, Mr S A G Anderson, in a letter on 6 February 1989.[85] Anderson added that the Council nevertheless continued to feel strongly that South African universities must remain autonomous. Nevertheless, the Council recognised the right of the Minister to call at any time for discussions with the University on any matter he wished to raise.

Clase responded to this letter a year later, on 5 February 1990,[86] noting 'with regret' that the Council was not prepared to give an undertaking to administer the University in the spirit of the four aims; and that the University was not prepared to accept the procedures to be followed when this undertaking was not effectively applied. He insisted that those procedures must be followed but hoped that it would not be necessary to implement them.

It seems clear from this letter and from the fact that a whole year had passed before it was written – a year in which no further action had been taken – that the Government had lost heart. Anderson responded by repeating what had been written in previous letters, expressing concern about the 'serious misunderstanding'.[87]

Clase grabbed this lifebelt with gratitude. The essential difference, it would appear, was that between 'undertake to administer the University ...' and 'continue to govern the University ...' He wrote to Anderson on 26 March 1990[88] that he had taken full cognisance of and noted with appreciation Council's confirmation of its intention to continue to govern the University as it had always done, in a manner consistent with the four aims which he had enunciated. He had understood and still understood the tenor of the letter of 6 February 1989 to be that the Council was not prepared to give the undertaking since it considered that this would amount to an infringement of the University's autonomy. 'I on the contrary do not consider that a request for a voluntary undertaking from your Council would in any way impinge on the autonomy of the university and in that light expressed my regret that your Council was not willing to give such an undertaking.'

This was, in effect, the last word on the subject, and no further threats were heard from the Government. By this time De Klerk had succeeded P W Botha as State President and was fully occupied with other matters following his important speech on 2 February 1990 which opened the way for free political activity.

At the meeting in his office on 20 November 1986 when the matter had first been raised with representatives of Wits, De Klerk had opened the discussion by saying that 'it was the wish of the State President that he and his colleagues talk to representatives of some of the universities'. It is possible therefore that it was Botha, rather than De Klerk, who was behind this relentless and obdurate action against the English-language universities. Nevertheless it was De Klerk who had ministerial responsibility for the policy, and he defended it vigorously. In pursuing it he had poor advice from the permanent members of his department and from his legal counsel. He was misled by the orchestrated campaign of letter-writing in the press, and by some misguided editorials, into believing that he would have massive public support for his actions. His greatest mistake however, was believing that the English-language universities would be a push-over and would succumb meekly before the power of his authority. It was a serious error of judgement.

Postscript

I wonder whether De Klerk was conscious of the irony of what he was saying or of the audience he was addressing, or did he believe that we all had short memories when, as Deputy President, in an address to the students of the University of Pretoria on 15 May 1995, he said that universities should resist any attempt by the state to undermine their autonomy and academic freedom. The autonomy of tertiary institutions was enshrined in the interim constitution, he told them.[89]

CHAPTER 9

The Struggle Reaches a Climax

The state of emergency was exacting a horrific toll on the forces of resistance in South Africa, including the student movements. Large numbers of troops were being deployed in the townships to assist the police. Thousands of people had been detained including substantial numbers of children. In March 1987 Vlok had admitted that 43 people had died in detention and 263 detainees had been treated in hospital. An investigation by doctors of the National Medical and Dental Association (Namda) in 1988 found that 73 per cent of a group of 131 detainees had been mentally abused by threats and humiliation during interrogation. Restrictions on the press imposed by emergency regulations prevented the reporting of detentions, disturbances or activities of the security forces.[1] A report of the International Commission of Jurists in May 1988 based on the findings of a team of lawyers from Western Europe the previous year, condemned the widespread use of torture and violence by security forces with the connivance of the Government.[2]

Although the Government had lost ground to the Conservative Party during the 1987 elections for the white House of Assembly because they were perceived by the political right to be moving away from the Verwoerdian apartheid principles, P W Botha was telling the party faithful at the annual congress in August 1988 that he was not considering the possibility of a black majority government. Instead he was contemplating various constitutional devices such as a National Council that would have only advisory powers. This was contemptuously rejected by black leaders as were segregated municipal elections which in October 1988 were boycotted and supported by a mere 3 per cent of voters from the entire African population of South Africa, including the homelands.³

While the conflict between the universities and the Government on the subsidy issue was being resolved in the Supreme Court in February 1988, the start of the new academic year was clouded by amendments to the emergency regulations on 24 February. These amendments and the orders published under them empowered the Government to 'name' seventeen organisations, which effectively banned them. Among them were Sansco, the United Democratic Front (UDF), the Detainees' Parents Support Committee (DPSC), the National Education Crisis Committee (NECC), Azapo and the South African Youth Congress (Sayco).

Charlton strongly condemned the action, which violated the basic freedoms of association and expression. The named organisations included several in which students had a particular interest, and the Government's action would seriously undermine attempts at peaceful resolution of the political impasse in South Africa. It denied students who were members of the named organisations the right to political expression through those organisations and was likely to provoke protest and the disruption of academic activities. This was a contradiction of the Government's recently professed commitment to the maintenance of freedom of speech and the prevention of unrest on university campuses.⁴

Student reaction was swift, and by early afternoon they had gathered and were singing in the concourse of Senate House. A meeting attended by about 2 000 people was held in the arcade of the Students' Union on the following morning. I was asked to prepare a statement to be read to the meeting and wrote: 'Whatever restrictions are inflicted on you by a government which sought to impose pressure on the universities on the pretext of defending freedom of speech, this University will continue to support your rights of freedom of assembly and a freedom of speech that may be denied you outside its walls. The University shares your anger at the new restrictions imposed on organisations which represent you and the majority of South Africans. We shall continue to speak out against all forms of oppression of our people and the denial of basic human rights.'⁵

After the meeting there was a march to the periphery of the campus and although the police were present they took no action against the students who turned around after about half an hour and returned to the piazza, singing solemnly.[6]

Another large meeting took place in the Students' Union arcade on 17 March 1988, in protest against the impending execution of six people convicted of murdering a town councillor in Sharpeville. After the meeting about 250 students wearing black armbands and bearing posters and placards moved to the Jan Smuts Avenue steps with the intention of picketing along the road. They were prevented from doing so by a squad of riot police who pursued them back onto the campus. In the course of the chase four students were injured. Plans to attend a protest meeting in Sharpeville were cancelled when the buses which were to transport them did not arrive.[7]

During the morning, Charlton and his deputies sent a telex to President Botha that read:

> We, the Vice-Chancellor and Deputy Vice-Chancellors of the University of the Witwatersrand, Johannesburg, urge you, Sir, to exercise mercy by commuting the sentence that the so-called Sharpeville Six be hanged tomorrow. We believe such an act of clemency would have a healing effect in this land that would far transcend any narrow sectarian criticisms that might be voiced by a few. We believe such an act of mercy would be statesmanship of the highest order and we implore you to follow such a course in the interests of justice and peace in our country.

Appeals for clemency also came from numerous human rights groups and from some newspapers. At 3.30 that afternoon it was announced that a stay of execution had been granted until 18 April 1988. On 23 November 1988 the Sharpeville Six were reprieved.

On 21 March 1988 there was another police incursion on campus. On this occasion three members of the security police came to the Barnato Hall residence looking for Michael Avidan, a member of the SRC. Without approaching the warden, they went to Avidan's room and when there was no response to their knock they discharged teargas under the door. This seeped into the corridor and affected other students in the vicinity.[8] A letter of complaint from Charlton to the head of the Security Police at John Vorster Square was ignored.[9]

On the same morning, the President of the SRC, Rosemary Hunter, was detained by security police. Three days earlier, Tiego Moseneke, a past president of the BSS had been detained. A General Assembly of students on 24 March was held to protest against the detentions of the students and of Mr Raymond Suttner, a lecturer in the School of Law. Charlton addressed the meeting, strongly condemning the process of detention without trial, and expressing the University's support and sympathy for staff and students who had been detained and for their families. He promised that the University would continue to follow every avenue open to it to try to secure their release and until that had been achieved would supply them with study materials and whatever other means of support they were allowed.[10]

Among the speakers was Mrs Winnie Mandela who called for unity across racial barriers on campus. 'It should not be necessary for me to belong to the BSS because of the colour of my skin and for my white counterparts to be in the SRC and NUSAS.'[11] This call was seen as important at the time because of the BSS's strategy of non-participation in established student structures and it was hoped that Mrs Mandela's call might trigger some unity moves.[12]

On 30 March an impressive demonstration, led by the President of Nusas, Steve Kromberg, took place at the Union Buildings, Pretoria, when student leaders from Wits joined a group of about seventy-five from eight universities throughout the country who had come together to deliver to President Botha personal notes of protest at the banning of the seventeen organisations. I was asked by Nusas to be present to keep a watching brief. I attended the students' pre-demonstration briefing and was impressed by their careful planning and strategising as well as by the unanimity of purpose shown by the Nusas supporters who included delegations from three Afrikaans universities – Stellenbosch, Pretoria and Rand Afrikaans University.

Botha did not receive them himself, but their notes were handed to a police brigadier in front of the Buildings. So as not to infringe the security laws, the students marched up singly, twenty metres apart, in the course of some hours, rather than as a group. They wore academic dress and the exercise was conducted peacefully and with dignity. I watched the southern end of the large lawn where the marchers assembled and grouped themselves before starting out on the long walk.

The demonstration proceeded without a hitch, although there was some provocation by members of the NSF who had come to observe the proceedings, angered, they claimed, at having been excluded from participating in the protest. A 150-strong police contingent was present but did not interfere, although every student was filmed and photographed and representatives of the media were instructed to leave the grounds.[13]

Towards the end of the demonstration, with the light fading and the temperature dropping on an early autumn evening, the security police were joining in the light-hearted banter, relieved, I thought, that it had not been necessary for them to engage the students in the usual confrontation. It was rewarding for me to have the opportunity to talk to these men about mundane everyday matters and to see how ordinary they were. It interested me that I would not have been able to pick them out as security police on a crowded train, whereas at political meetings they were so conspicuous they might as well have been wearing a large label.

MSA vs SAUJS

From time to time, conflict of a somewhat different nature took place between students on campus. These were clashes between members of the Muslim Students' Association (MSA) and the South African Union of Jewish Students (SAUJS), which were usually associated with days such as Al Quds Day[14] or Holocaust Day,[15] which were of particular significance to their members. The confrontations reflected the strife between the Israelis and the Palestinians and it always seemed strange and rather unreal seeing them played out in South Africa with all its own immense political problems. In their day-to-day association on campus there was little overt antagonism, but when one of the associations recognised a sensitive day the other would frequently organise a counter-activity. Representatives of the Muslim and Jewish communities in Johannesburg were as concerned as we were about the clashes, and discussions were usually held with them in anticipation of these events, often at their request, to try to work out strategies for defusing any conflict. Interestingly, the student leadership of the two groups participated constructively in such talks and their personal relationships with each other were good, but they seemed to be able to do little to influence their members to avoid confrontation.

One such occasion was on 11 May 1988 when the MSA arranged a meeting on the occasion of Al Quds, and announced it as a 'Palestine Solidarity' gathering. In anticipation of problems we had discussions with Mr Rael Lissoos, Chairperson of SAUJS Wits, Rabbi S M Moffson, the Orthodox Jewish Chaplain on campus, Mr A Goldberg, Executive Director of the SA Jewish Board of Deputies, and leaders of the Muslim community in Johannesburg, Mr M S H Cachalia and Dr E Jassat. Lissoos was anxious to avoid confrontation, Mr Goldberg said representatives of the Zionist Federation would be sent to the campus in case of conflict, and Mr Cachalia and Dr Jassat undertook to be present themselves.[16]

About an hour before the MSA meeting was scheduled to start a large number of Jewish students gathered outside the Social Sciences Building adjacent to the library lawns. Someone was holding up an Israeli flag and there was a board with posters and a table from which pamphlets were being handed out. In accordance with the recommendation of the Browde Commission of Inquiry of 1985 that rival meetings and displays should not be allowed on sensitive days, the SAUJS group was told to remove their display.

When the MSA meeting ended their members formed a long procession out onto the piazza, bearing posters, chanting and singing. Within minutes the SAUJS group came up towards the piazza holding aloft an Israeli flag and singing and chanting in Hebrew and approached the MSA group. The University's peace-keeping group, community members, members of the SRC executive and members of the BSS stood between the opposing factions, and held hands to form a human chain separating them. However, there was so much pushing and jostling from both sides that the chain fragmented.

Slogans, chants and insults from one side led to a similar but louder response from the other. Attempts were made to speak to the leadership on both sides but this was made difficult because individual members continually involved themselves in these attempts at negotiation and numerous people were shouting at the same time. It was clear that the leaders did not have mandates to speak on behalf of their respective groups. For the first twenty to thirty minutes, the main concern was to prevent the opposing sides from attacking each other physically. Gradually, however, it became possible for us to start discussions with the leadership. It was obvious that the roles of Rabbi Moffson and Dr Jassat were extremely important and valuable. Both were held in high esteem by the respective constituencies and both were anxious to maintain peace and defuse the situation.

After what seemed like a long time it became possible to separate the two groups, metre by metre. One of the posters being held by the MSA students was provoking some of the SAUJS students, and the Israeli flag was provoking members of the MSA group. We tried to negotiate that if the offending poster was handed over to the administration, the flag would be taken down. Then we negotiated that if the MSA students withdrew and sat down, the SAUJS students would withdraw to the library lawns, provided that the Muslim students did not cheer or clap. After some to-ing and fro-ing, this happened. Ten minutes later, the SAUJS students dispersed from the lawns, and the MSA students dispersed from the piazza to attend a prayer service in the Muslim Prayer Room.

It seemed that the honour of both sides had been preserved, and there had been no injuries or damage to property.

Unfortunately that was not the end of incident. About fifteen minutes later there was a confrontation between Muslim students inside the Yale Road fence and a number of Jewish students together with a group of young men who, it was alleged, were not students but members of the 'Jewish Defence Organisation', on the other side of the fence. Insults were hurled across the fence and some Muslim students alleged that they had been attacked and that some women had had their faces slapped. I instructed Wits Security to remove the outsiders and threatened the use of the Wits dog patrol. They moved up Yale Road where they were seen talking to some people in a Toyota Corolla, and we noted the registration number of the car. Two others moved down Yale Road and were followed by University Security with the intention of noting the number of their car. When they saw that they were being followed, they jumped over a fence and were picked up by a car on the freeway.

The entire episode was most unedifying and it was distressing to see two groups of Wits students opposing each other in such an intensely antagonistic way. The matter of the outsiders was taken up with the Jewish Board of Deputies which deplored their intervention.

In a letter to me, Aleck Goldberg wrote that though the Board was not in a position to initiate any action against the persons concerned, 'should they belong to an organised Jewish group, the Board could contact the leadership to express its disapproval and strongly urge them to dissuade their members from engaging in similar activities in the future. If the persons concerned committed an offence then we believe the University should lay a charge against them with the police.'[17]

The University would have laid a charge had it been possible to identify any of the outsiders, but it was not. The Toyota Corolla was registered in the name of a person living at an address in Witbank, and a letter that I wrote to him there was returned unopened and marked 'unknown at this address'. Had the legitimate owner moved from his registered address or was this a false number plate being used in a covert operation by a dirty tricks brigade, taking the opportunity to foment dissension and conflict on the campus? The latter contingency could not be discounted.

ECC

There was a fair amount of overt support among white students on the Wits campus for the End Conscription Campaign (ECC) and probably a great deal more opposition to compulsory conscription from white students who were not prepared to take a public stand on the issue. Many young white men had left the country to avoid the call-up. The black student body in general was strongly opposed to the South African Defence Force (SADF) which was seen as the enemy propping up the apartheid regime and at war with the liberation movements.

The ECC had been established in 1983 by a Nusas group at the University of Cape Town after a campaign in 1982 against the extension of the period of military service to two full years followed by annual camps. Its purpose was to organise resistance among whites to the military and the Government.[18] The mission of the ECC was set out in a pamphlet, 'Stop the Call-up', issued in April 1986.[19]

> The SADF claims to be defending all South Africans. The End Conscription Campaign and a growing number of young people who object to service in the SADF

refute this claim – and so do millions of South Africans living in the townships. The fact is, the SADF is being used more and more to suppress opposition to apartheid, not only on the borders of the country, but in the townships and homes of ordinary South Africans. In anyone's language, this is civil war. And many patriotic young men are deciding that they cannot be part of this war. They are refusing to be conscripted to fight against unarmed citizens, their fellow South Africans. The numbers refusing to fight apartheid's war grow annually – so much so that the Minister of Defence, Magnus Malan, has refused to release the figures of those who have failed to report for duty.

ECC calls for an end to conscription because we feel that these young men should have the right to choose not to fight in a civil war on the side of apartheid. It is the right of all people to refuse to take up arms when their conscience dictates otherwise. The overwhelming majority of South Africans support us in our defence of this right.

A low-key picket demonstration organised by the ECC took place on Jan Smuts Avenue on 19 May 1988 in protest against the imprisonment of Dr Ivan Toms who had ignored a call-up, and the impending trial of David Bruce, a Wits student, who had made a public stand against conscription and had refused to report for military service.[20] Another picket by a small group on 30 May, protesting against conscription and a range of other apartheid measures, was harassed by the police. A police van moved slowly down Jan Smuts Avenue, its hazard lights flashing and stopped at each student to allow the policeman in the passenger seat to read over his radio the slogan on each poster. This was followed by another unmarked car which moved slowly down the row of picketers allowing the passenger, in plain clothes, to photograph each of them.[21] This was arrant intimidation.

The position of the ECC infuriated the Government and the SADF and there were numerous attempts to discredit the organisation. On 3 August 1988, following the conviction of David Bruce, who was sentenced by a magistrate to the maximum term of six years imprisonment, 143 young white men from all over the country, including many Wits students, called a press conference and announced their refusal to do military service. This blatant defiance of state authority made a substantial impact, particularly as the repressive measures imposed by the state of emergency and restrictions on the press had had a profound effect on the opportunities for protest.

Defence Minister General Magnus Malan was enraged, accused the ECC of threatening the security of the state, and was reported as saying that the movement was the 'vanguard of those forces that are intent on wrecking the present dispensation and its renewal'.[22] He accused the ECC of making a 'sick attempt to try to create a martyr image ... National security is the top priority for South Africa and is above political prejudice ... The SADF is representative of the full spectrum of South African society. Its members have divergent political, ethical, moral and religious convictions but they stand shoulder to shoulder in solid camaraderie in the service of South Africa.'

Of course this was fallacious. The SADF did not represent the full spectrum of South African society. Only white males were conscripted and conscripts were subjected to powerful propaganda which attempted to convince them that there was a total onslaught against the country and that to serve in the SADF was to serve the country. The blatant untruth of this contention was evident from February 1990 when De Klerk announced that the policy of apartheid was to be abandoned and that the country would move to a democratic dispensation. The so-called 'total onslaught' dissipated overnight.

Mr Alistair Teeling-Smith, National Secretary of the ECC, responded by saying that the SADF had become a political vehicle because of the role it had played in the townships and in neighbouring states. Many young South Africans faced a crisis of conscience over participation in the SADF. 'We certainly do not see ourselves as the vanguard of outside forces and certainly not controlled by those forces.'[23]

There was speculation at the time that the Government might take action against the ECC and this is indeed what happened on 22 August when Law and Order Minister Adriaan Vlok used regulation

7 of the emergency security regulations to prohibit the organisation from carrying out or performing any activity or act.[24] This was the same emergency regulation that had been used earlier in the year to restrict the seventeen organisations. The ministry released a statement saying that 'South Africa is the target of a multi-dimensional revolutionary onslaught ... The SADF is responsible for safeguarding the borders of our country against terrorists. As a result of the ECC's campaigns, many liable for national service are influenced to refuse to do military service.'

Anger at the restriction order was expressed by opposition political parties and extra-parliamentary organisations, as well as by the opposition-supporting press, although it was supported by pro-Government media.[25] Charlton issued a statement criticising the restriction.[26]

> Conscription affects the lives of thousands of young university students, and even under the severe restrictions of the emergency regulations, remains a perfectly legitimate subject for debate.
>
> Many fine young people who want nothing more than to devote their energies and knowledge to building a better South Africa, leave the country because they cannot in conscience accept conscription at this time in South Africa's history, particularly service in the townships. Our country cannot afford the continuing loss of so many of its brightest and best educated young minds. The shortage of skilled young people is already a serious problem for the professions, for commerce and industry and for the universities.
>
> The introduction of a community service alternative to military service surely deserves careful consideration. This was one of the proposals advocated by the End Conscription Campaign, whose members, a number of whom have served in the South African Defence Force, put their views in a reasoned, dispassionate and sincere way which deserves an equally reasoned response. Instead their activities have been prohibited. This is not a productive way of addressing the concerns of millions

of South Africans. I call on the Government to lift the restrictions on the End Conscription Campaign, and to renew its discussions with its representatives in an attempt to resolve a matter of such fundamental importance to the country.

A mass meeting of students was called for 25 August 1988 in the Great Hall. I was asked to speak, and gave some thought to the question of whether a member of the University's senior administration should take a public position on a matter which excited such varying emotional reactions among South Africans. I knew that what I was going to say would be unpopular with many white South Africans and that some members of our own University Council would not be happy about it. However, I had strong objections to the involvement of the SADF in Namibia and Angola as well as to some of their activities in the townships and I empathised with the conscripts who were coerced into these positions irrespective of their personal ideologies. Moreover it seemed to me important that the young people who were exposing themselves to the risks of state retribution for their views should have some support, albeit only moral. I agreed to speak, as did June Sinclair then Dean of Law, and addressed this question first.[27]

> Why is it appropriate for me as the Deputy Vice-Chancellor in charge of student affairs to comment on the prohibition which has been placed on the End Conscription Campaign? The answer is simple: it is appropriate because conscription affects the lives of thousands of young men who are registered as students at this University and, secondly, because the University which I serve believes in the rights of all its members freely to express their views on any matter, provided that they do not promote racism, sexism or violence. Despite the severe restrictions imposed upon all citizens of South Africa by the emergency regulations, it remains perfectly legal to oppose conscription and I support without reservation those South Africans who wish to do so.
>
> The members of the End Conscription Campaign whom I have met have been concerned, mostly young,

people who put their views in a reasoned, dispassionate and sincere way. Many of them have already served in the South African Defence Force: many of them still have to do so. The ECC's recently published booklet 'Know your rights in the SADF' makes it clear that they were campaigning for a change in the law regarding compulsory military service and were not campaigning against the conscript himself. Nor were they calling on conscripts to refuse to render military service. They wanted conscripts to be given a choice of whether or not to serve in the SADF and if they had to serve, that they should be given a choice of whether or not to serve in the townships or outside South Africa. They believed that all conscripts who object to serving in the SADF should be allowed to do community service.

It is well known that conscription has not always been a feature of military service in South Africa. During the Second World War there was no conscription in this country because the government of that time appreciated the division of opinion in the white population on the war issue. So State President PW Botha was not conscripted during the Second World War. He did have the opportunity, of course, to volunteer, but he did not, and I venture to say that his contribution was not very substantial. And what did his predecessor, John Vorster, do during the Second World War? He was not conscripted. Did he volunteer? No, he spent a number of war years in an internment camp at Koffiefontein for reasons which are well known. And Vorster's predecessor, Dr Verwoerd? He was the editor of the 'Transvaler' during that war, writing editorials which did nothing to support the efforts of the young men and women serving in the Union Defence Force, as the armed forces were known in those days.[28]

I say these things about Mr Botha, Mr Vorster and Dr Verwoerd, not because I want to heap contempt on their decision not to fight in the SADF. They were not conscripted. It was perfectly legal for them not to enlist.

They chose, in good faith, not to go to war against Hitler and the forces of Nazism and Fascism. I defend their right to have taken this decision, whether I admire it or not. I ask only for the same right for today's young men to make the same individual choice.

What really irks me is the fact that people with records such as these can take up high moral positions and tell us what constitutes a loyal South African. I do not believe that one demonstrates one's loyalty to South Africa by serving in the townships. And may I emphasise that I am not criticising those conscripts who are ordered to serve there. They have no choice. Nor does one have to demonstrate one's loyalty to South Africa by being forced to serve in Angola or Namibia. For the past ten years young South Africans have been fighting and dying in Namibia and Angola in order to postpone agreement on the implementation of Security Council Resolution 435, which the South African government agreed to in 1978. As we all know, negotiations are in progress now and a date of implementation has been set. Ten years of war for no purpose! Has this been in South Africa's best interests?

And now, because of the ECC's massive public protest after the imposition of a six-year sentence of imprisonment on David Bruce, there has been this totally unacceptable response from the government. Quite absurdly, the government has accused the ECC of being part of the 'revolutionary onslaught', and in an attempt to discredit it, has linked it to the South African Communist Party.

The restrictions placed on the End Conscription Campaign will not, however, change the views of those who believe with sincerity that they cannot in conscience serve in the South African Defence Force in order to implement the present government's policies. Many of the country's finest minds are leaving for other lands which will derive the benefit of their expertise. Some of them will accept the option, as did David Bruce, of a punitive term of imprisonment. These are people committed to South Africa and all its peoples and who want nothing more than to stay here and an opportunity to devote their energies and knowledge to building a new South Africa.

None of this can be of benefit to South Africa. This country is in a parlous state, with our economy in a major decline; millions of unhappy, desperately dissatisfied citizens; and a constitution in tatters while this floundering government's response to any positive contribution which does not accord with its own philosophy is handled with an iron fist and smear tactics.

The End Conscription Campaign has been disabled by the recent prohibition on its activities, but the right of individual South Africans to continue to campaign for the right to alternative service remains intact. I support and defend their right to do so.

The day after this speech was reported in the press my secretary received a call asking what I had done in the war. I suggested that if the caller were to call back she should tell him that I was fourteen years old when the war ended but that I had spent many hours after school, as most school children did during the war years, raising funds and going from door to door selling raffle tickets and collecting empty bottles and tins, used toothpaste tubes, old newspapers and the like for the war effort.

Conscription of white males persisted even beyond the repeal of apartheid legislation but over the years increasing numbers of men simply ignored the call-up and there were no further prosecutions. On 22 August 1989 the ECC called a press conference at Wits to announce that the organisation would no longer obey the restriction orders. Exceptionally brave statements were made by two Wits students, Roddy Payne and Lindsay Falkov, who knew that they could face severe penalties, as well as harassment, for their stand. At about 3am on the day of the meeting ten security police broke into Falkov's bedroom through a window and interrogated him about the ECC campaign. Payne and others were raided at about the same time.[29] I was asked by the organisers to say a few words, and spoke as follows:

My involvement with student affairs at this University over the past seven years has made me share the anguish felt by many young men when conscripted for military service. Their love for and loyalty to South Africa have never been in doubt. They have not, however, been able to accept the 'total onslaught' propaganda which has been used to justify military service in the townships, where conscripts may be expected to operate against fellow South Africans for whose political aspirations they have sympathy. Nor, during all the years of the Namibia-Angola conflict, did they feel able to commit themselves to operations in those countries with any conviction. And their views have now been vindicated. No longer, according to the South African government, is a war in those regions necessary for our survival. On the contrary, peace in that region is now essential, we are told, and in the meantime countless young men have lost their lives and who knows how many others have been wounded. How many citizens have perished or lost their homes in Angola and Namibia and in cross-border raids into neighbouring countries?

The hearts and minds of thinking young people will never be won unless they are convinced of the justice of the cause, which is why many young white men are opting for exile and some of the country's finest minds are leaving for other lands which will derive the benefit of their expertise. Still others are accepting the option of a punitive term of imprisonment.

None of this can benefit South Africa.

Until all South Africans have negotiated a new constitution, and the country can proudly take its place in the commonwealth of nations, young South Africans must be given the option of alternative community service so that they, in all conscience, can serve their country and all their fellow South Africans.

Afterwards, I was challenged by a reporter for the *Financial Mail* who commented on the fact that I, an establishment figure, was calling on youth to commit an act of defiance. In response I suggested simply that he should read my statement carefully, a copy of it was in his information package.

On 21 September 1989 a national register of conscientious objectors was launched and 771 men from all over the country declared publicly that they would not serve in the SADF.[30]

On 25 August 1993 it was announced that compulsory National Service for white South Africans would be replaced in 1994 by an all-race voluntary system. Mr Chris de Villiers, chairman of the ECC announced that once the organisation was certain that callups were really being phased out, it would almost certainly dissolve.[31]

The Detainees

In the meantime, meetings and demonstrations protesting against detentions without trial continued on campus while the Advisory Group on Detentions (AGD) continued its work for the Wits detainees. On 2 June 1988 a meeting in the Great Hall was addressed by, amongst others, Kathleen Satchwell, the attorney who was representing the Wits detainees; the mother of student Chris Ngcobo who had been in detention for two years without any charge having been brought against him; the Rev Francois Bill who had shared a cell with law lecturer Raymond Suttner who had also been in detention without trial for two years; and Debra Nails, one of the conveners of the AGD.

After the meeting a march and demonstration was broken up by the police, some of whom carried automatic weapons. Teargas and rubber bullets were fired at the students.[32] Charlton wrote a letter to Brigadier Schnetler, Divisional Commissioner of Police complaining about this action against a relatively small group of students who could not be regarded as any threat to public order. He expressed particular concern at reports that some of the police were carrying automatic weapons. 'A member of even a highly disciplined unit may open fire without orders if sufficiently provoked, and the consequences would be too horrible to contemplate.'[33] A follow-up letter from Charlton to Schnetler on 14 July led to a meeting between Charlton, myself and the Commissioner on 5 August at police headquarters.[34] In his letter suggesting some dates, Schnetler indicated that he looked forward to a 'constructive meeting during which we may eliminate any possible misunderstandings'.

It was clear from this meeting that Schnetler did not have the authority to decide whether or not to react to any particular student protest or what the nature of the police response should be. We were surprised that he spent some time telling us how much he was looking forward to his impending retirement. A professional police officer, he was disillusioned by the role he was called on to play. My distinct impression was that his orders came from Pretoria and the local Security Branch and that despite his high rank and responsible position his authority was limited.

Protest in Hospital Street

Though many changes had been made since the days when black medical students could not work in 'white' teaching hospitals, one area remained closed to them. By 1988, the Departments of Gynaecology and Obstetrics were still no-go areas. In response to this ban, most black and many white students had resolved not to rotate through the teaching hospitals of the University.

In August 1988, the Medical Students' Council (MSC) and the Black Students Committee (BSC) of the Faculty of Medicine approached the Dean of the Faculty, Professor Clive Rosendorff, with the request that on Friday 19 August students and staff of the faculty should march down Hospital Street, which runs through the entire length of the Johannesburg General, and deliver a petition to the superintendent of the hospital in which a resolution of the Board of the Faculty of Medicine of 10 June 1985 would be reiterated, namely that:

> The Board of the Faculty of Medicine reaffirms its rejection of ethnically segregated facilities in the delivery of health care and in the teaching of students in health professions. Further, this Board commits itself to strive for fully integrated teaching hospitals as a first step towards a fully integrated health service.

Rosendorff had the support of Charlton in holding a General Assembly of the faculty in the lobby of the Medical School building followed by the march down Hospital Street and the presentation of the petition. It was to be a silent march with students in white coats and staff in academic dress. The day before the demonstration was to be held, I received a phone call from Dr R Brockman, Chief Superintendent of the hospital, who told me that he would not allow the march to proceed and that, if necessary, he would get a court injunction preventing it. Although I assured him that the University would not allow the march to go ahead without his approval, Broekman, on instructions from his superiors in Pretoria, obtained the injunction which was served on the Dean and the Presidents of the MSC and the BSC later that day.

Before this happened, I had attended, at their invitation, a meeting with the Dean and Deputy Dean and representatives of the two student organisations. The students had agreed that if an injunction was obtained the march would not take place. Their alternative plan was to proceed with the General Assembly followed by a march through the Medical School grounds, onto the road and then to the Hospital entrance. On the morning of the meeting Brigadier Schnetler informed Charlton that the students would not be allowed to leave the Medical School grounds but that the police would not interfere with a march in the grounds. Another route was planned that would terminate with the presentation of the petition to Broekman within the boundary of the Medical School.

The General Assembly was addressed by the Dean and medical student leaders after which a dignified silent march took place led by the Dean, professors, the student leaders and myself. We were supported by a few members of the diplomatic corps who frequently showed their countries' solidarity with protests on the campus by their presence. A police contingent was present outside the gates which were kept closed. At about the time that the petition was being handed to Broekman, a message was received that someone had telephoned saying that there was a bomb in the Medical School building. This was searched by a member of the bomb squad with a sniffer dog accompanied by members of University security staff. No bomb was found, and staff and students slowly drifted back into the Medical School.

Raymond Suttner

In September 1988 Mr Raymond Suttner was released after spending two years in detention without trial. He was nevertheless still severely restricted as to where he could live; he was not allowed to be on the University campus; he could not be with more than two people at any time and he had to report to the police every morning and evening. These restrictions were obviously extremely onerous and depressing for Suttner after the prolonged period in detention. In particular, the fact that he would be effectively prevented from teaching and would have great problems finding somewhere to live that would be acceptable to the security police, would make it difficult for him to readjust.

In discussions with Professor June Sinclair we decided that she would try to arrange academic work that Suttner could do at home and that I would place him in one of the University's flats. It was necessary to meet Suttner in order to discuss his problems and possible solutions with him. We decided to meet for lunch at a small restaurant in Parktown North, about nine kilometres from the University, where we would be able to talk freely. Sinclair phoned him to make arrangements and we planned to meet outside the restaurant at 12.30 on 22 September.

The place was almost empty when we entered and were shown to our table for three immediately adjacent to the only occupied table. As we sat down we were astonished to observe that the occupants of other table were Brigadier G Erasmus, head of the Security Police on the Witwatersrand, his deputy Colonel Piet du Toit and four others whom I did not recognise. Clearly, the arrangements for the lunch had been overheard on a tapped line and the six were enjoying an excellent lunch at taxpayers' expense to see whether Suttner was breaching his restriction order.

We had our lunch and our discussions as if they were not there, but when we got up to leave we could not resist going over to their party and greeting them. I used the opportunity to tell Erasmus that I wanted to arrange accommodation for Suttner in a University flat and trusted that this would be acceptable to the Security Police. A somewhat embarrassed Erasmus undertook to send someone around as soon as possible to check on the premises. Apparently their requirement was that there should be no entrance or exit which could not be observed at all times by the police.

I phoned Erasmus on 28 September and he told me that he would send a man around immediately to inspect the flat. The flat was in a converted house and had an interior door. If that was sealed, he informed me after the inspection, the flat would be approved.[35] During the call Erasmus asked me what we were discussing with Suttner (as if he did not know) and I told him that we had talked about his accommodation problems and the work he could do for the Law Faculty without breaching his restriction orders. Erasmus also took the opportunity to inform me that a group known as the 'Wit Wolwe' (White Wolves), who had recently been responsible for a number of right wing acts of sabotage, had phoned the *Beeld* newspaper and told them that Wits was their next target and that they would attack meetings. He did not sound particularly put out about the matter, and did not indicate that the Security Police would assist the University in preventing any such act of terror. Perhaps he believed that the mere thought of such right wing terrorism would deter our students from holding any more meetings.

Nevertheless, we took precautions. The student leadership was informed and it was felt that the threats should remain strictly confidential to a small group in order to obviate alarm. After discussions with Wits security and student representatives, it was decided that with immediate effect, only staff and students who produced cards would be allowed to attend meetings; venues would be searched by security before the meetings, and bags and brief cases would be searched; Campus Health would be alerted whenever a meeting of a political nature was to be held; and that security would maintain their link with Civil Defence. Fortunately, the threat was never carried out.

Municipal Elections

Municipal elections for racially segregated local councils were due to be held on Wednesday 26 October 1988. Not only were these apartheid-based elections offensive to millions of South Africans, their scheduling during the state of emergency mitigated against a free election campaign and there was a ban on any call to boycott them. While it appeared that the majority of the black community would boycott the elections, the white community was expected to vote as usual.[36]

On the Wits campus, black students were solidly opposed to the elections, whereas white student opinion was split. Some refused to vote because it would give credibility to a 'dangerous and politically unacceptable system'; while others wished to record their vote against the National and Conservative Parties.[37]

During a long discussion with the executive committee of the BSS on 21 October they told me that they planned protest action on the following Tuesday and believed that it was incumbent on the University to provide support for the proposed demonstration.[38] They indicated that there would be a mass meeting at 11.30 in the Old Mutual Sports Hall and asked that the University be closed from 11.30 to 13.30 to enable students to attend. Immediately after the meeting there would be a march along a route within the campus and the administration was asked to lead it. The University was also asked to issue a statement objecting to the conditions under which the municipal elections were being conducted.

When the BSS's plans and requests were considered by an advisory panel called together by Charlton, it was agreed that the strong feelings they and other constituencies involved expressed were fully justified and that the state of emergency would undoubtedly prejudice the holding of free and fair elections. There was concern, however, that the timing of the proposed protest would be seen by the general public as an encouragement to boycott the elections and it was felt that the University should maintain its policy of being scrupulously careful not to involve itself in electioneering. Any protest should therefore remain a manifestation of student opinion. The effect of this was that although members of the University staff were free to take part in their personal capacities, the administration would not participate in their official roles.[39]

Charlton issued a statement[40] on the morning of the planned protests in which he pointed out that the University was a community of scholars embracing a wide range of political views and that the University fully supported both the rights of those who wished to vote and that of those who wished not to do so. On the morning of the meeting, we were informed that community organisations in

Soweto had been invited to attend. This was a contravention of the provisions of the 'Freedom of Speech' document because if we had known of this earlier, we would have invoked the paragraph which restricted attendance at political meetings on campus to staff, students and a limited number of guests. The logistic problems associated with having large numbers of representatives of non-University organisations at such meetings were immense and beyond the capacity of university security to control. Although arrangements had been made with the SRC and BSS to have student marshalls assisting security in ensuring that only people with cards or *bona fide* guests would be admitted, there was no control over admission.[41]

The meeting took place in the arcade of the Students Union. It was peaceful and was addressed by student leaders and prominent persons from the black community.[42] After the meeting a crowd of about five hundred people gathered outside the arcade. Numbers of them were schoolchildren in uniform. The march got going, and although the peace-keeping group persuaded it not to move off campus at the Yale Road gate, there was a violent confrontation with police at the Station Street exit. In response to a stone thrown at the police by someone from the back of the crowd, teargas was fired and, as the demonstrators ran back towards the campus, more stones were thrown. A flag with horizontal blue, white and red bands, not a South African flag, was set alight but was dropped in the rush and was extinguished by members of staff. After regrouping on the piazza the students marched to the steps on Jan Smuts Avenue where they were again met by the police. At this stage bricks and bottles were hurled at the police, again from the back of the crowd. The police then charged towards the demonstrators, firing teargas and rubber bullets.

The police chased one student into the nearby Oppenheimer Life Sciences Building and arrested him, thereby provoking another rallying issue for the students, some of whom called for a march back to the police to demand his release. When the demonstrators returned to Jan Smuts Avenue, more stones were hurled at the police, this time by individuals who had their faces covered and appeared to be swopping headgear and shirts to avoid being identified.

The demonstration eventually fizzled out and it was subsequently determined that eleven students had been treated in Campus Health

Picture courtesy Mayibuye Centre

A familiar sight in the 1980s and 1990s – toyi-toying students head across the piazza and up the steps of the Central Block en route to a meeting in the Senate House concourse

for injuries sustained during the afternoon. The arrested student was released later in the afternoon without being charged.

Charlton convened a meeting on 31 October of some administrative and academic staff together with SRC and BSS leaders to discuss the events of the 25th.[43] He wished to discuss the booking of the venue; problems that arose when student protest meetings were not restricted to staff and students; planning of routes for marches if staff were to participate; the burning of the flag; and the throwing of rocks and bottles.

The student leaders present were angry and their responses were indicative of the general mood of the majority of black students as well as the black community off-campus and the white students whose opinion the SRC represented. They indicated that they could not agree to the proposed agenda as it appeared to be accusatory in tone. As the administration had declined to participate in the march, they felt that there was no need to be accountable to it for the day's events. They would, however, reply to the Academic Staff Association in another forum. There had been no intention on the part of the organisers of the day's events to call on University constituencies to boycott the elections but they had wanted the University to make a declaration regarding the unfair and unfree nature of the elections as this was considered to be a distinctly apartheid issue. Although they recognised that the University took a clear stand against apartheid it was felt that more positive action was required than merely the issuing of a statement.

They pointed out that it was necessary for us to recognise that the members of the BSS perceived themselves first and foremost as members of their community rather than as Wits students and, as such, felt an obligation to invite members of community organisations to be present, especially as the University was one of the few places where peaceful protest could still take place. In this regard, student leaders would find it impossible to support a blanket ban on outsiders attending protest meetings.

The students rejected the view that the protest had been violent. Although stones and a bottle had been thrown, the protest had started with a peaceful meeting and it was only after the police had provoked the students by ordering them to disperse that the mood had changed. They pointed out that the mere presence of the police was sufficient incitement as they were considered to be symbols of oppression. It was necessary to understand that the march had been dictated by the mood of the marchers at the time and that there had not been a deliberate intention to go off campus or to mislead us over the route taken. It was not always possible for the student leadership to adopt an authoritarian control over marches and it was necessary that there be constant assessment of a number of factors once a march got going. They believed, however, that given the mood on the day and the militancy of the marchers, the leadership had maintained mature control.

Both the SRC and BSS supported a policy of peaceful protest but considered that the day's events should be viewed in a broader context and that it must be expected that violence would erupt from time to time. It was necessary for people to understand the root causes of such violence before condemning it. The SRC thought it important to hold in-depth discussions of all issues involved before future meetings in order to gauge the climate and context of situations so as to understand how meetings might be expected to develop. The University must understand that student militancy against apartheid had not diminished and the emotion generated by this issue must not be underestimated. Their organisations believed that it was time for all institutions to take a clear stand and to take an active part in measures to end apartheid.

Our response was sympathetic but firm. The right of all students to peaceful protest was recognised. The purpose of the meeting was to analyse what had happened during the demonstration and there was no intention that it should be a disciplinary hearing or that it should provoke confrontation between the students and the administration.

Although the administration did not participate in the march, this should not be interpreted as upholding the apartheid system. The question of participating in the municipal election had deeply divided the white community and the BSS and SRC should appreciate that we had to represent the interests of all communities within the University. We would have been placed in an untenable position if we had been perceived to have supported an election boycott. This did not mean that we were unsympathetic to the problems involved, but the University must primarily concern itself with academic matters.

While we understood the view of student leadership that there was a need to open facilities to members of the community who would otherwise be denied a vehicle for protest, it was important to have some prior knowledge of who would be attending so that the necessary arrangements could be made. This had been the first occasion in nearly two years on which stones had been thrown and it appeared that this might have some connection with the number of non-University people who had participated in the march.

We emphasised that the University could not countenance any acts of violence and that anyone who was positively identified as having taken part in such activities would be charged by a University disciplinary committee.

We accepted that there had been no deliberate intention to mislead the administration about the route of the march and it was appreciated how difficult it was to control and dictate actions to an emotive crowd. The student leadership was commended on its attempts to control the march and it was acknowledged that matters would have been far worse without this control. We did not consider it wrong that students should have marched off campus but felt that we should try to protect marchers in these circumstances. Our concern was to ensure that future protest meetings, which would be protected by the University, should be organised and conducted in a peaceful manner and maximum cooperation between student leaders and administration would be necessary to accomplish this. It was necessary that established procedures be followed in order that we be fully aware of possible problems which could arise so that plans could be made accordingly.

Once everyone who wanted to speak had been given the opportunity to do so, and more importantly to be listened to, much of the anger was defused. It is notable that this was the first occasion on which the student leadership had attempted to justify stone throwing, a factor which could be ascribed to the accumulated bitterness arising from the prolonged state of emergency.

Criminal Violence

The last political incident on campus during 1988 saw criminal violence from another source, this time directed against Nusas. The Nusas offices were located on the first floor of the D J du Plessis Building on the West Campus. During the early hours of Saturday 12 November, unknown persons gained entry to the building, smashed a hole in the door of one of the offices and stole the telephone answering machine and pages of a message book.[44] They then set fire to the room using a long fuse leading from the corridor to detonators and inflammable liquid. The office and its contents were badly damaged by the fire and by water from the automatic sprinkler system which extinguished the flames before they could spread.

The wall of the corridor outside the office and the walls outside the lecture theatre on the floor below, were daubed with crude graffiti. The lecture theatre was to have been the venue that evening of the fourth annual Desmond Tutu Lecture.

Later the same day, after Radio 702 had broadcast news of the fire, they received a call threatening a car bomb attack on the West

Campus. An extensive search was conducted but no bomb was found.

The police were called to investigate the incident, but no one was ever arrested, let alone prosecuted. Since the Government and the Security Police were the most ardent foes of Nusas, the Security Police must be the main suspects.

Meeting the ANC

One of the diplomats who regularly attended student demonstrations on the campus to demonstrate support and to provide some sort of 'protection' in the event of excessive reaction by the police, was M Gilbert Erouart, the Cultural Councillor of the French Embassy in South Africa. Erouart was a warm and sympathetic person and his presence on these occasions was very welcome. During the course of 1988 he asked whether I would accept an invitation from the French Foreign Ministry to go to France during the coming December. The object would be to visit some universities and talk to their presidents, student leaders, civil servants with responsibilities for tertiary education and spokespersons of different shades of political opinion in France. If I wished, they would also arrange for me to meet the ANC and the anti-apartheid movement.[45]

I was delighted to have this opportunity and was particularly glad to be able to make contact with the ANC. South Africans were still being flooded with anti-ANC propaganda and for most whites the organisation and its leadership were shrouded in mystery. Yet large numbers of our students were ANC supporters and, I believed, were in clandestine communication with the organisation and were probably getting secret instructions from it. Moreover more and more white opinion formers believed it was of the utmost importance to recognise that the ANC could not be excluded from discussions on the political future of the country and that the constitutional stalemate could only be resolved by drawing the ANC into political negotiations.

In pursuance of this objective and much to the rage of the Government, successive delegations representing business, non-governmental organisations, the press, the churches, opposition politicians, the trade unions, the universities, student organisations, the legal profession and others had, since 1985, been meeting with representatives of the ANC in Lusaka, Harare, London and elsewhere.[46] I wanted to speak to ANC representatives about the requirements of increasing numbers of black students coming into the universities and their dire need for financial aid. My hope was that the ANC might assist us in raising funds for this purpose from foreign governments and non-governmental organisations. This visit was to be another opportunity.

I had in fact already had an opportunity to speak to ANC representatives on 29 August 1986 while I was in London on the way to a meeting of the International Association of Oral Pathologists in Edinburgh. It seems absurd in retrospect to recall how nervous I was at that time about making this contact; such was the fear that had been instilled in ordinary South African citizens about involving themselves in such ordinary peaceful activities as discussions about the needs of university students. My meeting was with Mrs Frene Ginwala, now Speaker of the National Assembly, then responsible for educational matters in the London office of the ANC. She was accompanied by Dr Francis Meli, editor of the ANC publication *Sechaba*, who was also on the education desk. There I was having a clandestine meeting with two of the country's 'mortal enemies'.

Meli was rather quiet but Mrs Ginwala was forthright, absolutely charming and very interested in hearing about the tertiary education scene 'back home'. Meli had earned his doctorate at a university in East Germany and it struck me as weird that two compatriots should, through political circumstances, have received their higher education in two such different cultural environments from my own. They were not as impressed as I had hoped they would be with the increasing numbers of black students at Wits and indicated clearly and courteously what they believed still had to be done to transform the institution into a truly South African one. In particular they emphasised issues such as curricular changes, more democratic governance, many more black staff in academic and senior management, and student numbers that more accurately reflected the demography of the country.

Interestingly, on the occasion of his installation as Vice-Chancellor on 8 June, Charlton had addressed some of these issues when he made a commitment that the University would respond to the needs of all the people of South Africa and that he would consult widely in addressing these problems. 'It is vital that that consultation does not neglect sections of the community who are not represented on the decision-making bodies of the University ... Such consultation is, of course, no substitute for adequate representation on University bodies. It is particularly to be deplored that there are so few blacks occupying senior positions in the University, and none on the University Council, whatever the historical or sociological reasons for that deficiency may be. I pledge myself and my administration to work to correct this imbalance.'[47] Charlton kept this pledge and initiated discussions that led to the amendment of the University's Private Act and enabled the appointment to Council of credible representatives of the black communities served by the University.

On 1 December 1988 I was taken to the ANC offices in Paris where I met ANC representative Solly Smith and Breyten Breytenbach, the exiled writer and artist. As we walked through the courtyard I saw the gendarmes who had been brought in as guards since ANC stalwart Dulcie September had been assassinated there by South African agents. They hardly gave me a glance. Smith and Breytenbach were supportive of attempts to raise bursary money and Smith gave me the names and telephone numbers of organisations and people who might be helpful. They also gave me the numbers of ANC contacts in Brussels, Stockholm, Denmark and London.

We spent some time talking about the academic boycott and I pointed out that we thought it very important that post-apartheid South Africa must not inherit universities that were academically destitute. Smith's response was that the ANC in Paris did not have much to do with the academic boycott since there was little academic exchange between France and South Africa, and that it was the people inside South Africa who should make these decisions. They suggested that Wits second someone to teach at the Solomon Mahlangu College in Tanzania, about 100 km inland from Dar-es-Salaam, which was an educational centre for the children of ANC exiles, and asked whether we could assist them with distance education courses.[48]

I took up the question of the widespread detention without trial of students with M Larivaille, President of the University of Paris X, Paris-Nanterre. The University was strong on human rights and had recently established an organisation, *La Maison des Droites de l'Homme*, jointly with the League of Human Rights. Larivaille indicated that they would raise the matter at the next meeting of the Commission of University Presidents and propose that a letter be written and signed by all the presidents and directed to F W de Klerk as Minister of National Education urging him to use his influence to secure the release of detained university students. The letter was subsequently delivered to the SA Embassy in Paris.

My meeting and lunch with M Bouillon, President of the French anti-apartheid movement and M Michel Mallet, a member, was informative. It was not a large structure like its sister organisation in Britain, but by means of meetings, newsletter and a bi-monthly newspaper it tried to maintain an awareness in France about apartheid, and cooperated closely with students, workers and churches in organising national campaigns, often about disinvestment. Members also campaigned vigorously for the release of detainees and convicted political prisoners and had a solidarity campaign with victims of apartheid. I was particularly anxious to gauge their views on the academic boycott. Their view was that although they could not support official ties with any of the universities their policy with regard to individuals was flexible and any academic who was supported by the democratic movement would be supported by them. Nevertheless, their ability to monitor the coming and going of individual academics was limited.

The French Government was prepared to provide direct funding for black students at Wits and similar support was later also given by the Finnish government. The Commission of European Communities office in Brussels received our application with sympathy but Dr Wim Blonk, who was responsible for financial aid programmes sponsored by the EC, explained that it was their policy not to support institutions individually. Their financial aid for black students was channelled through the Kagiso Trust. They were anxious to provide support for people in detention and also wished to finance a programme for Namibian students to be trained at Wits.

There was considerable sympathy for the plight of black students both from the Foreign Ministry and from the Swedish aid organisation SIDA, but they did not want to fund projects that would relieve the South African Government of its educational obligations and enable it to channel money elsewhere. They had discussed this dilemma with the ANC who suggested that these funds be sent through NGOs that were part of the democratic movement, such as the Kagiso Trust. They were concerned about impending legislation in South Africa to control foreign funding, a matter that was raised again in Copenhagen.

In Stockholm I also had an interesting discussion with Mrs Ulla Ström of the political department of the Foreign Ministry. She was responsible for matters relating to Southern Africa, Swapo and the ANC. She confirmed the policy on funding projects in South Africa but regarded the question of financial aid to black South African students as a humanitarian one and felt that if the funds could be channelled through an NGO this would not conflict. Aspects of the academic boycott worried her. The Swedish government had directed that there should be no scientific or academic contact between Swedish and South African universities, and there was an instruction that government officials must not take part in conferences if South Africans were present or attend conferences abroad if there were South African participants. Her dilemma was that even ANC members were running into problems with boycotts. There was also the humanitarian problem of excluding South African scientists from meetings where findings of major medical developments might be reported. It might then be the very people whom the boycott was intended to assist who would be deprived of these benefits. She therefore believed that there was a need for flexibility. She was also anxious to provide support for students in detention.

I encountered a similar conflict of well-intentioned principles in the course of a discussion at a lunch with Mr Kiljunen who was chairperson of the Finnish organisation 'Isolate South Africa'. The organisation aimed both at trying to persuade white South Africans not to pursue apartheid policies and to influence public opinion and foreign policy in Finland. Although they preferred to maintain contacts they believed that trade, sport and academic isolation were the only tools available to the international community to sway white South African opinion. He was impressed by the admissions policies of the open universities and although he was dubious about the academic boycott because he saw the value of contacts, he was convinced that all contacts with South Africa should be broken. Nevertheless there was considerable support for the proposal for financial aid for black students at a meeting in the Finnish Foreign Ministry with Mr Kimmo Pulkkinen, director of the division for humanitarian assistance of FINNIDA, Mr Frank Egman of the political division and Ms Eija Silvola also of the division for humanitarian assistance.

Mr Knut Vollebaek in the Norwegian Foreign Ministry told me that they would like to support efforts to provide funding for black tertiary education but Norway did not send any funds directly to South Africa. They did however do so through churches – especially the Church of Norway, trade unions, and other smaller organisations. He arranged for me to see someone in the Council on Foreign Relations of the Church of Norway. She was also helpful but wanted to consult the anti-apartheid group in the University of Oslo and also anti-apartheid groups in South Africa. It was also important to them that any students assisted by them have some contact with students in Oslo.

There were similar responses in Denmark. Again I was received most cordially and was told by Mr Birger Nielsen of Danida, the foreign aid arm of the Foreign Ministry, that assistance to South Africa would be channelled through other organisations such as the churches and the World University Services (WUS) which received substantial grants each year. But another problem was highlighted during this meeting that had also been raised in Stockholm. This was the concern in the Foreign Ministry about the South African Government's 'Disclosure of Foreign Funding' Bill, in terms of which Wits would become a 'reporting organisation' and it was unclear to them what the implications would be. It was not clear to me either although we had heard of the proposed legislation and realised that it was yet another attempt to intimidate democratic movements which were receiving increasing amounts of financial support from abroad, including legal aid intended for the support of detainees and political prisoners.

A few days later Mr M Bendtsen of WUS in Copenhagen told me that the organisation had been encouraged by the reaction in some of the South African universities to the apartheid government. They did support a small number of independent projects in some universities, but through indirect sources. They regarded our academic support programmes for educationally disadvantaged students as important and suggested that these be given high priority in any proposals for financial assistance.

A clear message was coming through. Much as they might want to provide financial aid for disadvantaged students at open universities, only Finland was able to commit direct aid to the universities. It was also important for them to have the approval of the anti-apartheid movements in their own countries and of the Mass Democratic Movement in South Africa before identifying a project for support. Before leaving South Africa I had had numerous discussions with leaders of the BSS and prominent figures in the UDF and I carried with me letters of support from them for fund-raising efforts towards financial aid for black students. These letters proved to be immensely useful in my European discussions.

While in Copenhagen I had some other interesting meetings. My frustration with the enormity of human rights violations in South Africa made me hungry to be in contact with some human rights organisations, and Denmark, which I had often thought of as the mother of human rights, seemed to be the place to seek this connection. I met Mr Lars Adam Rehoff, the Director of the Danish Centre of Human Rights who was very interested in the work of Wits's Centre for Applied Legal Studies (Cals).[49] On my return I arranged contact between Rehoff and Professor John Dugard, the Director of Cals, and Rehoff visited them and other institutions in South Africa during 1990. He was enthusiastic about obtaining financial aid from Danida for black South African students and helped me to draw up a proposal. Rehof told me that there were varying views in Denmark on the academic boycott but the intensity of feeling against apartheid and the South African Government was such that not even right-wingers in Denmark would dare to speak against it.

Another rewarding meeting was with the Rector Magnificus of the University of Copenhagen, Professor Ove Nathan. He was previously a professor of nuclear physics, played a leading role in the release of Andrei Sakhorov from the Soviet Union and was prominent in human rights issues in Europe. He was concerned to hear about the detentions and asked me to send him a letter about this which he and his colleagues would sign and send to De Klerk. I was amused to hear him say that he would act without bringing the matter up at a formal meeting because 'there was always someone who wanted to add something else'. When I got back I followed this up and Nathan had acted as he had promised. A translation of his letter appeared in a Danish newspaper. This sort of international support was invaluable in backing up the pressure that was being applied within the country.

I had been given the telephone number of the ANC representative in Copenhagen, Mr Aaron Mnisi, and I phoned him to see if I could arrange a meeting. He was understandably very suspicious of an unknown white South African but I gave him some references, including that of Birger Nielsen in the Foreign Ministry and asked him to call me back if he was satisfied. He phoned about two hours later and we arranged an appointment in the ANC offices at 3pm. I was there on time and found the office locked. Although I waited in the corridor for over half an hour, nobody arrived. There was clearly considerable fear of assassination among ANC representatives since the Dulcie September murder in Paris.

In London I had much more success. I renewed my acquaintance with Frene Ginwala and Frances Meli and they were accompanied by Dr Essop Pahad and Mr Harold Wolpe. My appointment with them was in the ANC offices and I was revisited with paranoia as I walked up the few steps to the door and wondered whether members of the South African Security Police were observing and filming from behind a curtained window on the other side of the road. After a friendly welcome I was told that there was no office available for a meeting and we walked to a café around the corner and sat at a bare table sipping tea and discussing the future of Wits.

I started by giving them a resumé of the position of black students: our selection policy, the committee that was trying to develop tests that would identify educationally disadvantaged students with potential to succeed, our academic support programme, the need of black students for financial aid, our support for black students in detention, our support of our students' right to express themselves freely on campus other than on racism, sexism and violence, our support of the community in providing facilities for meetings, and of some of the academic-related activities such as the Cals, the Centre for Continuing Education and the Education Policy Unit.

Their views were a let-down for me and they put them very clearly. They were not impressed with the 20 per cent black student enrolment which they considered far too low. They were insistent that the curriculum should be 'more relevant' to the needs of South African society and they were concerned about the involvement of some Wits academics with defence research. There was considerable antagonism towards the Council for Scientific and Industrial Research because they were anxious about the uses to which the results of the research were put.

They wanted to know whether there were programmes to get white students to understand the fundamental changes necessary in South Africa and whether we had courses in women's studies. Although they approved of the positive steps that Wits had taken, they felt the University had not identified itself sufficiently as had the universities of Natal and the Western Cape with the anti-apartheid struggle. I wonder whether our decision earlier in the year not to take De Klerk to court on the subsidy issue had influenced this perception. These issues informed their position on the academic boycott which was that no one might visit South Africa for academic purposes. If an institution identified with the struggle to eliminate apartheid, it should consult with the democratic movements in South Africa and at a properly-constituted meeting with an agreed agenda, the ANC could make its views known.

They were very anxious that we should have a meeting in Lusaka with the ANC leadership but believed that the initiative for the meeting should come from us. They would arrange for the University of Zambia to issue an invitation. The delegation, they emphasised, must include students and trade union representatives and at such a meeting it would be possible to discuss the academic boycott.

The ANC's stand on the academic boycott was reinforced at a meeting a few days later with Drs Peter Borcherds, Bill Stevenson and Martin Hughes of the Association of University Teachers (AUT). Although the official policy of the AUT was strongly in favour of the academic boycott, Borcherds, who was dovish on the issue, believed that the majority of members did not support it. They had reservations and suspicions about South Africa but they depended for their information mainly on what was reported and most of them knew very little about developments in the liberal universities. Generally though, they felt that if the open universities were to organise a joint meeting with the ANC in Lusaka, AUT members would see this as a sign of goodwill. They seemed to be under the impression that the open universities regarded the ANC as an adversary whereas this was far from being the case.

I found all these meetings immensely informative and rewarding and was gratified that I had been able to break the ice in making contact with the ANC. The black student leaders were clearly delighted when I told them about the contacts and this was helpful in breaking down yet another barrier between them and the University administration. Unfortunately I could not evoke much support for the proposal that we take a delegation to Lusaka.

It came as a considerable surprise when I learnt, not so long ago, that two of the ANC representatives I had met, Solly Smith in Paris and Francis Meli in London, had been exposed as spies for the Security Police. Details of their involvement had emerged in 1991 and 1992 after both of them died suddenly.[50]

The opportunity for a visit to Lusaka materialised when I was invited to join a large group of white South Africans at a conference organised by the Five Freedoms Forum from 29 June to 2 July 1989. It was an extraordinary experience.[51] We were received warmly, and mixed and talked freely to the ANC representatives during the sessions and in the course of many breaks for meals and at functions arranged by President Kenneth Kaunda and the diplomatic corps in Lusaka.

For many of us this meeting demystified the ANC as we met and spoke to people whom the Government propaganda machine had for so long demonised and vilified as mortal enemies of the country but who were regarded as heroes by black South Africans and whose names we had heard sung in praise during many student demonstrations. ANC President Mr Oliver Tambo led the ANC delegation and I also met Thabo Mbeki, Joe Slovo, Ronnie Kasrils, Reg September, Steve Tshwete, Pallo Jordan, Barbara Masekela, Jeremy Cronin, Max Sisulu, Ray Simons, Wally Serote, Derek Hanekom and Hein Grosskopf. In their presentations, in their contributions to discussion sessions, in informal conversation, they came across as so reasonable and so pleasant that it reoriented everyone's attitudes. There was much discussion on the possibility of negotiations and on cessation of the armed struggle, and during the leisure periods, in a spirit of camaraderie, with arms around each others' shoulders, we talked about how it would be when they returned to a post-apartheid South Africa. Few of us in Lusaka for those four days could have believed it remotely possible that only seven months later, De Klerk would make his dramatic speech in Parliament unbanning the ANC and that these compatriots would return home to negotiations, and not so long after that, into government.

BSS Restricted

In a further clamp-down on black student political activity, the BSS was restricted towards the end of 1988. A similar restriction had incapacitated black student activity at Rhodes University. Representatives from Wits and Rhodes had a meeting with Law and Order Minister Vlok on 31 January 1989 at which the Commissioner of Police and the head of the Security Police were present.[52] At the meeting Vlok enunciated the three main reasons for restricting organisations. These were that the safety of the public was being threatened; that the maintenance of law and order was placed in jeopardy; and that the activities of those organisations being restricted were contributing to the extension of the state of emergency. According to his information, the two black student organisations posed such threats. Vlok said the BSS could appeal against the restrictions and would be given a proper hearing, and he was also prepared to receive representations from the BSS for *bona fide* university activities to continue.

He gave permission for the organisation to hold a meeting to discuss his offer. Not surprisingly, the BSS rejected the Minister's offer because they did not accept his definition of a *bona fide* student society. They wished to continue to debate political issues.[53] They formed the Black Students' Interim Committee (BSIC) which was mandated to try to have the ban on the BSS lifted unconditionally. New office bearers were elected to the BSIC so, in theory, the leadership of the BSS no longer held office.

The types of activities regarded by the police as endangering the internal security of the state continued to defy belief. In January 1989, political detainees in Diepkloof, some of whom had been in prison for two-and-a-half years, had embarked on a hunger strike. The strike soon spread to other parts of the country. By 23 February, negotiations had taken place with Vlok on behalf of detainees in the

Transvaal, Western Cape and Port Elizabeth areas, and these detainees had suspended their strike until 2 March and were awaiting release. Nevertheless, over 200 detainees remained on hunger strike in Natal and the East London areas. Five Wits students were among those taking part in the hunger strike. The national executive committee of Nusas had held an eight-day solidarity fast. A meeting was planned at Wits on 23 February to be addressed by Lindsay Falkov, President of Nusas, Bettina von Lieres, President of the SRC and Dr Ivan Toms, a conscientious objector.[54] On that day a statement endorsing the demand that all detainees be released or charged and calling for the abolition of detention without trial, would be signed by a large number of student and staff groups on the Wits campus.[55]

Two weeks before the scheduled meeting an order under the Security Emergency Regulations had been published in the *Government Gazette* prohibiting gatherings organised or advertised 'as a protest gathering against the detention of persons in terms of the provisions of the Security Emergency Regulations, 1988; or as a gathering in solidarity with persons detained in terms of the Security Emergency Regulations, 1988'.[56]

About twenty minutes before the lunch-hour meeting was scheduled to start, Charlton received a telephone call from a Major Venter who told him that the police had obtained an order in terms of the Criminal Procedures Act from the Chief Magistrate of Johannesburg and that uniformed police would be entering the Great Hall. In the words of the order, which was issued in Afrikaans, the reasons for preventing the meeting were that: '... on the grounds of information provided under oath, it appears that a "keynote address" dealing with the hunger-strike of detainees and detention without trial is likely to be held on the premises of the University of the Witwatersrand, Johannesburg at 1pm on Thursday, 23 February 1989. And ... there is reason to believe that the internal security of the Republic or the preservation of law and order will be in danger as a result of the said meeting ... or that during the meeting an offence will apparently be committed or that preparations or arrangements will be made for the commission of an offence ...'[57]

Once again, one or more of the numerous police informers on campus who had access to information about the meeting had, apparently 'under oath', embroidered a report to give the Security Police ammunition to prohibit an expression of political opinion opposed to that of the state authorities. It was to lead to an outrageous intrusion of police into the Great Hall at the start of the meeting.

Charlton urged Venter not to send police onto campus saying this was not only unnecessary but likely to provoke disturbances which would not otherwise occur. He also contacted the head of the Security Police at John Vorster Square with the same request.

By the time the meeting started the Great Hall was only half full. As I was anxious about the information that the police would enter the hall, I kept in touch with the acting head of campus security who was in contact, by radio, with his staff throughout the campus. At about the time the meeting was scheduled to start, he told me that police had entered the campus and, a minute or two later, that they were moving toward the Great Hall from the library lawns. There was also a large force of police at the periphery of the campus. I immediately went to the piazza where I intercepted the advancing squad of police. I tried to speak to Colonel van der Walt who was in charge of the squad. He would not stop but when I asked him the purpose of the incursion, he thrust at me without comment the order signed by the Chief Magistrate.

Without giving me an opportunity to read it, he and the squad moved rapidly onwards. When I asked what he intended to do, he said that the meeting could not proceed. I told him that I thought his action extremely irresponsible and that he would be held personally responsible for any injury caused to anyone in the hall. I said that I would like an opportunity to address the meeting and ask the audience to disperse. My great anxiety was that the police might fire tear gas in the Great Hall in order to force the assembly to disperse and that there could be serious injuries in the ensuing panic. He then changed his attitude and said that he would give me time to do this.

By the time I reached the doors of the Great Hall, the police were already moving in, and they lined up at the back of the hall in a menacing manner. They were in riot gear and their arms were drawn. Moving to the front of the hall, I ascended the stage and asked the chairperson whether I might take the microphone. I told the meeting that I was very sorry to have to announce that there were riot police in the hall and that I had been handed a magistrate's order prohibiting the meeting. I called on the assembly to stand up and slowly file out of the hall. To my relief, there was an immediate response, and the students and staff left the hall very quietly and with no panic.

Out in the foyer, Van der Walt approached me and said that if I would give him my word that the students would not come back into the hall, the police would leave. I said that I could not promise that, but I would give him an undertaking that I would try to persuade them not to do so. He said that in that case he would remain. The foyer at that stage was packed with people who were gradually moving out towards the piazza. Van der Walt said he would not allow a gathering anywhere in the University and people must leave the front of the Central Block. The Vice-President of the SRC asked me whether I would address the students on the piazza, who were very restive. I told Van der Walt that I would call on the students to disperse but that I was going to be very critical of the police action. He told me to go ahead.

Speaking from the top of the steps of the Central Block, I told the crowd in the piazza that the University took the strongest exception to the police incursion onto our campus, and would make the strongest representations to the authorities about it. I told them that the police were still on campus (at this stage they were not visible, having remained in the foyer) and asked them to disperse in order to avoid anyone being hurt. Many students were angry at being asked to disperse from the piazza, calling out that this was where they normally spent their lunch-hour, which was, of course, quite true. While some did peel off from the crowd, substantial numbers of others remained behind and some of them started to sing 'Nkosi Sikelel' iAfrika'.

This appeared to incense Van der Walt who accused me of not keeping my word and objected to the fact that 'the people were singing freedom songs and giving the black power salute'. At this the police squad materialised, arms at the ready, and moved down the steps onto the piazza. The crowd then ran away, chased by the police, who, a few minutes later regrouped and moved away off campus.

Charlton issued a statement to all staff and students on the same day informing them what had happened and condemning it.[58]

> I regard this episode as outrageous and wish to register the strongest possible protest at this intrusion into the campus and the interruption, by a strong show of force, of a peaceful meeting. Under no circumstances could the police justify their view that there were reasonable grounds to think that the internal safety of the Republic or the maintenance of law and order were endangered by this meeting. If there was any reason for believing that a crime would be committed during this meeting, then this information should have been conveyed to me, with the evidence therefor.
>
> This action was either precipitated by demonstrably inaccurate information, or else was an attempt to intimidate the student body and to dissuade them from exercising their democratic right to express themselves on fundamental principles such as detention without trial.
>
> The Minister of National Education has in the past criticised the University for not allowing freedom of speech on campus. It is ironic that the police, controlled by the government which he represents, should today have acted by force to prevent the freedom of expression as well as of assembly on this campus.
>
> I call on the Minister of Law and Order to direct the police not to act in a similar manner again.

Charlton expressed the same objections in a letter to Law and Order Minister Vlok on the same day, and a special meeting of the University Council was called for 2 March in order to discuss the matter. Council expressed deep distress at the police action and was particularly concerned at the possibility that teargas might have been released in the hall with subsequent injury to students. Chairman of Council, SAG Anderson wrote to Vlok expressing Council's objections to the police action and asking him to receive a delegation.[59]

Council was concerned that the police had acted on the basis of information which was grossly at variance with the information we had, and had made no attempt to verify the information. The view that the police information was misleading was reinforced by the presence of a strong police contingent on the periphery of the campus the following day. On enquiry the University was told that they were there because 'a meeting of certain students was being held'. That meeting was to discuss failures in the recent examinations and the consequential exclusion of a number of students from the University and it was absurd that the police should have considered it necessary to be on the alert.

There were also statements of outrage from the Senate Academic Freedom Committee and the Academic Staff Association. The response of the press, which had had a great deal to write about infringements of freedom of speech on the campus, was appallingly inadequate. Unlike the students, who had been extraordinarily courageous in their condemnation of human rights infringements, much of the press had been cowed by the restrictions imposed during the states of emergency. Nevertheless *The Star* published a letter from Lorraine Chaskalson on behalf of the executive committee of the Academic Staff Association.[60]

> ... The meeting was an entirely peaceful gathering designed to provide information and discussions on detentions. There were no signs of disruption at all. The meeting was consonant with the best traditions of intellectual inquiry and social responsibility. University members came together on campus to discuss an issue of importance, and all too closely affecting some of them. It is an issue which concerns all South Africans living, with limited access to the rule of law, in a state of emergency.
>
> The entire university community has condemned this action. It is undemocratic, unnecessary and consistent only with the desire to intimidate. It was also precipitate and ill-considered and could easily have led to disturbances on campus.
>
> We deplore all invasions of the university's autonomy and wish to express our outrage at such arbitrary and provocative measures. We call on the Minister of Law and Order to keep the police off our campus and let us pursue, without hindrance, the business of educating future leaders of South Africa.

Surprisingly, because the police seldom felt it necessary during the state of emergency to be accountable to the public, there was a response from a police spokesman in Pretoria.

> The meeting in question was prohibited in terms of section 25 of the Criminal Procedure Act. Those people who intended attending the meeting on February 23 were warned accordingly. The people then present left the hall and gathered outside. They were again informed that the meeting was prohibited. No police action was taken.
>
> While those concerned are entitled to their views on the matter, we deny that the police acted with the desire to intimidate.

In a further act of intimidation, Bettina von Lieres had an order served on her by a detective warrant officer in which she was informed that she was suspected of having committed a crime in terms of 'regulation 10 of the Emergency Act read with GC No 11705 dated 1989-02-10. Gathering at Wits University on 89-02-23 in solidarity with hunger strikers in detention'. Von Lieres was ably represented by Kathleen Satchwell and no prosecution was brought.

The students were not convinced that a delegation to see Vlok was an adequate response and called for a General Assembly to make a public protest. They rather unfairly indicated that they considered the administration's response to have been inadequate. Charlton pointed out the vigorous responses of the University and claimed that these had achieved some success.[61]

Anderson and Charlton saw Vlok on 4 April 1989. They did not achieve very much. Vlok was accompanied by the Commissioner of Police, the head of the Security Police and a third police general who agreed that there had been an over-reaction on the part of the police and indicated that the police commander of the area was new or a locum. They gave an undertaking that this would not happen again.[62] They must have been referring specifically to the police invasion of the Great Hall, because there had been another confrontation with students on 21 March, Sharpeville Day, and further incursions occurred subsequent to the meeting with Anderson and Charlton.

On Sharpeville Day, five students, including Von Lieres were injured, and large numbers of students and staff were tear-gassed during a commemoration meeting on campus.[63] Von Lieres was hit on her shoulder by a teargas canister and was overcome by teargas as she lay injured. She required treatment in the Campus Health Clinic. The police claimed that the tear gas and rubber bullets were fired in response to two stone throwing episodes but they also reacted to students who were chanting 'ANC' and other slogans, carrying banners and an ANC flag. In response to questions from the press, Charlton said that action would not be taken against people carrying what looked like ANC flags as they were not contravening any University disciplinary code by doing so.[64]

There were indeed episodes of stone throwing during this demonstration, and while I was moving across to stop a person whom I saw about to throw a missile, a student intercepted me and gave me a hard shove, throwing me off balance. I was very angry and demanded his student card. Before we were able to note his name and student number he started to shout at me, demanding the return of his card and calling on the other demonstrators to assist him in getting it back. He was whipping up the mood of the crowd and there was an ugly atmosphere for a while, but I refused to return the card; nor was I prepared to move away from the scene, as advised by our security, until the tension had subsided and while student leaders were addressing the crowd.

At a meeting with SRC and BSIC leaders two days later, the students were not prepared to condemn stone throwing despite evidence emanating from the University of Cape. Town that an *agent provocateur* had been inciting students to throw stones. Although we were again unable to identify any of the stone throwers, the student who had shoved and abused me was brought before a University disciplinary hearing and was sent down for the remainder of the year. Although I was called to give evidence at the disciplinary hearing I played no part in the decision to prosecute him, nor in any of the subsequent proceedings. While expressing their personal regret that I had been shoved around, the student leaders brought a lot of pressure to bear on the University, firstly that he should not be prosecuted and later that he should not be sent down. The following year the student in question was blown up by a bomb that he was carrying.

In the course of the Five Freedoms Forum conference with the African National Congress in Lusaka I was surprised to find that the ANC knew of the incident. I was told by Ronnie Kasrils that the ANC did not support campus violence and was opposed to stone throwing as it discredited the democratic movement as well as the universities, and brought the police onto campuses. They preferred a more constructive form of peaceful protest.[65]

Assassination

On 1 May 1989, David Webster, a senior lecturer in the Department of Social Anthropology was murdered in front of his home by assassins who fired a shotgun from a passing car. Webster had played a leading role in the establishment of the Five Freedoms Forum, the Detainees' Parents Support Committee (DPSC) and the Detainees' Support Committee (Descom); and he had assisted in setting up the Human Rights Commission when the DPSC was banned in 1988. He had written a report on political assassinations shortly before his murder. His death was a tragic loss to the University and the country. He was greatly respected by many of his colleagues and by students throughout the institution, and the University community turned out in large numbers to pay tribute to him in a memorial service on the Library Lawns on 10 May 1989. A new student residence on the West Campus was named the David Webster Hall in his honour in 1992.

No arrests resulted from police investigations into his death. The University offered a reward for information leading to a conviction and the Academic Staff Association invited contributions to a fund for the same purpose. They also opened a telephone line where people might call and offer information anonymously. Dr Debra Nails, an office-bearer of the Association, monitored this line and received numerous anonymous death threats, but no useful information. The Harms Commission of Inquiry into 'murder and acts of violence allegedly committed with political motives' identified the existence of a covert branch of the South African Defence Force known as the Civil Cooperation Bureau (CCB). Evidence presented to the Commission, and a later inquest into Webster's death, suggested that he had been spied on and murdered because of his political activities.

Although suspicion was cast on the role in the murder of certain individuals in the CCB, no one has ever been charged.[66]

Despite Vlok's assurances, another outrageous Security Police incursion occurred on an extensive scale on the campus during much of the day of 15 June 1989. Using a warrant issued in terms of section 25 of the Criminal Procedures Act, about 200 police accompanied by dogs raided and searched eight buildings including several residences.[67] Entry to the Students' Union was barred as the security police under the command of a conscientious and committed Captain van Huysteen searched rooms occupied by the SRC, BSS and other student societies and clubs. Numerous items were confiscated, including many books from the SRC's Resource Centre. Books, pamphlets and other items were taken from students' rooms in the residences, and the Nusas offices received special attention. Pin-ball tables were confiscated from one of the recreation rooms.

I hurried to the Students' Union when I was told what was going on and found groups of students and staff hanging around, looking disconsolate and bewildered as the police moved arrogantly from room to room, opening cupboards, drawers and filing cabinets, removing everything, then sorting and packing things that they were confiscating, leaving the rest lying around. In the residences there was the same picture. Students who were in the throes of mid-year examinations were also wandering about aimlessly, discussing the invasion, comparing notes. They all had stories to tell me.

The police held a triumphant press conference that evening, claiming that they had removed banned books, pornographic literature and a pamphlet on how to make bombs, and their anti-Wits propaganda was reported zealously by those branches of the media inimical to the University. I asked the University Librarian to check the titles of the books removed against *Jacobson's Index of Objectionable Literature*. Of fifty-eight books confiscated, only one was banned, *War and Conscience in South Africa*, and this was on the shelves of the Jan Smuts Library, shared by the South African Institute of International Affairs and the Department of International Relations. It was not possible to identify any works on the list that could be considered pornographic unless two scholarly studies, *The Left and the Erotic* and *Lesbians, Women and Society* were construed as such by the Security Police.

The South African Broadcasting Corporation gave the press conference extensive coverage, and their morning propaganda programme 'Comment', through some devious reasoning, concluded that 'the literature uncovered on the campus of the University of the Witwatersrand last week underlines once again the intimate link between the African National Congress and the South African Communist Party'. The programme also used the opportunity to cast a slur on the University for its tolerance of radical political views and an intolerance of moderate political views. Von Lieres and Falkov described the press conference as 'little more than a collection of lies, rumours, crude stereotyping and factual inaccuracy'.[68]

At the press conference, a spokesman for the Minister of Law and Order said the search was the result of information received.[69] The validity of this information may be gauged from the fact that no one was arrested, nor were any prosecutions brought as a result of the raid. Some months after the raid I telephoned Brigadier Erasmus of the Security Police to ask whether the confiscated material could now be returned. He told me that he no longer had any interest in the material and I should direct my question to Attorney-General Mr Klaus von Lieres und Wilkau. When I did I got a brusque and unhelpful response. The material was returned about eighteen months later. The only item of note that was not returned was an ANC flag.[70]

Defiance

After two earlier postponements, the students planned to hold a meeting on 31 August 1989 in the Sports Hall to express solidarity with the defiance campaign of the MDM.[71] A mass meeting planned for 20 August was aborted after it had been banned, but once again police presence sparked trouble when groups of demonstrators gathered and there were confrontations throughout the morning.[72] The BSIC had informed the University that from 31 August it intended to unban itself. Its leaders also asked the University to express its support publicly for the BSS. Charlton issued this statement on 31 August:

> The Black Students' Society (BSS) was constituted legally in terms of the constitution of the Students'

Representative Council, approved by the Council of this University. When the BSS was restricted in December last year 'from carrying on or performing any activities or acts whatsoever,' the University Council expressed its dismay and deep disquiet and asked the Chairman of Council and the Acting Vice-Chancellor to seek an appointment with Minister Vlok in an attempt to persuade him to withdraw the restriction order. The Minister was informed that it was in the best interests of good and organised student government that the BSS be allowed to function as the representative organisation of black students on our campus. Unfortunately, the Minister did not accede to our request that we wanted the total and complete lifting of the restrictions, although he invited the students to write to him asking that the restrictions be relaxed to allow bona fide university activities to continue. As a result, an organisation known as the Black Students' Interim Committee (BSIC) was established on campus, which represented the interests of our black students.

The organisation has now decided to function under its original name. The University will continue to recognise the leadership of the black students on campus whatever the name of their organisation.

Other student organisations which were to participate in the campus meeting on 31 August were Sansco, Cosas, Sayco, the Transvaal Students' Congress (Transco), the Soweto Youth Congress (Soyco) and the Soweto Students' Congress (Sosco). The meeting was scheduled to start at 11am, but at 10.45 a banning order was received, signed by Brigadier Erasmus, now the Divisional Commissioner of Police for the Witwatersrand. News of the banning was immediately conveyed to the SRC but could not be communicated to all students at such short notice and at 11.00 it was still being advertised by loud-hailer.

This led to a confrontation on the campus between large numbers of students and the police that continued throughout the day. The police used teargas on a number of occasions to disperse groups of students gathering in different parts of the grounds. There was a particularly anxious period when a large gathering of about 600 students packed into the concourse of Senate House and started singing freedom songs. A large force of uniformed riot police and Security Police in plain clothes entered the concourse from different directions. There seemed to be a very real danger that if the police were to use teargas in the close confines of the concourse, a panicky rush for the exits could lead to serious injuries.

I negotiated with the officer in charge for time to try to disperse the crowd by persuasion. Some members of the diplomatic corps were present to give moral support to the students and prominent among them was Mr John Schram of the Canadian Embassy who often attended these events. Quietly spoken, modest and self-effacing, Schram was a very tall thin man who towered above a crowd and was clearly visible to all. Perhaps because of the diplomats' presence, the police agreed to withdraw to the door on the north side of the concourse to allow me and some of the student leaders to address the crowd, which then sat down on the floor.

The atmosphere was exceptionally tense, but after what seemed a very long time the crowd, extremely angry but responding to persuasion by BSS leader Chris Ngcobo who had recently spent two-and-a-half years in detention, began slowly to move outside where confrontation with the police continued. Keeping a watching brief on behalf of the police was Captain van Huysteen of the Security Police who had special responsibility for student activism at Wits and who had done such a thorough but meaningless search of the Students' Union and the residences on 15 June.

Only after 4pm was what had in effect been an ongoing battle finally over. I witnessed some extraordinary events during the course of the afternoon. I saw one security policeman with his revolver drawn rotating himself menacingly, Hollywood style, as if he were about to be shot after students had jeered as teargas was blown back towards the police by the wind; I saw wave after wave of teargas canisters thrown by the police and students running up to where they had dropped and dousing them with buckets of water. I saw groups of students gathering close to groups of security police who were just standing around, and toyi-toying and jeering at them; but the police stayed on.

Gary Wilson, a Springbok cyclist was standing next to a friend when the friend was struck by a rubber bullet and injured. Gary took him to the Campus Health Clinic and on his return found the bullet and hurled it in the direction of the riot unit. He was spotted doing this, arrested and detained for two weeks under the emergency regulations. Released on bail, he was charged with assault with intent to commit grievous bodily harm. At his trial in December 1989 a prosecution witness, Constable Goosen, testified that he had seen Wilson pick up a stone and throw it towards the riot squad, but conceded in cross-examination that the squad was 150 metres away and that it could never have reached them.[73]

Eventually the police began to withdraw and the students gradually drifted away. Forty casualties were treated in the Campus Health Clinic of whom twelve were not registered students of the University. Most had been affected by teargas, but some had been injured by rubber bullets or teargas canisters and some when running from the police.[74] In addition to Gary Wilson, one other Wits student, one from Khanya College and a 14-year-old scholar from Soweto were arrested. The first two were also detained for two weeks.

In the course of the day journalists and television crews were warned by the police to leave the area because they anticipated a security action. Not surprisingly they ignored this call. Two foreign television crews were taken for questioning and video cassettes were removed for further investigation. In an interview with the South African Press Association, the police liaison officer for the region, Captain E Opperman, warned journalists that it was an offence to be at the scene of an unrest incident, restricted gathering or security action. 'In fact, journalists are not even permitted to be within sight of any of the above-mentioned situations or actions without the prior consent of the Commissioner of the South African Police or a member of the security force who serves as a commissioned officer in that force.'[75]

Once the BSS had unbanned itself, it set about restoring the non-racial unity towards which it and the SRC had been working. In a statement issued on 1 September, the organisation said:[76]

> ... Yesterday a meeting that was convened to get the BSS together with other banned organisations unbanning themselves was banned. In what will go down in

history as a demonstration of the greatest unity on campus the students, both black and white, protested strongly against this. This is the kind of unity that we want on campus and it must continue... We condemn in the strongest possible terms the banning of our meeting and the subsequent police aggression.

Nevertheless as the BSS we are not prepared to comply with the restrictions imposed on us. As from yesterday we declare our organisation unbanned. We will continue where we left off when we were banned and we will continue to operate fully under our own name.

Comrades and friends, let us work for unity on campus. It is becoming increasingly clear that the unity of black students alone is not enough. Let us unite all the anti-apartheid forces on campus. Let us build the broader anti-apartheid front which will involve all the clubs and societies, organisations and staff members who are committed to a non-racial future.

The BSS defiance of its banning order was extremely courageous given that over fifty students at Wits alone and hundreds more throughout the country had been detained during the states of emergency, and many student leaders were being sought out and harassed by an unidentified force, thought by many to be right wing groups within the security forces who had access to detailed information about their personal lives. There was soon to be a spate of these incidents. The car of Anton Roskam, President of the SRC was firebombed. Nikkie Howard, Vice-President of the SRC, had the tyres of her car slashed; Steven Silver, Nusas Regional Organiser for the Transvaal, had acid thrown over his car and the tyres slashed; Angus Stewart, Secretary-General of Nusas, had his car's tyres slashed, graffiti painted on the bonnet and green, yellow and black stripes spraypainted around it; Lael Bethlehem, an SRC member, had her car tyres slashed, glue thrown over the windscreen and the word 'Nurden' painted on it; David Storey, an SRC member, had his car's tyres slashed and so did his mother; the house-mate of Bettina von Lieres, former SRC President, had her car's tyres slashed and the word 'Nurden' painted on it; and Paul van Zyl, SRC member, had the words 'ANC lives here' sprayed on the wall of his house.[77] On 27 October I issued a press statement condemning these incidents.[78]

> The University regards the attacks on the property of seven students, office-bearers of our Students' Representative Council and of NUSAS, as outrageous. There have been numerous incidents of this kind in recent times and it is imperative that the perpetrators of these deeds be hunted down and brought to justice. Failure to apprehend people who carry out such cowardly acts against the property of our students encourages those who attempt, and tragically sometimes succeed, in assassinations of individuals. This latest series of terrorist attacks was obviously carefully planned and took place in different parts of the city against targets which had been clearly identified.
>
> The University urges the police to act with vigour in this case before these terrorists commit a more dastardly act of violence.

No one was ever apprehended or charged with these offences.

The demonstration of political resistance by the BSS was part of the successful defiance campaign of civil disobedience that had been organised by the MDM to challenge segregated, state-controlled facilities such as hospitals and schools.[79] It was a campaign which would contribute in large measure to the eventual move of the National Party Government towards a democratic dispensation.

P W Botha resigned as State President on 14 August 1989 and De Klerk became acting State President the following day. On 20 September 1989 he was inaugurated as State President.[80] A student protest demonstration the day after the inauguration and the police response to it were so different from the many that had preceded it that it was difficult not to deduce that there had been a fundamental shift in the direction of South African politics, and that a move towards reconciliation had begun. A number of peaceful marches had taken place in different parts of the country in the preceding weeks, the first legal processions since all outdoor gatherings had been prohibited in 1986 in terms of the Riotous Assemblies Act.[81]

Picture courtesy Mayibuye Centre

Armed and ready, a phalanx of riot police in Jan Smuts Avenue don't know quite what to make of the peace sign

The theme of the mass meeting and march of students and staff on 21 September was a familiar one. A staff member, Willem Liebenberg, and a member of the SRC, Michael Avidan, had recently been detained, restrictions on students and staff persisted and so did police action on the campuses.[82] Students had requested that the University be closed between 12 and 2pm and that the administration take part in a march to the Hillbrow Police Station. They did not intend to seek permission for the march and would leave it to individuals to decide whether to participate in what would be an illegal gathering in terms of the emergency regulations.

Early on the morning of the march, four Wits students, including Bettina von Lieres, were detained. A statement was issued, endorsed by twenty-seven student organisations, registering outrage at the continued repression suffered by South Africans in general and the university community in particular.[83] The statement demanded the immediate release of students and all others in detention; the unbanning of student and all other organisations; the right to peaceful anti-apartheid protests; the right to a university free from police incursion and harassment and the immediate arrest of those responsible for underhand attacks on anti-apartheid leaders.

There was, of course, never any likelihood that the police would allow the march to go beyond the campus limits. Nevertheless, it had been well planned and, to the extent that it proceeded, was efficiently controlled by student marshalls. When confronted by police on the first occasion and advised that they would be allowed no further, the organisers turned the demonstration back towards the piazza. On the second attempt to leave campus by way of the steps onto Jan Smuts Avenue, they were met by police who stationed themselves on one side of the steps while the students remained on the steps. A further contingent of police arrived and stood directly in front of the demonstrators who sat singing and chanting, holding placards with slogans such as 'Police – we want peace,' 'Where is Mike?' and 'Free Liebenberg'. The students at the front of the crowd sat on the edge of the pavement at the feet of the policemen, each holding aloft a single flower.

When the police officer in charge called on the students to disperse they remained seated chanting 'We want peace'. Eventually, after some negotiation and consultation, I was able to advise the crowd that the police had agreed that if the students would move back to the steps, they would withdraw. This was accomplished to cheers and claps from the students. Not long after this, the crowd sang the anthem and dispersed.[84]

It had been a striking example of disciplined peaceful protest and impressive student leadership and organisation, and the police, who seemed somewhat unsure as to how to respond, showed considerable restraint. Interestingly and surprisingly, on this occasion the police operation was led by Captain Eugene Opperman, a member of the police public relations department who handled it with skill and diplomacy.

At about this time the Student Affairs Office documented for the information of Council all the incidents of political activity that had led to police action on the campus and against students during the period 1986-1988. There were fifty-two such incidents.[85]

At the next Council meeting I expressed great anxiety about the welfare of Michael Avidan who was still being held. I had received information that he was being physically abused and taunted with anti-Semitic jibes. I suspected that this might rouse Dr Leslie Frankel, an appointee of the State President to the Council, who was well-known for his philanthropy to the National Party and to the Hebrew University Jerusalem which had awarded him an honorary PhD. He had frequently mentioned his friendship with Adriaan Vlok and Security Police chief General Basie Smit. As expected, Frankel was incensed, and said he would phone Smit and complain about the treatment of Avidan.

As the matter was urgent and it was getting late on this Friday afternoon I suggested that we leave the meeting and go to my office to phone Smit. Smit was not in but Frankel spoke to his deputy and said that he wanted to talk to Smit urgently about a student who was in detention. As we walked back to the Council Chamber a very angry Frankel told me that he had recently given the National Party R500 000 for its election campaign. I was not able to listen to his call to Smit, but Frankel phoned me at the weekend to tell me that Avidan would be released, and indeed he was, early the following week.

No further student demonstrations took place during the 1989 academic year. By the time the University reconvened for the 1990 academic session, President De Klerk had delivered his celebrated address to Parliament on 2 February 1990.

CHAPTER 10

Transition to Democracy

1990 was not without political incident at Wits but the campus was very much more peaceful than it had been for many years. Ironically, the police clashed with students who went onto the streets on 2 February to celebrate De Klerk's announcements in Parliament that day.[1]

By the end of February, shortly after the start of the new academic year, a new direction in student politics had become apparent. As part of a nation-wide two-day period of mass action to protest against the crisis in education, the BSS and Sansco organised a class boycott at Wits. Anger was directed against the University administration with the BSS demanding a moratorium on all exclusions and the appointment of a commission of inquiry to investigate admissions and exclusions; an opportunity to make representations on how the University should redress imbalances created by apartheid education and a solution to the accommodation problem.[2]

Charlton was sympathetic, agreeing that the inferior education provided by the Department of Education and Training was an important factor in determining students' academic performance, and acknowledging that the University had an obligation to provide the academic support necessary to overcome the resulting educational disadvantage. Nevertheless, he said, 'once it becomes clear that (students) will not be able to complete a degree course, there really is no alternative to excluding them from the University'. He could therefore not agree to a moratorium on exclusions.

The University was experiencing an accommodation crisis similar to that of many other universities at the beginning of an academic year. The large influx of new students, most of whom had no alternative accommodation, was a grave problem. Past experience had shown that within a few months many residence beds would be vacated as some students moved into flats and communes and others dropped out of their studies. The University had to find a balance between providing new residences in the face of stringent financial constraints, and over-providing and having subsequently to administer residences that were only partly filled. It was clear however, that accommodation needs would increase steadily as black student numbers climbed in subsequent years, and strenuous attempts were made to raise financial aid to support a residence acquisition programme.

In order to cope with the immediate crisis, some students were given subsidised accommodation in nearby hotels and plans were made to extend the Esselen Street residence to provide rooms for an additional 200 students. The SRC, BSS and the Student Affairs Office arranged to get tents from the Red Cross and agreed after negotiations to erect them adjacent to the residences, so that those who lived in them would have ready access to the ablution facilities and dining halls. As a form of protest and in defiance of their agreement with me on their location, the students erected the tents on the library lawns and, with a tension-reducing display of humour, named the resultant squatter camp 'Charltonville'. Names were given to the streets between the tents, and some of the tents were given names such as Lusaka House. The 'night club' was called 'Shear Ecstasy'!

On 7 March, about 300 students started a three-day boycott of all academic activities to push their demands.[3]

The administration held numerous discussions with staff representatives and student leaders and the National Education Coordinating Committee (NECC) was consulted. On 22 March, following extensive negotiations, the Senate appointed a Committee of Inquiry into Admissions and Exclusions.[4] The Senate was the largest constituency represented. Others were the Academic Staff Association and the Union of Democratic University Staff Associations (Udusa), the African National Congress, the NECC, the SRC, the BSS and Sansco.[5]

The Committee's brief was to examine the University's selection and admission policy and procedures; to examine the University's exclusion criteria and procedures and to examine the reasons for the

People are living here ... in a novel protest, the library lawns are tranformed into the Charltonville informal settlement

poor academic performance of some candidates and what the University could do to improve it.

It should not be thought that the establishment of this Committee implies that Wits acted solely in reaction to pressure. For some years many faculties had been using innovative selection procedures to ensure that prospective black students should not be unfairly disadvantaged in their competition for limited numbers of places. This enabled students who had not gained automatic admission on the basis of their matriculation results to be selected by other forms of evaluation. Some faculties raised the number of points required on the matriculation examination for automatic admission, thereby reserving space within the faculty for discretionary admission.

Substantial progress had been made in the development of academic support programmes both in a centrally-located departments and in individual faculties; and many academic departments and research units were directing their curricula and research programmes increasingly towards addressing southern African issues and problems. Tober had established supernumerary positions enabling black academics to be brought into departments before actual posts were available.

The appointment of representatives of the ANC and the exclusion of other political parties evoked some controversy in the University and in the media. However Senate had decided to appoint community organisations to the Committee and student representatives who were consulted advised that the ANC was the organisation that best represented the interests of black students.

Written and oral representations were received from a wide range of internal and external bodies. A draft report dated 10 June 1991 was circulated to all members of the Committee and through them to the organisations they represented, and to all members of Senate and Council. Comments were debated by the Committee and most of the original recommendations were accepted. Where agreement could not be reached on certain points, this was recorded at the end of each section.

In its preamble the report refers to the growing awareness of the potentially damaging effects of apartheid education on Wits and the fact that dissatisfaction among those most severely affected by issues such as admissions and exclusions had generated conflict which if not seriously addressed, would be detrimental to the long-term development of the institution. The preamble continues:

> ... In order for the University to overcome the legacy of apartheid, it has become an urgent priority that, in so far as its resources allow and without sacrifice of standards either in the quality of its graduates or of research, it should vigorously persist in, and indeed go further in, implementing a programme of positive actions and intervention.
>
> Such a programme is necessary to reduce the effects of discrimination because mere equality of treatment in all respects would not redress the effects of past inequalities. It would simply maintain them, particularly against a background where it has become clear to those

involved in admissions procedures that black and white applicants' matriculation results are not comparable. To offset the results of apartheid education it is necessary to create mechanisms for implementing equal opportunity on the basis of a potential to succeed rather than on a past performance where the opportunities for performing have been unequal. Ensuring that disadvantaged students have an equal opportunity to succeed has meant and will continue to mean developing appropriate selection procedures, including alternative admissions procedures in faculties and departments; improving teaching; providing academic and social support for the disadvantaged; and refining the exclusion procedures with the new situation in mind. It is in this precisely defined sense that Wits supports the principle of affirmative action.

An affirmative action programme of this kind for overcoming inequalities is in the interests not only of the disadvantaged constituencies but of the institution itself; and failure to continue to develop such procedures will be seen by the majority as an attempt to entrench minority privileges. Such a programme does not imply reverse discrimination. Nor does it mean that different academic standards are being applied in respect of different groups of students, for, as must be stressed, the requirements a student must meet to gain credit for a course, or to be awarded a degree or diploma, remain common for all students...

The committee made recommendations on admissions; the changing context of teaching and learning; exclusions and readmissions; and on monitoring the outcome of the inquiry.

Its starting point was the 1980 Academic Plan in which Senate had agreed that 'the selection of undergraduates must be done in such a way as to constitute a student body which is closer than at present to being representative of the South African population'. Providing academic support to students whose educational background had been grossly inadequate enabled the standard of the

University's degrees to be maintained. The committee believed that both traditional and alternative admission procedures should continue to be used to admit students with the ability to succeed and that this 'should result in the distribution of students admitted reflecting that of the applicants who meet all the requirements for admission'.

Certain factors were essential if students were to succeed.[6] Among them were academic ability, motivation, a minimum level of knowledge, skills and the ability to communicate, adequate financial support for fees, books, accommodation and subsistence; and acceptable accommodation. The University was committed to doing its utmost to assist those offered admission to obtain adequate financial support and acceptable accommodation, but it recognised that it might not succeed in every case. It recommended that students who had difficulties should enrol in academic support programmes. Research into the validity of existing admissions policies and into alternative procedures had to be undertaken.

The 'points on which no consensus was reached' reveal that tension existed between the Senate members and the other members of the committee on some issues. For example, the staff and student organisations felt strongly that goals should be set in implementing an affirmative action admissions policy and the NECC commented that 'affirmative action without a programme of action means little more than rhetoric'. The Senate members believed however, that 'setting a target of a particular gender and ethnic mix which is to be achieved by a certain year takes no account of factors beyond the University's control ... The admission of students who have little or no chance of succeeding, in order to meet the target, would be disastrous ...' Another point of difference was that the student groups and the NECC felt that the alternative selection procedures should be open only to students from a disadvantaged educational background; whereas the Senate members pointed out that no evidence had been presented to suggest that any applicants who were able to demonstrate potential were being denied access to the University. In response to the NECC's concern that the report did not make a clear commitment to social support services such as the provision of accommodation, financial support, career guidance and psychological counselling, the Senate members indicated that financial constraints prevented the University from going beyond its commitment to 'do its utmost'.

Recognising that the low graduation rate of black students was a cause for concern and might indicate the need for a comprehensive re-evaluation of course curricula and teaching strategies, the committee made recommendations which would modify the processes of teaching and learning in the University.[7] Each faculty, it directed, should establish a teaching and learning committee which would include student members and be charged with the task of promoting an integrated approach to teaching and learning. Faculties should consider introducing an alternative extended degree course structure which should not merely consist of an extended first-year curriculum but should include enrichment programmes to develop language competence, study skills and discipline-specific skills. They should also consider introducing preliminary level courses in key areas such as mathematics.

Academic support should be recognised as a faculty responsibility and each academic department should accept responsibility for identifying students in need of support and for developing appropriate support activities. Methods of assessing student performance should be continually and systematically reviewed, and the teaching staff should be encouraged to evaluate the success of their teaching. All new staff should be encouraged to take some form of training for their teaching roles. Other recommendations dealt with supplementary examinations and proposals about extending the scope of academic support.

On the question of 'Exclusions and Readmissions' the committee stated that:[8]

> There are more qualified applicants than there are places in many courses. Readmission of a student who has failed to meet the minimum academic requirements therefore often means denying one of those applicants a place. A readmitted student requiring bursary support and/or a place in a residence will be in competition with another student for these limited resources. The decision whether or not to readmit a student who has failed to meet the minimum academic requirements is

therefore always a matter of judgement. The decision must be based on (a) an assessment of the likelihood of the student succeeding if given a further chance, and (b) an evaluation of where the University's limited resources will be most effectively deployed.

The position of students who have failed to meet the minimum academic requirements is best considered and handled at faculty level even though legally the exclusion of a student must be a Council decision. The recommendation of the FACE (Faculty Advisory Committee on Exclusions) and the decision by the CCE (Council Committee on Exclusions) must be based on the academic performance, the reasons for failure to meet minimum academic requirements and the likelihood of success if readmitted.

A number of recommendations related to policy and procedure, to FACE activities and to CCE activities.

Other contentious issues related to the membership of the exclusion committees and the monitoring of the outcome of the recommendations. The non-Senate members wanted the NECC or its representatives to sit on the exclusion committees and pressed for a review committee or some form of joint monitoring body. The Senate members believed that 'to suggest that it is necessary to include external members in a watchdog committee to monitor progress in implementing recommendations accepted by Senate and Council indicates lack of confidence in either their will or their ability'. They saw the suggestion of outside bodies being represented on Senate or Council committees as a threat to their jealously guarded autonomy. 'The University should be sensitive and responsive to articulated community concerns but ... even with a more representative and democratically based government, it is essential for the effective pursuit of truth that the University retains its academic integrity and autonomy.'

After the Committee's report was approved, the Senate decided to amalgamate two of its standing committees – on 'Teaching and Learning' and 'Admission and Selection' – into a Senate Advisory Committee on Student Development.[9] This committee was to co-ordinate and monitor progress in respect of admissions and selection tests, academic support and development, teaching and learning, and to receive reports from faculties on examinations and exclusions and from the committee on the Vice-Chancellor's Teaching Award. In recent years, all faculties have established committees on teaching and learning.

The College of Science was introduced by the Faculty of Science in 1991 to provide a development programme for students selected for admission. The Faculty of Engineering has followed suit and has linked itself to the College structure. Academic development programmes, which were originally centrally based in a separate department, are increasingly being extended into the faculties and individual departments.

Education Development Officers have been appointed in six faculties. Their main role is to work under the direction of the Dean, the Director of the Academic Development Programme (previously the Academic Support Programme) and the relevant faculty committees to initiate and coordinate research into admissions, to facilitate the development of teaching structures and strategies in ways responsive to the changing student population. It is also envisaged that the development officers will act as facilitators with groups of staff working on curriculum innovation, and will be involved in research relating to student admissions and development, and in the preparation of creative and imaginative teaching material.

The question of admissions and exclusions became an urgent political issue again in May 1993 when Sasco issued a list of demands, some of which related to the inquiry and called for 'the implementation of the committee's recommendations concomitant with an independent monitoring process', and for a 'readjustment of admission requirements with a strong bias towards affirmative action. In particular the University must commit itself to a quota of African students whom it will accept in 1994. At the very minimum we demand that at least 60% of those admitted should be African.'[10]

These demands were part of a country-wide campaign by Sasco for the transformation of the universities. A detailed account of the events following these demands and the disruption that occurred on the Wits campus, is beyond the scope of this book.

March Against Violence

Although campus politics transformed considerably in the months after De Klerk's speech,[11] there were a few more student demonstrations in the second half of 1990. On 29 August a march was planned from the Johannesburg City Library to the John Vorster Square Police Headquarters as part of a national campaign being organised by Nusas, Sansco, and Cosas (Congress of South African Students) to draw attention to the violence in the townships.[12] According to Bettina von Lieres, spokesperson for the organisers, the students intended to present a memorandum to the police demanding a public inquiry into the origins of township conflicts and the role of the police and Inkatha supporters, and the immediate prosecution of those responsible. Other demands were the lifting of the state of emergency in the townships, the establishment of an international peace-keeping force and the removal of Chief Mangosutho Buthelezi as leader of the KwaZulu police. Some fifty-one students, not all from Wits, were arrested.

For a follow-up open-air demonstration and march planned for 19 September, a detailed application was submitted to the Chief Magistrate of Johannesburg and the Johannesburg City Council. A carefully-planned march from the campus to the Hillbrow Police Station was proposed. At the police station a petition would be handed to the Station Commander calling on the State to take 'urgent steps to end the violence currently rampant in the black townships of South Africa and with the particular demand that the role of the South African Police in failing to terminate this violence be assessed and that allegations of partiality on the part of the South African Police be addressed as a matter of urgency.'[13]

The response from the City Council was that, in view of the short period of notification, the Council would not be able to assist with the march in respect of such matters as traffic control. 'If you decide to continue with the march it will be at your own risk and you will be held responsible should any problems occur.'[14] The Chief Magistrate gave permission for the open-air meeting but made no reference to the march.[15]

After a well-attended meeting on the library lawns, a group of about 150 to 200 students decided to march. The result was another confrontation with the police during which the students were dispersed with teargas and rubber bullets.

As usual, in attempting to defuse the tension, I was moving between the students itching for a confrontation, and the officer in charge of the riot squad), again Colonel van der Walt. I had just been speaking to Van der Walt and been told that I had two minutes to get the students off Jan Smuts Avenue onto the campus, and was hurrying back to convey this message, when I was hit in the back with a rubber bullet fired from no more than 10 metres away. It knocked me over with what felt like considerable force and I lay on the ground for a while in fairly severe pain. A few people ran to assist me, but photographs of the incident show most of the students scurrying up the steps to the campus. The force of the bullet was such that it tore a hole in the jacket of my suit and left a round punched-out wound that penetrated the skin over my sacrum; and extensive bruising that took some months to heal.[16]

Professor June Sinclair who was standing nearby was almost hit on the head by another missile. When I got up and hobbled away, surrounded by reporters, Van der Walt ran across the road and asked whether I was all right. I replied, rather angrily, that of course I wasn't all right; I'd just been shot in the back by one of his men! I refused his offer to have me taken to hospital – the students had by then regrouped, the riot squad was still there, and intercession was still going to be needed.

A short while later I was over the road again, by now in a rather better humour. I showed a somewhat chastened Van der Walt and some of his men the hole that the bullet had made in the back of my jacket) and asked him how he would feel if I had shot him in the back. With just a glimmer of a smile he replied, 'Well I'm bigger than you are'. And that he was.

The incident hit the headlines that night and the next day. In the USA the report led to someone asking my son who was a graduate student at Northwestern University, whether he knew this Mervyn Shear at Wits who had been shot by a police rubber bullet. An alarmed Keith phoned my wife the next morning to find out whether I was all right and was told that I was at work. Of course a lot of fuss was made of it because of my position, whereas students were being shot by rubber bullets all the time without

I become a victim of police tactics when I am hit in the back by a rubber bullet fired at short range

raising any particular comment and in the townships live ammunition was often used.

I have no doubt that the rubber bullet was fired at me intentionally. Charlton wrote a letter of complaint to Major-General G N Erasmus, by then the Divisional Commissioner of Police for the Witwatersrand, and asked that the incident be investigated.[17] Erasmus refused, responding that 'it would be appreciated, in those instances where the South African Police deems it necessary to take steps to enforce law and order, that personnel attached to the University do not intervene. This will prevent a re-occurrence of the events which had taken place on 19 September 1990.'[18]

However, a leading article in the Government-supporting newspaper, *Beeld*, criticised the police over the incident and Minister of Law and Order Adriaan Vlok gave instructions that it should be investigated.[19] The investigation was done internally by Brigadier Blignaut of the Regional Commissioner's office, Johannesburg – the same Blignaut we had taken to court in May 1986 because of his refusal to grant bail to forty-eight of our students.

Four months later Charlton received another letter from Vlok's secretary stating that 'I regret to inform you that a departmental enquiry has not been held into the incident. In spite of the video recordings of the incident having been closely scrutinised by senior officers, it is impossible to identify the person or persons responsible for shooting Professor Shear, and the matter can consequently not be taken any further. The incident is however sincerely regretted.'[20]

The concern in the University about the violence in the townships persisted and it was decided that there should be a meeting of the University Community on the library lawns on 27 September which would be addressed by the Vice-Chancellor and representatives of Udusa/ASA, SRC, Sansco, Nehawu and Dr Beyers Naudé. This would be followed by a march around the perimeter of the campus ending at the Jorissen Street entrance adjacent to the Wits Theatre when a memorandum and joint University statement would be handed to the police.[21] The statement read:[22]

> The University of the Witwatersrand is deeply concerned and troubled about the violence that has occurred in our neighbouring communities. It wishes to

express its sympathy to the victims of the violence and its concern about the traumatic effect that the violence has had upon all sections of our community. The University joins the call of many South Africans for peace and an immediate end to the violence.

The University sees the violence as a legacy of years of racial division, poverty, social justice, poor education, unemployment, inadequate housing and the barbaric hostel system caused by the evil order of apartheid. The University rejects the simplistic view that some have espoused, for their own political ends, that the violence of the past few months is the result of tribal or ethnic division. We dismiss the crude portrayal of the events of the past months as 'black on black violence'.

The identity of the forces responsible for the violence is as yet unknown. However, we believe that there is evidence to support the view that the violence is orchestrated by forces opposed to the abandonment of apartheid and to the creation of a just political order in South Africa.

While it is clear that there is a desperate need for peace to be restored and for the Government to be seen to be taking strong measures to restore peace, we are not convinced that the drastic measures contained in 'Operation Iron Fist' will provide a lasting peace.[23] The name of this operation – 'Iron Fist' – is in itself an unfortunate one. The whole black community is seriously affected by these measures. They cause hardship and inconvenience to the whole community, including many of our own staff and students.

The role of the police in this violence is controversial. However, there are serious allegations of police partiality that are believed by many to have contributed to the violence. This surely calls for impartial investigation. In this context we wish to express our concern that certain groupings, such as the CCB,[24] in the security forces that were created to enforce apartheid rule, have not been disbanded and may still continue their operations.

The University of the Witwatersrand believes that there is a need for an urgent impartial investigation into:
the socio-economic causes of the violence
the impartiality and effectiveness of the police in controlling this violence
the persons and groupings responsible for the violence. We believe that it is essential that those responsible for the violence be brought to justice as soon as possible.

We therefore call for the establishment of a commission of inquiry presided over by a judge, whose members will be qualified to make a proper investigation into the issues we have raised. The members of the commission of inquiry should be selected on a non-racial basis and should include credible leaders from the affected communities.

The University calls for peace. However, it believes that a just peace is not possible until the causes of the recent violence have been explored and the persons responsible for the violence have been identified and brought before the courts.

The speakers at the meeting condemned the 'Iron Fist' policy and the associated curfew that was causing much disruption of life in the townships. After the meeting a march up Station Street was intercepted by the riot police at the Jorissen Street intersection. There was tension between the antagonists facing each other across the road but, accompanied by June Sinclair, I interceded with Captain Buitendach who was in charge of the police operation (what had happened to Colonel van der Walt of the rubber bullet incident?) and he agreed not to take any action against the students as long as they did not cross Jorissen Street. He allowed a student delegation of five people to present the petition after which the demonstration ended peacefully.[25]

In the years before the democratic election in April 1994, the violence in the townships escalated to an appalling extent and thousands of people were killed. There was a substantial drop in violence after the elections except in Kwazulu-Natal where it is still severe.

The concerns and suspicions about the causes of the violence have not changed, and pitifully few people have been charged for the many atrocities that have been committed.

A Happy Ending

The year ended on a happy note in respect of non-racial student representation. In the course of 1990, several non-racial house committees were elected in the residences. After extensive debate and discussions between the SRC and the BSS, the BSS had held a referendum in which 75 per cent of its members had supported a proposal for an end to the BSS policy of non-participation in SRC affairs. Following a decision at its annual general meeting the BSS dissolved and a transitional committee, the BSTC was formed to operate until the next SRC elections. Sansco and Nusas had also taken a decision to disband when a new national student body was formed. They did so during 1991, and a non-racial student organisation known as the South African Students' Congress (Sasco) was established.

By the time I had the responsibility for sport there was no longer a policy of social segregation in the University but the BSS, like other similar organisations throughout the country, had developed a strategy of non-participation. Of course, like many whites, I was extremely naïve at that time about the dynamics of black political strategies and I tried hard, but obviously in vain, to persuade black student leaders that it was tragic that black students should be deprived of the excellent sports facilities available at Wits.

I was delighted therefore when, in April 1987, the BSS asked me to convene a meeting with the sports administration and representatives of the SRC, BSS and the All Sports Council to discuss the sports issue on campus. Dali Mpofu and Moss Mashishi presented the BSS position. Mashishi later played a prominent role in the National Sports Congress (NSC), the campaign against the 1989 rebel cricket tour led by Mike Gatting and in the development of sports unity in the country. He is now an influential figure in the national sports scene.

He told the meeting that in the past black students had comprised too small a percentage of the student body to organise themselves at

Wits under the non-racial South African Council on Sport (Sacos).[26] Now that there were more black students on campus and in the residences, the BSS had held a referendum and this had indicated that its members were strongly in favour of using 'sports facilities on campus under the auspices of the BSS in order to advance the struggle for non-racialism and democracy'.

Extensive and protracted negotiations led to the decision that two sporting bodies would exist – the old All Sports Council and the South African Tertiary Institutions' Sports Congress (Satisco), later to become Satisu, and both would fall under the general control of Sports Administration. The road to the establishment of Satisco was a rough one. At first the sports administrators were against it, but were later persuaded that it was the way to go in the transition phase. Some of the executive of the All Sports Council were supportive, others were not. Some national and provincial sports administrators who thought they knew it all, also had to have a say, and expressed strong opposition to the development. They were to learn very quickly in the next few years what the political realities were if South Africa was to get back into world sport. Mr John Baxter, Wits head of sports administration, played a leading role in educating white sports administrators about these realities.

The Wits Council took a lot of persuading on the Satisco issue and I was given a hard time in some very difficult debates by a few of the conservative members who, insensitive to the national debate that was raging on the sports issue, were adamantly opposed to the idea of separate sports bodies. They could not or would not understand why the black students refused to be absorbed by the existing all-white All Sports Council. Nevertheless Satisco/Wits was formally approved on 11 September 1987. In the meantime, black students started to use the sports facilities for the first time in the University's history. After the establishment of Sasco the ASC and Satisu unified[27] and an Agreement on Unity in Sport was signed on 22 October 1992.

CHAPTER 11

Epilogue

During 1990 I had taken the decision not to make myself available for reappointment when my second term as DVC expired at the end of that year and I was succeeded by Professor June Sinclair in January 1991. I was sad to leave the student affairs portfolio but was feeling stressed at the perpetual crisis management that the job entailed. There was very little time left for creative thinking about the development of student affairs at the University. Moreover, I wanted to have the opportunity of engaging in other activities while I was still feeling energetic enough to pursue them. Finally, I had often said that I wanted to go while people were still wanting me to stay, rather than hang on until I had lost all insight into my own incompetence.

I went through a series of warm and emotional farewell parties and early in 1991 my wife Caryll and I moved to Simon's Town where we had built a holiday home sixteen years before and had enjoyed many happy and restorative vacations. I was not long out of my job and still revelling in my independence as a pensioner when I began to feel the withdrawal symptoms associated with 'no longer being needed'. Nevertheless I was able to do some writing in my old discipline, go back to part-time teaching in the Oral Pathology Department of the University of the Western Cape, become involved in a little political activity and in assisting with the development of the Kwazulu-Natal tertiary institutions' Regional Institutional Cooperation Project. And to write this book.

I had not intended to include any personal memoirs but have been persuaded to do so by several people who read early drafts of the

Farewell party for the Presidents of the SRC and the BSS between 1983 and 1990.
Front Row (Left to Right): Claire Wright, Chris Ngcobo, Lloyd Vogelman, myself Tiego Moseneke, Brendan Barry, Dali Mpofu
Back Row (Left to Right): Jonathan Stead (a past Deputy Registrar Student Affairs), Dan Mashitisho, Anton Roskam, Rosemary Hunter, Etienne Marais, Pauline Cuzen (Deputy Registrar Student Affairs), James Maseko, Bettina von Lieres, Terry Tselane, David Jammy, Jocelyn Cairns (SRC Administration Coordinator). Grant Rex was unable to be there.

manuscript. This was not easy and in writing about the events of the 1980s I hope that I have not tended to inflate my personal contribution. So many Wits people were involved during that turbulent decade as were students and dedicated staff at other South African educational institutions and I am very happy to have had the opportunity of being one of them.

In my introduction I point out that there are conflicting views on the University of the Witwatersrand, particularly with regard to the extent to which it opened its facilities to all South Africans; what its contribution was to the transformation of South Africa to a non-racial and democratic society; and the positions it took in the fight against social injustice, infringements of fundamental human rights and the struggle for academic freedom and university autonomy. While Wits has always had a considerable body of loyal supporters, it has also been reviled for doing either too little or too much in these respects.

The purpose of the book was to examine Wits's record in order to determine, if possible, where the truth lies.

The University has gone through a number of fairly well-defined phases. There can be little doubt that the institution was established to provide education and professional training for white South Africans. Although J H Hofmeyr had expressed the view in 1919 in his inaugural address as Principal that the University should know no distinctions of class or wealth, race or creed, there was consternation among some members of the Council when applications for admission were first received from pitifully small numbers of blacks. In the 1920s the Council was anxious to know whether it had the power to refuse admission to 'non-Europeans' and if not, what would have to be done to give it that power. Fortunately the Government at that time was more progressive in this respect than the Wits Council and it was clear that it would not be given this power.

During the next phase, black students were admitted to some faculties but excluded from others. At the same time, the policy of 'academic non-segregation but social segregation' was rigidly applied by Hofmeyr's successors, Raikes and Sutton. For all these limitations on access and integration for black students, a conviction developed in the institution that Wits was an 'open university' and the Senate rejected a motion proposed in 1954 by some of its more conservative members that it should not endorse even the policy of 'academic non-segregation'.

It was however, the actions of the apartheid government during the 1950s in imposing racial segregation on the universities that mobilised the collective conscience of a majority of the Council, staff, students and Convocation and initiated a struggle that was waged with varying degrees of intensity and conviction until 1990.

MacCrone, who succeeded Sutton as Vice-Chancellor, determinedly pursued the 'social segregation' policy despite his considerable reputation as a liberal. He was however bitterly opposed to academic apartheid and fought it fiercely. The advent of Bozzoli to the Vice-Chancellorship coincided with the introduction by the Government of increasingly repressive legislation and at the same time, in response, angry, vocal and visible opposition from the students. Bozzoli provided impressive support for this student activism which was detested by the state and its media minions, who pilloried both him and the students, particularly Nusas. Many members of staff took courage from Bozzoli's example and became more outspoken in their opposition to apartheid and state oppression. Bozzoli was prepared to do away with social segregation on the campus, arguing that social activities were part of a student's academic development. Unfortunately he was forced by the Government to abandon the new policy when conservative students took the story to the Afrikaans press.

Du Plessis, Tober and Charlton have all put their individual marks on the Vice-Chancellorship since 1977. Du Plessis, unlike Bozzoli, delivered little memorable rhetoric, but he was strong and determined and effected fundamental changes.

Tober and Charlton presided over the University during a much more turbulent period and much of their energy was directed towards conflict resolution. Nevertheless, the process of transformation has progressed inexorably. Not surprisingly, this is not obvious to many young black students who have recently come to the University for the first time, but to those who have been associated with Wits for many years it is strikingly apparent. During their years in office, the University fought and won, together with the Universities of Cape Town, Natal and Rhodes, two major battles against the Government. It also endured the oppressive states of emergency during which many of its students suffered detention, torture and harassment. It was during this period that the University finally opened its doors and facilities to all and became a truly non-racial institution.

Although it has still not met all the expectations of its black constituency, the will to do so is there. The Council however, still projects the image of being dominated by white businessmen and increasing pressure is being exerted for the appointment of more women and more blacks and for a restructuring of the constituencies represented on it. Another considerable bone of contention is the pitifully small number of blacks who fill academic and senior administrative positions. The increasing numbers of black students continue to be plagued by their apartheid heritage: appalling primary and secondary education, poverty and inadequate housing. There are expectations of the role that a university like Wits must play in redressing the legacies of apartheid and in addressing the needs of a South Africa in transition and in the future.

What is Wits doing about it? In November 1992 the Senate considered a discussion document *Developing a Mission for Wits* which argued for 'a process of wide consultation both inside and outside the University, with a view to uncovering Wits' strengths and determining what the institution could do to make a major contribution to national reconstruction.'[1] Senate appointed a small project group to consult widely and to draft a new Mission Statement for its approval. The new Mission Statement would provide the guidance to 'preserve the University as a centre of excellence and demonstrate that, as a national resource, Wits would contribute to the development of a tertiary education system accessible to communities previously denied opportunities to benefit from it. The task would require the selection and ranking of priorities, the identification of specific objectives and a commitment to the implementation of appropriate strategies to achieve those objectives. This would involve a set of short- and medium-term goals, supported by management structures and decision-making mechanisms which would permit rapid and effective responses to unexpected shifts in the environment.'

The project group consulted widely during 1993, both within and outside the University.[2]

It concluded that Wits should continue to commit itself to excellence in teaching, learning and research; to courses of study which served the needs of South Africa and to increased access and appropriate academic development for South Africans from disadvantaged backgrounds. The group believed that a dynamic vision for Wits could yield a Mission Statement and a strategic plan that would allow the University to address all these commitments while making a major contribution to the reconstruction of South Africa.[3] In setting out its views on what the University's priorities and goals should be, the group concluded:

> Wits is a public institution and national resource with special responsibilities to the region and the country. Its

central task is the provision of outstanding university education, and its primary products are its graduates and research.

In order to meet its public responsibilities, Wits must remain committed to its high exit standards. Our graduates must be comparable in their level of skill, knowledge and understanding to graduates with equivalent degrees from top universities anywhere. At the same time, our curricula must be re-examined and updated continuously to ensure that they serve the multifarious long-term needs of the country as well as the personal development need of our students.

Wits has an obligation to participate in a massive national effort to undo Apartheid. Its pursuit of excellence must therefore be balanced by continued commitment to a policy of increased access and improved success (through academic development) for members of disadvantaged communities, especially in important disciplines in which they are seriously underrepresented. Academic development models may differ from one subject area to another. The College of Science model has merits which seem to make it an attractive option for coherent subject groupings outside of the natural sciences. Alternative initiatives will, however, be required in disciplinary areas where it is inappropriate.

It is widely agreed that South Africa suffers from a shortage of skilled people in science, engineering and technology (SET). The University has a distinctive capacity in this area, which should be developed as a high priority. There are also opportunities for Wits to broaden access to SET by producing and upgrading school teachers in the key subjects of mathematics and physical science.

In the humanities (broadly understood) the University's priorities should be the production of more and better black managers, personnel appropriately educated for the public service and teachers of English. Quality postgraduate studies and research should be fostered by Wits and there is a need for a new research policy embracing broader criteria for the evaluation of research.

Wits must be a vigorous affirmative action employer. Its policies for the recruitment, development and promotion of its staff must be adjusted and managed in pursuit of demonstrable progress in redressing racial and gender imbalances without compromising standards. This effort should be facilitated by a major initiative to produce more black postgraduates in order to provide a pool of potential academics, researchers and high level professionals from which Wits and other institutions could benefit.

Wits should prepare itself to accommodate a potentially growing demand for part-time tertiary education. It should also recognise a need for flexible degree structures that permit an accumulation of credits over time and facilitate cross-disciplinary studies and mobility between institutions. A uniform credit-rating system within the University is needed for these innovations, and Wits should take the initiative in promoting regional co-operation between institutions in the post-secondary education sector.

The Mission Group saw these goals as achievable provided that a strategic plan was formulated and vigorously implemented. The plan should involve structure, systems, culture and leadership. As they put it:

> Organisations with inappropriate structures and systems are likely to be frustrated in the pursuit of their goals. In mature organisational structures, there is a danger of energy being wasted on minor changes within existing structures and systems when major revisions are required. Culture and mind-set are often invisible, and influence the decision-making process without the individuals concerned being aware of the assumptions underpinning their decisions. Finally, if the leadership of

an organisation is unable to focus on and respond flexibly to the external realities driving its future, failure can result.

After the report was approval in principle by both the Senate and the Council, a forum, comprising representatives of all the constituencies of the University and communities it served was convened in order to consider it before the Mission Statement was drafted.[4] The definitive document *Towards the twenty-first century: the University's Mission*, is reproduced in Appendix 16.

It would be a mistake to believe that the sole contribution made by South African academics in the prolonged and oppressive process that led to a non-racial democracy was in the issuing of antiapartheid and anti-Government statements, and in silent, dignified demonstrations.

Over many years, teachers and researchers in the open universities made substantial contributions towards redressing the appalling disadvantages suffered by South Africans who were not white. Their work, particularly in the fields of education, medicine, law, sociology, trade unionism, history, social anthropology, political studies, African literature, social work, community dentistry, human geography and applied psychology, alleviated to some extent the conditions under which the victims of apartheid were forced to live, and modified the thinking and approach to many of the established norms and problems of the country. For many of these academics, these studies have been a career-long commitment. Their contributions richly deserve to be recorded, but regrettably I am unable to do so within the scope of this book.

Notes

Preface

1 Lawrence Boya, *History of Black Student Organisation*, an address at the Nusas July Festival, 1987.
2 The term 'liberal' is difficult to define in the South African context because those who describe themselves as such in this country range widely from liberal conservatives to liberal democrats. A common thread in the apartheid era might be that all South African liberals and liberal organisations would have claimed to be opposed to apartheid although those on the left would have supported a universal adult franchise whereas those on the right and even some on the centre-right would have supported a qualified franchise.
3 Student Political Activism and Student Movements, in *The International Encyclopedia of Education*, Husen T and Postlethwaite T N (Eds-in-Chief), 2nd ed. Pergamon Press 1994, vol 10, pp 5778-5782.
4 Article by Professor Kenneth Keniston, Department of Psychology, Yale University, in the *New York Times Magazine*, 27 April 1969; reproduced in volume. 2 of *The University Crisis Reader: Confrontation and Counterattack*, Immanuel Wallerstein and Paul Starr (eds), Vintage Books 1971, p 453.
5 *The University Crisis Reader* vol 2, pp 495-515.
6 Student Political Activism and Student Movements, p 5780.
7 Ibid.
8 *Newsweek* magazine, 12 June 1989, No 24, p 24.
9 The Mervyn Shear Festschrift, *Journal of the Dental Association of South Africa*, vol 47, p 182, May 1992.
10 Utasa was one of a number of national university staff associations at that time. It was a liberal organisation and its members came only from the four English-language 'open' universities. It functioned by committee, held occasional conferences, issued statements on academic freedom issues and lobbied for improved salaries for academic staff. It had little influence with the Government but we thought it important. It gradually faded away and was disbanded when the Union of Democratic University Staff Associations (Udusa) was established in the 1980s.
11 Toyi-toyi n. A militant dance expressing defiance and solidarity especially during mass demonstrations; as v. especially in form toyi-toying. From Branford J and

Branford W. *A Dictionary of South African English.* 4th ed 1991, p 339, Oxford University Press. The toyi-toyi, with its accompanying singing, is frequently frightening and intimidating to white South Africans, particularly those observing it for the first time. It certainly had that effect on many white staff and students at the University, until they learned to understand that it was directed at the enemy, the apartheid regime, and not at whites as a group.
12 'Nkosi sikelel' iAfrika' (God Bless Africa) was regarded by many millions of South Africans as the national anthem and, since the inception of the Government of National Unity, has indeed become a part of the national anthem.

Introduction

1 Sasco came about through a merger of the black student body Sansco with the predominantly white Nusas in 1992. A more detailed discussion of these organisations is to be found in subsequent chapters.
2 Doc C93/332, Statement to all Staff and Students on Sasco Protest Action, from Acting Vice-Chancellor June Sinclair, 20 August 1993. The interdict itself is Case No 13884/93 in the Witwatersrand Local Division of the Supreme Court, C93/326.
3 Doc C93/333, a circular issued by Sasco, 'Boycott for transformation. Reject the admin's resort to police brutality', 20 August 1993.
4 *Wits Reporter,* 13 February 1995. The hostage-taking incident had occurred on 20 October 1994.
5 Numerous contributors. *The Role of the University in a Changing Society. Perceptions of Wits.* University of the Witwatersrand, June 1986. Usually referred to as the *Perceptions of Wits* document.
6 The use of the generic term 'black' to describe African, Coloured and Asian South Africans is preferred in this publication, although the words 'non-white' and 'non-European' have been used in order to avoid confusion, when referred to in official documents.
   The authors of *Perceptions of Wits* state (p 2) that 'the community participants consisted of organizations from the disadvantaged or black communities in the PWV (Pretoria, Witwatersrand, Vereeniging) area. When we use the term "disadvantaged community" we mean to refer to these groups of people who are deprived of equitable access to the resources of the country and of equitable access to the decision-making processes of the country. In South Africa these groups constitute the majority of the population. A community usually consists of individuals grouped into a variety of organizations. For this reason we thought it would be much more fruitful to interview a broad range of organizations, rather than survey selected individuals ...'
7 *Sunday Times,* 29 October 1995, *The Star,* 1 December 1995, *Business Day,* 16 February 1996.
8 Communication to the author, February 1996.

Chapter 1

1. *The Open Universities in South Africa*. Johannesburg, Witwatersrand University Press, 1957, Preface.
2. Murray, B K. *Wits. The Early Years: A History of the University of the Witwatersrand Johannesburg and its Precursors 1896-1939*, Ch 9, p 297ff, Johannesburg: Witwatersrand University Press, 1982. Hereinafter *Wits. The Early Years*.
3. Hofmeyr, the first Principal of Wits, was a notable liberal whose thinking was well ahead of the times in South Africa. He was later a Minister in the cabinet of J C Smuts.
4. Doc N.5f. Admission of Non-European Students: the Legal Position. Signed with initials W H, 11 March 1954.
5. Ibid.
6. Ibid.
7. Murray, B K. Wits as an 'open' university 1939-1959: black admissions to the University of the Witwatersrand. *Journal of Southern African Studies*, 16: 649676, 1990. See also Misc S/403/55, a report of an investigation done in all the faculties of the University to determine 'the provision necessary to admit non-European students to the full courses of study leading to degrees, diplomas and certificates in each faculty'. Supplementary Doc Misc F.M.S. 332/55 deals with the 'admission of non-Europeans to the Faculty of Medicine'. Murray's African Studies Seminar Paper No 350, World War II and Wits Student Politics, presented 11 October 1993; and Seminar Paper No 352, Raikes, Student Politics, and the Coming of Apartheid, Institute for Advanced Social Research, presented 28 February 1994, are other useful sources of reference.
8. Murray. Raikes, Student Politics and the Coming of Apartheid, p 14.
9. Ibid. The motion was proposed by Sydney Brenner and Phillip Tobias.
10. Murray. Wits as an 'open' university, pp 661-665.
11. Ibid, pp 666-667
12. Misc S/394/54. Statement requested by the Senate ... in regard to the admission of non-European students to the Faculty of Dentistry, p 2.
13. Ibid, p 3.
14. Ibid, p 5.
15. Ibid, p 6.
16. Ibid, p 7.
17. Murray. Wits as an 'open' university p 652 and Davenport, T R H. *South Africa. A Modern History*. 3rd ed. Macmillan, 1987, p 533.
18. Murray. Wits as an 'open' university, pp 671-672; and Raikes, Student Politics and the Coming of Apartheid, p 15.
19. Council minutes C/73/53, para 5, 24 April 1953.
20. Murray. Wits as an 'open' university, p 673; and Raikes, Student Politics, p 17.
21. Now the Department of Speech Pathology and Audiology.
22. Murray. Wits as an 'open' university, p 674.

23 Murray. Raikes, Student Politics, p 4.
24 Harold Wolpe was a co-accused in the Rivonia Trial with the leadership of the ANC. He escaped from prison, went into exile and taught at the University of Essex while playing a prominent role in the ANC in the UK. George Bizos became a prominent advocate much of whose work was in the human rights field. He was a member of the defence team in the Rivonia Trial. Michael O'Dowd became Chairman of the Chairman's Fund of Anglo American and De Beers. Godfrey Getz emigrated to the USA where he became an eminent academic biochemist.
25 Personal communication from Professor Trevor Arendorf.
26 University Archives file 111, to 1959, ref 142/a.
27 Ibid.
28 Murray. Raikes, Student Politics, p 11.
29 Murray, BK. Wits University, student politics, and the coming of apartheid. *Perspectives in Education*, 12, 1990, p 56.
30 Murray. Raikes, Student Politics, p 12.
31 Ibid, p 12 and footnote 37.
32 Ibid, p 59 and SRC minutes, 13 May 1952. See also Murray. Raikes, Student Politics, p 12 *et seq*.
33 Ibid, p 61 and SRC minutes 8 October 1952.
34 Murray. Raikes, Student Politics, p 15, and *Wits Student*, 6 March 1953.
35 Murray, ibid, p 16.
36 Murray, ibid.
37 Memorandum on Academic Non-segregation, 15 September 1953. University Archives file 111, to 1959.
38 Murray. Raikes, Student Politics, p 18.
39 Council minutes C/94/54, p 3, 23 April 1954.
40 Murray. Wits University, student politics, pp 64-67.
41 Council minutes C/145/54, para 7(b), 25 June 1954.
42 Misc C/39/62.
43 Council minutes C/48/62, 22 February 1962, para 12.
44 Council minutes C/256/62, 25 October 1962, para 8.
45 *Transvaler*, 19 May 1969; *Rand Daily Mail*, 20 May 1969.
46 University Archives file 113.
47 Ibid.
48 *Rand Daily Mail*, 28 May 1969.
49 *The Star*, 29 May 1969.
50 Letter from Bozzoli to the author, 12 February 1993.
51 Council meeting 15 September 1944, para 8(b) and Convocation Bulletin, No 5, March 1945. The Minister of Native Affairs was invited to lay the foundation stone and it was he who suggested that the building be called 'Douglas Smit House'. Smit was Secretary of Native Affairs and chairman of an interdepartmental committee which investigated the social, educational and health conditions of urban Africans in 1942. The Smit Committee also recommended the abolition of the pass laws. (*South Africa. A Modern History*, p 339).

52 Minutes of Finance Committee, 17 April 1963, doc 68/63, para 11. See also *The Star*, 26 September 1963.
53 *Eastern Province Herald*, 4 October 1963.

Chapter 2

1 *Hansard* 83, col 3576, 17 September 1953. Cited by Helen Suzman, *In No Uncertain Terms*, Jonathan Ball Publishers, 1993, pp 34-35.
2 The sequence of events following publication of the original Bill, called the Separate University Education Bill, in March 1957, are described in Academic Freedom Committees of University of Cape Town and University of the Witwatersrand. *The Open Universities in South Africa and Academic Freedom 1957-1974*, Chapter 2, pp 8-24, 1974, Juta. The provisions of the Bill and the reaction to it are detailed in South African Institute of Race Relations. *A Survey of Race Relations in South Africa 1956-57*, pp 196ff, cited in above reference.
3 Misc C/57A/54, University Archives file 113, N.5f, signed W H, 15 April 1954. The commissioners were Dr J E Holloway, Dr R W Wilcocks and Dr E G Malherbe.
4 Signed by S S Israelstam, President of Convocation. University Archives file 111, to 1959.
5 The full text of the motion is to be found in the University Archives file 111, to 1959.
6 An open letter to the public, dated 29 October, 1956, and written by E M Wentzel, President of Nusas (University Archives file 111, to 1959) provides a useful account of events at that time and in particular, the reactions of the students. See also discussion in the Council of the resolution, Council minutes C/209/56, para 6B, 14 September 1956.
7 Minutes of the first meeting of The Open Universities Liaison Committee (Witwatersrand) held on 23 October 1956. University Archives file 111, to 1959.
8 The full texts of these addresses are to be found in the University Archives file 111, to 1959. Hoernlé was Professor of Philosophy and had been the Senate's choice for Principal when the Council appointed Raikes in 1928 (*Wits. The Early Years*, p 132); I D MacCrone was Professor of Psychology and later Vice-Chancellor. W F Nkomo was a medical doctor and one of the founders of the ANC Youth League, who died in 1972 while President of the SA Institute of Race Relations (*South Africa. A Modern History*, p 347); W Pollak was an eminent member of the Johannesburg Bar who was closely associated with the University's Faculty of Law.
9 University Archives file 111, to 1959.
10 Council minutes C/261/56 pp 1 and 5, 14 December 1956.
11 Held in Cape Town, 9, 10, 11 January 1957. The Wits delegates were F G Hill, I Glyn Thomas, L M Lachmann, G H L Le May, J S Marais, I D MacCrone, M W Richards, S S Israelstam, P V Tobias, A Welsh. The UCT delegates were B Z Beinart, D V Cowen, J H O Day, F Forman, M Grant, F G Holliman, W E Isaac, E N Keen, L Marquard, T W Price, H M Robertson, L M Thompson, M van den Ende, S van der Horst, M Wilson.

12 *The Open Universities in South Africa and Academic Freedom 1957-1974.*
13 Universities in South Africa. *Nature 179(4563)* pp 745-747, 13 April 1957.
14 Council minutes C/59/57 p 1, 22 February 1957. For a report of the Council's 'Open Universities' Liaison Committee, see Misc C/48/57, 25 March 1957 and Misc C/151/57, 26 June 1957.
15 Misc C/49/57.
16 Council minutes C/53/57 pp 2-3, 25 March 1957.
17 Ibid, p 4. See also Misc C/47/57 for the wording of the petition to be heard at the Bar of the House to be submitted on behalf of the Universities of Cape Town and the Witwatersrand.
18 Misc C/66/57. Record of the interview between the Council's deputation and the Hon the Minister of Education, Arts and Science, at Cape Town on Monday, 1 April 1957, from 10.15 to 11.20am.
19 Misc C/93/57.
20 Ref 04. Substance of the petition to Parliament sent by the Registrar to all members of the academic staff, dated 23.4.57. It was also signed by 2 200 students.
21 *The Open Universities*, p 8. Also to be found here are further useful references, including one to *A Survey of Race Relations in South Africa 1956-57*, pp 196ff which contains an account of the provisions of the Bill and the responses to it.
22 The Council document *Evidence for submission to the Commission on the Separate University Education Bill* dated 29.10.57, is Misc C/276/57. The documents submitted by these bodies are in University Archives file 111, to 1959.
23 *The Open Universities*, pp 8-9. It was the student who would be prosecuted and the universities who were required to implement the policy.
24 Ibid, p 10.
25 Wits Registry L9/6.
26 According to Professor Noel Garson, Sutton did not take part in the procession.
27 Various documents in the University Archives file 111, to 1959. The addresses of Sutton and MacCrone are to be found in this file.
28 University Archives file 111, to 1959. The signatories were Saul Bastomsky, Hugh Isaacs, Dawn Jacobson, Justin Joffe, Mariemootho Pillay and Rose Innes Phahle.
29 The proceedings of the ceremony are reported in the *University Gazette*, July 1959; *Convocation Commentary*, No 2, 1959; *Wits Student*, April 16 1959.
30 University Archives file 111, 1960-69.
31 *The Open Universities*, p 12. The Chancellor's Lecture has been delivered by Sir Eric Ashby, Master of Clare College, Cambridge (1962); Sir Robert Birley (1965); Lord Butler, Master of Trinity College, Cambridge (1969); Dr Leo Marquard (1973); Mr Harry Oppenheimer (1979); Dr Clark Kerr, Berkeley, California (1976); Professor Harry Hinsley, Vice-Chancellor, University of Cambridge (1985). Feetham Memorial Lectures have been delivered by Dr the Hon O D Schreiner (1963); the Hon Garfield Todd, former Premier of Southern Rhodesia (1964); Sir Edward Boyle, British parliamentarian (1966); Lord James of Rusholme, Vice-Chancellor of the University of York (1967); Lord Walston,

Chairman of the British Institute of Race Relations (1968); Baroness Wootton of Abinger (1969); Sir Robert Birley (1970); Miss Joan Lestor, British parliamentarian (1971); Jeremy Thorpe, Leader of the British Liberal Party (1972); Dr Manas Buthelezi (1974); Professor Ronald Dworkin, Oxford (1976); Mr Percy Qoboza, Editor of *Sowetan* (1977); Mr Justice J Didcott (1978); Dr David Owen MP (1979); Senator Garfield Todd (1980 – not delivered as visa was refused. An address was given instead by Professor D J du Plessis, Vice-Chancellor of the University. Todd's lecture was published in *The Rand Daily Mail*, 25 July 1980); US Congressman John Anderson (1981); Mrs Helen Joseph (1982); Mr Jacobo Timerman (1983 – visa refused and Lecture given by Mr Allister Sparks); Mr Jeremy Cronin and Rev Beyers Naudé (1984); Archbishop Desmond Tutu and Attorney Priscilla Jana (1985); Mr Eric Molobi and Mr Mluleki George (1986); Professor Hugh Phillpott (1987); Mr Jan van Eck MP and Mr Vusi Khanyile (1988); Mr Ihron Rensburg and Mr Govan Mbeki (1990); Professor Njabulo Ndebele (1991); no speaker (1992); Professor Mervyn Shear (1993).
32 *Rand Daily Mail*, 17 April and *Star* 16 and 17 April 1969.
33 *Rand Daily Mail*, 6 September, 1969 covered the court proceedings; and *Sunday Times*, 7 September, 1969 published a leading article critical of the action of the police.
34 *Rand Daily Mail*, 16, 17 April 1969.
35 *The Universities and the State 1959-1969*. Edited by Richard Beynon. Copy in University Archives file 111, 1959-69.
36 University Archives file 111, 1959-69. Various notices and booklets, including the full text of Tobias's paper, Freedom and the Universities.
37 *The Open Universities*, p vii.
38 Ibid, p x.
39 Bozzoli's memorandum is Doc C76/209; Council Doc is C76/222.
40 Draft Working Paper on Admission of Black Students, dated 16 September 1976. In University Archives file 111, 1970 to 1979.
41 Memorandum on the Admission of Black Students, signed by Bozzoli but not dated. University Archives file 111, 1970 to 1979.
42 S76/922.
43 Memorandum from the Senate Academic Freedom Committee, dated 14 September 1976, entitled 'Re-opening the University'.
44 Undated document issued and printed by the Wages and Economics Commission, c/o SRC. In University Archives file 111, 1970 to 1979.
45 Address to the University. Meeting on academic freedom held in the Great Hall at lunch-time on Wednesday 15 September 1976. University Archives file 111, 1970 to 1979.
46 Circular from Bozzoli to all members of the staff, 16 November, 1976. University Archives file 111, 1970 to 1979.
47 Report to Council meeting on 29 October 1976, Doc C76/469.
48 Personal communication, February 1993.

Chapter 3

1. Frederikse, Julie. *The Unbreakable Thread: Non-racialism in South Africa.* 1990, Ravan Press, p 273.
2. Meeting of Council 25 October 1962, Doc C/256/62, para 2(c).
3. *Convocation Commentary,* November 1969, p 19.
4. Statement by Vice-Chancellor MacCrone, *Sunday Times,* 20 December 1964.
5. *Rand Daily Mail,* 13 May 1966.
6. *The Star,* 13 May 1966.
7. *Rand Daily Mail,* 26 May 1966.
8. *The Star,* 19 August 1968.
9. *Rand Daily Mail,* 20 August 1968. At that time the newly-established Rand Afrikaans University occupied temporary premises directly opposite Wits.
10. Ibid, 19 August 1969.
11. Ibid, 17 August 1968.
12. Ibid, p 32, which cites Section 15 of Act 92 of 1970.
13. *The Star,* 18 May 1970.
14. *The Star,* 15 July 1970.
15. *Rand Daily Mail,* 8 October 1970.
16. *The Open Universities,* p 38 provides details of the 90-day and the 180-day detention laws and the Terrorism Act detention provision.
17. Address by Bozzoli, 29 February 1972. University Archives file 111, 1970 to 1979.
18. Statement to the academic staff by the Vice-Chancellor, Ref S.5/lf dated 2 May 1972.
19. *The Open Universities,* pp 32-34, which cites Act 17 of 1956.
20. Ibid, p 33. 7 June 1972. The Minister was acting under section 2(3) of the Riotous Assemblies Act.
21. Davenport T R H. *South Africa. A Modern History.* 3rd ed. Macmillan, 1987, p 427. Tiro was subsequently killed by a car bomb in Botswana, and his assassin has never been identified.
22. *Convocation Commentary,* September 1972.
23. The full text of Bozzoli's address to the Assembly of the University, Thursday 8 June 1972, is in the University Archives.
24. *Rand Daily Mail,* 10 June and *Sunday Times,* 11 June 1972.
25. Press statement to *Rand Daily Mail* 9 June, *Star* 10 June 1972.
26. *The Open Universities,* p 34.
27. *Rand Daily Mail,* 10 June 1972.
28. The full text of the letter from Bozzoli to Vorster is published as an Appendix, pp 48-49, in *The Open Universities,* and in *Convocation Commentary,* September 1972, p 1.
29. Personal communication from Bozzoli to the author, February 1993.
30. *Rand Daily Mail,* 13 June 1972.
31. The Rapportryers was formed as an Afrikaans counter to organisations such as Lions and Rotary. It was regarded as an ideal training ground for future members of

the exclusive Afrikaner Broederbond. From: Strydom H and Wilkins I. *The Super-Afrikaners: Inside the Afrikaner Broederbond.* 1st ed, Jonathan Ball, 1978, p 420.
32 *Vaderland,* 14 June 1972.
33 *The Star,* 16 June 1972 and *Sunday Tribune,* 18 June 1972. Open letter to parents in University Archives file 111, 1970 to 1979.
34 *Vaderland,* 14 June 1972.
35 *Transvaler,* 17 April 1969.
36 Ibid
37 Telex from Rectors of six Afrikaans Universities to SAPA, 20 June 1972. The full text of the statement is in University Archives file 111, 1970 to 1979. The statement was signed by Professors H J J Bingle (Potchefstroom University for Christian National Education), J N de Villiers (Stellenbosch), E M Hamman (Pretoria), B Kok (Orange Free State), E J Marais (Port Elizabeth), G V N Viljoen (Rand Afrikaans University).
38 Strydom H and Wilkins I. *The Super-Afrikaners.*
39 *The Star,* 13 June, 1972.
40 *The Open Universities,* pp 36-37.
41 Suzman. *In No Uncertain Terms,* p 132.
42 *The Open Universities,* p 37.
43 *The Unbreakable Thread,* p 144.
44 Ibid, p 145.
45 The full statement is to be found in University Archives file 111, 1970 to 1979.
46 *South Africa. A Modern History,* p 428.
47 *Rand Daily Mail,* 26 August 1975.
48 *The Star,* 25 August 1975 and *Rand Daily Mail,* 26 August 1975. Also detained were a member of the extra-mural studies department of the University of Cape Town and his girlfriend.
49 *The Star,* 26 August 1975.
50 *Rand Daily Mail,* 27 August 1975.
51 Ibid.
52 *The Star,* 27 August 1975.
53 *Main Report of the Commission of Inquiry into Universities.* Department of National Education, RP 25/1974. Obtainable from the Government Printer, Private Bag X85, 0001 Pretoria.
54 Bozzoli, G R. *Commission of Inquiry into Universities. Minority Report in Respect of Certain Chapters of the Main Report, and Having Reference Also to the Second Interim Report,* 26 November, 1973. See also the statement to overseas press on the Van Wyk de Vries Commission from Professor G R Bozzoli, Vice-Chancellor and Principal, 12 November 1974. Both documents in University Archives file 111, 1970 to 1979.
55 Bozzoli. *Commission of Inquiry.* Ch 4, p 87, para 8.8.
56 Radio interview with Van Wyk de Vries, 3 November 1974.
57 Interview with Bozzoli, *The Star,* 6 November 1974.
58 Council minutes C/75/118, para 75.25.3, p 48, 21 March 1975.
59 Senate minutes, Doc S75/463, p 9, item 75.49 in which Senate supported the

contents of Doc S75/434 which sets out the response of the University to the report of the Van Wyk de Vries Commission, for submission to the Committee of University Principals.
60 The statements from these bodies are to be found in the University Archives file 111, 1970 to 1979.
61 *The Unbreakable Thread*, p 151.
62 *Academic Freedom. Message from the Vice-Chancellor, 23 August 1977.* The document is to be found in University Archives file 111, 1970 to 1979.

Chapter 4

1 Steve Mufson in the Introduction to Tom Lodge and Bill Nasson (eds) *All, Here and Now: Black Politics in South Africa in the 1980s*, co-published by the Ford Foundation and David Philip, 1991, p 6.
2 Ibid, p 7.
3 *South Africa. A Modern History*, p 418.
4 A succinct but graphic description of the circumstances surrounding Biko's detention, aspects of the inquest into his death, the debates in the House of Assembly on the matter and subsequent events are to be found in Suzman, *In No Uncertain Terms*, pp 224-231. For a detailed account and analysis see Hilda Bernstein, *No. 46 - Steve Biko*, International Defence and Aid Fund, 1978, reprinted in 1987.

To the shock and distress of many members of the medical profession, the South African Medical and Dental Council (SAMDC), after a disciplinary inquiry, took a decision more than two years after Biko's death that there was no *prima facie* evidence of improper or disgraceful conduct on the part of the three doctors – Benjamin Tucker, Ivor Lang and Colin Hersch – who had treated Biko before his death. At a meeting on 27 June 1980, the Board of the University's Faculty of Medicine resolved unanimously to dissociate itself from the decision of the SAMDC. The Faculty endorsed the guidelines for doctors concerning detainees and prisoners adopted in 1975 by the 29th World Medical Assembly of the World Medical Association in Tokyo and known as the 'Declaration of Tokyo'.

In November 1984 a group of doctors, including the Dean of Medicine at Wits, Professor Phillip Tobias, Professor Trefor Jenkins of Wits's Department of Human Genetics and Professor Frances Ames of the University of Cape Town, took the matter to court and obtained an order against the SAMDC which compelled it to set aside the disciplinary committee's decision and to hold an inquiry. Tucker and Lang were both found guilty of misconduct but received absurdly light sentences. Further public criticism by Tobias and Mrs Helen Suzman resulted in an order from the full SAMDC that Tucker's name be struck off the medical register.
5 *Illustrated History of South Africa*, p 440.
6 *Illustrated History of South Africa*, pp 442-4.
7 *South Africa. A Modern History*, pp 433-4.
8 Ibid, p 434.
9 This and following paragraphs referring to events during this period are from minutes of the Council meeting 2 July 1976, Doc C76/280, item 76.64.

10 Dan 'Gorbachev' Mashitisho (BSS Executive), 1990. A Challenge to Non-participation Strategy. The paper is in the University Archives. Mashitisho gives 1969 as the date of the breakaway from Nusas, but Davenport (p 418) dates it as 1968. See also Lawrence Boya (Sansco NEC) History of Black Student Organisation in *Let Us Speak of Freedom*, Nusas July Festival Speeches, 1987, Education for a free South Africa, p 46, which describes the major black student movements in South Africa from the early 1940s to 1987.
11 Report by the Deputy Vice-Chancellor (Student Affairs) to Council, 15 November, 1990, Doc C90/566, para 90.89. A transitional committee was formed to operate until the next SRC elections in 1991, and this would fundamentally change the nature of campus life. Sansco and Nusas had also agreed to disband when a new national body, known as the South African Students' Congress (Sasco) was formed.
12 The non-participation strategy is expounded in detail in the Mashitisho document.
13 *Citizen*, 7 August 1980, *The Star*, 8 August 1980 and *Transvaler*, 12 August 1980.
14 *Transvaler*, 28 August 1980.
15 Interview with Peta Thorneycroft, *Sunday Express*, 31 May 1981.
16 Crystal in interview with Marc Dobson, *Sunday Times*, 31 May 1981.
17 Crystal to the author in 1983.
18 *Report of the Commission of Inquiry into events on the campus of the University of the Witwatersrand between August 1985 and October 1986*, 17 November 1986. Hereinafter referred to as *Commission of Inquiry, 1986*. The Commissioners were Advocates G Bizos SC (Chairman), W H R Schreiner SC and E Cameron of the Centre for Applied Legal Studies of the University. An earlier Commission of Inquiry into the events which occurred on the campus of the University of the Witwatersrand on Tuesday 14 May 1985 (hereinafter referred to as *Commission of Inquiry, 1985*) had reported on 20 June 1985. This report is Doc C85/321. The Commissioners were Advocates J Browde SC (Chairman), G Bizos SC and E Cameron. Both reports will be considered in more detail in subsequent chapters.
19 *Weekly Mail*, 26 July 1991; *Wits Student*, August 1991; *Beeld, Business Day, Citizen* and *The Star*, 2 August 1991; *Sunday Star*, 4 August 1991; *The Star*, 16 August 1991.
20 *Wits Student*, August 1991.
21 Phillip van Niekerk, *The Sunday Independent*, 16 July 1995.
22 *South Africa. A Modern History*, p 441-442. The Department of Co-operation and Development was previously the Department of Bantu Affairs, and briefly, the Department of Plural Relations. The Bill was scrapped in 1984.
23 Council minute 81.60, 8 May 1981, *Rand Daily Mail*, 21 March 1981, and *Sunday Times*, 31 May 1981.
24 Council meeting 8 May 1981, para 81.60.
25 Council meeting 12 June 1981, Doc C81/315, minute 81.74.3.
26 Dated 26 March and 23 March, respectively. University Archives.
27 *The Star*, 21 March 1981 and *Sunday Times*, 31 May 1981.
28 A few years later the SMA issued a pamphlet which cast the actions of the police at Sharpeville in 1960 in a sympathetic light and suggested that the events had been

'manipulated to produce anti-SA propaganda'. *Commission of Inquiry,* 1986, p 46, para 85.
29 The *Commission of Inquiry, 1986,* p 47, para 8.7 stated: 'It seems to us that the anger evoked in BSS members and amongst many other students by the prominence of SMA displays, particularly at or near certain occasions, cannot be seen in isolation either from the tragic events which are occurring in this country at present or from the University's own avowed stance in relation to these events ...'
30 *Sunday Express,* 31 May 1981.
31 Interview with Boraine by Julie Frederickse, *The Unbreakable Thread,* p 173.
32 Report by the Vice-Chancellor to Council on 12 June 1981, Doc C81/315 para 81.73.
33 *The Reporter,* 8 June 1981.
34 Council meeting, 12 June 1981, para 81.73.4.
35 Ibid, para 81.73.9.
36 Council meeting 24 July 1981, Doc C81/373, para 81.91.
37 See *Sunday Times,* 14, 21 June; *Citizen,* 22 June 1981.
38 *The Reporter,* 8 June 1981.
39 President P W Botha appointed General Magnus Malan, Chief of the Army, as Minister of Defence. Under him the concept was developed of a 'total strategy' against what the Government and its various agencies presented as the 'total onslaught' by Marxist enemies against South Africa. This became the mainspring of Government policy. See *South Africa. A Modern History,* p 438. Propaganda pushing this slogan was most effective in influencing the attitudes of many whites, particularly young white men conscripted into the armed forces.
40 *Citizen* and *The Star,* 3 June, 1981.
41 Article by Ameen Akhalwaya, *Rand Daily Mail* 19 June 1981.
42 *Citizen,* 20 June 1981.
43 Ibid. See their leading article. Also *The Star* and *Vaderland,* 19 June 1981.
44 Press statement 27 November 1981. Archives file 116. Those detained were Nicholas (Fink) Haysom, a research officer in the Centre for Applied Legal Studies, Firoz Cachalia, Keith Coleman, Debbie Elkon, Ben Greyling, Barbara Hogan, Leslie Lax, Elaine Mohammed, Michael O'Donovan, and Clive van Heerden.
45 Aggett was an organiser for the Food and Canning Workers' Union. *Illustrated History of South Africa,* p 455. An inquest into his death exonerated the Security Police despite evidence from a fellow detainee that he had been beaten shortly before he was found hanged in his cell. Note in Frederikse, *The Unbreakable Thread,* p 224.
46 S82/597. Press statement by the Senate Academic Freedom Committee.
47 News Release, University of the Witwatersrand, 25 August 1983.
48 Interview with Du Plessis in *Zoo Lake Advertiser,* January 1978.
49 Report of the Enquiry into Admissions and Exclusions, Doc S91/1218, 29 August 1991, Table 1, p 4.
50 *Zoo Lake Advertiser,* January 1978. See also reports in *The Star,* 4 December 1978, of an address at a graduation ceremony of the College of Education; *Citizen,*

18 May 1981, of an address at a University graduation ceremony; in *Citizen*, 25 November 1983, of a speech at a luncheon soon before his retirement.
51 *Zoo Lake Advertiser,* January 1978.
52 The Academic Plan. Doc S80/945.
53 Report of the Enquiry into Admissions and Exclusions, Table 1, p 4.

Chapter 5

1 See *South Africa. A Modern History*, pp 468-471.
2 *Rand Daily Mail,* 3 June 1983.
3 *Rand Daily Mail,* 30 and 31 May 1984.
4 *Rand Daily Mail,* 30 November 1984.
5 *Rand Daily Mail,* 1 December 1984.
6 Report of the Commission, doc C85/321, (referred to as Commission of Inquiry, 1985).
7 Ibid. A full description of the events is to be found in the Report of the Commission, p 6ff. There are also detailed reports by the Deputy Vice-Chancellor (Student Affairs) dated 17 May 1985 and the Registrar, Mr K W Standenmacher, dated 29 May 1985. See also reports by students in *De minimis*, May 1985, and by Glen Kruger, Chairman of the Student Moderate Alliance in a letter to Tober dated 16 May 1985.
8 Jan Smuts Avenue is the main thoroughfare on the eastern boundary of the University and is a favourite venue for student demonstrations (see map p xx).
9 Another main thoroughfare on the southern border of the campus often used for demonstrations.
10 Professor Karl Tober, previously Deputy Vice-Chancellor and Professor of German Studies, had succeeded Du Plessis on 1 January 1984.
11 From personal notes prepared by the author, 17 May 1985. There are also detailed reports by Mr Ken Standenmacher, Registrar, and Mr Cliff Hurst, Head of University Security.
12 *Commission of Inquiry, 1985,* pp 23-24.
13 Ibid.
14 Ibid, pp 43 and 44.
15 Council meeting 2 August 1985, doc C85/362, para 85.75.1. See also doc C85/427, Précis of recommendations of the Commission of Inquiry into events on campus on Tuesday 14 May 1985 and the response to them of the University Council. Also unnumbered document dated 22 April 1986 prepared by Deputy Registrar (Student Affairs), Mrs Pauline Cuzen, which reports on a series of meetings with individual students and student organisations arranged to attempt implementation of the Commission's recommendations.
16 Ibid.

Chapter 6

1 The Deans at the time were L J Suzman (Arts), C F Cresswell (Science), M McGregor (Medicine), R N Brits (Commerce), L A Tager (Law), J F van

Reenen (Dentistry), J G Muller (Architecture), D R White (Education), and G S Andrews (Business Administration).
2 For details of the events of 12 August, see the incident report dated 12 August 1985 from Mr C Hurst, Head of Security, to the Vice-Chancellor. The week's events are outlined in Don's Diary, written by the author, published in *The Times Higher Education Supplement*, 6 September 1985, p 4.
3 A stout rhinoceros or hippopotamus hide whip. From *A Dictionary of South African English*, Oxford University Press, p 289.
4 Letter from author to Advocate S Kentridge SC, 3 October 1985, affidavit sworn on 26 September 1985 by Mr V T Maphai and letter from author to Assistant Supervisor, Campus Law Clinic, 24 December 1985.
5 General Assembly: University of the Witwatersrand, Johannesburg: Friday, 16 August 1985: Address by the Vice-Chancellor and Principal. Unnumbered document.
6 In fact Tober had quoted the 1972 resolution verbatim in his address.
7 Special Meeting of the Boards of the Faculties of Arts, Education and Science, 9 October 1985, doc S85/1339A.
8 Cresswell was also Professor of Botany at Wits, and later Vice-Principal and Deputy Vice-Chancellor of the University of Natal.
9 Special meeting of the Boards of the Faculties, doc S85/1339A. According to Professor Cresswell, the persons responsible for drafting the statement were himself, Professors J Booyens (Chemistry), R Crewe (Zoology) and H Garnett (Microbiology).
10 Meeting of ABEX 22 October 1985, doc S85/1438.
11 Report at meeting of Additional Academic Board, 3 March 1986, doc S86/447, para 86.10. Senate meeting 3 December 1985 doc S85/1669, see para 85.91; Council meeting 6 December 1985 doc C85/656, see para 85.137.
12 Doc S85/1303A.
13 See statement from Vice-Chancellor dated 25 March 1986, on events during the week 17 to 21 March 1986; and report from Head of Security on incidents on Friday 21 March 1986. I have also used personal notes made for a report to a Special Meeting of Senate 2 April 1986.
14 The incidents considered by the *Commission of Inquiry, 1986* took place on 1, 20, 25 March; 1, 20, 29, 30 May; 9, 15, 20, 27 June; and 28 August 1986. The general tenor of these demonstrations was very similar, and two previous incidents have been reported *in extenso* earlier in this work. Without wishing to diminish the importance of the effects of each episode on the persons involved, or on the University, it is not intended to give detailed accounts of all of them. They are well-documented in the University Archives.
15 *South Africa. A Modern History*, p 485.
16 Author's personal notes. The BSS leadership was under great pressure from the grass roots membership and policy determination was from the bottom up.
17 A free translation from *Die Vaderland*, 21 March 1986.
18 On 21 March 1985 forty-five people had been killed by police in Langa township, Uitenhage.

19 See report and annexures dated 24 March 1986 from C F Hurst, Head of Security, to Col S Smith, Registrar (Administration).
20 Doc C86/95.
21 See the article in *The Observer* by Neal Ascherson and extracts from the correspondence columns of *The Times* and *Guardian* cited in Ucko, P, *Academic Freedom and Apartheid. The Story of the World Archaeological Congress*. 1st ed, 1987, Gerald Duckworth & Co, pp 239-240.
22 *The Times*, 6 September 1986.
23 *Guardian*, 9 October 1986.
24 John O'Leary in *The Times Higher Education Supplement*, 5 December 1986.
25 Personal communication from Debra Nails to the author.
26 The statement headed 'Disruption of Academic Meetings' was issued on campus and circulated to all staff on 20 October 1986.
27 According to a report in *Die Burger*, 25 March 1986, Lambson was principal of the Bordeaux Primary School in Randburg (near Johannesburg) and was a past-chairman of the Transvaal Teachers' Association.
28 In April 1987 Lambson challenged Tober about a letter, quoting the reference number, that the Vice-Chancellor had sent to the acting-chairman of the SMA.
29 For example, letters from R Dexta, Parkwood in *Citizen*, 2 April 1986 and *The Star*, 4 April 1986. He found that 'most of the leftists views are both ridiculous and naïve' and considered that 'one-man-one-vote' rule would mean the end of true freedom for the white population. Also, identical letters from Lambson to *The Star*, 9 April 1986 and *Citizen*, 11 April 1986.
30 Under the headline 'Wits not immune from this pain'.
31 Chaplinsky v New Hampshire 315 US 568, 62 S Ct 766 (1942). Cited by the Commission.
32 pp 59-60 of the report.
33 pp 72-75 of the report.
34 Senate minutes S86/1246, para 86.45.3.
35 Academic Board minutes, doc S88/1558, para 88/12615 November 1988.
36 Doc S88/711.
37 Zellick, G. Freedom of Speech in Universities, Polytechnics and Colleges. *Patterns of Prejudice*, 22, 36-38, 1988.
38 Ibid.
39 *Daily Dispatch*, 3 March 1988.
40 Fax from Jackson Mthembu, chairperson Namibia Solidarity Committee to Charlton, 17 October 1989.
41 Fax from Charlton to Mthembu, 18 October 1989.
42 From report prepared by P M Stevens, 31 July 1989. Personal file, 'Student Unrest 1988-1990'.
43 *E P Herald*, 1 August 1989.
44 Letter from the author to Keith Shear, 2 August 1989.
45 Personal file, 'Student Unrest, 1988-1990'. Note on an informal discussion held on 18 September 1989.

46 Statement by the Registrar, KWS/SA/15/13, 9 October 1989.
47 Ibid.

Chapter 7

1. Report of a meeting of representatives of the BSS with the Student Affairs Office, 17 April 1986.
2. From a report made to the author soon after the incident and contained in a telex from the acting Vice-Chancellor, Professor R W Charlton to the Minister of Defence, General Magnus Malan. Charlton frequently acted for Vice-Chancellor Tober during this period because the latter was in ill-health.
3. *Vaderland, Citizen* and *Business Day*, 27 May 1988.
4. From Mrs Jocelyn Cairns, SRC Administration Co-ordinator, to the author.
5. Sparks, Allister. *The Mind of South Africa*, Heinemann 1990, pp 351-354.
6. From a minute prepared by the author the following day.
7. *The Mind of South Africa*, p 247. In May 1983 a car bomb explosion in downtown Pretoria outside a building housing the headquarters of the South African Air Force, killed 19 people and injured nearly 200, many of them civilians. The military wing of the ANC, Umkhonto we Sizwe, accepted responsibility.
8. The Vice-Chancellor's Graduation address, 24 May 1986 is published in full in the booklet *Providing for the Needs of Black Students in the University*, revised ed 1986, pp 40-42.
9. See statement dated 3 June 1986 from the Vice-Chancellor and Principal on events during the week 26 to 31 May 1986.
10. The film was donated to the University by the BBC and is housed in the Archives.
11. A detailed account of the events of 30 May, as described by students who were involved, is to be found in *Wits Student*, 38(8), 3 June 1986.
12. Adv Martin Brassey, instructed by Kathleen Satchwell, appeared for the University.
13. *Citizen*, 31 July 1986.
14. The full resolution of the general meeting and the statement of the executive committee, signed by the chairman, Mr D A Young, are in the records of the Academic Staff Association.
15. *The Star*, 21 May 1986.
16. *The Star*, 3 June 1986, p 13.
17. Forcefulness, also figurative of political 'steamroller' tactics. *A Dictionary of South African English*, p 165.
18. The request was made through Mrs Helen Suzman MP.
19. Report by the author dated 25 June 1986, headed 'Raid on Glyn Thomas House Residence – 15 June 1986, and on Mofolo Residence – 20 June 1986,' and report by Dr S Sibisi, Warden of Glyn Thomas House, stamped 26 June 1986.
20. The residence had been established for black students at the time that the University practised social segregation and continued as such during the period that the Group Areas Act was rigidly applied. However, white medical students

were given overnight accommodation there when they had duties at Baragwanath Hospital. When the University wished it to become an integrated residence, this was opposed by the residence house committee and the BSS who considered that it should continue to be exclusively for blacks because the housing needs of black students were so great. In any case it is unlikely that many white students would have elected to stay there in view of its geographic location. The residence was finally closed at the end of 1993.

21 Letter from the Warden, Dr M A Marais, to the author, 27 June 1986.
22 From a statement by the Deputy Vice-Chancellor (Student Affairs) at a meeting called by students: 6 August 1986. The Minister of Education and Culture was not a member of the Cabinet. In terms of the constitution he was responsible to the House of Assembly for the education of whites.
23 Guidelines for Wits Departments: Disappearances, Detainees, Release. University Archives file 116.
24 Senate meeting 2 December 1986, doc S86/2130, para 86.95.
25 See Emergency Law. Papers presented at a workshop, Johannesburg, April 1987. Nicholas Haysom and Laura Mangan (eds), p 4 *seq*, 1987, Centre for Applied Legal Studies, University of the Witwatersrand.
26 Report by Tober 29 August 1986 and *Wits Student* 38(13) September 1986. Powell is now a Senator, representing the Inkatha Freedom Party.
27 p 23ff of the report.
28 pp 37-56 of the report.
29 Council meeting 5 December 1986, doc C86/544, para 86.132.2.2.
30 Notes of meeting, prepared by J Stead, 28 November 1986.
31 *Weekly Mail* 26 July 1991, *The Star*, 2 August 1991, *Sunday Star*, 4 July 1991.
32 *The Star*, 16 August 1991.
33 Letter to *The Star* 26 August 1991.
34 Circular headed 'Meeting Banned', issued by the BSS, 8 October 1986.
35 Various letters in the author's file – Student Unrest, July 1986-Dec 1987.

Chapter 8

1 Council meeting 3 December 1982, doc C82/668, para 82.145 and special Senate meeting 8 March 1983, doc S83/422.
2 Council meeting 3 December 1982, doc C82/668, para 82.145.
3 Doc S83/422. See also doc C83/103A dated 16 March 1983, which summarises the statements and documents relating to the proposed amendment to the Act. The definitive document setting out the University's opposition to the proposed quota system was sent to Members of Parliament.
4 Ibid.
5 Council doc C83/162, para 83.24.3.
6 News Release, University of the Witwatersrand, 12 April 1983.
7 Council minutes, doc C83/205, para 83.47.1. The addresses are published as a booklet *A General Assembly of the University*, University Archives file 111, 1980 onwards.

8 Council minutes, doc C83/312, para 83.84.
9 See Senate doc S83/1160, para 83.67.3.5 and *Government Gazette,* 217(8790), 6 July 1983.
10 Doc C83/312.
11 Council meeting 5 August 1983, doc C83/383, para 83.102.2.
12 Letter dated 1 August 1983 from Stutterheim to the Minister.
13 Doc C83/383. At the second meeting the Chairman of Council and Dr Steyn represented the University.
14 Senate meeting 30 August 1983, doc S83/1160, para 83.67. See letter dated 25 August 1983 from the Minister to Stutterheim.
15 Ibid.
16 University Policy, 1983 Calendar, pp 30-31.
17 This and the following paragraphs from doc S83/1160.
18 Ibid para 83.67.5 and SRC Motion E: Resol 194/83.
19 S83/1160, para 83.67.6.
20 Council meeting 2 September 1983, doc C83/476, para 83.109.4.
21 Although the racial composition of the student body did not influence the subsidy formula, this device was used by the state to obtain the figures. For all this, the University found it useful to maintain a record of black student numbers, as these were invariably required by funding bodies that wished to support the studies of black students.
22 News Release, 8 September, 1983. Academic Freedom file 111, 1980 onwards.
23 Report of the Enquiry into Admissions and Exclusions, Table 1, p 4.
24 Ibid, Table 2, p 4.
25 Interim registration figures on 17 February 1995.
26 Report of the Enquiry into Admissions and Exclusions, Table 5, p 6.
27 Clase ref M3/4/5/1.
28 Tober to Clase, ref (5)83.
29 Chief Executive Director to Registrar, ref 14/4/2/1/7/5.
30 Council meeting 17 May 1991, doc C91/225, para 91.28.
31 The report was compiled from notes made by the author at the meeting.
32 Tober, who had been on a visit to universities in the USA, was reported to have made the remark to a gathering of students at one university.
33 Ampie Coetzee was an Associate Professor in the Department of Afrikaans and Nederlands. The author had not heard nor read of Professor Coetzee making this statement.
34 Council minutes C87/286, para 87.81.3, 7 August 1987.
35 In terms of the 1983 Constitution, the House of Assembly had responsibility for 'white own affairs', the House of Representatives for 'coloured own affairs', the House of Delegates for 'Indian own affairs' and the Department of Education and Development Aid for 'black' education.
36 Minister's ref 3/4/12/1; 14/5/B.
37 Notes of the meeting were compiled by the author, 'De Klerk's regulations' file 1.
38 S88/711.
39 Minutes of Exco of Council, doc 87/308, p 2, para 87.47, 14 August 1987.

40 Doc S87/1222, headed 'The Senate's response to the Minister's letter concerning conditions determined under section 25(1) of the Universities' Act, 1955 (Act 61 of 1955)'. The minutes of the Special Senate are doc S87/1213.
41 Minutes of Special Meeting of Council, 21 August 1987, doc C87/333.
42 Doc C87/319. Academic Staff Association. Statement by the Executive Committee on the conditions which the Minister of Education and Culture intends to determine as a basis for the allocation of subsidies. Signed by Peter Randall, Chairperson, 18 August 1987. Reported in full in *The Star*, 16 September 1987.
43 Doc C87/320.
44 Paragraph 1(b)(iv)(aa) placed restrictions on 'the promotion of the aims or public image of any unlawful organisation ... or of any affected organisation as defined in section 1 of the Affected Organisations Act, 1974'.
45 A copy of the letter was included in the documents for the Special Senate meeting on 21 October 1987.
46 Meeting of Senate, doc S87/1582.
47 S87/1588.
48 Author's personal notes made at the meeting.
49 *Sunday Star*, 1 November 1987.
50 *Business Day*, 19 November 1987 and *Financial Mail*, 13 November 1987, p 57.
51 Riglyne vir die reeling van orde op US-campus. Part of a press release from the office of the Rector of the University of Stellenbosch, 7 November 1987.
52 *Cape Times*, 3 September 1993.
53 From an article in *Die Vaderland*, 9 December 1987.
54 *The Star*, 10 November 1987.
55 Leading article 'Academic suicide in South Africa', *Nature* 12 November 1987.
56 *Citizen*, 11 November 1987.
57 *Business Day*, 11 November 1987.
58 Statement issued by Professor John Reid, Acting Vice-Chancellor of the University of Cape Town. In the author's file, De Klerk's Conditions, file 1.
59 Authors' personal notes. De Klerk's Conditions, file 1.
60 *The Star*, 17 October and 23 October 1987.
61 This, and what follows, from a report prepared by Mrs Pauline Cuzen, Deputy Registrar (Student Affairs), 3 November 1987. Also reported in the *Weekly Mail*, October 30 to November 5 1987.
62 Whitecross's responsibility for Wits student matters during the state of emergency have been referred to earlier in the book.
63 June Sinclair was a professor in the School of Law and succeeded me as Deputy Vice-Chancellor (Student Affairs) in 1991.
64 Circular from Charlton to all staff, 12 November 1987.
65 *The Star*, 29 October 1987. A fuller report of the interview is in *The Star* 30 October 1987.
66 Meeting of Senate 1 December 1987, doc S87/1/19, para 87.83. Chancellor Rosholt, Charlton as Vice-Chancellor Designate, and Acting Chairman Steven Anderson had represented the University.

67 Meeting of Council 11 December 1987, doc C87/517, para 87.142.
68 Letter from Kentridge to Tober, 17 December 1987.
69 Doc S87/1582, para 87.74.9.
70 *Citizen*, 14 November 1987.
71 *Citizen*, 8 December 1987.
72 *SA Law Reports* 1988 (3) 203-217.
73 Ibid, pp 204-206.
74 University of Natal (Applicant), Minister of Education and Culture in the House of Assembly (First Respondent) and Minister of National Education (Second Respondent). Case No 3302/87. I am grateful to Professor C Cresswell, Vice-Principal of the University of Natal, for providing me with a copy of the judgement.
75 Additional memorandum: Executive Committee of the CUP for discussion with the Minister of National Education, signed by C F Crouse, chairman of the CUP. Annexure 2 to circular 61/88 of the CUP, 16 March 1988. (Crouse was Rector of the Rand Afrikaans University.)
76 Letter from Charlton to De Klerk, 25 March 1988.
77 Letter from the Chief Director CUP to Saunders, with copy to Charlton, 8 April 1988, ref 2/1/1/8 x 1/7/1.
78 Letter from De Klerk to Charlton, 25 April 1988, ref 2/1/1/1/1.
79 *The Star*, 5 April 1988.
80 *The Star*, 20 April 1988.
81 Ibid.
82 *Citizen*, 4 May 1988.
83 *The Star*, 4 May 1988.
84 Council doc C90/63, Gl.
85 C90/64, G2.
86 G90/65, G3.
87 C90/64, G2.
88 C90/136, C.
89 *Business Day*, 16 May 1995, p 3.

Chapter 9

1 Thompson, L. *A History of South Africa*, 1st ed, Yale University Press 1990, p 236.
2 Ibid.
3 Ibid, p 237.
4 Statement issued 24 February 1988.
5 Personal notes.
6 Report prepared by Mrs P L Cuzen, Deputy Registrar (Student Affairs), 25 February 1988.
7 From a report prepared by Mrs P M Stevens, Student Affairs Officer, 23 March 1988.
8 Letter from Warden to author, 21 March 1988. Personal file, Student Unrest 1988-1990.
9 Letter from Charlton to Brigadier G M Erasmus, 22 March 1988.

10 Address by Professor R W Charlton, Vice-Chancellor and Principal, concerning the detention of students, on 24 March 1988. University Archives.
11 From a report by P M Stevens. Personal file, Student Unrest 1988-1990; and *Business Day*, 25 March 1988.
12 Mashitisho. A Challenge to Non-participation Strategy.
13 *Business Day, Citizen* and *Star*, 31 March 1988.
14 Al-Quds Day, on the last Friday of the Fast of Ramadan, commemorates the Israeli denial of access to the Al-Aqsa Mosque in Jerusalem to Muslims. The Day of Quds was declared in 1979 by Imaam Khomeini as an International Day of the Oppressed to create awareness of the plight of the Palestinians.
15 Commemorating the murder of six million Jews by the Nazis.
16 Report prepared by the author for Council, Doc C88/190.
17 Letter from Aleck Goldberg, Executive Director, to the author, 18 May 1988.
18 Interview with Janet Cherry, Secretary-General of Nusas in 1982. Reported in Frederikse. *The Unbreakable Thread*, p 214.
19 Ibid, p 216.
20 Report by P M Stevens, 2 June 1988.
21 Ibid.
22 *The Star*, 4 August 1988.
23 Ibid.
24 *The Star*, 22 August 1988.
25 *The Star* and *Citizen*, 23 August 1988.
26 Prohibition on the Activities of the End Conscription Campaign, 25 August 1988.
27 Published *in extenso* in *Sunday Star*, 28 August 1988.
28 During the war, Vorster was assistant chief-commandant of the Ossewa Brandwag, a pro-Nazi organisation. Under Verwoerd's editorship, the *Transvaler* took a distinctly pro-Nazi position. *The Mind of South Africa*, pp 172 and 194.
29 Letter from the author to Keith Shear, 23 August 1989.
30 *Weekly Mail*, 22 September 1989.
31 *Cape Times*, 25, 26 August 1993.
32 Report by the author, 2 June 1988 and P M Stevens, 8 June 1988.
33 Charlton to Schnetler, 8 June 1988, with copy to Brigadier G Erasmus, head of the security police, John Vorster Square.
34 Schnetler to Charlton, C 2/642, 25 July 1988.
35 Author's personal notes, file 'Student Unrest 1989-.'
36 Report of a Nusas press conference, *The Star*, 23 September 1988.
37 Ibid.
38 Report of a meeting of the Vice-Chancellor's advisory panel held on 21 October 1988 at 15h00. Prepared by P M Stevens.
39 Ibid.
40 The Municipal Elections, RWC/sa/10/099, 25 October 1988.
41 Report by head of campus security to Vice-Chancellor, 26 October 1988.
42 Report to Council, Doc C88/501, prepared by Peta Stevens.
43 A88/192.

NOTES

44 Circular letter to staff from Professor P D Tyson, Acting Vice-Chancellor, 15 November 1988.
45 A full report on this visit is housed in the University archives.
46 Raymond Louw, *Four Days in Lusaka*, published by the Five Freedoms Forum 1989, p 161.
47 Installation Address as Vice-Chancellor and Principal, 8 June 1988.
48 These comments are from personal notes made during discussions. Mr Reg September MP told me recently that the college prepared the children for admission to a university. In the early days in exile, before the ANC enjoyed widespread international support, only universities in the eastern bloc countries would accept them. Later, they were welcomed into universities in western Europe.
49 Rehoff is the author of *Guide to the Travaux Préparatoires of the United Nations Convention on the Elimination of all Forms of Discrimination against Women*, Martinus Nijhoff Publishers, 1993, and joint editor with Claus Gulmann of *Human Rights in Domestic Law and Development Assistance Policies of the Nordic Countries*, Marthinus Nijhoff Publishers, 1989.
50 Article by Gavin Evans in *Leadership*, 13(5), p 8, 1994.
51 Louw. *Four Days in Lusaka*.
52 Council meeting 3 February 1989, C89/24, para 89.2.5.
53 Council meeting 17 March 1989, C89/94, para 89.19.3.
54 This report from personal notes prepared on the same day. See also circular letter from Charlton to all staff and students, 23 February 1989, doc S89/225.
55 Statement on the hunger strike, handed out at the meeting on 23 February 1989.
56 *Government Gazette*, 284(11705), 10 February 1989.
57 Lasbrief ingevolge artikel 25 van wet 51 van 1977. Signed by the Landdros van die Distrik, Johannesburg (Magistrate of Johannesburg), 23 February 1989.
58 Police Action on Campus, S89/225.
59 Anderson to Vlok, 3 March 1989. The delegation was to comprise the Chairman, Chancellor, Vice-Chancellor and Mr L Frankel.
60 *The Star*, 9 March 1989.
61 Circular letter from Charlton to staff and students, 8 March 1989 and author's personal notes of meeting with delegation of students, 8 March 1989, following a student meeting on the previous day.
62 Letter from the author to Keith Shear, 5 April 1989.
63 *The Star*, 22 March 1989.
64 *Citizen*, 23 March 1989.
65 Letter from the author to Keith Shear, 13 July 1989.
66 See *The Unbreakable Thread*, pp 212 and 283, and *Illustrated History of South Africa*, p 497.
67 *The Star*, 15 and 16 June 1989; *Citizen*, 16 June 1989; and letter from author to Keith Shear, 21 June 1989.
68 *The Star*, 16 June 1989 and letter from author to Keith Shear, 21 June 1989.
69 *Citizen*, 16 June 1989.
70 Personal communication from Mrs Jocelyn Cairns, SRC Administration Coordinator.

71 From a report by P M Stevens, 12 September 1989, doc 89/175. See also *Star, Citizen* and *Business Day,* 1 September, 1989.
72 *Citizen,* 21 August 1989.
73 *Citizen,* 8 December 1989.
74 Report from the head of the Campus Health Service, 4 September 1989. Personal file, 'Student Unrest, 1988-1990'.
75 *Citizen,* 1 September 1989.
76 BSS document *Close Ranks and Build Unity on Campus,* 1 September 1989. In personal file, 'Student Unrest 1988-1990'.
77 *Citizen,* 18 September, 28 October 1989 and personal notes made when the incidents were reported to me.
78 Copy in personal file, 'Student Unrest 1989-1990'.
79 Lodge T. The Rebellion Resurgent: 1988-90. In Lodge, T and Nasson, B (eds) *All, Here and Now: Black Politics in South Africa in the 1980s,* pp 110-5.
80 *Illustrated History of South Africa,* p 491.
81 *Weekly Mail,* 22 September 1989.
82 Notes in personal file 'Student Unrest 1988-1990'.
83 *The Star,* 21 September 1989.
84 From file note on the events of the day in personal file, 'Student Unrest 1988-1990'. See also reports in *Citizen* and *Star,* 22 September 1989.
85 Doc C89/480.

Chapter 10

1 *Citizen,* 3 February 1990 and *City Press* 4 February 1990.
2 *Citizen* and *Star,* 28 February 1990.
3 *Citizen, Star* and *Sowetan* 8 March, *Citizen* 9 March and *City Press* 11 March 1990.
4 See Report of the Enquiry into Admissions and Exclusions, 29 August 1991, Doc S91/1218.
5 The committee consisted of: Professor R W Charlton (Chairman), Professors P D Tyson, B D Cheadle, C J R Dugard, D J Freer, A R Kemp, G Mitchell, W D Reekie, M Sears (replaced by J C A Boeyens in 1991), Ms J Hawarden (ASA and Udusa), Dr R Levin (ASA and Udusa), Mr G Mashamba (ANC) (later replaced by Ms F Potgieter,) Dr A Msimeki (ANC), Dr A S Nkomo (NECC) (later replaced by Dr N Cloete), Mr K Shubane (NECC) (later replaced by Mr J Maseko), Ms L Bethlehem (SRC), Mr B Kelobonye (BSS) (later replaced by Mr S S Mabotja (BSTC), later replaced by Mr K Ngema (BSTC)), Mr J Maseko (Sansco National) (later replaced by Ms P McKenzie).
6 pp 11-12 of the report. Only a précis of the recommendations is given here.
7 Ibid, p 16.
8 Ibid, p 21.
9 This follow-up information on University action to implement the recommendations of the Commission of Inquiry has been provided by Mrs Felicity Eggleston from the office of the Registrar (Academic).
10 The document in which these demands were made was headed *Ke Nako!.*

Attached to it was a document headed *Memorandum to Administration*, which recorded a resolution adopted at a meeting of students on 26 May 1993. It was signed by the Chairperson, General Secretary and Education and Transformation Officer of Sasco Wits Branch. The resolution also called for a 1994 admission of a minimum of 60 per cent African students. Documents in personal file, 'Student Unrest, 1989-1990'.
11 Letter from author to Keith Shear, 3 June 1990.
12 *Citizen* and *Star*, 30 August 1990.
13 Personal file 'Student Unrest, 1989-1990'. Fax from attorney Kathleen Satchwell on behalf of the SRC to Chief Magistrate, 17 September 1990.
14 Ibid. Town Clerk to Vice-Chancellor, 19 September 1990.
15 Ibid. Fax from Chief Magistrate to SRC, 19 September 1990.
16 Ibid. Report on the events of 19 September 1990, Student Affairs Office, file G.2. Also *Sunday Star*, 23 September 1990.
17 Ibid. Charlton to Erasmus, 21 September 1990, S5/21.
18 Ibid. Erasmus to Charlton, 13 October 1990, his ref 30/1/2(41).
19 *Financial Mail*, 12 October 1990 and letter from Vlok's administrative secretary to Charlton, 23 November 1990, ref 3/A10/12/1 (207/90).
20 Administrative secretary to Charlton, 14 February 1991, ref 3/A10/12/1 (207/90).
21 Personal file 'Student Unrest, 1989-1990'. Report on the meeting, file K.7.
22 Ibid. The major contributor to the drafting of this statement was Professor John Dugard.
23 'Operation Iron Fist' had been announced by the Ministry of Law and Order as a plan to control the violence.
24 Civil Cooperation Bureau, a covert branch of the South African Defence Force unmasked by the Harms Commission in 1990. De Klerk had appointed the Harms Commission early in 1990 to probe 'murder and acts of violence allegedly committed with political motives'. *Illustrated History of South Africa*, p 497.
25 *Business Day* and *Citizen*, 28 September 1990.
26 Sacos was a militant national sports organisation whose slogan was 'no normal sport in an abnormal society' and who refused to associate with any of the established all-white sports bodies in the country. The NSC was the sports body set up as part of the Mass Democratic Movement.
27 Council meeting 15 November 1990. Doc C90/566, para 90.89.

Chapter 11

1 C93/515. Mission Statement Project. Report to the Senate Planning Committee, Senate and Council, November 1993. The report is signed by Professors June Sinclair, David Freer, Alan Kemp, Michael Pendlebury, Michael Sears and Eddie Webster.
2 Ibid. Appendix 1, p 30, for list of individuals and bodies consulted.
3 Ibid, pp 28-29.
4 Charlton to the author, 4 January 1994.

Appendices

APPENDIX 1

THE GOVERNANCE OF THE UNIVERSITY OF THE WITWATERSRAND

In the course of this book there are numerous references to the structures known as the Council and the Senate and to officers of the University known as Vice-Chancellor and Principal and Deputy Vice-Chancellors. These structures and individuals and the authority that they carry are similar throughout the university system in South Africa in the post-apartheid era. In the period about which I write they were similar for the English-medium so-called 'open universities' but were under much greater state control in those institutions established by the National Party government for the development of apartheid tertiary education.

The Council

In terms of the University of the Witwatersrand, Johannesburg, (Private) Act and the statutes that fall under it, the government and the executive authority of the University is vested in the Council. The Council elects the chairperson from amongst its members. The Council has statutory authority to administer all the property of the University and has general control (including financial) of the University and of all its affairs, purposes and functions, except as otherwise provided in the Act. Council appoints all persons considered necessary for the efficient conduct of the University and determines the title, status, powers, privileges, functions and duties of the people appointed. The Vice-Chancellor and Deputy Vice-Chancellors are appointed by the Council after it has consulted with various constituencies of the University. It also determines the fees to be paid by students, but only after consultation with the Senate.

During the 1980s the Act provided for the following composition of Council: Vice-Chancellor, Vice-Principal and Deputy Vice-Chancellors, the Mayor of Johannesburg, eight members appointed by the State President, four members elected by the Convocation (graduates, academic staff, professors emeriti and retired academic staff who have had ten years continuous full-time service), five members elected by the Senate, three members appointed by the Council of Education of the Witwatersrand, two members elected by past students and donors, two members appointed by the

City Council of Johannesburg, one member appointed by the Johannesburg Chamber of Commerce, one member appointed by the Transvaal Chamber of Industries and two members appointed by the Chamber of Mines of South Africa.

In 1995 the composition changed to allow the inclusion of three students appointed by the Student Representative Council, seven members of Senate, four persons appointed by the Council and one member from the Johannesburg Chamber of Commerce and Industry.

The Senate

In terms of the Act the organisation and superintendence of instruction and examinations, and of lectures and classes, is vested in the Senate which determines the standard of proficiency to be attained in examinations and decides who has satisfied the requirements for obtaining degrees, diplomas or certificates. Subject to the approval of Council it makes the rules and regulations governing the requirements for these qualifications. It reports to Council on aspects of its work that may be required by Council.

During the 1980s Senate was composed of the Vice-Chancellor and Deputies, all the full professors, the heads of department who were not professors, two members appointed by the Council, and eight lecturers. In the latter part of the 1980s there were ten student observers. In 1995 the lecturer membership was stipulated as six per cent of the constituency of lecturers, there were eight students appointed by the SRC and two by the Postgraduate Association of the University.

The Academic Board and the Academic Board Executive carry out responsibilities delegated to them by the Senate.

The Vice-Chancellor and Deputy Vice-Chancellors

The Vice-Chancellor exercises general supervision over the University and is chairperson and chief executive officer of the Senate. The Vice-Principal and Deputy Vice-Chancellors have responsibilities and duties allocated to them by the Vice-Chancellor. The powers, privileges, functions, duties and period of office of the Vice-Chancellor are prescribed by the statutes and those of the Deputy Vice-Chancellors by the Council.

APPENDIX 2

RECOMMENDATIONS OF THE BROWDE COMMISSION

1. The use of dogs to control crowd behaviour on campus should, at almost any cost, be avoided.
2. Where a group of students appear intent on leaving the University campus in order to march into a predictable confrontation with the South African Police, senior University officials, including Mr Hurst and his security officers, should do all in their power to persuade the marchers to desist; in the end, however, the decision cannot be taken from those who wish to proceed. Professor Shear

implicitly agreed with this point of view in his evidence. It was indeed pointed out to us by student witnesses that many black persons are fully aware of what taking a decision to march into a confrontation with the South African Police entails. In our view, the University is constrained to recognise that many black students are heirs to a tradition of activism which is maintained sometimes at very great personal cost. The University would err, in our view, if it attempted to coerce them to a different point of view. It should, however, reserve to itself the right to discipline students who deliberately disobey instructions and where there have been clear breaches of University discipline.

3. The BSS and SMA should, if possible by mutual agreement but if necessary by the authoritative intervention of the University, be prevented from holding meetings in response to each other. Moreover, the SMA should be prevented from deliberately provocative behaviour such as setting up tables in the path of the BSS members who have attended a particular meeting, or attempting to photograph BSS members. It would obviously be desirable if these tables, if they are set up at all, should be placed so that they are not conspicuous to many students who may be offended by them.

In this respect the University must take account of the fact that certain days are of especial emotional importance to black students. Mr Mayet recited a list of eight such days: This may be too extensive, but that certain days are of emotionally charged significance to black students is obvious and it is our view that they should be accommodated to this extent that, on them, SMA should be prevented from holding its own meetings. The manner in which the details of the suggestions is worked out is something which must of necessity be left to the administrative and academic officers of this University. What is clear to us is that, without essential infringement of the rights of all students to express and propagate their views freely, incidents can and should be avoided in which any group of students is deliberately provoked in a manner which can only bring the University into discredit and which could ultimately damage the fabric of what the University is seeking to attain.

Liaison between the University authorities and the BSS; the BSS and University Security; and University authorities and Security should be improved. Two telling pieces of information emerged in the course of the hearings which, in our view, demonstrated the urgent need for improved liaison in the above three respects. First, it appeared that Mr Hurst and his security officials have been completely unaware that that Mr Russel Crystal was not this year a registered student at this University. The fact that he had no right to be on campus was therefore unknown to them. Secondly, it was privately communicated to the Commission by a senior security official that he had been unaware that regular meetings were held between BSS and the University administration before any particular 'sensitive day.' It seems manifest to us that Security, if it does not attend those meetings, should at least be informed of their outcome.

The need for improved trust and understanding between Security and the BSS was universally acknowledged in evidence before us.

The positive steps which can be taken in this regard do not seem to us to be in our province to recommend. What we can affirmatively say, however, is that the security officers who testified before us as well as the past and present leadership of the BSS seemed to us to be entirely capable of effecting a closer and more successful relationship. Moreover they are willing to do so. Regular meetings may be of assistance in this regard. We have already referred above to the individual aspects of security officials' behaviour which we feel requires improvement.

Mr Russel Crystal should be informed that he will not be permitted access to the campus on certain days of especial sensitivity to the BSS. It is plain that Mr Crystal's mere presence on campus, symbolising as it does all that he stands for, is a tremendous provocation to the members of the BSS. We consider that a BSS witness effectively answered a challenge from the Commission to the effect that banning Mr Crystal access to the campus on certain days could lead to demands for a whole spate of such bans. The witness pointed out that Mr Crystal was in an entirely unique position and that he seemed to appear on campus only on extraordinary days and that his appearance seems deliberately calculated to provoke reaction. Indeed, the whole tactic of the SMA seemed to be one of deliberate provocation through apparent passivity. Mr Crystal, not being a registered student, has no right to be on this campus and his presence seems to us to be calculated to do harm to the life of this University. It should therefore be prevented.

5. The SRC and the University authorities should, in conjunction with the BSS, launch a campaign to bring home to students the great importance of their carrying their student cards with them at all times. Mr Hurst, rightly in our view, complained of the difficulty he and his officers more frequently now than in previous days experienced in persuading students to display their student cards to identified officials of the University. It seems to us to be of the highest importance that every person present on campus should be identifiable as either a member or a non-member of the University. Failure on the part of students to cooperate in this immensely important matter complicates the task of campus Security and makes it easy for intruders and deliberate provocateurs to be present on campus.

The University should greatly increase the penalties for a student who declines to display his student card to an identified official of the University when required to do so. It is implicit in what we have said above that the officials entitled to demand such a display of a student's card should be clearly identified themselves.

6. Finally, it seems to us of great importance that no prosecutions or disciplinary proceedings should follow from the events of 14 May 1985. Professor Shear and the Vice-Chancellor agreed to hold an open and independent enquiry into the events of the day. The two days we spent in holding the enquiry constituted a remarkable experience for us. We were enormously impressed with the calibre of a number of the witnesses who testified before us. They greatly assisted us in the enquiry. At the same time, the openness and manifest dedication of some of

the University officials who gave evidence before us was notable. It seemed to us, in itself, to have been remarkable that the University should permit its Deputy Vice-Chancellor, its Academic Registrar and its Chief Security Officer to be subjected indirectly to questions in the manner which occurred on the two days of the enquiry. Even more impressive was the manner in which these questions were at all times answered. We concluded that the enquiry in itself may have been a therapeutic experience and that it may possibly constitute the start of a cure to some of the ailments which were referred to before it.

At this juncture, to persist in disciplinary hearings would, in our view, undo a great deal of what has so far been achieved. This should not be allowed to happen.

We think, however, that the students who were responsible for drafting the carefully prepared and presented report on behalf of the SMA are deserving of censure. Many of the statements of fact we find to be palpably false and we regret to say that the report appears to have been drafted in an attempt to mislead us into making wrong findings of fact against their fellow-students (members of BSS). That the SMA chose not to participate in the viva voce proceedings, in our view, renders their motives in submitting the report suspect.

7. At the same time, our concern at the outbreak of stone-throwing on campus on 14 May 1985, is immense. It cannot be tolerated in the future. This should be made as plain as the University is able to make it to all students.

The student leaders in the SRC, BSS and SMA and those involved in University publications should be called upon to publicly condemn violent or even unruly behaviour such as was deposed before us. They should take steps to ensure that intemperate students do not resort to such behaviour in the future. To be able to withstand provocation is part of the process of learning. Students at this University should try not to allow themselves to be provoked. If they are provoked and perform acts of violence as a result, those who provoke them may have succeeded in their aim better than they had hoped to do.

The Commission drew the following conclusions:

The black students involved in the events of the day must be severely criticised for their unruly and even dangerous reaction to the provocation already referred to. Their leaders who are young men of undoubted calibre must ensure that this does not happen again. They in turn will be greatly assisted if-
  (i) the deliberately taunting and inciting conduct of the members of SMA is not allowed to coincide with meetings, on commemorative days, of the BSS, and
  (ii) the security guards, without dogs, treat black students with greater sensitivity.

The Administrators of the University and more particularly Professors Tober and Shear and Mr Standenmacher could not have done anything to prevent the events of the 14th May. They showed concern for all the students of the University and did whatever was possible to defuse the situation as soon as it was reasonably possible. All the student witnesses who were asked the question agreed that the doors of those responsible for the administration of the University were always open to them, including those of the Vice-Chancellor. Needless to say, it is highly desirable that this state of affairs, which is a credit to Wits, continues in the future.

APPENDIX 3

STATEMENT OF PRINCIPLE

The Original Document

PREAMBLE
The moral indignation of the civilised world is turning upon the South African academics' inaction in the face of political outrage both here and abroad, which has brought to an end an era of relatively mild protest. High-minded silence could in some situations be a valid response, but certainly not to this positive challenge. Continued silence implies collusion and invites censure.

We must admit accountability and voice our opposition to whatever threatens to impair the scholarly freedom of any individual on the campus. As often as we fail to insist on free access for all to our instruments of learning; as often as we tolerate harassment for voicing an opinion; as often as we stand by, albeit in anger, as silent witnesses to the implementation of perverse laws; as often as the legitimate function of this University and service to its community is allowed to be frustrated; as often as we accept any form of discrimination while proclaiming our belief in equality and freedom; and as often as we permit our silence to be construed as condonation of a system that we condemn; just so often must we expect to be censured.

Thus we are moved to consider afresh the position of our Faculties within the society in which it is located. In the past the University of the Witwatersrand has concerned itself with what were considered 'the four essential freedoms' of a university, namely the right of the university to determine for itself on academic grounds who may teach, what may be taught, how it shall be taught, and who may be admitted to study. However, even at the time of the 'Open Universities' document, this narrow interpretation of academic freedom was questioned by members of this University. After a lapse of a further 11 years, and in the midst of political crisis, it is essential to re-evaluate our position and to re-affirm that 'Academic and human freedom are indivisible' (In *The Open Universities in South Africa and Academic Freedom 1957-1974.*)

After 25 years of resistance, all but two faculties of the University may now admit students without regard to race. This has all the appearance of a victory for university autonomy, but is largely a hollow one, both because the 'Quota Bill' remains on the statute book and because the social and educational conditions in a racist state lead to inherent inequalities of opportunity. It is thus clear that, while the University should not assume the role of '...a kind of unofficial political Opposition', there are certain conditions that must exist in a society for universities to function adequately. Where such conditions do not exist, it is the function of the University to highlight these deficiencies and to take what positive steps are within its power to alleviate them.

The opening of many faculties of the University to all South African students and attempts to recruit staff on a non-racial basis bring the effects of apartheid on university life into clear focus. Its effects consist of both direct activities and indirect influences; deleterious activities include provisions which interfere with free selection of staff and students, State censorship of study materials, and interference with rights of discussion and congress. Less direct, but no less harmful, are conditions in which there is a lack of interaction between communities, a situation of poverty, an escalation of unemployment, a climate of repression and a state of emergency.

These problems must be urgently addressed by the University. Only by promoting and achieving freedom will the University of the Witwatersrand be able to function as a true university and provide for the long term future of South Africa.

STATEMENT OF PRINCIPLE

We recognize that we are part of Africa, operate in an African context and must be committed to serve our Society as a whole.

We acknowledge that we have not been able to perform our functions adequately. There are two reasons for this, one is a lack of sensitivity on our part to the needs of the Society we seek to serve, and the second is the socio-political structure within which we operate.

THEREFORE

We condemn:

any political dispensation which makes use of group criteria as a basis for the allocation of political and social rights and resources;

the view that the safeguarding of the interests of minorities be elevated to a non-negotiable principle in any future political dispensation even though the legitimate interests of minority groups are recognised;

the continued implementation of all laws and practices (e.g. Population Registration Act, Group Areas Act and segregated education) which entrench the basic principles of apartheid;

the operation of these laws which have culminated in the present state of emergency with its attendant repression.

We call for:

the immediate ending of the state of emergency;

the repeal of all apartheid legislation and of all security legislation designed to maintain it;

the release of all political prisoners;

the removal of bans on organizations and individuals;

the cessation of hostilities on and across the borders of the Republic;

the institution of negotiations with the ANC and SWAPO and other legitimate representatives of the disenfranchised citizens in South Africa and Namibia.

We affirm:
that academic freedoms and general freedoms are indivisible and that true academic freedom can only be fully realized, and the University perform all its functions, in a society in which all people are free;
that the rights of the individual are the only basis on which society should be structured;
that all individuals have the right to equal educational opportunities within a single educational system based on non-segregation.
We commit ourselves with a sense of urgency:
to voice our opposition to injustice and to create forums for the purpose of striving for its elimination;
to explore the ways in which our Society sees the role of this University in its future, and create the necessary forums to achieve this end;
to reconsider all our activities within our subject areas and disciplines and to examine their relevance to our role as a University in Africa;
to seek constructive opinion and assistance internationally to support the implementation of all these commitments.

The Second Document as Approved by Senate and Council in December 1985

UNIVERSITY POLICY AND THE CURRENT CRISIS
Today we witness the consequences of apartheid, a policy that has brought about not just restrictions on freedom of movement, but the forced removal and resettlement of whole populations; not just restrictions on freedom of expression, but the banning of books, of organizations and of people; not just infringements of personal liberty, but detention without trial and even torture; not just denial of political liberties, but the exclusion, on the ground of race, of people from their common and effective democratic rights. The outcome is the current tragedy: burnings and lynchings, intimidation and looting, the boycott and destruction of schools and the consequences of the cry 'liberation before education'; the shooting of men, women and even children, the use of excessive force by those seeking to maintain order, indemnity for agents of the state who do wrong and further restrictions on rights and liberties. This entire scene bears grim testimony to the fruits of the policy of apartheid and the need for rapid and sweeping change.

Universities generally have hitherto tended to take an official position only on matters that bear directly and narrowly on their nature and function. The University of the Witwatersrand has a record of resistance to academic apartheid and to the denial of civil liberties. Its deep concern over the present impasse in the affairs of our land demands that it now speak out on the broader issues that affect South Africa as a whole. Not only is it morally obliged to protest at gross injustice, but a failure to speak at this time could wrongly be taken to imply tacit acquiescence in an outrageous state of affairs.

The aims of the University are the pursuit of truth, irrespective of its consequences, and the academic advancement of the individual, irrespective of race. These aims cannot be attained where discriminatory practices prevail and provoke violent action and reaction.

The Council and Senate of the University therefore call for the repeal of all apartheid legislation and the security laws that are designed to maintain it, and for the negotiation of a new, just and democratic constitution, built on the rule of law and the protection of human rights.

For years the University has been involved in the pursuit of equal access to educational opportunities. It has, for half a century, enrolled black students, among whom have been several who are now political leaders. The University has undertaken projects aimed at redressing some inequalities of education for blacks. It was a prime mover in securing the suspension of restrictions on its right to admit students without regard to race, in all but two of its faculties, a significant, albeit incomplete, achievement. Even an unqualified right to admit students freely to any faculty would be inadequate to attain our ideals, because of the manifold inequalities suffered by so many of our members and fellow citizens under apartheid.

The University of the Witwatersrand rejects racism and racial segregation. It is committed to non-discrimination in the constitution of its student body, in the selection and promotion of its staff, and in its administration.

Black education under apartheid is a focus, a symbol and a cause of the present national crisis. There is a need for reconstruction of the entire educational system. Particular attention will have to be paid to those whose education over the years has been neglected or disrupted. The University bears its own responsibility in the process of reconstruction and reform. It commits itself to extend assistance to those from educationally disadvantaged backgrounds and those condemned by the policy of apartheid to conditions of life not conducive to a full realisation of the opportunities offered by a university education, so as to enable them to attain their true potential.

Accordingly, we commit ourselves to the cause of equal educational facilities and prospects for all, including the repeal of the entire body of legislation requiring separate facilities in education, health and welfare on the ground of race.

APPENDIX 4

SENATE RESOLUTION

This meeting of Senate of the University of the Witwatersrand, noting the recent events on campus, reaffirms its commitment to the principle and practice of freedom of speech and fair debate on the University campus. At the same time, Senate notes that the age in which we live is characterized, in many parts of the world, by a tendency to abandon consensus for confrontation and by widespread intolerance, insecurity, fear and alienation: this is especially true in South African society at present. Senate is aware too that the purposes of higher education can prosper only in a free and tolerant society – and this we do not have in South Africa.

In view of these conditions in our country at large, it would be inconceivable if higher education here were not affected by this insecurity, fear and intolerance. Such encroachments on our campus, with its 18 000 students of many backgrounds and beliefs, may from time to time make it difficult for university students faithfully to carry out the University's commitment to free speech and fair debate on campus. The central focus of the problem lies in the structure of South African society. Even if deviations from the practice of free speech in the University are seen as a spillover or spin-off from society on our campus, they are to be deplored and discouraged.

Senate reiterates its belief in free speech on the campus and, in the face of the growing crisis in our land, re-dedicates itself to do all it can to work towards the continued observance of that principle. Senate appeals to the members and leaders of our University communities to exercise restraint and tolerance in the face of the many provocations of life in South Africa and to refrain from behaviour which infringes the claims of all opinions to be heard on campus and which might encourage a spirit of intolerance or even violence. Senate unequivocally rejects violence in all its forms.

APPENDIX 5

PART OF THE MINORITY REPORT BY ADVOCATE EDWIN CAMERON ON THE ISSUE OF FREEDOM OF SPEECH AND DISRUPTION OF MEETINGS ON CAMPUS

As a general principle, and one of high importance, there is no doubt that a university should be open and available for the expression of all views. Even those which are unpopular or unfashionable or which give credence to repressive ideologies, movements or regimes should be heard. The students' choice of strategy in this case, however, must in my view be seen against the background which the Commission recognizes necessarily impinges on the practical ways in which effect is given in the South African context to principles such as academic freedom and freedom of expression.

Here it is impossible to leave out of account either (i) the barrage of publicity which is given to the ideological affiliations, military strategies and individual personalities of the UNITA movement in all sections of the media in South Africa; or (ii) the active suppression in South Africa of most viewpoints which are sympathetic to the legitimate government in Angola. What the students did at the UNITA meeting on Wednesday 19 March 1986 reverberated throughout Southern Africa and echoed, I suspect, in some other parts of the world as well.

The point they made was to them crucial: that many people in South Africa feel solidarity with the legitimate government of Angola in its eleven-year war against UNITA; that the credence and indeed commendation given to UNITA by most organs of expression in South Africa is by no means universally shared; that many South Africans find UNITA's unique association with and extensive reliance upon the South African security apparatus repellent ...

Much of the above reasoning may be thought to be applicable to the disruption by Wits students of two meetings which were to have been addressed by Dr Conor

Cruise O'Brien on Thursday 9 October 1986. The students involved, again, were giving expression to moral viewpoints based on principles of profound importance to them. The national struggle for liberation in their view necessitates an isolation of this country without exception; this includes prominent figures like Dr O'Brien. Again, the point made by the disruption of the meetings in question here and at the University of Cape Town reverberated widely and received very extensive publicity in many Western media. Again, the point could perhaps not have been made adequately elsewhere or in other ways.

However, I share the view expressed by the Academic Staff Association's statement that the coercive approach adopted by the students in question was in all the circumstances inappropriate. There must always be less justification, in my view, for the disruption of genuine academic meetings, even when the viewpoints sought to be expressed by the disruption are inadequately vented elsewhere or where feelings about the content of the views which would otherwise have been aired at the meeting in question run very high.

The viewpoint I have expressed holds dangers. Lines have to be drawn; distinctions made. That seems to me to be no answer to the view I have expressed. I have yet to meet the protagonist of 'freedom of speech' whose viewpoint does not involve drawing some line somewhere. That defending the principle inherent in the true concept of freedom of speech in South Africa over the next ten and more years will involve anxious decisions and painstaking moral debate does not fill me with dismay. That the debate should be occurring on the Wits campus in as vibrant and as passionate a way as seems to be the case is also no cause for dismay. What is in my view a cause for far greater disquiet is the attitude of many of this University's critics whose rhetoric seeks to create the impression that no issues of moral difficulty are involved at all.

APPENDIX 6

MEMORANDUM ACADEMIC FREEDOM AND FREEDOM OF SPEECH
Professor Jonathan Suzman

1. There are two general theories about academic freedom...
2. The first of these theories sees academic freedom as merely a special branch of general rights to freedom of expression which are held to be valid in all society. On this basis, universities, being committed to free enquiry and free expression, are bound to uphold, particularly on their campuses, the right of free speech, and to act firmly against any inroads into it. If this were the only justification for academic freedom, then universities would be honour bound to intervene at once on inroads into the rights of free speech, on behalf of anyone whatever, on or outside the campus.
3. The alternate theory sees the particular claims of academic freedom to arise from the special role of universities, although it accepts that these claims are

connected with freedom of expression. In brief, such a view suggests that the advancement of knowledge requires that its pursuit be untrammelled, and that the teaching of even heterodox views is an intrinsic part of this search. Knowledge is good, therefore what is necessary for this pursuit will also be good. Academic freedom is necessary for this pursuit, therefore it is good and is independently justified.

4. On this latter view academic freedom consists of the freedom of academics – teachers and students – to hear and expound those views for which they regard the evidence as being best, independently of any external pressures with respect to their unpopularity or even their dangerousness. Although notable discoveries and innovations have been made by people outside of the academy, and although general freedom of expression is of advantage to this, academic freedom proper, and the particular role of the University, is primarily connected to this rather narrow view. A university is therefore primarily concerned with the protection of the rights of expression of its own members, or members of other universities, rather than of outsiders. Clearly the University will view with concern any inroads on freedom of speech in general, but it is not committed to formally taking action, or using such authority as it has, in defence of this right, even if the right has been infringed on its campus.

5. The question then arises as to how far such a right extends to those invited, even though they are not members of the University community, to speak to its members. Again, I believe a distinction can be drawn. Those who are formally invited to give lectures on academic questions to members of academic courses by a member of academic staff, ought to expect the same privileges as those who are formally employed by the University. They have a right to such protection as the University offers to its own members, and this protection ought to be firm, clear and committal. When however, we talk either of invitations by non-academic bodies which operate on campus, such as student societies, or invitations by academics to people who are not themselves academics, but perhaps represent some special viewpoint or have some special skill, the matter becomes a little more obscure.

6. In this kind of context, I believe the deciding criteria rest on the following considerations:
    a) What are the speaker's qualifications?
    b) Who invited the speaker?
    c) Who does the audience consist of?
    d) What is the point and purpose of the invitation?

If in all cases the answer to these four questions is an academic answer, then I believe that such people should enjoy the full protection of the University. To the extent that they are not, claims for academic freedom on their behalf are muted or even perhaps absent, and the requirements on the University to exercise its powers and prerogatives in defending such rights are to that extent lessened.

7. I believe therefore there is an absolute requirement on the University to defend the rights of freedom of speech with respect to its full members, but that that

obligation does not hold with respect to any of the other categories to the same extent, and with some of the categories it does not hold at all. In such cases the University may allow and even encourage the use of its campus by groups even with a tenuous connection with its membership, because of the University's commitment to the ideal of free speech. But it is not required to ensure that its members provide a hearing under such circumstances. It may deprecate any interruptions to a citizen's general right to freedom of speech, wherever this is exercised, but it is not required to enforce these. In particular, where such a right of free speech poses what Judge Oliver Wendell Holmes called a 'clear and present danger' to the public order, it has a right, insofar as it is the custodian of order on its own campus, to postpone or even to prevent, on particular occasions, certain views from being expounded on its own campus. This is not a general prevention, but a prevention of a particular occasion of expression at a particular time, in view of particular circumstances. It has to be used very sparingly and not as a general rule...

APPENDIX 7

FREEDOM OF SPEECH ON CAMPUS

1. PREAMBLE
   The University accepts the Universal Declaration of Human Rights which states, inter alia, that 'everyone has the right to freedom of opinion and expression; this right includes freedom to hold opinions without interference and to seek, receive and impart information and ideas through any media and regardless of frontiers ... Everyone has the right to freedom of peaceful assembly and associations ... In the exercise of his rights and freedoms, everyone shall be subject only to such limitations as are determined by law solely for the purpose of securing due recognition and respect for the rights and freedoms of others and of meeting the just requirements of morality, public order and the general welfare in a democratic society.'
2. THE UNIVERSITY'S COMMITMENT TO FREEDOM OF SPEECH
   The University of the Witwatersrand is committed to human rights and freedoms, one of which is academic freedom. While recognising that basic freedoms are violated in this country, the University must continue to do all that it can to ensure that freedom of expression and freedom of enquiry, the core of academic freedom, prevail within its walls, exposed neither to restriction nor to intimidation, neither to disruption nor to censorship. At the same time, the University requires that academic freedom be exercised with responsibility. While the University is dedicated to ensuring the free expression of views and the peaceful continuation of teaching and research, it must protect life, limb and property, the integrity of the institution and the rights and dignity of its members. In its pursuit of academic freedom, the University will not countenance racism,

sexism or violence or the advocacy thereof.

The purpose of meetings, functions and displays on campus should be in keeping with the aims of pursuing knowledge and encouraging debate.

3. PROCEDURES TO BE FOLLOWED

These procedures deal with meetings, functions and displays on the East and West campus. The same procedures will apply to meetings held at the Medical School, the Graduate School of Business Administration or residences, where the Deans, Principal Administrative Officers or Wardens will be responsible for administering them.

3.1 An application for a venue on campus, whether for the holding of a meeting or function, or for the erection of tables or boards for the issuing or displaying of pamphlets, posters, photographs, etc., shall be submitted to the office of the Deputy Registrar (Administration). If permission is sought for an outside speaker to address a meeting or function, or if in the opinion of the Deputy Registrar (Administration) the meeting or function or the material to be issued or displayed is of a political or potentially contentious nature, at least three clear working days must elapse before the day in question. Under special circumstances, for good and sufficient reason, all or part of this period may be waived.

3.2 Applications must be in writing and specify the following information:

3.2.1 Date, time and exact place requested.

3.2.2 Name of any speaker(s) or possible alternative speaker(s).

3.2.3 Time of expected arrival and departure of any speaker(s).

3.2.4 Subject and/or nature of the meeting, function or material to be issued or displayed.

3.2.5 Approximate number of people expected at the meeting, function or display.

3.2.6 Copies of any proposed poster or notice announcing or advertising the meeting or function and of any pamphlets, posters, photographs, etc., to be issued or displayed.

3.2.7 Name of the organisation involved and name, designation, address and telephone number of the chairperson and the organiser who will be responsible for communication and liaison with the administration.

3.2.8 Whether it is the intention that the meeting, function or display should be open to the public and/or the media.

3.2.9 Details of any concern which the organisers might have about possible disturbance.

Notwithstanding anything required in 3.2.1 – 3.2.9, the Deputy Vice-Chancellor, in his discretion, may dispense with any of the information required in those clauses, or require that additional information be furnished.

3.3 If a meeting, function, display, or any of the material to be issued or displayed is considered by the Deputy Registrar (Administration) to be likely to conflict with the principles as stated in paragraph 2, he shall refer the matter to the Deputy Vice-Chancellor. If the Deputy Vice-Chancellor is also of the opinion that there is likely to be conflict with the principles as stated in paragraph 2, he shall call a meeting of a special Panel constituted for the purpose, as set out in paragraph 3.4. No further arrangements shall then be made by the organisers without the express permission in writing of the Deputy Registrar (Administration). In particular, no advertisement of or promotion of the meeting, function or display shall be made without appropriate authorisation.

3.4 The panel constituted for this purpose shall consist of: the Chairperson of the Senate Academic Freedom Committee (or alternate), three persons from among the Vice-Chancellor and Deputy Vice-Chancellors, the Registrar, two members of the Senate nominated by the Vice-Chancellor, the Chairperson of the Academic Staff Association (or alternate), the President of the Students Representative Council (or alternate), the Chairperson of the Student Academic Freedom Committee (or alternate), and additional persons nominated by the Deputy Vice-Chancellor at his discretion. The Deputy Registrars (Administration) and (Student Affairs) shall be in attendance.

3.5 Any person or organisation within the University may make representations as to why a particular visiting speaker should not be welcome in the University, or why a particular meeting or function or display or the issuing of particular pamphlets should not be allowed. Such representations shall be in writing and submitted to the Head of the appropriate Department, or to the President of the SRC, or to the Deputy Registrar (Administration), who shall report to the Deputy Vice-Chancellor. If the representations are not frivolous or unfounded they shall be referred to the Panel.

3.6 The Panel shall convey its recommendation to the Vice-Chancellor if he is not present at the meeting of the Panel. The Deputy Registrar (Administration) shall convey the final decision to the applicant.

3.7 If the application referred to in 3.1 is refused, a statement setting out the reasons for this decision shall be furnished to the applicant.

4. PROCEDURES TO BE FOLLOWED IF PERMISSION IS GRANTED FOR AN OUTSIDE SPEAKER OR FOR A MEETING, FUNCTION OR DISPLAY OF A POLITICAL OR POTENTIALLY CONTENTIOUS NATURE

4.1 If permission for the meeting, function or display is granted, it will have been done after careful consideration and it must therefore be accepted that the meeting, function or display has the formal approval of the University. The speakers at such a meeting, function or display, therefore, are entitled to the protection of the University.

4.2 Such protection does not preclude a reasonable amount of heckling, nor reasonably vigorous questioning during the discussion period nor possible demonstration outside the venue. Attempts to prevent a speaker from delivering his or her address are not acceptable.

4.3 The Deputy Registrar (Administration) may require the organisers to amend or withdraw any advertisements or notices, and/or to comply with

specified instructions about the conduct of the meeting, function or display.
4.4 The organisers may be required to comply with any of the following conditions, if the Deputy Registrar (Administration) believes that these are necessary:
- 4.4.1 Only students and/or members of staff of the University shall have the right to attend. Student or staff identity cards shall be produced for admission to the venue. The Security Division shall be responsible for checking these cards at the entrance.
- 4.4.2 Only those guests whose identity is known to the organisers shall be admitted. The organisers shall nominate one person in advance to liaise with the Security Division on this matter. Names of the guests invited to attend shall be submitted by the organisers to the Security Division not later than 30 minutes before the scheduled start of the meeting, function or display. No blank visitors' cards shall be supplied and the names of the guests shall be ascertained in advance to avoid problems. In exceptional cases, the organiser referred to in paragraph 3.2.7 may request visitors' cards after the above deadline if he/she appears in person at the Security Division office (CB 1) No vouching by a member of staff or student for any other person shall be permitted.
- 4.4.3 If, in the view of the Deputy Vice-Chancellor, it should be necessary for security reasons, bags, parcels or similar items may, on occasion, not be permitted into the meeting or function or may be permitted only after a security check.
- 4.4.4 A number of stewards shall be provided by the organisers and they shall be required to be present throughout the meeting, function or display and also while the audience is assembling or dispersing.
- 4.4.5 The names and addresses of stewards shall be supplied in advance by the organisers to the Head of Campus Security.
- 4.4.6 The admission of representatives of the press, radio or television shall be prohibited or shall be subject to specified restrictions.
- 4.4.7 The date or time of the meeting, function or display shall be changed if there is the possibility of conflict.
4.5 On a trial basis it is permissable for fixed displays of flags, banners and posters to be **erected** by the organisers of the event inside the venue. However, the prohibition in terms of Rule R.7(e) of the General Rules for Student Conduct still applies to the **taking into** the venue of flags, stickers, posters, stickers, weapons or objects of any kind that can be thrown.

Organisers of meetings in the Great Hall are required to liaise in advance with the Stage Manager regarding the erection of any flags, banners or posters in the venue.
4.6 The chairperson and/or organiser shall ensure that no speaker or other person present at a meeting, function or display uses language or behaves in a manner which conflicts with the principles as stated in paragraph 2 and if,

in the opinion of the chairperson or organiser of the meeting, function or display, such conduct continues after a warning, the chairperson or organiser shall close the meeting, function or display and request those present to disperse in an orderly manner.

4.7 The Deputy Registrar (Student Affairs) shall, prior to such a meeting, function or display discuss details with the Head of Campus Security. If it is considered necessary, there shall also be a preliminary meeting of members of the administration and student leaders. The Deputy Registrar (Student Affairs) shall alert the Peace-keeping Group to assemble outside the venue at the time that the meeting, function or display was scheduled to start.

5. ACADEMIC LECTURES, SEMINARS, TUTORIALS AND PRACTICAL CLASSES

5.1 The procedures for inviting lecturers to give lectures, seminars, tutorials or laboratory classes are dealt with in a separate document.

5.2 Academic activities shall take precedence, at all times, over all other meetings and activities.

5.3 Lectures, seminars, tutorials and practical classes given by a member of the staff of the University shall under no circumstances be interrupted without the permission of the lecturer.

5.4 Marching, singing and any other disturbances in the corridors and other public spaces in academic buildings during normal University hours shall not be permitted.

5.5 Visiting academics or speakers, if invited by a properly constituted University authority or academic authority in terms of the document referred to in 5.1 above, are guests of the University and will be afforded its protection.

5.6 Visiting academics or speakers participating in departmental activities shall be accorded all the normal courtesies and their classes shall not be interrupted.

5.7 Venues for academic lectures, seminars, tutorials and practical classes which are to be conducted outside the normal timetable, must be booked through the office of the Deputy Registrar (Administration).

6. GENERAL RULES FOR STUDENT CONDUCT

Students are reminded that the General Rules for Student Conduct which appear annually in the Calendar apply at all times. Infringements may render those responsible subject to disciplinary proceedings. Paragraph 2 of this document clearly states the guiding principles by which behaviour is judged.

7. OTHER MEASURES

Nothing in the procedures set out above shall prevent the officers of the University from taking such steps as may be necessary at any time to ensure the safety of students and staff of the University or other persons, or to safeguard the premises and property of the University.

8. DAMAGE

Organisers of meetings, functions or displays who fail to comply with any provisions of this document, may be required to pay any costs incurred by the

University in making good any loss or damage caused as a direct result of such meeting, function or display.
9. OTHER REQUIREMENTS
The Vice-Chancellor may impose such other requirements as he deems necessary.

APPENDIX 8

PROCEDURES TO BE FOLLOWED BY A DEPARTMENT WHEN A STUDENT OR MEMBER OF STAFF ARE REPORTED TO HAVE BEEN DETAINED

IF A STUDENT IS MISSING:
* Notify the Student Affairs Office.
* If the student has teaching responsibilities in the department, arrange for these to be covered.

IF A MEMBER OF STAFF (ACADEMIC OR NON-ACADEMIC) IS MISSING:
* Notify Academic or Non-Academic Staffing.
* Arrange for classes, tutorials and other responsibilities to be covered.

IF A STUDENT HAS BEEN DETAINED:
* Notify the Student Affairs Office.
* Nominate a member of the department to do the following:
* Contact any member of the Advisory Group on Detentions who will help you to undertake the following: (Don't wait. Contact *someone* immediately.)
* Monitor student's DP and records.
* Collect study materials: books, handouts (including tests) and classnotes.
* Write to the detainee frequently.
* Arrange additional support.
* If needed, make the trip to the place of detention.

IF A MEMBER OF STAFF HAS BEEN DETAINED:
* Notify Academic or Non-Academic Staffing.
* Nominate a member of the department to coordinate the following:
* Contact any member of the Advisory Group on Detentions who will help you to undertake the following: (Don't wait. Contact *someone* immediately.)
* Collect research and other materials required for work in prison.
* Write to the detainee frequently.
* If needed, make a trip to the place of detention.

WHEN A STUDENT HAS BEEN RELEASED:
* Contact the student and offer intensive academic support within the department, remaining sensitive to the likelihood that concentration and memory difficulties will occur following detention. Post-traumatic stress syndrome may be acute, chronic, or delayed in its onset (three-month delay is common).
* Suggest the student make use of counselling and/or therapy available through

Professor Straker's office (Detainees' Counselling Service), the Counselling and Careers Unit, the Academic Support Program, and/or Campus Health.
* Arrange peer support and notes.
* It may be useful to compare marks before and after detention.
* If necessary, guide the student toward requesting a deferral of examinations.

WHEN A MEMBER OF STAFF HAS BEEN RELEASED:
* Be aware that the staff member may not be able to assume full responsibilities immediately.

APPENDIX 9

LETTER FROM DEPARTMENTS OF EDUCATION TO ALL UNIVERSITIES, 5 AUGUST 1987

Dear Sir

CONDITIONS DETERMINED UNDER SECTION 25(1) OF THE UNIVERSITIES ACT, 1955 (ACT 61 OF 1955)

With reference to the discussions held on 5 August 1987 between members of Cabinet and members of the various Ministers' Councils on the one hand and representatives of universities on the other hand, I wish to inform you of my intention to determine the following conditions by virtue of the powers vested in me under section 25(1) of the above-mentioned Act to serve as a basis for the allocation of subsidies to your University:

1. The Council of your University shall take all reasonable steps directed towards –
   (a) the prevention of wrongful or unlawful interference with or discrimination against students or staff members of your University in the pursuit of their normal and lawful activities as such students or staff members;
   (b) the accomplishing of the undisrupted and undisturbed continuance of the teaching and research activities and of all related supporting activities, of your University in accordance with the pre-determined academic calendar;
   (c) the deterring on the premises of your University of gatherings which are unlawful by the provisions of any law, the boycotting of classes or examinations, any other disruptive or seditious conduct or the commission of any act of intimidation, as contemplated in section 1 of the Intimidation Act, 1982 (Act 72 of 1982), in respect of any student or staff member;
   (d) the prevention of staff members or students of your University or other persons from using –
      (i) any supplies (including stationery);
      (ii) any equipment (including vehicles, office equipment, printing presses, recording equipment, sound amplifying equipment or notice boards);
      (iii) any buildings; or
      (iv) any land improvements other than buildings, of your University for any of the following purposes, namely:

(aa) the promotion of the aims or public image of any unlawful organization as defined by section 1 of the Internal Security Act, 1982 (Act 74 of 1982), or of any affected organization as defined in section 1 of the Affected Organizations Act, 1974 (Act 31 of 1974);
(bb) the promotion, support or organising of a boycott action of any kind against –
  (aaa) any particular firm or against firms of any particular nature, class or kind; or
  (bbb) any particular product or article or against products or articles of any particular nature, class or kind; or
  (ccc) any particular educational institution or against educational institutions of any particular nature, class or kind;
(cc) the incitement or encouragement of members of the public to stay away from work or to strike in contravention of the provisions of any law;
(dd) the promotion, support or organising of any campaign of civil disobedience in terms of which members of the public are incited or encouraged, or which is calculated to have the effect of inciting or encouraging members of the public –
  (aaa) to refuse to comply with or to contravene a provision of, or requirement under, any law;
  (bbb) to refuse to fulfil any obligation towards a local authority, as defined in regulation 1 of the regulations published by Proclamation R.97 of 1987, in respect of rent or a municipal service;
(ee) the printing, publishing or dissemination of any publication in contravention of a notice issued under section 5(1) of the Internal Security Act, 1982 (Act 74 of 1982); or
(ff) the commission of any act which endangers or which may endanger the safety of the public or the maintenance of public order;
(e) the disciplining of any student or staff member who, to the satisfaction of the Council, is found to have –
  (i) been guilty of conduct intended as or constituting interference or discrimination as contemplated in paragraph (a);
  (ii) been guilty of conduct which disrupted or could have disrupted the teaching, research or related supporting activities contemplated in paragraph (b);
  (iii) organised, promoted or taken part in any unlawful gathering, boycott, other disruptive or seditious conduct or act of intimidation contemplated in paragraph (c); or
  (iv) used any supplies, equipment, building or land improvement referred to in paragraph (d) (i) to (iv), inclusive, for any of the purposes set out in paragraph (d) (aa) to (ff), inclusive;
(f) the disciplining of any student or staff member who conducts himself in a seditious or riotous manner within a radius of two kilometres from the perimeter of the campus of your University;

(g) finding whether you have complied with the above conditions. If I find that my conditions have not been met, you will be notified accordingly and afforded 10 days to furnish me with your submission relating to the finding. If the submission fails, the formal procedure in terms of section 27 of the Universities Act, 1955 (No. 61 of 1955) will commence.

In accordance with the verbal assurance given to you, your Council is afforded the opportunity to comment on the abovementioned conditions before 31 August 1987. You will be notified in writing of the final conditions.

PJ CLASE
MINISTER OF EDUCATION AND CULTURE,
ADMINISTRATION: HOUSE OF ASSEMBLY

APPENDIX 10

LEGAL OPINION SUBMITTED TO COUNCIL BY H C NICHOLAS, S KENTRIDGE AND D ZEFFERT, 12 AUGUST 1987

LETTER FROM MINISTER OF EDUCATION AND CULTURE DATED 5th AUGUST, 1987

ADVICE

1. We have considered the Minister's letter of the above-mentioned date addressed to the chairman of council, and have the following comments.
2. In this letter the Minister gives notice of his intention to determine certain conditions by virtue of the powers vested in him under sub-section (1) of section 25 of the Universities Act, No. 61 of 1955.
Under this sub-section the Minister is empowered to grant subsidies to a university –
   '... for such purposes and on such basis and subject to such conditions as may, in respect of each university, be determined by the Minister and with due regard to the requirements of each university in relation to the general requirements of higher education in the Republic.'
Section 27 of the Act provides –
   '(1) If any Council fails to comply with any provision of this Act under which subsidies from moneys voted by Parliament are paid to universities or with any condition subject to which any such subsidy is paid to its university, the Minister may call upon such Council to comply with the said provision or condition within a specified period.
   (2) If such Council thereafter fails to comply with the said provision or con-

dition; the Minister may, notwithstanding anything to the contrary in any law contained, withhold payment of the whole or any portion of the subsidy voted by Parliament in respect of the university concerned...'

The proposed conditions are set out in two numbered paragraphs in the letter.

Paragraph 1 of the letter sets out **substantive conditions** dealing with preventive measures to be taken by the University Council (sub-paragraphs (a), (b), (c) and (d)); disciplinary measures relating thereto (subparagraphs (e), (f), and (g)); and measures for ensuring strict compliance with the provisions of section 17 of the Joint Statutes of the universities for denial of admission to students who have been expelled from another university on the ground of misconduct as contemplated in paragraphs (e), (f), and (g) (sub-paragraph (h)).

Paragraph 2 of the letter sets out **procedural conditions** designed to ensure that the substantive conditions are complied with.

3. CONDITIONS ULTRA VIRES OF THE MINISTER

In our opinion the Minister does not have the power to make Conditions such as those set out in the letter.

It is a fundamental principle of South African administrative law (ie. the law governing the exercise of the powers of Ministers and other administrative officials) that when a public body or a public official is, by statute, given a power for a particular purpose, that purpose cannot be used for obtaining any other object, however laudable. If a person exercising a power avowedly uses it for some purpose other than that for which alone it has been given, he acts contrary to law. (See Van Eck, N.O. & Van Rensburg, N.O. v. Ema Stores, 1947 (2) S.A. 984 (A.D.), at 996 and 988; The Firs Investments (Pty) Ltd v. Johannesburg City Council, 1967 (3) S.A. 549 (W), at 551H-552B.)

Under section 25 (1) the Minister is not at large to impose any conditions which he may choose to make. He may not, for example, make it a condition for the payment of a subsidy that women should be excluded from a university or that the university does not teach the theory of evolution. To be valid, conditions must be germane to the subject matter of the section, namely, the payment of subsidies. They must not have as their object the promotion of extraneous matters, such as the maintenance of law and order. Section 25 (1) is a purely financial provision. Under it the Minister may determine the purposes for which a subsidy is granted; the basis on which it is granted (eg with reference to a formula); and the conditions subject to which it is granted. And in granting a subsidy to a particular university, the Minister is required to have regard to the requirements (sc. financial reqirements) of that university in relation to the requirements of higher education in the Republic generally.

Clearly the section does not authorise the Minister to impose conditions which are in no way related to finance. More especially, it does not authorise him, by way of conditions, to dictate to the University Council in regard to matters which the legislature has entrusted to the organs of the University and particularly the Council.

Thus, sub-section (1) of section 9 of the University of the Witwatersrand, Johannesburg (Private Act), No. 15 of 1959 provides that, subject to the provisions of the Act, the government and executive authority of the University shall be vested in the Council. Sub-section (6) provides inter alia that the Council shall have the general control of the university and all its affairs, purposes and functions. Section 20 provides that a student of the University shall be subject to such disciplinary provisions as may be determined by the statutes (ie. the statutes made by the Council under the authority of Act 61 of 1955.

In terms of sub-section 1 of section 17 of Act 61 of 1955 a council has power to frame:
   (a) statutes for giving effect to any law relating to its University in relation to matters not specifically prescribed by any law; and
   (b) regulations for the better carrying out of such statutes.

Again, section 11 of Act 61 of 1955 provides that 'a council shall have the right to refuse admittance to any student who applies for admission should it consider it to be in the interests of the university concerned to do so.' This means that the Council must decide each application on its merits in the light of the interests of the University.

The conditions contemplated in the letter trench on the autonomy of the University and would encroach on, and interfere with powers which Parliament has vested in the Council alone. They would interfere with the **exclusive** authority of the Council; with the Council's 'general control of the university and all its affairs, purposes and functions'. They would prescribe to the Council what disciplinary provisions would be the first and necessary step towards the achievement of the objects set out in paragraph 1 of the letter. The condition set out in the proviso to paragraph 1 (h) is not one which the Minister is competent to impose: the university would be acting illegally if it were to refuse to register a student merely on that ground.

There can be no doubt in our opinion that the Minister does not have the power under section 25 (1) of the Act to determine the proposed conditions.

4. CONDITIONS IN PARAGRAPH 1 VOID FOR VAGUENESS

Paragraph 1 of the letter enjoins the University Council to 'take all reasonable steps' directed towards the achievement of the matters there set out.

No guidance is provided as to what is meant by 'reasonable steps.'

The Council is not informed with sufficient certainty what are the steps it is required to take. They are presumably not restricted to steps which the Council considers reasonable, and the Minister does not say what steps he considers reasonable. What are 'reasonable steps' is not capable of objective ascertainment; it involves a value judgement, and is something in regard to which different views may well be held by different people.

That being so, the Council would be left in ignorance of what it would be required to do in order to comply with the conditions. The problem may be illustrated by reference to section 27 (1) of Act 61 of 1955. Under that section the Minister can do no more than call upon the Council to comply with the conditions. He would be entitled at that stage to issue directions in regard to specific matters. And if the Minister were merely to direct compliance, the Council would not know what it had to do.

The Minister cannot lawfully require a council to take any steps which are not within its powers under the relevant Acts of Parliament or any statutes framed by the Council thereunder; or which it is not, by its nature, capable of taking. The Council can express its corporate will only by means of resolutions. It follows that the only steps which the Council could take would be to pass resolutions making rules and regulations in regard to the matters set out in paragraph 1 of the letter and instructing that they be enforced by the responsible officers of the University.

If, therefore, the letter contemplates any other steps, they should be spelt out in order that Council can consider whether such steps are within its powers, and regulate its conduct accordingly.

For these reasons we are of the opinion that the conditions are void for vagueness.

5. COMMENT ON PARTICULAR PROVISIONS OF PARAGRAPH 1

If we are right in the views expressed in either paragraph 3 of paragraph 4 hereof, then the conditions as a whole would be null and void, and liable to be set aside by the court. Nevertheless we deal specifically with certain of the provisions. (It should be observed that there are other questionable provisions, with which for the sake of brevity we do not deal.)

(i) It would appear from sub-paragraph (b) of paragraph 1 of the letter that the Council would be precluded from authorising any departure from the 'predetermined academic calendar' even if it considered that to be proper in the interests of the University. If that is so, this would constitute an unwarranted interference with the Council's responsibility for the general control of the affairs of the University.

(ii) The reference in paragraph 1 (c) of the letter to 'seditious' conduct gives rise to difficulty and uncertainty. The definition of 'sedition' is one of the more difficult problems in South African law.

(iii) In paragraph 1 (d) (aa) the phrase 'the promotion of the ... public image' of any unlawful organisation is likewise uncertain: while the promotion of the aims of an unlawful organisation is a criminal offence, there is no offence known to the law of 'promoting the public image of an unlawful organisation.' In the same sub-paragraph there seems to be a misunderstanding of the nature of an affected organisation. An affected organisation is not illegal under Act 31 of 1974. It may be lawfully joined or supported; the only offence in relation to an affected organisation is the collection or receipt of funds from abroad.

(iv) Sub-paragraph 1 (d) (bb) relates to boycott action. This is so wide that any regulation which embodies it is unlikely to be valid. What, for example, of a boycott against a firm which exploits or mistreats the students of a university? What of the boycott of a product which is believed on good grounds to be harmful?

(v) Sub-paragraphs (e) and (g) of paragraph 1 of the letter provide for the disciplining of any student or staff member who, to the 'satisfaction of the Council,' is found to have committed specific acts. Sub-paragraph (f) does not provide a similar qualification. The reason for the omission is not apparent and it may be an oversight.

Sub-paragraphs (e) and (g) misconceive the role of the Council in disciplinary proceedings in the University against students.

Such proceedings are governed by 'Rules for Student Discipline'. The Council does not exercise original jurisdiction in any disciplinary proceedings against students. It only has powers of review. It is therefore inappropriate to refer to 'the satisfaction of the Council' in regard to such disciplinary proceedings.

(vi) It would appear from sub-paragraph (e) (i) of paragraph 1 that a person should be subjected to discipline merely because of his intention, even though his conduct falls short of interference or discrimination (or an attempt) as contemplated in sub-paragraph (a). In our system of justice a person is not punishable because of his bare intention. It is conceived that such a provision would be *ultra vires* of the Council and would not be enforceable.

(vii) It would appear from the words 'could have disrupted' in sub-paragraph (e) (ii) of paragraph 1 that such conduct would be punishable even if disruption would be no more than a possible consequence (however remote) of the conduct concerned. A disciplinary provision in that form would be *ultra vires*.

(viii) In regard to sub-paragraph (f) of paragraph 1, it is open to serious question whether the Council could lawfully discipline a student or staff member who conducts himself in the manner referred to outside the campus of the University, unless such conduct is in some way connected with the University. Moreover, the expression 'a radius of two kilometres from the perimeter of the campus' is unintelligible. A radius is a straight line between a centre and a circumference; it is difficult to see how there can be a radius measured from a perimeter. Moreover, in the case of this University, while there is a main campus, the campus includes other premises, eg. Frankenwald which is 20 kilometres from the main campus.

(ix) Sub-paragraph (g) of paragraph 1 covers acts committed by **any** student or staff member, committed **anywhere** in the Republic against **any** other student or staff member even though such acts have no connection with the University or its activities. Any provision in such wide terms in the University's code of discipline would clearly be *ultra vires*.

6. COMMENT ON PARAGRAPH 2

Paragraph 2 of the letter sets out the procedure to be followed in the event of

'Any incident of unrest or disruption or any other occurrence against the happening of which the preventive or disciplinary measures contemplated in paragraphs 1 (a) to (g)...are directed... '

Such incident or occurrence is to be notified to the Minister within a specified period. The notification is to be accompanied by an explanation of the circumstances giving rise to the incident or occurrence and by a report submitted by or on behalf of the Council setting forth what steps were taken in respect of the incident or occurrence and what steps, if any, are intended to be taken in order to prevent a recurrence of similar incidents or occurrences in the future.

On receipt of such report, the Minister will notify the University of his finding whether the University has complied 'with the above conditions' (sc. the conditions set out in paragraphs 1 (a) to (g) inclusive).

There may then follow certain steps leading up to action by the Minister in terms of section 27 of the Universities Act.

It would appear from paragraph 2 that the only matter to be considered by the Minister is a specific incident or occurrence and the steps taken thereto. Hence it is only in regard to such incident or occurrence that the Minister will make a finding whether the University has complied with the conditions. The underlying assumption appears to be that the happening of an incident or occurrence shows *prima facie* that there has not been compliance. Such an assumption would not be justified, as is illustrated by the fact that even though there has existed for many months in the Republic a state of emergency, and there have been brought into operation all the powers of the State (including emergency regulations, detention without trial, and coercive action by the police and army) incidents of 'unrest' still occur. There is no reason to believe that in the case of a university, with its limited powers and different approach, 'unrest' will not occur, even though all 'reasonable steps' are taken.

The terms of paragraph 2 of the letter are such that the Council will be required to notify the Minister of every incident or occurrence, however limited and trivial, and even though it involves only a single person.

Is it really contemplated that such a burden should be placed upon the University, or that the Minister should be troubled with such cases?

In order to enable the Minister to consider whether the conditions have been complied with, the Minister should, it is suggested, call for information on what steps have been taken by the Council and not concern himself with particular incidents. The relevant enquiry, it is submitted, should be into the nature generally of the measures taken and not in regard to the facts of a particular case. Moreover it appears to us that what the Minister has in mind is that he may exercise his powers under section 27 if he considers that disciplinary steps taken by the University in any particular case are inadequate. The undesirability of putting pressure on the University to take this factor into account when considering the proper punishment for a disciplinary offence hardly needs emphasising.

Moreover, the requirements of the paragraph are unrealistic and impractical.

It has happened in this University in the past that it has been possible to ascertain the 'circumstances giving rise to an incident or occurrence' only after a detailed and time-consuming investigation, sometimes by an independent commission of inquiry. In such cases it would be impossible for an explanation to be given within the prescribed period. Nor is it practicable for a report by or on behalf of the Council to be submitted within that period. Disciplinary steps take time (sometimes a considerable time) for the investigation and formulation of charges and the disciplinary hearing.

7. CONCLUSION

Our conclusion is, therefore, that the conditions as a whole are *ultra vires* of the Minister; that they are void for vagueness; and that they are likely to be set aside by the Court. The conditions are moreover open to attack on numerous points of detail.

H C NICHOLAS
S KENTRIDGE
D ZEFFERT
12 August 1987

APPENDIX 11

RESPONSE OF CHAIRMAN OF COUNCIL, DR N STUTTERHEIM, TO THE MINISTER OF EDUCATION AND CULTURE, MR PJ CLASE

25 August 1987

Dear Mr Minister
CONDITIONS DETERMINED UNDER SECTION 25(1) OF THE UNIVERSITIES ACT 1955 (ACT 61 OF 1955)
I refer to the meeting between members of the Cabinet and members of the various Ministers' Councils, on the one hand, and the Chairmen of Councils and Vice-Chancellors and Rectors of the Universities, on the other, on 5 August 1987, and to your letter of 5 August 1987 (reference 3/4/12/1 and 14/5/B). The Council of the University of the Witwatersrand has considered your letter carefully and has reached unanimity in its views. In response to your invitation, the Council comments on the letter as follows:

1. University Autonomy

    The principle of autonomy is central to the very being of a university and has been so for centuries. In those countries where university autonomy exists standards are highest and universities are able to achieve excellence; in lands where universities are controlled centrally standards suffer and their achievement levels fall short.

    The University of the Witwatersrand, Johannesburg (Private Act), No. 15 of 1959 states that the government and executive authority of the University, 'the general control of the University and all its affairs, purposes and functions', shall be the responsibility of the Council. In these matters Parliament has vested exclusive authority in the Council.

2. Academic Freedom

    Academic freedom is a fundamental principle of universities. The Council has affirmed this principle with vigour since the inception of the University of the Witwatersrand; its commitment to this essential freedom is undiminished. The Council welcomes the Government's public commitment to academic freedom. It must be pointed out, however, that what would be required of the University in terms of your letter itself involves a curb on academic freedom on campus and constitutes an invasion of the autonomy of the University.

3. The aims of the University

    The University is dedicated to the acquisition, advancement and imparting of knowledge through the pursuit of truth in balanced dispassionate teaching, in tolerant and scholarly discourse, in free and open debate and in the undertaking of research. In all these activities the University strives for nationally and internationally recognised excellence, the maintenance of the highest standards and the greatest possible contemporary and local relevance.

4. Council's attitude to the letter
   In the opinion of Council, the conditions contemplated in your letter would
   (a) constitute an invasion of the autonomy of the University;
   (b) involve curbs on academic freedom; and
   (c) be inconsistent with the University's aims and the values that it expresses.
   That being so, the Council cannot voluntarily accept the conditions. It submits in addition that, for reasons which appear from the following paragraphs, the imposition of such conditions would be unjustified, unwise and counter-productive.

5. Attainment of aims
   That the institution has standards of excellence equal to the highest in South Africa in the educating of students, in scholarship and research has been established by the Committee on Standards of the Advisory Committee on Universities and Technikons, the Committee of University Principals' Academic Planning Committee's comparisons of SAPSE returns and by various independent statutory bodies such as the Human Sciences Research Council. They show that standards are being maintained and that the productivity of the University has never been higher. They make apparent that the research done at Wits is the most cost effective of all South African university research and is a national asset of great and increasing value at a time when links with the outside world are becoming ever more difficult to maintain. Over the years the proportion of undergraduates and postgraduates who complete studies for degrees has increased. The University is making a substantial contribution to the country's high-level manpower need. Taxpayers' money is not being wasted: on the contrary, it is being invested wisely.

6. Existing policy with respect to disruption
   It is the policy of the Council to eschew outside interference in the running of the University and in the conduct of its activities, whether such interference comes from individuals, sectarian groups, business or professional interests, or other sources.

   Any forms of violence, intimidation, harassment, incitement, discrimination, or wilful disruption of University activities (particularly teaching and research, classes and meetings) are not acceptable. Abrogation of the freedom of speech whether it be by students, staff or outsiders is rejected by the academic community, and the principle of freedom of speech is instilled in our students throughout their stay in the University. The University responds when any members of the academic community, by their activities, reject this principle and takes action against those who break the rules of the University.

7. Handling of disruption
   It is submitted that under extremely difficult circumstances, and contrary to some uninformed public opinion, a good deal of success has been achieved in the handling of unrest in the past. While it is conceded that on some occasions minor disruption has been tolerated to avoid greater disorder, overseas experience proves that such a policy is wise, effective and should be followed judiciously.

In the past the Council has appointed independent Commissions of Inquiry into various incidents of unrest, has accepted many of their recommendations for improving procedures to handle such incidents and has supplied the Government with copies of the reports. It would be prepared to submit such reports in the future.

The Council wishes to assure the Minister of its intention to govern the University to the best of its ability with the object of achieving the aims of the University as set out. The Council will, after formal disciplinary procedures, continue to take measures against those who, in terms of Point 6 (second paragraph) above, attempt to disrupt the University's activities. It will take strong disciplinary action when this is necessary and appropriate. However, indications are that *agents provocateurs* linked to outside agencies have been active on campus. Under such circumstances the currents of unrest cannot always be excluded whatever measures may be taken.

8. Future disruption

   Apart from the problems of principle that they raise, it is possible that the conditions the Minister wishes to impose could in fact open the way to far greater systematic disruption of University activities than hitherto by individuals or groups wishing to exploit the University for their own ends. The conditions could easily become counter-productive and become the means by which malevolent action might be taken against both the University and the Government.

   It is also suggested that implementation of the conditions would be administratively unmanageable, both for the University and for the office of the Minister, which would have to consider every incident.

9. Outside intervention

   It cannot be stressed enough that when disruption does occur on the campus, police intervention, however well intended, simply exacerbates the situation. The police should come onto the campus only at the request of the University authorities.

10. Legal considerations

    The attached legal opinion holds that the conditions of the Minister's letter as a whole are *ultra vires*.

11. Recommendation

    It is recommended that the Minister should accept the Council's assurance that it intends continuing to implement its existing policy in a vigorous and appropriate manner, and that the Minister takes the matter of the conditions as stated in his letter of 5 August 1987 no further.

Finally it must be mentioned that the Council, the Senate and the University as a whole stand united in their wish to see full university autonomy preserved. The University is committed to providing a forum for untrammelled, rational and unrestricted enquiry into and debate upon the many sensitive issues that must be aired if solutions are to be found for the pressing problems that the country faces. This it cannot do unless it retains its autonomy and preserves its academic freedom. It is resolute in wishing to do both.

Because the Minister of National Education chaired the meeting on 5 August 1987, I thought it a necessary courtesy to send him a copy of this response.

The Vice-Chancellor and I would be grateful for an opportunity to discuss the contents of this letter with you.

APPENDIX 12

THE REVISED CONDITIONS

CONDITIONS DETERMINED UNDER SECTION 25(1) OF THE UNIVERSITIES ACT, 1955 (ACT 61 OF 1955)

1. The Council of the University of the Witwatersrand shall within the scope of the powers and duties conferred or imposed upon it by law with regard to the government and the general control of the affairs and functions of the University, take steps directed towards-
    (a) the prevention of wrongful or unlawful interference with, intimidation of, or discrimination against students or staff members of the University in the pursuit of their normal and lawful activities as such students or staff members;
    (b) the accomplishing of the undisrupted and undisturbed continuance of the teaching and research activities and of all related supporting activities of the University in accordance with a pre-determined academic calendar as determined by the responsible authority of the University;
    (c) the deterring on the premises of the University of gatherings which are unlawful by virtue of the provisions of any law, the boycotting of classes or examinations or any other disruptive conduct;
    (d) the prevention of staff members or students of the University or other persons from using –
        (i) any supplies (including stationery);
        (ii) any equipment (including vehicles, office equipment, printing presses, recording equipment, sound amplifying equipment or notice boards);
        (iii) any buildings; or
        (iv) any land improvements other than buildings, of the University for any of the following purposes, namely:
        (aa) the promotion of the aims or public image of any unlawful organization as defined in section 1 of the Internal Security Act, 1982 (Act 74 of 1982);
        (bb) the promotion, support or organizing of a boycott action against –
            (aaa) any particular firm or against firms of any particular nature, class or kind;
            (bbb) any particular product or article or against products or articles of any particular nature, class or kind; or

(ccc) any particular educational institution or against educational institutions of any particular nature, class or kind;
(cc) the incitement or encouragement of members of the public to stay away from work or to strike in contravention of the provisions of any law;
(dd) the promotion, support or organising of any campaign of civil disobedience in terms of which members of the public are incited or encouraged, or which is calculated to have the effect of inciting or encouraging members of the public to refuse to comply with or to contravene a provision of, or requirement under, any law;
(ee) the printing, publishing or dissemination of any publication in contravention of a notice issued under section 5(1) of the Internal Security Act, 1982 (Act 74 of 1982); or
(ff) the commission of any act which endangers or which may endanger the safety of the public or the maintenance of public order;

(e) ensuring that disciplinary steps be taken against any student or staff member who, to the satisfaction of the responsible disciplinary body, is found to have –
　(i) been guilty of conduct constituting interference or intimidation or discrimination or an attempt at interference or intimidation or discrimination as contemplated in paragraph (a);
　(ii) been guilty of conduct which disrupted the teaching, research or related supporting activities contemplated in paragraph (b);
　(iii) organised, promoted or taken part in any unlawful gathering, boycott or other disruptive conduct contemplated in paragraph (c); or
　(iv) used any supplies, equipment, building or land improvement referred to in paragraph (d)(i) to (iv), inclusive, for any of the purposes set out in paragraph (d)(aa) to (ff), inclusive;

(f) ensuring that disciplinary steps be taken against any student or staff member who is found, to the satisfaction of the responsible disciplinary body of the University, on proof furnished by the Minister of Education and Culture at any place to have committed any act of which the Council is notified by the Minister, which constitutes an act in respect of which the Council is in terms of these conditions required to take preventive or disciplinary measures;

(g) ensuring that disciplinary steps be taken against any student or staff member who, to the satisfaction of the responsible disciplinary body, is found to have at any place intimidated any other student or staff member; and

(h) ensuring strict compliance with the provisions of section 17 of the Joint Statute of the Universities regarding the submission of a certificate of conduct by a student who was previously registered at another university: Provided that the University shall not register any student who has been expelled from another university on the grounds of misconduct contemplated in paragraphs (e), (f), and (g) above as long as such expulsion is of force and effect.

2. Any incident of unrest or disruption or any other occurrence against the happening of which the preventive measures contemplated in paragraph 1 (a) to (c), inclusive, are directed, involving the University or a student or staff member thereof and of which the Council is aware or which has been brought to the attention of the Council shall be notified to the Minister of Education and Culture in writing within twenty-one days of the date on which it took place, or in the event of such incident or occurrence coming to the notice of the Council only after the expiration of such period of twenty-one days, within such further period, not exceeding twenty-one days, as the Council can conveniently so notify the Minister. Should the Council not be in a position to comply with this requirement within the stated period, the Council may request an extension of the aforesaid period.

The notification of the Council shall be accompanied by an explanation of the circumstances giving rise to the incident or occurrence, as well as by a report submitted by or on behalf of the Council setting forth what steps, if any, were or are to be taken in respect of the incident or occurrence, including disciplinary steps and what steps, if any, are intended to be taken in order to prevent a recurrence of similar incidents or occurrences in the future.

On receipt of such a report the Minister will notify the Council of his finding whether the Council has complied with the above conditions. If the Minister finds that any condition has not been met, the Council will be notified accordingly, the reasons for any finding will be given and the Council will be afforded twenty-one days to furnish the Minister with a submission relating to the finding.

If the submission fails, the formal procedure in terms of section 27 of the Universities Act, 1955 (No. 61 of 1955) will commence.

APPENDIX 13

LEGAL OPINION OF PROFESSOR D ZEFFERT ON THE REVISED CONDITIONS

1. CONDITIONS DETERMINED UNDER S 25(1) OF THE UNIVERSITIES ACT 61 OF 1955.
... The new conditions are substantially the same as the draft conditions but have been modified in certain respects. I have been asked, in the light of the changes that have been wrought, whether I am still of the opinion that the conditions are liable to be set aside by the court.
2. CONDITIONS ULTRA VIRES OF THE MINISTER
In my opinion the Minister does not have the power to make conditions such as those set out in the amended conditions. The conclusion that the conditions initially proposed were, as a whole, ultra vires of the Minister, was based upon an application of the principle that when a public official is, by statute, given power for a par-

ticular purpose, that purpose cannot be used for obtaining any other object however laudable.

As s 25 does not authorise the Minister to impose conditions that are in no way related to finance, it follows that it does not authorise him to dictate conditions to the University Council on matters that the legislature has entrusted to the organs of the University and, particularly, the Council, that are not financial matters.

... We concluded that (in terms s 17(1) of the Universities Act 61 of 1955 and s 9(1) of the University's Private Act) the conditions initially contemplated by the letter trenched on the autonomy of the University and would encroach on and interfere with matters within the exclusive authority of the Council.

The most significant concurrence between the new and the old conditions is as follows. Both the old and new conditions require the Council to notify the Minister about certain incidents of unrest or disruption. In both the old and the new, the Council is required to give an explanation of the circumstances giving rise to the incident or occurrence as well as a report setting out the steps, if any, that were or are to be taken, including disciplinary steps. When the Minister gets the report he has to notify the Council of his finding and whether the Council has complied with the conditions. If he finds that they have not been met, the Council has to be given time to furnish the Minister with a submission relating to the finding and, if the submission fails, the formal procedure in terms of s 27 of the Universities Act of 1955 (the procedure by which the subsidy can be attacked) will commence.

The difference lies in the scope of the conditions. The conditions that were initially contemplated referred to incidents and occurrences contemplated in paragraphs 1 (a) to (c).

The duty to report incidents or occurrences, on pain of incurring 'the formal procedure' in terms of s 27, is now confined to the taking of steps directed towards –

'(a) the prevention of wrongful or unlawful interference with, intimidation of, or discrimination against students or staff members of the University in the pursuit of their normal and lawful activities as such students or staff members;

(b) the accomplishing of the undisrupted and undisturbed continuance of the teaching and research activities of the University in accordance with a predetermined academic calendar as determined by the responsible authority of the University;

(c) the deterring on the premises of the University of gatherings which are unlawful by virtue of the provisions of any law, the boycotting of classes or examinations or any other disruptive conduct;'

I am of the opinion that these conditions interfere with the exclusive disciplinary authority of the Council and with its 'general control of the university and all its affairs, purposes and functions.' They prescribe to the Council what disciplinary provisions it must adopt, since proper disciplinary provisions would be a necessary step toward the achievement of the objects set out in paras 1 (a) to (c) inclusive of the new conditions. Their intrusion into the Council's power of general control is obvious.

I am, accordingly, of the opinion that the Minister does not have the power under S 25(1) of the Act to determine the conditions.

3. CONDITIONS VOID FOR VAGUENESS
Paragraph 1 of the original conditions enjoined Council to 'take all reasonable steps' directed towards the achievement of the matters set out. The new conditions omit the word 'reasonable'. They enjoin the Council to 'take steps directed towards' certain objects.

I am of the opinion that the Council has still not been informed with sufficient certainty on what steps to take. I iterate that the Minister cannot lawfully require a Council to take any steps which are not within its powers under the relevant Acts of Parliament or any statutes framed by the Council under them; or which it is not by its nature capable of taking. The Council can express its corporate will only by means of resolutions. It follows that the only steps the Council could take would be to pass resolutions making rules and regulations in regard to the matters set out in paragraph 1 and instructing that they be enforced by the responsible officers of the University. If, therefore, the conditions contemplate any other steps, they should be spelt out so that Council can consider whether such steps are within its powers and regulate its conduct accordingly.

I am still of the opinion that the conditions are void for vagueness.

4. PARTICULAR PROVISIONS
I do not intend to comment on particular provisions of paragraph 1 of the new conditions. Some of the worst instances of unreasonable demands of vague and imprecise drafting have been removed; some of the other defects, previously alluded to, remain. I would add the following point as it seems to me to be an almost text-book illustration of ultimate unreason. The University is precluded from registering any student who has been expelled from another university on the basis of certain acts of misconduct. This presupposes that the student was expelled on good grounds. What if there had been fraud in expelling him from the other university? What if no reasonable man, applying his mind to the facts, could possibly have expelled him? He must be refused admission.

5. CONCLUSION
My conclusion is, therefore, that the new conditions are, also, as a whole ultra vires of the Minister, void for vagueness; and, consequently, liable to be set aside by the court. The conditions remain, moreover, open to attack on some points of detail.

APPENDIX 14

ADDRESSES DELIVERED AT THE GENERAL ASSEMBLY OF THE UNIVERSITY ON 28 OCTOBER 1987

Address by Professor M Shear in opening the Assembly

It is exceedingly rare that a General Assembly of this University is called. The first of these was in the Great Hall on 16 April 1959 when we met to make the solemn affirmation that a university is a place where men and women, without regard to race and colour, are welcome to join in the acquisition and advancement of knowledge. The second was held on 16 April 1969 on the tenth anniversary of the historic dedication. The third was on 8 June 1972, called to express the University's attitude towards events relating to universities in South Africa, when the Minister of Justice at the time prohibited by proclamation, all protest meetings. On 26 August 1975, a General Assembly of the University protested against the detention of our students without charge or trial. Four years ago, on 3 May 1983, the University met to express its objection to the Government's intention to impose a racially based quota for the admission of students. On 16 August 1985 we met in General Assembly to reaffirm the University's academic principles and on 15 August last year, a General Assembly of the University expressed its abhorrence of the state of emergency and the detention without trial of staff and students.

Therefore we are gathered here today, as a General Assembly of the University of the Witwatersrand, for the eighth time in our history: Council, Senate, Convocation, students, the academic staff and the support staff, to express to South Africa and to the world, our gravest concern at what is regarded as the most serious threat ever, to the autonomy of the University.

The present ministerial regulations, like previous assaults on our autonomy, have been imposed because we are perceived as vulnerable and weak. Vulnerable we may be, but weak we are certainly not. The thousands of members of our community, present here today, bear witness to this. While we are meeting here today, similar gatherings at the Universities of Cape Town, Natal and Western Cape are expressing their own rejection of these ministerial edicts.

Messages of support from members of the public are pouring into the University, and expressions of solidarity have come from our sister universities.

Previous attacks on this University have not deterred us. Let no-one underestimate our resolve. We shall not be cowed.

Address by the Chairman of the Council, Dr N Stutterheim

Since the establishment of our University, by Act of Parliament, sixty-five years ago, the University Council has successfully carried out the statutory mandate entrusted to it. The testimony to this success is not only the nationally and internationally recognised standards of the University's undergraduate and postgraduate degrees and the quality of its research output, but also the universally perceived commitment to liberal values and equal human rights. Throughout its existence, Wits has continued to provide a dynamic academic environment which has stimulated generations of students and staff to high intellectual achievement.

The present University Administration has, as did its predecessors, run the day-to-day affairs of the University with dedication, sensitivity and responsibility. The normal activities of the institution proceed productively and the occasional breaches of the code of defined proper behaviour, which occur in every dynamic university, have been dealt with sensibly and with the best interests of the institution and its community uppermost in mind. During the years the funds allocated to the

University have been utilised solely for the purposes intended. The Administration has the full confidence of the Council.

The recent unilaterally imposed Government interference in the administration of our University is an abrogation of the autonomy assigned to it by Parliament. This encroachment is, we sincerely believe, unwarranted and will inevitably prove to be counter-productive. The Council therefore earnestly requests the authorities to reconsider their arrogation to themselves of functions of Council.

Address by the Chancellor of the University, Dr A M Rosholt

We are gathered today in response to the gravest threat to its autonomy the University has ever had to face. This autonomy was first violated in 1959 when racial segregation was forced on the University. In 1983 the Universities Amendment Bill (the so-called 'quota Bill') gave the Minister power to impose racial quotas on universities and to withdraw subsidies from those not complying with imposed conditions. The Law remains on the Statute Book. The latest threat to the University is being presented in the guise of help from the Government in the preservation of academic freedom on campus. Let no one be taken in by this stratagem. The University needs no external assistance in the running of its affairs. It is committed to the upholding of free speech and to the prevention of intimidation, disruption of its activities and violence. It has always taken timeous and appropriate action against those who have broken its codes and will continue to do everything possible to ensure that its members behave in a manner befitting the great institution it is recognised to be both nationally and internationally. Our record of achievement in scholarship and in service to all the people of South Africa is second to none and I am proud to be its Chancellor. I think the Council has done an excellent job of guiding University policy in the past and see no reason to doubt its ability to do so in the future. I reject the implication that it is unfit to control the affairs of the University.

No rational person can take exception to the Minister's wish to see the right of free speech protected or the public's desire that orderly behaviour be safeguarded on campus. These are things every member of the University believes in. Let nobody doubt this. What we find objectionable is the method the Minister wishes to use to force the University to comply with his manner of attaining these ends. His method we find to be repugnant and unnecessary. It must be rejected. By his threat to withhold the subsidy if the University Council does not meet certain conditions he has laid down and by requiring Council to report all so-called 'incidents' to him within 21 days for his further action should he so decide, the Minister is imposing political control on the University. It is a tragic irony that a government so opposed to financial sanctions seeks to impose them on an institution which demonstrably does so much for so many in this country. We cannot allow the University to become an agent of Government in the disciplining of its members. We find the Minister's conditions unacceptable. We must do all we can to ensure that full autonomy is restored to the University. We must continue to govern the University as we have up to now. Wits is a great university. External control of its affairs is unwarranted and unacceptable.

Address by Professor P V Tobias, Head of the Department of Anatomy, as the representative of the Senate

The Senate of this great University deplores the Government's conditions attached to the granting of university subsidies; moreover the Senate is angry. It takes a lot to make Senate angry, for it is the cool-headed, supreme academic body of the University. It is angry because the Government has instructed the University to betray traditional educational values, to enforce on our campus the ideology of the white ruling party, to become a Star Chamber smelling out the political views and activities of students and staff members both on and off the campus, to become an implement of State security, a tool of government policies, an instrument of repression. These are the implications of the newly imposed conditions. No wonder Senate is angry.

The Minister's conditions constitute the most serious assault on university autonomy, as well as on freedom of speech, freedom of assembly, freedom of thought and freedom of the academy. These principles, so dear to our University, are being butchered to make a Roman holiday for the apostles of intolerance and tyranny.

The Senate of Wits University finds the Minister's conditions totally unacceptable. We declare solemnly that we decline to comply with them. We are utterly convinced that we cannot continue to function as a university in the true sense of the word, unless the Minister forthwith cancels these objectionable fetters. We have full confidence in our University's disciplinary procedures and are proud that we have continued to produce outstanding results in teaching, research and scholarship. We are confident that the Council of Wits does not need dictation from outside on how to run this University.

In our protest we stand shoulder to shoulder with the Universities of Cape Town, Natal, Rhodes and Western Cape. It should be with *every* university in this country. Alas, it is not so. Not often does Senate criticise other universities, but on this occasion Senate is not only surprised but bitterly disappointed that several universities seem sublimely unperturbed by the new conditions. For example, Stellenbosch 'can go along with them' (*The Star*, 17 October), while Potchefstroom gives 'full support' to the new regulations (*The Star*, 23 October). Can they really fail to appreciate the sinister implications of the restrictions?

Are they really blind to the national and international damage our universities will suffer? What do they know of conditions on this campus, which they think have justified the Minister's draconian rules? It is the mark of the true academic to determine the facts first. Small wonder that Senate has called on these universities to reconsider their positions and not be party to the betrayal of these essential educational freedoms. This is a time for all universities in the country to show the Government the error of its ways.

Senate joins with all other constituents of the University in demanding the withdrawal of the Government's drastic rules. We shall *not* subjugate ourselves to these savage conditions; we shall *not* prostitute our calling as academics to become a spying and policing agency; we shall *never* cease our struggle for autonomy and freedom, nor our determined opposition to racism, apartheid and authoritarianism.

Address by the Vice-Chancellor Designate, Professor R W Charlton

The Government's action in usurping the authority of the University Council is totally unacceptable. History teaches that universities flourish when they are autonomous, while in those countries where they are under direct government control academic standards suffer. The long-term consequences of the breaching of the autonomy of the University will be disastrous for the quality of university education and the international status of South African degrees. It is ironic that the sort of control which is now being imposed is typical of those countries which the Government opposes most strongly.

We have been subjected to a propaganda campaign that has created the impression in the minds of the general public that the taxpayers' money is being wasted. The Government's own objective comparisons demonstrate that Wits is one of the most cost-effective of all the universities: indeed, it is easily the most productive and cost-effective in research. Equally false are the absurd allegations that we are allowing academic standards to drop. Our academic standards have always been high, and they will certainly be maintained. The third thrust in the program of disinformation has been repeated accusations that our academic work is continually disrupted by unruly behaviour. Everybody on campus knows that this is completely false. While there have been instances of unacceptable behaviour, I reject unequivocally assertions that discipline is not being adequately upheld. We shall continue to apply the principles of natural justice in disciplinary matters. I refuse to collaborate in the stifling of legitimate dissent and peaceful protest.

Far from requiring Ministerial intervention, the University has been fulfilling its obligations to our complex society with distinction, and I intend to see that it continues to do so. That will be achieved by administering the University in the same way as it has always been administered.

APPENDIX 15

JUDGEMENT IN THE CASE OF THE UNIVERSITY OF CAPE TOWN AND THE UNIVERSITY OF THE WESTERN CAPE AGAINST THE MINISTERS OF EDUCATION AND CULTURE OF THE HOUSE OF ASSEMBLY AND OTHERS IN THE CAPE PROVINCIAL DIVISION OF THE SUPREME COURT 12 FEBRUARY 1988

Section 25 of the Universities Act 61 of 1955 (as amended) makes provision for the grant of subsidies to universities, 'subject to such conditions as may ... be determined by the Minister and with due regard to the requirements of each university in relation to the general requirements of higher education in the Republic.' Section 27 of the Act provides *inter alia*, that upon failure by a university council to comply with certain conditions, the relevant Minister may withhold all or part of that university's subsidy. Pursuant to the provisions of s 25, the first and second respondent Ministers imposed certain conditions upon all universities with effect from 19 October 1987. Paragraph 1 of the conditions required the university councils to notify the relevant Minister of the occurrence of 'any incident of unrest or disruption or occurrence' to which the preventive measures in para 1 were directed, and to report on the disciplinary steps taken or intended to be taken to prevent similar incidents, etc in future. Finally, para 2 provided that 'the Minister will notify the council of his finding whether the council has complied with the ... conditions.' The first and second applicant universities brought an application against the respondent Ministers for an order declaring such conditions invalid on the grounds that:

(a) their imposition exceeded the powers conferred by the Legislature in s 25 of the Universities Act;
(b) they were so vague that they did not convey with any reasonable certainty what universities were required to do in order to avoid non-compliance and its consequences; and
(c) they involved unreasonably oppressive or gratuitous interference in the applicant universities' rights.

In his speech motivating the imposition of the conditions objected to, the second respondent Minister, in reference to 'disturbances' and other events on certain campuses, stated that such conduct threatened 'responsible academic freedom;' that it posed 'a potential threat towards the maintenance of law and order;' and that 'there (had) been a shift towards our campuses amongst those behind the revolutionary onslaught.' As to the applicants' first ground of attack, it was contended by the respondents that any conditions imposed under s 25 would be *intra vires* if its purpose was to achieve optimal use, or to avoid unnecessary waste, of subsidy moneys. As to the applicants' second ground of attack, it was contended that, by implication, the steps required to be taken by university councils were such as would have the potential to achieve what had been set out in the subparagraphs to para 1 of the conditions and that, since university councils had expertise in regard to the running of their institutions and the application of disciplinary control, they must be taken to know what was necessary to attain such achievement. Furthermore, the respondents, pointing to the procedure prescribed in para 2 of the conditions, contended that the first respondent Minister would in any event be in a position to tell universities where they had transgressed and what steps would be required in future.

Held, as to ground (a), that the bulk of para 1 of the conditions imposed dealt solely with conditions germane to, if not bearing directly upon, the maintenance of law and order.

Held, further, that that factor, taken in conjunction with the second respondent's motivating speech, justified the conclusion that a dominant motive behind the imposition of the conditions had been the implementation of action to combat lawlessness and to counter what had been regarded as revolutionary conduct, and that such motive had been at least as strong as any motive to achieve the better functioning of the universities.

Held, further, that the imposition of the conditions in issue had been prompted substantially by the ulterior motive to achieve objects not empowered by s 25.

Held, accordingly, that the operation of such ulterior motive had rendered the conditions *ultra vires* and invalid.

Held, further, as to ground (b), with regard to the words 'take steps directed towards,' that it had been stated nowhere what steps were required: there had been nothing in the conditions laying down the quality or number of 'steps' to be taken, the accuracy or efficacy with which they had to be directed, or how far 'towards' the required goal they had to go. Consequently, nothing expressed in the conditions had provided a pointer as to the intended meaning or had assisted in determining where the line between compliance and non-compliance would be drawn.

Held, further, as to the respondents' contention that university councils would have to take such steps as would have the 'potential to achieve' the desired objectives, that since 'potential' conveyed such a range of contingencies, even if the suggested requirement of potentiality could properly be implied, it would leave the conditions as uncertain as they had been before such implication.

Held, further, as to the respondents' suggestion concerning the expertise of university councils, that the knowledge and skills required for the achievement of the goals stated in para 1 of the conditions were those appropriate to experienced and well-staffed law enforcement agencies and there was no justification for a conclusion that the applicants or any other universities possessed such skills: even if they did, that would still not enable them, on a proper construction of the conditions, to determine how far to go in order to achieve compliance or to avoid non-compliance.

Held, further, as to the respondents' reliance on the procedure prescribed in para 2 of the conditions, that, firstly, quite apart from the fact that the first respondent's reservation to himself of the power to determine, *ex post facto*, what constituted non-compliance had not been authorised by the Act, the very fact that there had been such a purported reservation had served to emphasise that what had preceded para 2 had no reasonably certain meaning; secondly it could not be the law that someone could be pronounced in default without his ever having been told what to do; thirdly, assuming that the first respondent had had every intention of implementing a benevolent application of para 2, once he had found 'non-compliance,' such finding would blot the 'errant' university's record, even if the s 27 sanction were not then imposed; and fourthly, the first respondent's successor would not be bound to adopt a benevolent attitude and a subsidy could then quite easily be unjustifiably imperilled.

Held, accordingly, that the conditions were void for uncertainty.

Held, further, as to ground (c), that para 1(e) of the conditions, requiring university councils to 'take steps directed towards ... ensuring that disciplinary steps (were) taken' placed the university disciplinary tribunals under pressure to pass or sanction sentences which might or might not, depending on their severity, stave off the withdrawal of the university's subsidy, which amounted not only to an unwarranted intrusion upon the council's powers to administer discipline, but also an intolerable interference with its duty to exercise those powers freely.

Held, further, that the provisions of para 1(e) of the conditions constituted oppressive or gratuitous interference with the unhindered imposition of punishment according to the merits of each case, free from extraneous influence.

Held, accordingly, that the provisions of para 1(e) were invalid and, since they formed so integral a part of the conditions as a whole, that, even if the conditions as a whole had been *intra vires* in the strict sense and enforceably clear in meaning, they would nonetheless be void for unreasonableness.

JUDGEMENT OF MR JUSTICE N S PAGE IN THE NATAL PROVINCIAL DIVISION OF THE SUPREME COURT IN THE APPLICATION BROUGHT BY THE UNIVERSITY OF NATAL

Although the decision of the Cape Provincial Division is not absolutely binding upon me, it is persuasive authority of the most cogent kind. As I have already remarked during the hearing, the applications giving rise to that decision appear to me to be *in pari materia* in that the facts are not materially different and the legal issues identical to those in the present application.

Counsel for the Respondents, whilst reserving their right to contend in another tribunal that the Cape decision is wrong, have very properly conceded that they are unable to argue before me that it is so clearly incorrect that I should decline to follow it. Indeed, after studying the reasons for that decision I am of the respectful opinion that it is correct, insofar as it held that the conditions were ultra vires for being attributable to an ulterior motive; were void for uncertainty; and were unreasonable ... I propose to follow it, and, having decided to do so, I find it unnecessary to consider such additional grounds of invalidity as were advanced in the case before me.

I make the following order:

1. It is hereby declared that the conditions imposed by the First Respondent and set out in his letter to the Chairman of the Applicant dated 13th October 1987 are invalid and of no force and effect;
2. The Respondents are ordered, jointly and severally, to pay the costs of this application, including those consequent upon the employment of two Counsel.

TOWARDS THE TWENTY-FIRST CENTURY:
THE UNIVERSITY'S MISSION

The University of the Witwatersrand is located in the largest metropolitan area and the industrial and commercial heart of South Africa. Wits is recognised both nationally and internationally for the quality of its graduates and its excellence in teaching, research and service to society. It has a longstanding commitment to university autonomy, academic freedom and non-discrimination.

Vision

As democracy takes root in South Africa, Wits will
- develop its standing as a centre of excellence and academic freedom which fosters free and open enquiry and the search for knowledge and understanding
- continue to take decisive steps towards becoming representative of the society it serves
- make a fundamental contribution towards reconstruction and development in South Africa.

Central Goals

Wits is committed to
- ensuring that its graduates are comparable in their levels of skill, knowledge and understanding to graduates with equivalent degrees from leading universities worldwide
- continuing to develop its courses to serve the needs of South Africa, recognising that this requires a solid foundation in basic, theoretical and comparative studies
- broadening access to the University for students from disadvantaged communities who have the potential to succeed academically
- promoting student development, and increasing the success rate of students through improved teaching and learning and coherent academic development programmes
- continuing to support excellent basic, strategic and applied research, especially research of particular relevance to South Africa
- fostering staff development at all levels, and correcting imbalances in race and gender through affirmative action and equal opportunity policies.

Immediate Priorities

Recognising its history, its location, its strengths and the needs of South Africa, Wits aims to
- foster its capacity in science and engineering and increase its output of graduates in these areas, especially from under-represented groups
- prepare students for managerial positions in the public and private sectors, and produce social scientists with the capacity for skilled research on issues of critical importance to the country
- contribute substantially to the production and upgrading of school teachers in the key subjects of English Language, Mathematics and Physical Science
- produce more postgraduates, especially from under-represented groups, in its areas of strength
- develop flexible study programmes to facilitate interaction between disciplines, mobility between institutions in post-secondary education, and part-time study
- participate with other institutions and the State in developing a rational and effective system of higher education and research.

A National Resource

The University of the Witwatersrand has a distinctive capacity to contribute to the development of South Africa through research, social criticism, partnerships with the public and private sectors and the community – and, most importantly, through the production of skilled, critical and adaptable graduates. In order to maximise this contribution, Wits will maintain and foster its strengths, and pursue its goals and priorities with determination.

**UNIVERSITY OF THE WITWATERSRAND,
JOHANNESBURG**

APPENDIX 16
Mission Statement

Index

academic boycott 106, 231, 232, 234
Academic Freedom Committee
   (of Senate) 35, 38, 159
   condemns report of Schlebusch
      Commission 52
   advises on freedom of speech
      issues 114, 115
   opposes 'Quota Bill' 150
   on De Klerk's conditions 179
   on police incursion into
      Great Hall 243
Academic Non-Segregation
   Committee 22
Academic Plan 78, 79, 261
Academic Staff Association (ASA) XXV,
   10, 45, 55, 58, 75, 95, 156, 165, 246
   on O'Brien incident 112, 113
   anger at police action on campus
      128
   on De Klerk's conditions
      169, 171, 181, 183
   on police incursion into
      Great Hall 243
Academic support (development)
   programmes 259, 265
accommodation crisis 257-58
Adelman, Sammy 69, 70, 74
   banned for 5 years 74
Administrative and Library
   Staff Association 183
admissions and exclusions
   inquiry into 257-65
   membership of committee 258,
      260
   brief of committee 258, 259

   report on 260-64
admissions of black students
   Council restrictions 2, 5
   Government restrictions 1
   Restrictions by Faculties 3, 4, 5
   Senate policies 6
Advisory Group on Detentions
   (AGD) 134-36
Affirmation of academic freedom
   1959: 30-32
   10th anniversary 1969: 32
African Medical Scholarship Fund 3
African National Congress (ANC)
   120
   meetings with 228-38
   criticism of defence
      research at Wits 236
   views on academic boycott 236
   on relevance of curricula 236
Afrikaner Nationale
   Studentebond (ANS) 3
Afrikaner Studente Bond (ASB)
   XXI
Afrikaner Volksfront 182
agents provocateurs 174, 177
   incite students to throw stones 245
Aggett, Neil 75, 293 (n45)
All Sports Council (ASC) XXV, 13,
   272
   merges with Satisu 273
Al Quds Day 205, 302 (n14)
Ames, Frances 291 (n4)
ANC Youth League 12
Anderson, P M 5
Anderson, Steven 153, 159, 198, 199

complains to Vlok about
 police action 242
Angola
 war in 214
Annegam, Harold 134, 190
Anti-apartheid Movement (French) 231
apartheid
 Statement of Principle
  against 99-100, 311-14
Arendorf, Trevor 10, 18
Ashby, Godfrey 134
Association of University
 Teachers (AUT)
 academic boycott 236
 support for ANC 236, 237
Avidan, Michael 203
 detained 254
 abused in detention 256
Azanian Students' Movement (Azasm) XXI, 81
Azanian Students' Organisation(Azaso) XXI, 81

Bakke case in US 151
banning of 17 organisations 202
Bantu Education Act, 1953 20
Barnato Hall 131
 raided by security police 203
Barry, Brendan 275
Baxter, John XVIII
Becker, B J P (Bunny) 9
Beffon, Joyce XVIII
Bendtsen, M 233
Bernstein, B L (Birch) 53
Bethlehem, Lael 252
Biko, Steve 61, 62
 detention and death 291 (n4)
Bill, Francois 217
Bingle, H J J 49
Bizos, George 9, 86, 110, 284 (n24)
'black'
 use of generic term 283 (n6)
Black Consciousness
 Movement (BCM) 61
Blacking, John 41

Black People's Convention (BPC) 61
Black Sash 81
Black Student Committee (BSC)
 protest against hospital apartheid 218
Black Students' Interim Committee
 (BSIC) 118-20, 238, 248, 249
 formed when BSS restricted 238
Black Student Society (BSS)
 66-68, 71, 81, 90, 125, 147, 161,
 165, 166, 189, 206, 224-27
 established 66
 and Unita incident 100-102
 and Sharpeville incident 102-103
 and O'Brien incident 106
 and freedom of speech
  document 116-20
 protests against raids on
  ANC bases 122-24
 on De Klerk's conditions 183
 strategy of non-participation 204
 explain stone-throwing at police 225
 support fund-raising for
  black students 234
 restricted 238
 resuscitated as Black Students'
  Interim Committee 238
 offices searched by
  security police 247
 unbans itself 248, 251-53
 supports MDM defiance
  campaign 253
 on admissions and exclusions 257-65
 dissolves itself 272
 policy on sport 272, 273
 policy determination 295 (n16)
Black Student Transitional
 Committee (BSTC) 272
Black University Workers'
 Association (Buwa) 75, 183
Blight, Geoffrey XXIII
Blignaut (Colonel/Brigadier) 128, 269
Blurton, Geoff XVIII
Boesak, Allan 80
books confiscated 247
Booyens, Jan 295 (n9)

Boraine, Andrew 70, 74
Borcherds, Peter 236
Borkon, Libby XVIII
Botha, M C 61
Botha, P W 122, 159, 199, 204
  on black majority government 201
  and Second World War 213
  resigns as State President 25
Bouillon, M 231
Boya, Lawrence 136
Bozzoli, G R (Boz) 16-18, 32, 34, 35, 38, 43-48, 53-60, 63, 65, 66, 276, 277
  summoned by Minister 46
  open letter to Vorster 46
  calls General Assembly on detentions 53, 54
  minority report, van Wyk de Vries Commission 55-58
  on academic freedom 59, 60
  retires 60
Brassey, Martin 297 (n12)
Breytenbach, Breyten 230
British Broadcasting Corporation (BBC) 127
Broederbond 49
Broekman, Reg 219
Browde Commission of Inquiry 82-91
  recommendations of 307-11
Browde, Jules 86
Bruce, David 209, 214
Bruce, Nigel 146, 147
Brune, Derek 58
Brutus, Dennis 37
Buitendach, Captain 271
Bureau of State Security (Boss) 10
Buthelezi, Mangosutho 266

Cachalia, Azhar
  detained 74
Cachalia, Firoz 178, 293 (n44)
  detained 74
  arrested 94
Cachalia, M S H 206
Cairns, Jocelyn 190, 275

Callie, Neil 15
Cameron, Edwin 86, 110, 189
  minority report 113, 143, 315-316
Campaign for National United Action 147
Campus Health Clinic 93, 127, 223, 224, 245, 251
Canadian Embassy 250
Centre for Applied Legal Studies (Cals) 81, 86, 135, 234, 235
Centre for Continuing Education (CCE) 235
Chancellor's Lecture 32, 287 (n31)
Charlton, Robert (Bob) XVII, 85, 118, 119, 121, 129, 219, 222, 224, 277
  on De Klerk's conditions 177, 178, 184, 185, 190, 195, 196
  condemns 'emergency' restrictions 202
  condemns detentions without trial 204
  condemns restrictions on ECC 211, 212
  complains about police intrusions 217
  meeting with police Commissioner 217, 218
  commitment in installation address 229, 230
  reacts to banning of student meeting 239-42
  sees Vlok with chairperson of Council 244
  on waving ANC flag on campus 245
  recognises 'unbanned' BSS 249
  supports inquiry into admissions and exclusions 257
'Charltonville' tent town 258, 259
Chaskalson, Lorraine 134, 243
Chatkidakis, C 9
Chief Magistrate
  authority for General Assembly 184, 185
  bans protest meeting on detentions 239
Chinese students 16-17

Choral Society 18
    defies SRC motion 15
Civil Cooperation Bureau
    (CCB) 305 (n24)
    and assassination of David
        Webster 246, 247
Civin, Brian 67
Clark, Jeremy 74
Clase, P J (Piet) 159
    and the quota system 157
    and the De Klerk conditions
        164, 174, 175, 198, 199
coercion 124
Coetzee, Ampie 160, 299 (n33)
Coetzee, Kobie 159, 160
Coleman, Keith 76, 293 (n44)
Coleman, Max 81, 82
College of Science 265
Collen, Lindsey 17
Commission of Inquiry (Bizos),
    109-14
    on freedom of speech 110-
        13, 138, 315-16
    on disruption of meetings 111,
        112
    on the Unita incident 112
    on the O'Brien incident 112,
        113
    on media attacks on University
        114, 141, 142
    on campus unrest 138
    on the SMA and NSF 139-41
    on students 142
Commission of Inquiry
    (Browde) 82-91, 206
Commonwealth Eminent
    Persons Group (EPG) 122
conditions demanded of universities
    by Government 324-26
    legal opinion on 167-69, 175,
        176, 326-31, 337-39
    judgement on 343-46
    conditions revised 335-37
Congress of South African
    Students (Cosas) 81, 249
Conradie, J 194
    judgement against De Klerk 343-46

Convocation of the University
    5, 22, 28, 43, 58
Council 37, 71, 212
    restricted admission of
        black students 2
    opposes academic segregation
        24, 25
    deputation to Minister (1957) 25
    on Van Wyk de Vries
        Commission report 57, 58
    on Browde Commission report 90
    delegation to Minister of Law
        and Order 131, 132
    on Bizos Commission report 142,
        143
    on 'Quota Bill' 150, 153, 156
    deputation sees Minister
        on 'Quota Act' 153
    authority of 167-69
    divided on De Klerk's conditions
        169, 171-79, 183, 191-93
    dissatisfaction with Council's
        position on conditions 193
    black representation on 230
    reacts to police incursion
        into Great Hall 242
    opposition to Satisco 273
    functions and membership 306,
        307
Cresswell, Christopher
    XXIII, 99, 295 (n8,9)
Crewe, Robin 295 (n9)
Cronin, Jeremy 237
Crouse, C F 301 (n75)
Crystal, Russell 67, 68, 83, 89, 90
Cunningham, Jenny 45
Curtis, Neville 40, 51
Cuzen, Pauline XVIII, 190, 275

Danish Centre of Human Rights 234
Danish International Aid
    Authority (Danida)
    assistance to South Africa 233,
        234
David Webster Hall 246
Deans of Faculties
    protest against detentions 92
De Beer, Cedric 59

De Beer, Zac 33, 119
De Klerk, F W 48, 72, 92, 138, 158, 210
  announces end of apartheid XIX, 238, 256, 257
  last all-white election, 1989 XXVI
  threatens universities 159-200
  legal opinion on threats 167-69, 174-76, 326-31
  summons a delegation from Wits 159-62
  presents ultimatum to all universities 164
  conditions demanded 324-26
  defends his conditions 182, 183
  meets deputation from five universities 191
  taken to court by universities 194, 195, 343-46
  meets Committee of University Principals 195, 196
  responses to Supreme Court judgement 196, 197
  succeeds P W Botha as President 199, 253
De Klerk, Jan 16, 18, 33
Dentistry, Faculty of
  black admissions policies 3-5, 9-11
  black student numbers 1990 157
Deputy Vice-Chancellorships at Wits XXIII
Detainees' Parents Support Committee (DPSC) 81
  banned 202
  David Webster and 246
detentions 53, 70, 74-76, 91, 92, 130-38, 250, 254
  detained students allowed to study 92
  action on behalf of detainees 132, 323, 324
  Advisory Group on Detentions 134, 217
  abuses and deaths in 201

detainees embark on hunger strike 238, 239
De Vries, Mike 181
'Die Stem' 72
Dickson, Bruce XVIII, 85, 102, 190
Die Burger
  on De Klerk's conditions 181
Diepkloof Prison 92
Disciplinary Adviser 103, 104
Disclosure of Foreign Funding Bill 233
Dockrat, Ismael 10, 11
Dodds, A E 10
Don's Diary 294 (n2)
Douglas Smit Residence 18, 285 (n51)
Dugard, John 81, 82, 179, 190, 234
Du Plessis, D J (Sonny) XXIV, 35, 69, 71, 73, 157, 277
  condemns detention of Andrew Boraine 74
  assumes office as Vice-Chancellor 76
  initiates Academic Plan 76-79
  more residences for black students 77
  speaks against 'Quota Bill' 150, 152, 154, 155
Du Plessis, Michael 134
Durban Student Alliance (DSA) 69
Du Toit (Major) 186, 189
Du Toit, Piet 129, 220
Dworkin, R on racial quotas 150

Education Policy Unit 235
Egman, Frank 233
electioneering on campus 107, 108
Elkon, Debbie 293 (n44)
Emergency regulations 135, 202
End Conscription Campaign (ECC) 125, 208-17
  established by Nusas group 208
  mission of 208, 209
  143 white men refuse to serve in SADF 210
  restricted 210
  ignores restrictions 215
  conscription ends 217

INDEX

Ensor, Paula 51
Erasmus, G 220, 221, 248, 249, 269
Erouart, Gilbert 228
Esselen Street residence 258
European Commission 231
Extension of University Education Act of 1959 28

Falkov, Lindsay 215, 239
Feetham Memorial Lecture 32, 287 (n31)
Feetham, Richard 23, 25, 32
Financial Mail
　funding for NSF 146
Finnish Foreign Ministry
　financial aid for black students 233
Finnish International Development Authority (FINNIDA) 233
Finsen, Eyvind 185
Five Freedoms Forum
　conference with ANC in Lusaka 237, 238, 246
flag, ANC 245, 248
flag burning 71-73, 223, 224
Forder, Heather XVIII
Fort Hare 23, 33
Forum of Progressive Students (FOPS) 12
Frankel, Leslie
　intercedes for release of detained student 256
Fraser, Kirsty XVIII
freedom of speech issues 100-20, 161, 173
　Unita incident 100-102
　O'Brien episode 105-107
　Helen Suzman episode 107-108
　'Freedom of Speech on Campus' document 115-118, 120, 223, 318-23
　Senate resolution on 314-15
　minority report by Edwin Cameron 113, 143, 315-16
　memorandum on 316-18
Freer, David 190

French Commission of University Presidents
　letter to De Klerk on student detentions 231
French financial aid to black students 231
Friedman, Steven 119

Garnett, Helen 295 (n9)
Garson, Noel 190
Gatting, Mike
　leads rebel cricket tour 272
General Assemblies of the University
　first, 16 April 1959 30
　second, 16 April 1969 32
　third, 8 June 1972 43-44
　fourth, 26 August 1975 53
　fifth, 3 May 1983 152
　sixth, 16 August 1985 96
　seventh, 28 October 1987 183-90
　　march following 186
　　addresses at 339-343
Getz, Godfrey 9, 12, 13, 14, 285 (n24)
Gibson, Douglas 129
Ginwala, Frene 229, 235
Glaser, Daryl 76
Glasser, David 190
Glyn Thomas House 19, 297 (n20)
　raided by armed police and military 130-31, 297 (n19)
Glyn Thomas, I 12, 25
Goldberg, A 206, 208
Goldstein, Dan 14
Goldstone, Richard 135
Goosen, Constable 251
Gordon, Ian 59
Gordon, Victor XXVI, 190
Great Hall segregation 12, 13, 18
Greyling, Ben 293 (n44)
Grosskopf, Hein 237
Group Areas Act
　impediment to integration of University housing 77

Hamman, E M 49

Hanekom, Derek 237
harassment of student activists
   137, 244, 252, 253
Harber, Anton 68
Harms Commission of Inquiry 246
Harris, E 6
Haysom, Nicholas (Fink) 76,
   293 (n44)
Hazelhurst, Scott 171, 190
Hauptfleisch, G J 182
Hellman, Ellen 23
Hill, Francis (Pinky) 43
Hinton, Tim 134
Hoernlé, A W 23, 286 (n8)
Hoffenberg, Raymond
   banned by Government 38
Hofmeyr, Isabel 134
Hofmeyr, J H
   installation address as
      Principal 1, 276
   as Education Minister 4
Hogan, Barbara 293 (n44)
Holloway Commission 21, 22
Holocaust Day 205, 302 (n15)
Horsfall, David 190
Horwood, Owen 54
hospitals
   apartheid in academic
      hospitals 218, 219
Howard, Nikkie 252
Howie, J 194, 197
   judgement against De Klerk
      343-46
Hughes, Martin 236
Hunter, Rosemary 171, 185, 275
   detained 204
Hurst, Cliff 190

Inkatha Freedom Party (IFP) 120
International Commission of Jurists 201
International Freedom
   Foundation (IFF) 69
International support for
   'open' universities 24
Intervarsity against Pretoria
   University 8
Israeli flag 206, 207
Israelstam, Sam 23

Jagoe, Kathy XVIII
Jammy, David 275
Jassat, E 206, 207
Jenkins, Trefor 291 (n4)
Jewish Defence Organisation
   207
Johannesburg Democratic
   Action Committee 81
Johnson, David
   detained 74
Jordan, Pallo 237
Joubert, Danie 181
Jubilee Hall 131

Kagiso Trust 231, 232
Kahn, Ellison 43
Kane-Berman, John 41
Kasrils, Ronnie 237, 246
Kaunda, Kenneth 237
Kekana, Nepo 119
Kennedy, Robert
   guest of Nusas 1966 39
Kentridge, Sydney 164, 167, 191
Keyter, Barry 16, 17
Khanya College 251
Kiljunen, Kimmo 232
Klein, Adam 43, 47
Koffiefontein internment camp
   213
Kolk, Berend 190
Koornhof, Piet 34-36, 69, 70
Kriel, Danie 68, 146
Kromberg, Steve 204
Ku Klux Klan 159
KwaZulu police 266

Labour Day (May Day) 121
Lambson, J R 108, 296 (n27, n28,
   n29)
Larivaille, M 230-231
Larkin, Michael 190
Latter, Phyl XVIII
Law Students' Council 95
Lax, Leslie 293 (n44)
Laxton, Andrew 59
Lecturers' Association 55
Le Grange, Louis 92
Le Roux, Phillipe 51

INDEX

Lewis, Carol 190
liberal
    definition of term 282 (n2)
'Liberal Ticket' 30
Liebenberg, Willem 254
Lissoos, Rael 206
Lodge, Tom 106
Loubser, Nol 134
Love, Andrew 59

MacCrone, I D 23, 25, 30,
    41, 276, 286 (n8)
Machanik, Philip 190
Machel, Samora
    memorial meeting 147
Mafeje, Archie 39
Makgoba, W M XXXII
Malan, D F XIX
Malan, Magnus 121, 122,
    209, 293 (n39)
    enraged by ECC 210
Mallet, Michel 231
Mandela, Nelson XIX, XXX
    awarded LLD(hc) 1991 XXXI
    speaks at University of Pretoria
    182
Mandela, Winnie
    calls for student unity 204
Maphai, Vincent 94, 95
Marais, E J 49
Marais, Etienne 165, 171, 275
Marais, J S 6, 23
Marais, M A 298 (n21)
Maré, Gerry 53
Masekela, Barbara 237
Maseko, James XXVII, 165, 275
Mashishi, Moss 272
Mashitisho, Dan 275
Mass Democratic Movement 119,
    234
    students support defiance
        campaign 248
May Day 121
Mbeki, Thabo 237
McGiven, Arthur 58, 59
Medical Students' Council (MSC)
    protest on hospital apartheid 21,
    219

Medicine, Faculty of
    black admissions policies 3, 5
    deplores restrictions on
        black admissions 156
    black student numbers 157
    protest against hospital
        apartheid 218, 219
    action on death of Steve
        Biko 291 (n4)
Meli, Francis 229, 235
    alleged to be security police spy
    237
Mendelowitz, Michael 59
Metcalfe, Mary 134
Meyer, Roelf 159
Middleton Shaw, J C 5, 6, 10
Military Intelligence 69
Mission Statement 278-81, 347
Mji, Deliza 12
Mlangeni, Bheki 136
Mnisi, Aaron 235
Moelwyn-Hughes, Timothy XXIII
Moffson, S M 206, 207
Mofolo Residence 131
Mohamed, Jennifer 84
Mohammed, Elaine 293 (n44)
Moseneke, Tiego 106, 188, 275
    detained 204
Moss, Glenn 53, 59
Motlana, Nthato 12
Mphahlele, E XXXII, XXXIV
Mpofu, Dali 101, 103, 126,
    131, 272, 275
Mueller, Conrad 190
Mulder, Connie 52
Mulder, S P 18
Municipal elections boycotted
    201, 202, 221, 222
    demonstration against 222-27
Mureinik, Etienne 190
Murray, Bruce 1
Muslim community 206
Muslim Prayer Room 207
Muslim Students' Association
    205-208
Mutsi, Sipho 82

Nabarro, Frank 78, 79

Nails, Debra 106, 134, 190, 217
  receives anonymous
    death threats 246
Namibia
  war in 214
Namibia Solidarity Committee
  (NSC) 118
Nathan, Ove
  letter to De Klerk 234, 235
National Education Crisis
  Committee (NECC) 202
National Education Health and Allied
  Workers' Union (Nehawu) XXX,
  183
National Medical and Dental
  Association (Namda) 201
National Sports Congress 272
  announces restrictions on
    admissions, 1956 1, 23
  legislation for apartheid
    tertiary education 26-28
  threatens universities with
    subsidy cuts, 1972 48
  reprimands Wits for anti-
    Republic sentiments 71
  further threats of subsidy cuts 72
National Student Federation
  (NSF) 68, 69, 108, 161
  funding by Government and
    security police 68, 141, 146,
    147
  and the Unita incident 100-102
  link to security police 146
  funding by business
    organisations 146, 147
  observers at Nusas
    demonstration 205
Nationalist Government XXV
Naudé, Beyers 269
Nel, J 194
  judgement against De Klerk
    343-46
Ngcobo, Chris 84, 85, 136,
  137, 217, 250, 275
Nicholas, H C 164, 167
Niehaus, Karl 76
Nielsen, Birger 233, 235
Nkomo, W F 23, 286 (n8)

'Nkosi sikelel' iAfrika' 283 (n12)
Noero, Gill 134
Norwegian Foreign Ministry
  policy on financial aid to
    black students 232
Nusas XXI, 5, 33, 50, 53,
  61, 147, 172, 277
  President banned, 1966 38
  delegation sees Vorster 39
  investigated by Schlebusch
    Commission 50-52
  declared 'affected organisation' 52
  leaders detained 1975 53
  relations with BSS at Wits 66
  President detained, 1981 70
  smeared in anonymous letter 129
  leaders harassed and detained
    137, 252, 253
  opposes De Klerk's conditions 183
  demonstration at Union
    Buildings 204, 205
  office set alight 227, 228
  solidarity fast with detainees 239
  offices searched by
    security police 247
  campaign on violence in
    townships 266
  merges with Sansco and
    disbands 272

Oberholzer (Major) 143, 144, 161
O'Brien, Conor Cruise 105-107,
  159-61
O'Donovan, Michael 293 (n44)
O'Dowd, Michael 9, 127, 285 (n24)
'Open Universities' 1
Open Universities in South
  Africa, 1957 XX, 24, 28
Open Universities Liaison
  Committee 23
Operation Aristotle, 68
Opperman, Eugene 251, 256
Orkin, Mark 16, 32, 33, 47
Owen, Ken 162, 163, 183, 195

Page, N S 195
  judgement against De Klerk 346
Pahad, Essop 235

INDEX

Payne, Rodney 215
peace-keeping group 190
'Perceptions of Wits' study XXXI, XXXII
Pienaar, P de V 6
Pines, Noam 190
Pogrund, Benjamin 46, 47
police
  on campus XXIX, 33, 42, 45, 71, 83, 93-96, 100, 103, 109, 122-32, 137-39, 143, 144, 147, 148, 186, 203, 217, 223, 224, 239-42, 244, 245, 248-51, 254-56, 257, 267-69, 271
  raid meeting in Great Hall 239-40
  security police raid Students' Union 247
  raid concourse of Senate House 250
  Council told of 52 incidents 256
  meetings with 129, 143-44, 218, 238, 244
police code names 68
Pollak, W 23, 286 (n8)
Postgraduate Association 171
Powell, Phillip 83, 137, 138, 161
Pretoria bomb blast 122, 297 (n7)
Pretorius, Paul 51
Pulkkinen, Kimmo 233

'Quota Bill' 54, 149-59
  becomes law 152
  Senate and SRC pressure Council 152, 153

Raditsela, Andreas 82
Rag 8, 12
Raikes, Humphrey 3, 4, 5, 276
  affirmative action for ex-servicemen 8
  social segregation 11, 12
  retires 14
Rand Afrikaans University 78
  condemns protests at open universities 33
  Vice-Rector critical of De Klerk's conditions 182

students join Nusas demonstration 204
Randall, Peter 300 (n42)
Rapportryers 289 (n31)
referendum at Wits 34-36
referendum of white voters, 1983 80
Reeves, Ambrose 23
Regional Institutional Cooperation Project (RICP) 274
Rehof, Lars 234
Reid, John 300 (n58)
Republic Festival, 1981
Residences 18, 19
  raids on 130, 131
Rex, Grant 82, 84, 85
Rhodes University 33, 47, 70
  on 'Quota Bill'
  opposes De Klerk's conditions 183
Richard Feetham Memorial Lecture 32
Robertson, Ian 38
  banning leads to student march 38
Rosendorff, Clive 218, 219
Rosholt, Michael 153, 185
Roskam, Anton 252, 275
Roux, Eddie
  appointment terminated by Minister 38
Russell, Geoff 59

Sacos 305 (n26)
Sakhorov, Andrei 234
Sarbutt, Paul 59
Satchwell, Kathleen 125, 135, 217, 244
  urgent application to Supreme Court 128
  defends 5 staff and 36 students 128
Saunders, Stuart 196
Schlebusch Commission 50-52
Schnetler, Brigadier 217-19
Schram, John 250
Schreiner, W H R 110
Schroder H J 47
Schwarz, Jonathan 59
Science, Faculty of 5
Seabrook, Marian XVIII
Sears, Michael 190

Sechaba 229
Senate 5, 58
  rejects restrictions on black
    student admissions 6
  and freedom of speech 104, 107,
    115
  opposes 'Quota Bill' 150-
    52, 155, 156
  prepared to defy 'Quota Act' 155
  opposes racial classification
    of students 156
  on De Klerk's conditions
    170, 171, 179, 180, 192
  functions and composition 307
Senior Appointments Committee XXIII
September, Dulcie 230, 235
September, Reg 237, 303 (n48)
Serote, Wally 237
Sharpeville Day 102, 110, 111
Sharpeville Six
  protests against impending
    executions 203
  appeal for clemency 203
Shear, Mervyn
  appointed DVC XXII-XXVII
  elected to Council XXIII
  student at Rhodes and Wits
    6-9
  crisis in concourse 84-87
  Unita incident 100-102
  Sharpeville Day incident
    102-103
  writes guest column in
    Saturday Star 109
  asked to join student protest
    march 125, 126
  application to court for
    students' bail 128
  called to attend meeting
    with police 129
  circular on steps taken for
    detainees 132, 133
  addresses student meeting
    on detentions 133
  visits detained students
    in prison 136, 137
  meeting with Commissioner
    of Police 143, 144
  responds to De Klerk 160
  on De Klerk's conditions 185
  threatened with arrest 186
  and peace-keeping group 190
  condemns 'emergency'
    restrictions 202
  speaks on prohibition of ECC
    212-15
  urges alternative to conscription 216
  meeting with police
    Commissioner 218
  invitation to visit France 228-31
  meetings with ANC 228-30,
    235-38
  fundraising for black student
    financial aid 231-34
  visit to Lusaka 237, 238
  and police incursion into
    Great Hall 240-42
  abused by a student 245
  condemns harassment
    of students 252
  hit by police rubber bullet 267-69
  retires as DVC 274
Shochot, John 190
Sibisi, Sibusiso 297 (n19)
Silver, Steve 147, 252
Silvola, Eija 233
Simons (Alexander), Ray 237
Sinclair, June 189, 190, 220, 271
  condemns prohibition of ECC 212
  almost hit by police missile 267
  appointed Deputy Vice-
    Chancellor 274
Sisulu, Max 237
Sisulu, Walter
  prevented from speaking at
    University of Pretoria 182
Skeen, Charles 80, 153
Skuy, Mervyn 190
Slovo, Joe 8, 237
Smit, Basie 129, 256
Smith, Solly 230
  alleged to be security police spy
    237
Social segregation on campus 6-19
Solomon Mahlangu College
  230, 303 (n48)

South African Broadcasting
  Corporation (SABC) 34, 48, 127
  propaganda programme
    'Comment' 248
South African Council on
  Sport (Sacos) 273
South African Defence Force (SADF)
  harasses Wits students 121, 122
  launches attacks on ANC 'bases'
    122
  used to bolster police 147
  opposed by black students 208
  and ECC 208-17
  and Civil Cooperation Bureau 246
South African Jewish Board
  of Deputies 206, 207
South African Medical and
  Dental Council
  action after death of Steve
    Biko 291 (n4)
South African National Students'
  Congress (Sansco) XIX, 249
  opposes De Klerk's conditions
    183
  banned 202
  merges with Nusas and disbands
    272
South African Press Association
  journalists warned by police 251
South African Students' Organisation
  (Saso) XXI, 61
South African Students' Congress
  (Sasco) XXIX, XXX
  merger of Nusas and Sansco
    to form 272, 283 (n1)
South African Tertiary Institutions'
  Sports Congress (Satisco)
  established 273
  becomes Satisu 273
South African Youth
  Congress (Sayco) 249
Soweto Day 121
Soweto Students' Congress (Sosco) 249
Soweto student uprising 62-66
  Wits's response 63
Soweto Youth Congress (Soyco) 249
spies on campus 37, 38, 58, 59,
  102, 177, 178, 239, 240

Standenmacher, Ken XVIII,
  85, 101, 102, 190
Stadler, Alf 190
Starfield, Jane 134
Statement of Principle 311-14
State of Emergency, 1985 91 et seq.
  protests against 92-99
State of Emergency, 1986 130 et seq.
Stead, Jonathan XVIII, 101, 143, 190,
  275
Stent, Michael 53
Stevens, Peta XVIII, 190
Stevenson, Bill 236
Stewart, Angus 252
Steyn, AK 153, 159
Stiff, Peter
  addresses SMA meeting
    on 'terrorism' 82
Storey, David 252
Straker, Gill 134
Strijdom, J G XXVI
Strom, Ulla 232
Student Medical Council 5
Student Moderate Alliance (SMA)
  XXVII, 67-71, 81-84, 89, 90,
  108, 109, 125, 159, 161
  supports Republic Festival 71
  distributes SA flags and anti-
    Nusas pamphlets 81
  and Unita incident 100-102
  and freedom of speech
    document 116-20
  invites far-right speaker 118
  invites speaker on Swapo
    detention camps 118
  commemorates Pretoria
    bomb blast 122-24
  views of Bizos Commission
    on 139-41
  funding of 141
  begins to fade 145, 146
Student movements, international
  XXI
  Chinese XXII
  European XXII
  Nicaraguan XXI
  United States XXI, XXII, 161
  in India XXI

Student Representative Council
  (SRC) 4, 5, 9, 11-13, 17,
  33, 37, 89, 95, 97, 102, 119,
  165, 189, 206, 224-27
  loses motion of no-confidence
    (1953) 14
  new constitution imposed (1954)
    15
  organises marches (1970) 41, 42
  photograph of 1973-4 Council 59
  relations with BSS 66
  five members resign (1989) 120
  smeared in anonymous letter 129
  leaders harassed and detained
    137, 252, 253
  calls for 'Quota Act' to be defied 153
  opposes racial classification
    of students 156
  on De Klerk's conditions
    169, 173, 183
  explains stone-throwing at police
    225
  offices searched by
    security police 247
Students for Social Action XXVII
Students' Liberal Association (SLA) 12
Stutterheim, Nico 69, 71, 80,
  153, 159, 169, 185, 198
  letter to Minister on
    conditions 332-35
Supreme Court
  application for students' bail 128
  universities' action against De
    Klerk 194, 195, 343-46
Suttner, Raymond 85
  detention of 204, 217
  'secret' lunch with 220, 221
Sutton, W G 15, 23, 25, 30, 276
  becomes Vice-Chancellor 14
Suzman, Helen 105
  and freedom of speech issues
    on campus 107, 108, 162
  action on death of Steve
    Biko 291 (n4)
Suzman, Jonathan
  memorandum on freedom of
    speech 114, 115, 316-18
Swart, Andrew XVIII

Swedish Foreign Ministry
  and financial aid to black
    students 232
Swedish International Development
  Authority (SIDA) 231, 232
Swemmer, Derek 165
swimming pool saga 16-18

Tambo, Oliver 237
Technical Staff Association
  183
Teeling-Smith, Alistair 210
television crews
  questioned by police 251
Terblanche, J D V 159
Thom, H B 54
Tiananmen Square XXII
Tip, Karel 53
Tiro, Abraham 43, 289 (n21)
Tober, Karl 84-86, 90, 91,
  92, 95-99, 124, 127
  meeting with Minister of
    Law and Order 129
  on the application of a quota
    157, 158
  responds to De Klerk 159, 160
  on De Klerk's conditions
    164, 165, 169, 184, 186
  suggests collegial decisions
    on speakers 166
  establishes supernumerary
    positions 260
Tobias, Phillip 33, 53, 185, 291 (n4)
Toms, Ivan 209, 239
'total onslaught' 74, 293 (n39)
toyi-toying students 166, 282 (n11)
transformation issues XXIX, 120
Treurnicht, Andries 61
Tselane, Terry XXVII, 275
Tshwete, Steve 237
Turner, Richard 51
Tutu, Desmond
  addresses student protest meeting
    96
Tyson, Peter 159

Union of Democratic University Staff
  Associations (Udusa) 282 (n10)

INDEX

Unita 100-102, 161
United Democratic Front (UDF) 91
  banned 202
  supports fund-raising for
    black students 234
United Party
  participates in Schlebusch
    Commission 50
Unity in Sport Agreement 273
Universities XIX
  Afrikaans-medium XIX, 49
  defend separate education
    49, 50, 290 (n37)
  supportive of De Klerk's
    conditions 181
  'open' or historically white
    (HWUs) XIX, 33
  historically black (HBUs) XIX, 33
  international support from 193, 194
'University Freedom of Speech
  Association' 108
University of Cape Town
  33, 35, 42, 47, 57
  joint conference with Wits
    (1957) 23
  joint petition with Wits
    to Parliament 26
  visit of O'Brien 105-107
  on 'Quota Bill' 152, 154
  opposes De Klerk's conditions 183
  challenges De Klerk in court
    191, 194, 343-46
  agent provocateur at 245
University of Copenhagen 234
  Rector organises letter to
    De Klerk 234, 235
University of Durban Westville 33, 70
University of Natal 33, 47, 51, 70
  resists state takeover of
    medical school 28
  on 'Quota Bill' 152, 154
  opposes De Klerk's conditions
    183
  challenges De Klerk in
    court 191, 195, 346
  praise from ANC 236
University of Paris X, Paris-
  Nanterre 230, 231
University of Potchefstroom
  Rector satisfied with De Klerk's
    conditions 182, 185
University of Pretoria 72
  'cringing compliance' of students
    49
  Political Students' Union
    condemns bannings 74
  not concerned about De
    Klerk's conditions
  students join Nusas
    demonstration 204
University of the North 33
University of Stellenbosch
  on De Klerk's conditions 181, 185
  Rector under pressure on De
    Klerk's conditions 181
  students join Nusas
    demonstration 204
University of the Western Cape 33
  opposes De Klerk's conditions
    183
  challenges De Klerk in court
    191, 194, 343-46
  praised by ANC 236
University of the Witwatersrand
  racial discrimination at 1
  1957 protest march 27-30
  1981 anti-Republic
    demonstrations 70
  staff associations condemn
    detentions, 1981 75
  admits expelled black students 81
  culpability for consequences
    of apartheid 99, 311
  regarded by Government as
    centre of excellence 160
  rejects De Klerk's conditions
    180
  Private Act, amendment of 230
  call for end to detentions
    without trial 239
  conflicting views on 275, 276
  Mission Statement 278-81, 347
  academic contributions to
    anti-apartheid struggle 281
  governance of 306, 307
University of Zululand 33

University Teachers' Association
  of S A XXV, 282 (n10)

Van den Bergh, H J 48
Van der Merwe, Johann 159
Van der Spuy, J P 42
Van der Walt, Colonel 240, 241, 267
Van Eyck, Mulder 143, 161
Van Heerden, Clive 76, 293 (n44)
Van Huysteen, Captain 247, 250
Van Lingen, Hazel XVIII
Van Wyk de Vries Commission 48-58
  Bozzoli submits minority report 55
  and withdrawal of state subsidy 56
  condemns political activity
    in universities 56, 57
  strongly criticises Nusas 57
  condemned by university bodies 58
Van Wyk de Vries, J 54
Van Zyl, Paul 252
Van Zyl Slabbert, Frederick 119
Venter, Major 239, 240
Venter, Rue 159
Verwoerd, Hendrick 20, 21
  and Second World War
    213, 302 (n28)
Vice-Chancellor and Deputy
  Vice-Chancellors
  duties 307
Viljoen, Gerrit 49
  and 'Quota Bill' 149-59
  backs down on 'Quota
    Act' 154, 158, 159
Viljoen, J H 25
Violence in townships
  University demonstrations
    and statement 266-71
Visiting Lecturers Trust Fund 15
Vlok, Adriaan 201, 256, 269

prohibits ECC 210, 211
restricts BSS 238
Vogelman, Lloyd 82, 275
Vollebaek, Knut 233
Von Lieres, Bettina 119, 239, 266, 275
  attempt to intimidate 244, 252
  hit by teargas canister 245
  detained 254
Von Lieres und Wilkau, Klaus 248
Vorster, Henry 16, 17
Vorster, John 33, 40, 46-48, 54
  and Second World War
    213, 214, 302 (n28)

Webster, David 75
  assassinated 246
Webster, Glenda 134
Weekly Mail 146
Wessels, Albert 159, 162
West Rand Administration Board 77, 78
Whitecross, Robert 76, 186
Whitmore Richards, M W 42
Williamson, Craig 45, 58
Wilson, Gary 251
'Wit Wolwe'
  threaten Wits 221
Wolpe, Harold 9, 12, 235, 284 (n24)
  Motion against discrimination 13
World University Services
  (WUS) 233, 234
Wright, Ann 134
Wright, Claire 123, 126, 275
  detained 131

Young, Derek 297 (n14)

Zeffert, David 164, 167, 175,
  176, 191, 337-39
Zionist Federation 206

www.ingramcontent.com/pod-product-compliance
Lightning Source LLC
Chambersburg PA
CBHW030252100526
44590CB00012B/374